PUBLIC AND PRIVATE OWNERSHIP OF BRITISH INDUSTRY 1820-1990

PUBLIC AND PRIVATE OWNERSHIP OF BRITISH INDUSTRY 1820–1990

by

James Foreman-Peck
and
Robert Millward

CLARENDON PRESS · OXFORD

Oxford University Press, Walton Street, Oxford OX2 6DP
Oxford New York
Athens Auckland Bangkok Bombay
Calcutta Cape Town Dar es Salaam Delhi
Florence Hong Kong Istanbul Karachi
Kuala Lumpur Madras Madrid Melbourne
Mexico City Nairobi Paris Singapore
Taipei Tokyo Toronto
and associated companies in
Berlin Ibadan

Oxford is a trade mark of Oxford University Press

Published in the United States by
Oxford University Press Inc., New York

British Library Cataloguing in Publication Data
Data available

Library of Congress Cataloging in Publication Data
Foreman-Peck, James.
Public and private ownership of British Industry, 1820–1990 / by James
Foreman-Peck and Robert Millward.
p. cm.
Includes bibliographical references and index.
1. Government ownership—Great Britain—History.
2. Privatization—Great Britain—History. 3. Great Britain—Industries—
History. I. Millward, Robert E. II. Title.
HD4145.F67 1994 338.941—dc20 93–30848
ISBN 0–19–820359–4

3 5 7 9 10 8 6 4 2

Printed in Great Britain by
The Ipswich Book Company Ltd.
Suffolk

PREFACE

BRITAIN led the way for much of the world with industrial privatization during the 1980s. Yet the historical origins of the process that was being reversed have rarely been discussed. In the future we may therefore, relive earlier episodes, as the privatizations are unravelled. In any case, international similarities and striking differences in the pattern of state ownership of industry in the Western world at the end of the 1970s demand some form of explanation and scientific evaluation.

Reflections such as these led us to embark independently a decade ago on the quantitative study of the economic history of private and public enterprises in Britain. We adopted similar methods and found a pattern across a number of key industries that suggested the results could constitute a coherent monograph. The present book is the result. It includes quantitative estimates of the performance of various institutional arrangements as well as explanations of how they have changed over the period from about the beginning of the nineteenth century to the end of the 1980s. We have not written an exhaustive economic history of these industries nor are we advancing a new thesis about their role in British economic growth, though we hope to contribute to that debate. By offering a non-technical treatment with more specialized analysis consigned to appendices, it is hoped that the analysis will reach a wide audience of historians, economists, and others interested in how we came to arrive where we are today.

We are grateful to the following publishers for permission to reproduce material which appeared first in their journals or books: Blackwell Publishers for permission to use, in Chapter 4 and Appendix 4.1, extracts from Millward's article 'The Market Behaviour of Local Utilities in Pre-World War I Britain', in *Economic History Review*, 44 (Feb. 1991); Manchester University Press for permission to use, in Tables 9.1, 9.2, 9.3, 9.4, and the surrounding text of Chapter 9, material from Millward's chapter 'The Nationalised Industries', in M. Artis and D. Cobham (eds.), *Labour's Economic Policies 1974–79*; Oxford University Press for permission to use, in Chapters 2, 3, and 6 and Appendices 2.1, 3.3, and 6.3, extracts from Foreman-Peck's article 'Natural Monopoly and Railway Policy in the Nineteenth-Century' and Millward and Ward's article 'The Costs of Public and Private Gas Enterprises in Late Nineteenth Century Britain', both in *Oxford Economic Papers*, 39 (Dec. 1987); Cambridge University Press for permission to use, in Chapter 2, extracts from Millward's chapter 'The Emergence of Gas and Water Monopolies in Nineteenth-Century Britain: Contested Markets and Public Control', in James Foreman-Peck (ed.), *New Perspectives on the Late Victorian Economy*; Frank Cass & Co. for permission to use, in Chapters 2 and 3 and Appendix 3.1, material from Foreman-Peck's article 'Competition, Co-operation, and Nationalization in the Early Telegraph Network', *Business History*, 31 (1989); the publishers of *Histoire, Économie et Société*, Paris, for permission to use, in Chapters 3 and 7, material translated into English from Foreman-Peck's article 'L'État et le développement du réseau de télécommunications en Europe à ses débuts' published in their 1989 volume; the Royal Economic Society for permission to use, in Chapter 6, material from Foreman-Peck's article, with M. Waterson, on 'The Comparative Efficiency of Public and Private Enterprise in Britain: Electricity Generation between the World Wars', in the *Economic Journal*, 95 (1985 Supplement); Butterworth & Co. for permission to use, in Chapters 6 and 10, material from Foreman-Peck's article 'Competition and Performance in the UK Telecommunications Industry' in *Telecommunications Policy*, 9 (Sept. 1985); the Council of the Newcomen Society for the study of the history of engineering and technology, for permission to use, in Chapters 3 and 7, material from Foreman-Peck's article 'The Development and Diffusion of Telephone Technology in Britain 1900–1940' in *Transactions of the Newcomen Society*, 63 (1992–3).

The book is dedicated to the late H. M. Hallsworth, sometime student and member of staff in the University of Manchester. It was his bequest to the University which created a fund for scholars to visit Manchester and thereby afforded the environment, with the visit of Foreman-Peck in the Autumn Term of 1990, for the germination of the ideas which generated this book. Thanks are due to Martin Chick, Mark Casson, and Barry Supple for reading a first draft of Chapter 10 on privatization. We would also like to thank Jean Ashton, who typed Chapter 2, and Liz Dyckhoff, who typed two of the chapters and tidied up much more.

R. M.

J. F.-P.

February 1993

CONTENTS

Contents

LIST OF FIGURES

LIST OF TABLES

I

Introduction: Government and the Infrastructure in the Nineteenth and Twentieth Centuries

Direct involvement of government at both local and national levels in industrial activities of nineteenth- and twentieth-century Britain is largely a story of the infrastructure, or what might be called the network technology industries; from the first industrial revolution, railways, gas, water supply, and telegraphy, and from the second, electricity supply, telephony, tramways, and broadcasting. Each of these industries requires a substantial distribution network that 'channels' their service from the source to the destination. On the way, the service passes through processes that in information theory are called 'encoders' which transmit the service and 'decoders' which pass the service data to the destination. The telegraph employed relatively simple electrical encoders, decoders, and signals. The continuous wave form of the human voice posed a new range of problems for telephony. A railway channels people or freight, with varying degrees of reliability and speed, between terminuses. The water industry piped water under pressure from waterworks to the appliances of households and businesses in a manner similar to the 'piping' of information, in abstract terms.

These industries can be classified into 'large' and 'small' networks. When only moderately developed, telephony is a large network industry, with many nodes or switching points, like railways. By contrast a 'small' network has a single node from which radiate a number of channels, characteristic of nineteenth-century gas or water industries or the telephone before the development of trunk lines. The number of channels that can be supported by a given node may be insufficient for demand in an area and therefore a hierarchy of nodes may have to be arranged.

Network industries raise distinctive problems for government policy. They tend to require a unified system which has often seemed incompatible with the coexistence of a number of competing service suppliers. Yet competition has been the traditional guarantee of 'fair' and minimum prices in British industrial policy. Moreover the capital cost of the infrastructure accounts for a large proportion of its total costs. Pricing under competition in these circumstances is likely to be unstable and predatory, with a tendency for the largest firm to become a single supplier, at least in the absence of niche markets. A single supplier may have less reason to develop the technology than one driven by the spur of competition or may charge excessive prices. Entry of new firms will be difficult. In competition between an entrant and an established large network in one local node area, the established system operator can cut prices in the competitive zone to bankrupt the entrant, while supported by subsidies from other areas.

Problems such as these have provoked a variety of government policies over the last two centuries. The effectiveness of such intervention has been of vital importance to the British economy, for network undertakings have always been huge. At the turn of the century, as Table 1.1 shows, railway fixed assets alone were larger than those in the whole of manufacturing industry. From as early as 1850, as Table 1.2 shows, the capital stock in the network industries exceeded that in manufacturing and this was still the case in 1960.

Despite the obvious size of network industries, manufacturing industry and the institutions that surround it have been given a pre-eminent place in accounts of British relative economic

TABLE 1.1 *Net fixed assets in the UK 1850–1910* (1900 prices £m.)

	1850	1900	1910
Trams and light railways	—	15.0	42.0
Post and telecommunications	0.8	17.7	31.9
Railways	202.1	616.3	651.1
Electricity supply	—	21.2	45.0
Water supply	10.6	93.4	121.3
Gas supply	7.1	45.5	57.9
Manufacturing	165.7	478.7	679.8
UK total	1,229.0	3,515.0	4,324.0

Source: Feinstein and Pollard (1988).

TABLE 1.2 *Sectoral distribution of net fixed assets in the UK 1850–1960* (% of UK total)

	Network industries	Manufacturing
1850	17.9	13.5
1900	23.0	13.6
1910	21.9	15.7
1930	30.5	16.0
1960	23.6	22.6

Notes: Manufacturing includes construction. Network industries comprise transport, communications, gas, electricity, and water.

Sources: Feinstein (1965, 1972).

decline, as they have been in explanations and descriptions of the industrial revolution. The most noticed recent accounts have typically been qualitative rather than quantitative. Porter's influential *Competitive Advantage of Nations* (1990) cites Wiener (1981) and Elbaum and Lazonick (1986) as authorities for deep-seated British economic decadence. Like the economic interpretation of history the manufacturing industry interpretation of economic history has its weaknesses (the neglect of two-way causation) as well as strengths. In the 1980s a commonplace of government and others was that education and health services depended upon resources being generated by industry, with little acknowledgement that the converse was also true. So with the doctrine of manufacturing industry as an engine of growth. Manufacturing depends for its productivity in part on a host of other industries and services. Adam Smith's dictum that the division of labour is limited by the extent of the market points to the role of transport and communications. Abundant water supplies were essential for textiles. All of these industries, fundamental in the sense they provided inputs to manufacturing, shared the characteristics of being based on networks and on capital intensity.

  The precise role of these infrastructure industries in the economy and in particular in the long-term performance of the British economy has yet to be explained. We cannot claim this book fills that gap. Nor is it a general account of the infrastructure or of government–industry relations: roads, airspace, safety, quality control are not covered. Developments in the coal industry, not usually thought of as infrastructure, are included in the chapters on the twentieth century, because it figured in one of the major institutional changes directed at network industries in the British economy, the nationalizations of the 1940s. The main thrust of the book is to report on some new quantitative estimates of the performance of various institutional arrangements and on the reasons for their rise and fall. We assess the performance of public utilities by comparing them with private utilities within the same industry. We use as a yardstick the performance of the same industries in continental Europe and the USA, as well as considering the experiences of different regions and urban areas. We also chart and explain the growing role of government over the period *c.*1820–1980 with a postscript on the 1980s privatizations.

Two centuries of state policy and development of infrastructure industries fall into the following five phases.

PHASE I: THE COMPETITIVE ERA 1820–1860S

Railways, telegraph, and gas emerge as new industries and together with water supply expand rapidly under private ownership with joint stock companies to the fore. Regulation is absent or exercised by Parliament ineffectively through statutes which do not bind or are not enforced. Competition between companies in the same market and competition for particular markets give way to amalgamation, district agreements, and local private monopolies.

PHASE II: REGULATION AND MUNICIPALIZATION: 1860S TO THE FIRST WORLD WAR

This period sees closer railway regulation by Parliament, nationalization of telegraphy, and acquisition by the larger local government units of 40 per cent of gas undertakings and 80 per cent of water undertakings, together with roughly 60 per cent of the undertakings in the new industries of electricity and trams.

TABLE 1.3 *State employment and output in the Census of Production industries 1907*

	Employment	Gross output	Net output	% of industry net output
Government shipbuilding (incl. dockyards and lighthouses)	25,580	6.46	2.49	
Royal ordnance	14,533	3.36	1.45	
Naval ordnance	1,118	0.083	0.077	
Miscellaneous (army clothing factory, army bakeries, etc.)	2,329	0.51	0.18	
HM Telegraph and Telephone	10,171	2.87	n/a	
HM Post	202,193[a]	18.70[b]	n/a	
HM Office of Works	5,668	0.63	n/a	
Local authority (building)	185,286	20.02	n/a	
Gas (local authority)	28,574	10.77	5.73	33
Water (local authority)	17,389	8.46	7.35	81
Electricity (local authority)	14,119	5.73	3.59	64
Trams and light railways (local authority)	12,434	1.74	n/a	57[c] (73)
Total	519,394	79.33		
Total national	6,984,976	1,765.00	712.00	
State percentage of the total	7.4	4.5	—	

[a] 1910 total for post and state telecom. minus 1907 state telecom. employment.
[b] 1910.
[c] Proportion of gross output. Figures in brackets indicate proportion of employment. Values in £m.

Sources: *Census of Production 1907*; British Parliamentary Papers (1910).

Much was however still in private ownership. Taken in conjunction with the low labour intensity of techniques it is not surprising to find in Table 1.3 that employment in government-owned industries was still fairly small by the time of the 1907 Census of Production, a little over half a million; the price-regulated sector was however much larger. The move from Phase I to Phase II is a consequence, in part, of ineffective government regulation of monopoly and environmental spillovers; at the local level it reflects an extension of the tax base, by municipalizing utility profits

to finance public health and other nonrevenue-generating infrastructure services.

PHASE III: STATE-SPONSORED RATIONALIZATION FROM THE FIRST TO THE SECOND WORLD WAR

The collapse of the export staples and the technological weaknesses
revealed by the First World War prompt inter-war governments
to intervene in industrial organization, including manufacturing.
Railway rationalization was essential but an enormous task with
limited political pay-off. The state resists coal nationalization,
dabbles hesitantly with manufacturing, fails to overcome stubborn
local intervention in gas and water, but has some success with the
electricity grid and broadcasting.

PHASE IV: THE NATIONALIZATION ERA c.1945–1985

Perceived failures to promote amalgamation of companies and
related aspects of industrial organization in the inter-war period
generate a concern for drastic reorganization of the network
industries. The reconstruction needs of the British economy, the
success of wartime planning, and the Labour Party's commitment
to redistribution and economic planning pave the way for the
1940s nationalization of coal, railway, steel, gas, and electricity.
Productivity growth in these sectors compares favourably with
manufacturing industries 1950–85 and with similar industries
in the USA. But the 'national' framework of organization, the
use of the industries as a tool of income redistribution policy,
the confused objectives, and primitive accounting procedures
lead to financial problems and disillusionment.

PHASE V: PRIVATIZATION FROM THE 1980s

The option of arm's length regulation of private utilities is re-
sumed and injected with a stronger dose of competition. Privately
unprofitable services disappear. The need for public control is
not rejected, nor is the diagnosis of the market structure and
environmental problems of the network industries. Managerial

efficiency and stronger incentive arrangements come to the fore. Different forms of public control are chosen and a new complex regulatory system is established.

Within this chronology and framework, several broad conclusions emerge from the quantitative and analytical research reported in the following chapters. The first is that the economic performance of institutions does not fit readily into popular stereotypes. Technical and managerial efficiency can be measured in productivity and cost function studies. Private and public firms show a very similar performance in this respect in the gas and electricity industries in the early part of the twentieth century. The telegraph was nationalized in 1870 and unit costs rose with expansion of the system. On the other hand the private UK railway system of the late nineteenth century compares unfavourably with Continental systems with more government ownership. In the 1919–39 period the big difference in productivity between the USA and the UK in electricity generation and transmission was markedly reduced with the advent of the publicly owned Central Electricity Board. In the post-1945 period the UK nationalized industries' productivity growth record compared favourably with UK manufacturing and with similar infrastructure industries in the USA. But by the 1980s the privatized British Telecom was showing a slightly better productivity record than perhaps the Post Office would have achieved in telecommunications during this period.

The second conclusion, from the involvement of the British government with the infrastructure industries rather than manufacturing, suggests pragmatic rather than ideological explanations of changes in the institutional arrangements. It is true that in the 1960s iron and steel was renationalized and in the 1970s shipbuilding was taken over as well as the motor vehicle firm British Leyland. Even in this period, as Table 1.4 shows, the German, Italian, and French state ownership was more evenly, albeit more thinly, spread across the whole of industry including chemicals, tobacco, and glass. Looking at the whole period from 1820, regulation and government ownership have clearly concentrated in Britain on the fuel industries as well as the major sectors not shown in Table 1.4, transport, communications, and water resources. As we have suggested and will argue in more detail later, these sectors have intrinsic tendencies towards

TABLE 1.4 *Percentage of employment in state-owned enterprises in selected industries 1978*

	Electricity, gas, and water	Iron and steel	Shipbuilding	Motor vehicle manufacture	Industrial chemicals	Tobacco	Glass and glass products
UK	95	100.0	95.0	46.2	0.0	0	0.0
Germany	25	21.9	19.7	40.9	0.0	0	19.5
France	80	—	—	25.0	2.9	85	—
Belgium	18	0.2	0.1	0.2	0.2	0	1.0
USA	10	0.0	0.0	0.0	0.0	0	0.0
Denmark	60	30.0	0.0	0.0	0.0	0	0.0
Italy	93	75.0	70.0	14.0	16.3	5	34.0

Source: CEEP Review 1981 (European Centre of Public Enterprise), *Public Enterprise in the European Community*.

monopoly which undermine some of the advantages of *laissez-faire*. The incentives for collusion, amalgamations and price fixing are strong; the nineteenth-century experience reported in subsequent chapters brings this out clearly. When added to environmental and safety problems especially in water, gas supply, and coal-mining the pressures for government intervention become strong. It is these sectors which have seen extensive government regulation and ownership in Britain. Textiles, engineering, agriculture, construction have barely been affected, even in the 1940s nationalizations.

A third point is that the choice of instrument for public intervention may have been optimal at the time but with hindsight has often appeared inappropriate and hence been abandoned. Market failures and environmental effects in production do not necessarily require public intervention in the form of public ownership. Yet the desire to improve industrial organization was an important ingredient of the 1940s nationalizations, on the grounds that other instruments had failed in the inter-war years. By the 1970s a reassessment of policy instruments was in train. Municipalization in the late nineteenth century was partly motivated by local government's shortage of tax revenue and the consequent interest in utility profits which could be expropriated via municipal ownership. By the early decades of the twentieth century central government grants to local authorities were relieving the pressure on local taxes. At the same time local government boundaries were no longer coterminous with economic areas of production and delivery of services. Municipal ownership had lost much of its rationale. The above two periods when firms were transferred from the private sector to the public sector were both preceded by attempts at parliamentary regulation. Initially this was directed at prices, profits, and supply conditions. By the inter-war period it was used as a means of promoting protection and reorganization. Both regulatory phases were perceived as failures and were important ingredients in the switch to government acquisition of companies as a vehicle of change; the direction of acquisition was then reversed in the 1980s and 1990s.

Our story starts in the next chapter in the early nineteenth century when the industrial revolution was in full swing. It is the classic period for the study of private ownership of the infrastructure.

2

Competition in the New Network Technology Industries 1820–1870

INTRODUCTION

Despite Factory Acts and trade union legislation, British governments during the industrial revolution generally preferred policies of non-intervention in economic life, as long as national security and law and order were maintained. Water supply expanded rapidly in the first half of the nineteenth century, through competition between a growing number of joint stock companies. Gas was a new industry at the beginning of the century, but developed in a similar fashion. Railways took off in the 1830s and 1840s, with a deluge of new competing companies. Telegraph lines emerged in the 1840s and a competitive regime of sorts existed until 1868. In all these cases, companies needed rights of way for lines or tracks which necessitated approval from local government or Parliament, as did joint stock status. But so far as prices, profits, and many supply conditions were concerned, in the first half of the nineteenth century, competition was presumed to regulate the industries in the public interest.

Experience by the 1860s began to convince the public and official opinion otherwise. Networks with high fixed capital costs were inefficient to duplicate. Additional considerations for public regulation in gas and water were geographically inadequate extensions of supply and health and safety concerns, which were even more important than in rail travel. Like railways in requiring a national network but like gas and water in the network being comparatively cheap, the telegraph in private hands showed a lack of system integration and limited geographical spread. In short, state policy in these years allowed competition between networks and the public was dissatisfied with the results.

The fundamental problem faced by policy makers can be expressed in a simple form in Fig. 2.1. In carrying railway pas-

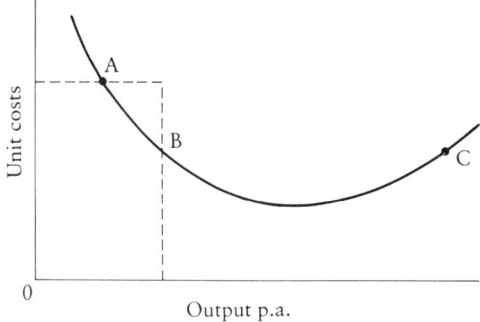

F I G. 2.1 Natural monopolies

sengers, gas, water, or telegraph messages between two points (minimum), unit costs tended to be lower the greater the volume sent. Fixed costs of the network of railways, gas or water pipes, or telegraph lines could be spread over a greater volume of through-put, while the variable cost of throughput was not high in relation to fixed costs. Consequently, if two equal-sized enterprises (A) maintained rival networks for carrying between the same points, their unit costs would be higher than a single cost-minimizing organization (B) that conveyed both. More generally, a *natural monopoly* is said to exist for any given constellation of product types and output levels when one enterprise can produce more cheaply than two or more enterprises. Competition between A-type companies could be indecisive for some time because each would be willing to cut prices in the short run so as only to cover variable costs if they thought they could drive their rival out of business by so doing. How long they could follow such a tactic depended on the durability of their fixed capital or the availability of reserves to meet the interest costs of their fixed capital. When eventually one company triumphed, the problem for state policy was how to prevent it raising prices to the maximum the market would bear. Upper limits on prices were one option, but typically they were fixed too high to be effective in technologically pro-gressive industries where unit costs were regularly reduced by new investment. A second ineffective policy was an upper limit on dividends. The intention was to constrain profit maximizing and therefore hold down prices. But more attractive for the company was letting costs rise, sometimes spuriously by expanding the capital on which the dividend was paid (later known as the Averch–Johnson effect). The upshot could be that the private monopolist was no more efficient than the competitors and perhaps less so.

Because there was no second-hand market for railway track, gas and water pipes under the streets, or telegraph lines, once the investment had been undertaken, the network company was committed to the industry; its fixed costs were often literally, as well as conceptually, sunk costs. An incumbent firm could not save any of these costs by leaving the industry and an entrant wishing to compete was obliged to undertake substantial investment. New entry into the whole range of an established company's activities was therefore unlikely to be successful unless the competitor was both large and much more efficient. The threat of entry was consequently only a weak incentive to efficiency for large established network monopolists. A second problem for public policy in these years was harmful 'spillovers' or negative externalities. Private companies did not necessarily include the full costs of accidents in their calculations because they did not always bear them entirely. Failure to make water readily available when there was a fire cost a water company little, but a town that was partly destroyed as a result paid a great deal. In the absence of additional incentives, such companies would not supply as much water as was socially desirable.

For networks with only one node or distribution point (water, gas), the effects of entry threats may have differed from those with many (railways, telegraphs). When a single price is charged and costs rise with distance from the node, profitability decreases with distance. The possibility that a rival may establish a node close to the boundary of the incumbent firm's area of profitable supply and be able to undercut the incumbent's cost-based prices within the boundary may deter extension of the distribution network as far as at first sight seems rational. In a multiple node network the threat of entry may encourage an extension of nodes by the incumbent and therefore extend the boundaries of supply further than profit maximization might appear to suggest. In such networks addition of more nodes increases competitiveness by raising the quality of services and thus deters or combats entry. How pervasive these different characteristics of network industries were in the half-century before 1870 is demonstrated in the following sections on railways, gas and water, and the electric telegraph.

RAILWAYS: COMPETITION AND EXPANSION

More than any other single industry, railways transformed the Victorian economy, by reducing transport costs and by their demands for capital. The embodiment of Victorian technical achievement, they presented fundamental problems for the Victorian doctrine that competition reconciled customer well-being with the pursuit of self-interest by suppliers (generally see Cleveland-Stevens 1915; Lewin 1925, 1936; Freeman 1988). The railway combined two discoveries. Running wheels in channelled rails was an old ploy used by the Romans to reduce friction and power dissipation. At the time of the Stockton & Darlington Railway opening, the granite quarries of Dartmoor were still employing the technique. The Victorian innovation depended upon a flanged wheel running on iron rails that created far less friction than cart road wheels. More radical, and dependent upon similar metallurgical advances, was the use of the steam engine to drive the wheels (Jackman 1916: 470–2; Lewin 1925).

At first when railways were employed only in collieries there were no new regulatory issues. But by 1841 a series of public trunk lines existed that allowed (first class) travel from Lancaster to London in a day. Stage coach and canal carriage competition was undercut and eliminated. Railways were left unchallenged for inland transport, and a sole railway in a locality therefore wielded considerable power. English railways had clearly come of age by 1842 when Queen Victoria took her first train journey. French railways had not yet attained a similar acceptance, for the following year Louis-Philippe was advised not to make his maiden train trip, probably because of a horrific accident at Meudon on the Paris–Versailles line. Braking and signalling were still minimal and travellers could expect to be locked in their carriages (which at Meudon was responsible for so many passengers being burned to death). An incident in Charles Dicken's short story 'The Signalman' turns on the impossibility of communication between passengers and drivers in emergencies. Self-regulation was the norm in the railway industry of the 1840s, and not all of it was clearly in the traveller's interest. The London & Birmingham forbade friends to see off passengers on the station, and tickets for numbered places were required to be bought well in advance of the train's departure. Restrictions on English lines were however mild compared to those imposed upon passengers from Vienna to Baden in 1842, where despite a lengthy unsatisfied queue, company regulations required ticket sales to cease fifteen minutes before the train left half-empty. At Berlin passengers were handed a list of twenty-five detailed regulations to which they were expected to conform (Acworth 1889: 51–2).

Apart from safety, legislation governing railways was primarily concerned with avoiding monopolistic behaviour. Parliament originally intended that the economic functions associated with the permanent way and with carriage should be separately owned. Then, like the canals and the turnpikes before, the monopoly provision of the track could be regulated by Parliament, while transport services remained competitive. The Stockton & Darlington Railway, on which Stephenson's 'Rocket' made its inaugural run in 1825, allowed independent operators to use their own horses for hauling on the tracks. But the Railway's decision to move over entirely to steam operation between 1833 and 1834 precipitated a change of policy. Under the terms of its 1826 Act, the Liverpool & Manchester Railway, whose successful operation from 1830 truly began the railway age, was obliged to make its track available to any user, and did so as late as 1838 (Jackman 1916: 575–6). Two years later the small Clarence Railway of County Durham was leasing the carriage of passengers to a Mr Walton. 'Mr Walton finds his own engines and carriages; and with regard to the latter they are but little inferior to those belonging to passenger-railways generally' (Wishaw 1969: 60). Leasing is not the same as allowing competing carriers on the track; the track owner may maintain monopoly profits. Because leasing out the supply of engine power was feasible it does not follow that competition on the track was. Engines may have been specific to particular lines because of the trade-off between gradient and engine power. Stationary engines, for example on the Liverpool incline through the tunnel on the Liverpool & Manchester, were an extreme case. Assets (steam engines) the profitability of which is solely dependent on the pricing policy and goodwill of one business (the track owners) are highly vulnerable. Technology may have combined with economics to eliminate multiple track users where engine power was concerned.

On the other hand enforcement of the right to run independent traffic on company railway lines was non-existent. Parliamentary maximum tolls were fixed too high for any but the railway company to run traffic profitably if the company decided that was what it wanted. It was therefore an easy matter for management to withdraw co-operation in signalling and the provision of sidings, and render such operations impossible. But inter-company agreements were reached. The Grand Junction Railway Company paid a fee per passenger and per ton of goods to the Liverpool & Manchester Railway for the use of the line between Newton and Liverpool and Newton and Manchester. Grand Junction carriages were employed but a Liverpool & Manchester booking office, stations, and stationary engines were part of the deal (Wishaw 1969: 206). Use of the company's track in a co-operative arrangement was often preferable to the threat of a new directly competitive line being laid. The Leeds & Selby was willing to take advantage of other management and lease its tracks to the York & North Midland for thirty-one years in 1840. Other railway companies experimented with leasing out track maintenance (Wishaw 1969: 445, 210, 252).

Railways claimed that competing use on their tracks was dangerous because of inadequate investment in engines and rolling stock. Equally possible is that, with the track service charges relatively easy to regulate (for technical progress was less marked), they wanted to take advantage of the profits on the lightly regulated carrier services. Freight was a minor source of revenue in the 1830s and therefore railway management's principal interest was in 'bundling' passenger services in with their track provision. Only later, from the mid-1840s, as freight assumed a greater role, did they aim to eliminate the services of independent freight carriers as well. One unfortunate legacy of multiple ownership of assets in railway services in this era that lasted into the inter-war years was the right of colliery owners to own their own trucks. This became an obstacle towards the end of the nineteenth century for attempts to increase train-loads. It suggests there were eventually social costs from multiple ownership of some components of railway services (though divided ownership is a necessary, not a sufficient, condition for competition on the track) (Clapham 1963: i. 413; Gourvish 1972: 31–3; Jackman 1916: 572–3).

After the abandonment of the separation of services, British railway policy, in contrast to those policies of continental Europe, for most of the time operated a market test for natural monopoly: if one firm was more efficient than two, then only one would survive in the market. A maximum ton-mile toll and maximum dividend (10 per cent) were imposed on the Liverpool & Manchester but so high was the toll maximum fixed that it was never binding and no other Railway Act contained dividend limits. Before it faced the market test, though, the aspirant railway was first obliged to leap a political hurdle. If companies were to obtain limited liability for their shareholders and be granted rights of way for their tracks with the associated compulsory powers for land purchase, they needed a private Act of Parliament. Under this procedure each new project was obliged to pass an examination of committees of both Houses, where it was necessary to buy off the opposition (Williams 1852: 88–94). Critics of the approach were quick to point out that British construction costs were higher than in the rest of Western Europe (Gourvish 1972: 23) but their claims were largely ignored, at least in part because of the strong representation of the railway interest in Parliament (Bagwell 1965; Alderman 1973). Traders' fears of monopoly pricing (on the London & Birmingham's lines) did prompt the creation of a supervisory body, the Railway Department of the Board of Trade, in 1840 but to little avail because the Department lacked effective powers (Parris 1965). Strengthened by the 1844 Railway Act, a group of five 'wise men' or 'kings' headed by the tenth Earl of Dalhousie and including G. R. Porter (author of *The Progress of the Nation*) sat in judgement on competing railway schemes. They claimed to apply the principle of public advantage under which no existing railway company could claim preference, but the public were to get the best railway lines (Board of Trade 1845: 32–5). The assessors believed that competition offered little advantage when there were only two or three competitors whose mutual interest drove them to collude; they knew of no instance of public benefit from direct competition between railway lines.

Such methods and conclusions were uncongenial to the railway interests, for whom huge sums of money were at stake. The 'wise men' were criticized and overruled by the House of Commons; Grinting's (1903) chapter on the Great Northern Railway entitled 'How the "Five Kings" Issued an Edict to "Strangle the Monster Infant at its Birth"' illustrates how many of the railway interest thought about the Railway Department. Dalhousie felt that if Peel and members of the government were prepared to vote against the Department's recommendations, its activities might as well be terminated, which they were in 1845 (Parris 1965). Thereafter schemes were effectively trusted to the play of political forces in Parliamentary Committee and 'railway mania' was given a boost. Within a year, replacement Commissioners of Railways were appointed, only to be absorbed into the Board of Trade as an economy measure in 1851.

Parliamentary consideration of railway schemes was likely to be less impartial, and more expensive, than that of the Board of Trade. A proposal for a 134-mile line by the Great Eastern Railway in 1864 was rejected by a Committee of the House of Commons on the grounds that the gradient was too favourable and costs too low for the established competition. The Committee protected the interests of the Great Northern Railway (Galt 1865: 153–7). The competitive process was worked out as much in the legislature and between members of different railway boards as in the open market. Payments to arrange mergers of competing lines, buying off competing interests, and conducting proceedings in front of Parliamentary Committees could prove expensive for the railways that emerged, quite regardless of whether they were optimally routed. In addition directors overcapitalized their companies, awarding themselves stock which they disposed of at the height of the 1845–7 boom, often fanned by paying dividends out of capital. Pamphleteers could call on official support for their allegations that the waste and corruption would have been sufficient to pay for a trunk system for the entire country.

By the end of the 1840s almost all companies were conducting or had conducted investigations into real or alleged financial irregularities by their officers. George Hudson the 'Railway King', midwife of the Midland, was unseated in 1849 when his propensity to conflate revenue and capital accounts, misappropriating some half a million pounds, was exposed. Despite these inquiries the 1850s were not free of railway financial scandals. Edmund Denison of the Great Northern told his shareholders in August 1856 that their property was perfectly sound, having known since January of that year that there were major discrepancies in the books. Three months later the company was obliged to announce that £200,000 was unaccounted for, expropriated, it eventually emerged, by the company registrar (Pollins 1969; Smith 1848; Grinting 1903). Such scandals, and the inadequate regulation that permitted them, contributed to the general unpopularity of limited liability companies for many years after they were permitted by the 1856 Act, and thus constrained investment in the development of the British economy (Foreman-Peck 1990).

Competition for shareholders' funds was obviously intense but competition in the market for railway services was confined to those few points between which there was more than one railway, where there was a credible threat of new entry, or where sea freight offered an alternative transport mode. Sea competition helped to hold down London–Southampton and London–Liverpool rates, and on the London–Birmingham route competitive railway lines reduced rates between the 1840s and 1860s. New entry to the industry as a whole occurred on the largest scale in the 1840s (Joint Select Committee 1872), when new lines or alterations of existing lines were projected as shown in Table 2.1. Such was the excessive optimism of these years that 1,560 miles of line proposed in Acts between 1845 and 1847 were subsequently not built. Judgements about the profitability of entering into head-on competition with established railway companies were revised downwards in the light of experience. Between 1850 and 1870 the national system was virtually completed, some of the expenditure having been authorized in the 1840s. Further booms ending in financial crises in 1857 and 1866 encouraged mergers. Seventy British companies controlled 2,100 miles of track in 1843, the London to Liverpool and Bristol to Leeds routes each being owned by three separate companies. Twenty-two years later the much larger network was owned by almost the same number of companies: 11,451 miles of line were worked by seventy-eight railways, the largest individual system consisting of 1,274 miles (Royal Commission on Railways 1867: pt. 1 p. lxxxii).

An alternative to mergers were the agreements to eliminate competition by other means that became increasingly common. Pooling arrangements divided up the country's traffic by the beginning of the 1850s. Under the agreement between the Eastern

TABLE 2.1 *New railways projected 1844–1847*

Year	Acts	Miles of line	Capital authorized (£m.)
1840	47	805	20.5
1845	120	2,700	59.5
1846	270	4,538	132.6
1847	190	1,354	39.128

Source: Royal Commission on Railways (1867: pt, 1, p. xvii).

and the Great Northern, the second company paid to the Eastern 60 per cent of any earnings from traffic passing over Great Northern lines between London and Hitchin and 20 per cent of earnings from Eastern Counties traffic sent from Peterborough to Newark, Lincoln, and Hull. The two companies further agreed to abstain from interfering in the district of the other and to interchange traffic for mutual benefit (Williams 1852: 269–70). Two decades later, normal price competition between established railways had disappeared. New entry could still temporarily lower rates, as the 1889 opening of the Barry Railway did for South Wales coal, but even this type of threat was emasculated as early as 1863 by agreements between companies covering new lines.

Operation of the large interconnecting British railway network required some inter-company co-operation in traffic management in the public interest. Without cajoling by the state, the directors of the London & Birmingham, in particular Charles Carr Glyn, took the initiative to persuade other companies that a Railway Clearing House was desirable (Bagwell 1963: 37–43). Established in 1842, the Clearing House encouraged a number of forms of co-operation. Carrying through traffic for other companies necessitated that lines be managed as if they belonged to one organization, from which, as we have seen, pooling agreements were only a short step. Voluntary agreement did not necessarily come easily in phases of expansion when companies were still fighting for territory. Only one-third of all goods traffic receipts passed through the Clearing House as late as 1857.

Refusal or obstruction of interconnection remained a competitive weapon that could operate against the public interest. The public wanted through traffic but a large network would see no advantage in interconnection with competing small systems; the private benefits would accrue principally to the small railways who gained access to a large volume of traffic (cf. Katz and Shapiro 1985). Common railway gauges, essential to interconnection, were to some extent enforced by shared engineering beliefs and personnel in railway planning and construction. But Brunel's broad gauge Great Western offered an alternative to George Stephenson's 4 ft. 8.5 in. gauge until the 1846 Railway Gauge Act legislated Brunel's ultimate defeat. With 274 miles of broad gauge and 1,901 miles of narrow in 1845, Stephenson's system was almost bound to win. The reasons given by the Commissioners for their decision were rather less convincing; that the capacity and power of the broad gauge was far in excess of what the traffic required and that traders found the narrow gauge more handy for their private sidings. More unsatisfactory, but consistent with the *laissez-faire* policy of the time, was the inability of the legislation to enforce uniformity or even prevent an increase in broad gauge mileage (Lewin 1936: 123–5; Parris 1965: 101).

The most glaring attempt to break with *laissez-faire* was Gladstone's 1844 Railway Act. This was intended to control railway pricing and services by the requirement that a return train be run on each company's lines each day at such a time and at such a price that it could be used by working men. The obligation was often fulfilled in a manner that was not helpful to anybody. But the Act did empower the government to buy out in 1869 all private railway companies established since 1844. The later 1860s therefore heard a public debate on the benefits and costs of state ownership, culminating in the first effective and substantial regulation of railways under the 1868 Act. By the beginning of the 1870s, when the network was largely completed, official opinion hardened against competition as a principle, and against parliamentary oversight, for regulating the railways. The 1872 Parliamentary Committee reported, 'Committees and commissions have for the last thirty years clung to one form of competition or another yet it has become more and more evident that . . . competition must fail to do for railways what it does for ordinary trade' (Joint Select Committee 1872: p. xviii). Manipulation of the regulatory and legislative system by the railway companies over the same period was also recognized within the Board of

Trade, whose Captain Tyler stated that the question was 'whether the state shall manage the railways or whether the railways shall manage the state'. As a director of the Grand Trunk Railway of Canada as well as a civil servant, Tyler was particularly well placed to judge (Cleveland-Stevens 1915: 259–60; Parris 1965: 131).

REGULATORY POLICY AND RAILWAY PERFORMANCE

Contemporaries found plenty of grounds for criticizing *laissez-faire* state policy towards railways throughout the period the national system was being built, and indeed before (Jackman 1916: 507–8). But whether railway performance was in fact much poorer than could reasonably have been expected has not been quantitatively demonstrated. Nor have the policies that would have generated more satisfactory results been identified, although alternatives were proposed by critics. The Post Office early offered a model for would-be railway reformers even in the 1840s when revenue had not recovered from the 1840 price cut (Galt 1844). Consolidation of systems, removal of state taxation of railway passenger traffic (5 per cent of gross revenue from 1842), and massive cuts in fares were the three principles of Galt's proposals of 1844 and 1865, each of which is considered below.

The first principle, consolidation, aimed to reduce costs to best practice levels, appealing to the great differences in running costs between British companies (Glasgow & Greenock's costs were allegedly one-quarter of the London & Birmingham's) and to the experience of the Belgian state railway trunk system. A plan of 1833 linked the major Belgian towns with the sea and with the French and Prussian frontiers in order to capture through traffic. By August 1838, 159 miles of the four branches centred on Malines were open. Construction costs and the accuracy of their estimates compared favourably with those for the English lines, even taking topography into account. Consequently Belgian rail fares on the Brussels–Antwerp line were less than half of those on the comparable Liverpool–Manchester line and more traffic was generated as a proportion of the population (Rawson 1839). Throughout the remainder of the nineteenth century Belgium's railway network continued to be the system most comparable with Britain's and one that consistently charged lower freight and passenger rates. In 1856 Belgian third class fares per mile were one-quarter lower than British fares (Chadwick 1859: 382) and in 1883 they were 40 per cent less, while freight was similarly cheaper (Mulhall 1892: 498). Baxter noted in 1866 that Belgian fares had always been much below those of English lines, but he did not allow this observation to qualify his panegyric on the British system. He maintained that the distribution of the Belgian population conferred an advantage. 'A system which will pay admirably between large cities at short distances from each other and on lines which cost little to construct might break down completely on lines of expensive construction in more thinly inhabited districts' (Baxter 1866: 583). One of the points at issue is precisely whether the more expensive construction was justified or whether the alternative systems offered different incentives to supply efficiently the desired quantity of railway services. Similar considerations apply to the claim that national construction costs were not comparable with each other because Britain had a higher proportion of double, treble, and quadruple track than, say, America. The only social justification for more multiple tracking is a correspondingly greater volume of traffic, although in fact competition between railways for business may lead to unnecessary duplication or underutilization of track. Competition or the threat of new entry could also overextend company networks as they built unprofitable branch lines (Gourvish 1972: 104). Such excess capacity made more credible the threat to cut rates if competitor lines appeared; the extra traffic generated by reductions could be accommodated. Geographical extension also reduced the possibility that a new entrant or competitor would find an untapped market to serve. The London extension of the Midland Railway in the 1860s after the end of the revenue-sharing agreement in 1857 with the London & North Western, and the war between the London Chatham & Dover and the South Eastern Railways from the 1860s to the 1890s, offer examples (Channon 1972; Pollins 1971: 110).

The second and third of Galt's principles were inspired by the elasticity of demand revealed for postal services, though some of that expansion may have been due to income growth rather than the price cut. Some railway price experiments supported and others cast doubt on Galt's belief that railway pricing policies were not making the most of the market. Glasgow & Greenock's price cuts of 1847 raised revenue (Harding 1848) but the Leeds & Selby price rise of 1836 did not lose revenue (anonymous railway pamphlet of 1844). Of course each railway may have been operating on different portions of the demand function for their services and so a uniform response should not be expected. The idea was that at lower prices existing trains would be more fully utilized and unit costs thereby lowered. Railway prices were a continuing source of public concern, for railways discriminated by region, and by type of good (Hawke 1969; Freeman 1988). Given the high ratio of railway fixed to variable costs and the importance of costs common to a number of services, price discrimination may have allowed more traffic to be carried, while revenue covered costs, than would uniform pricing. A single marginal cost price would not have covered total costs. Similarly the principle of the 'terminal charge', a two-part tariff, was entirely justified as a means of covering fixed costs. It permitted the second part of the tariff to be closer to marginal costs, and a greater volume of traffic to be carried. As the discussion above shows, less easy is to establish that the general levels at which these tariffs were fixed were as low as they could be. Galt (1865) suggested that average passenger rail fares were about the same as it cost for an outside stage coach passenger when the coach was fully loaded, but railway costs were far below such levels.

Hand in hand with proposals like Galt's went demands for state ownership (Eldon Barry 1965: 85–9). The contemporary economist W. S. Jevons (1867) concluded that the argument by analogy with the Post Office was not appropriate for the much more capital-intensive railways, but he conceded (Jevons 1874) that some form of more rigorous regulation was necessary and a number of influential persons continued to advocate nationalization (see Galt 1865 and Biddulph Martin 1873 and the debate on his paper). Others, such as the majority of the 1867 Royal Commission, contended that the existing regulatory framework, rather than competition, was responsible for the defects of the system. Parliamentary consideration of schemes 'on their own merits' had led to inconsistent decisions and, for example, sometimes required two stations serving a town when one would have been adequate. Quantitative investigation falsifies the common contemporary claim that high construction costs were primarily due to high land prices demanded by avaricious landowners. Land costs were generally less than one-fifth of company capital outlays before the mid-century (Pollins 1952). Some portion of the high construction costs could be attributed to the disadvantages of being first (Pollins 1971: 31–3) and during the 1850s and 1860s, consistent with this explanation, the ratio of railway company capital to railway mileage tended to fall. Construction costs may also have been raised by the speed at which the networks were built and the central location of city stations, though in both cases there could well have been social gains over and above the additional costs. The original terminus of the London & South Western at Nine Elms, Vauxhall, proved an inconvenient distance from London. The company therefore extended their line to Waterloo station, opened in 1848, at a cost of £800,000 for little more than two extra miles. Six bridges were needed and costs were further boosted by the pace of construction. The 90,000 bricks of the skew bridge crossing Miles Street, South Lambeth, were laid in forty-five hours (Clunn 1932).

Without an explicit theoretical framework as well as quantification, evaluation of such performance is usually problematic. At best foreign comparisons provide a range of alternative possibilities, although even there some theoretical principles are necessary to identify relevant influences that should be held constant. Chadwick's early attempt to link railway policy with theoretical analysis is of considerable interest for it was eventually implemented for commercial television stations more than a century later. Drawing on his experience with the water industry (see below), Chadwick (1859) proposed franchise bidding as a means of controlling railway monopoly power. Instead of competing 'within the field' and unnecessarily duplicating capital, companies would bid 'for the field', for the right to supply rail services at a specified price. French railway policy, Chadwick believed, followed this procedure (though in fact for very long leases). Not only were French operating and construction costs below those of British companies, despite more expensive iron, coal, and steel, but accident rates were also lower, he maintained. On the basis of his experience with the Post Office, Rowland Hill supported Chadwick, but the majority of his colleagues on the 1867 Railway Commission remained unconvinced, citing a

French report of 1863 as to the unsuitability of the leasing system in English conditions (British Parliamentary Papers 1867: pp. xxxv–xxxvii).

Closely related to Chadwick's proposal is the more recent recommendation (Baumol 1982) that policy should be directed to minimizing sunk costs so as to encourage the threat of 'hit and run' entry. The mere threat of competition then ideally encourages cost minimization and competitive prices without the expensive duplication of plant that actual competiton 'in the field' would require. As we have seen in the preceding section, in the absence of authoritative regulation and supervision, this strategy proved impossible. Even had sunk costs of the railway track been removed as an entry barrier, as in the original separation of services, the problem of regulating the track owner, the 'common carrier', would have remained.

By the end of the nineteenth century, the European solution tended increasingly to be 'internalized' regulation by at least some form of state ownership. That was not necessarily the motive for nationalization however. In Germany the state interest was primarily to acquire the railways profits (Fremdling 1980) and French state railway ownership originated with the Freycinet plan of 1882, intended to modernize the economy (Caron 1979, 1983). British railways by contrast remained privately owned but hedged in by increasingly detailed state regulations. Apart from the costs of nationalization, Victorian policy chimed with the modern view that state-owned (railway) enterprise was necessarily inefficient

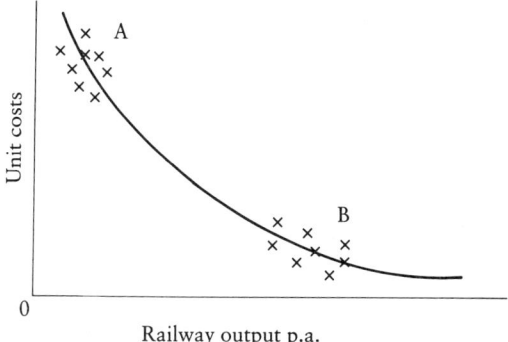

Railway output p.a.

FIG. 2.2 The railway test

because the ultimate paymasters of the state, the taxpayers, were and are unable to monitor performance as efficiently as private stockholders through the capital market (Millward and Parker 1983). On the other hand for a natural monopoly industry that has evolved through the market test, there may be more than offsetting inefficiencies in a regulated private industry. Duplicated and over-expensive plant built during the competitive era may be capitalized into industry costs by merger or cartels to form regional monopolies. In the following section a test is offered intended to resolve this issue of how well competition worked.

TESTING THE EFFICIENCY OF THE RAILWAY REGIME

Fig. 2.2 is a diagrammatic representation of the test. If railway company unit costs corresponded with cluster A, then they were consistent with a less than optimally organized industry emerging from the competitive process. Some form of integration would raise railway output and move surviving companies down the cost curve towards B. If railways were in cluster B then with the particular measure of output on the horizontal axis, there is no evidence of suboptimal company size. The dispersion of observations on each company around the best-fitting curve may be attributed to differences in the measurement of costs, as well as to unique company characteristics, such as management.

The test entails the estimation of a railway cost function of the diagram from cross-section data in the railway returns of 1865 (British Parliamentary Papers 1866). 1865 was chosen as one of the latest years before substantial regulation was introduced and for comparability with Hawke's (1970) classic study. Forty-six railways in Great Britain with ten miles of railway or more were found to have reasonably complete data. The returns provide working expenditure figures, capital costs (calculated from each railway's debenture rate times the sum of paid-up capital and debenture loans), and three output measures for each of the two types of traffic, passenger and freight. These are numbers of trains, volume carried, and train-miles. Ideally, we would have liked data on passenger-miles and goods ton-miles.

From the three output measures, we can infer the average

TABLE 2.2 *British railway systems' mean out-puts in 1865*

Goods train-load	104.8 tons
Passenger train-load	111.78 passengers
Goods train haul	32.73 miles
Passenger train haul	35.43 miles
'Maximum ton-miles'	91.04 million
'Maximum passenger-miles'	258.99 million

Source: 46 railways in the railway returns of 1865 (British Parliamentary Papers 1866).

load per train and the average distance travelled per train, but because passengers and freight did not travel the whole distance, we cannot deduce ton-miles and passenger-miles. The closest approximation to these variables is the rather large numbers obtained by assuming no intermediate loading or unloading of freight or passengers. Thus 'maximum ton-miles' for a railway company are found by multiplying the average goods train-load (in tons) by the average goods train haul (in miles) and by the number of trains. A similar procedure was used to calculate 'maximum passenger-miles'. For our purposes, the critical assumption is that there are no major differences between companies in intermediate loading and unloading. Mean values for British railways as a whole are shown in Table 2.2.

Railway companies' costs might differ because they faced different factor prices and these prices would often be beyond their control. Here again, in the absence of detailed data, the assumption was that there was no significant variation across the companies. Regional variation in railwaymen's pay was very limited, reduced in part by agreements between employers (Hunt 1973: 57, 351). Coal prices must have varied as much from one section of a railway to another as between railways, in view of the key role of transport costs in coal price determination. Consequently, no attempt was made to measure either factor price for individual railways.

The cost exercise therefore involved estimating how, across the sample of forty-six railway companies, total costs varied with the six output dimensions shown in Table 2.2. The results are shown in Appendix 2.1 and may be explored in more detail in Foreman-

Peck (1987*b*). The main features are as follows. Total costs rose only slightly less than proportionately to maximum passenger- and ton-miles, suggesting only small unexploited economies of scale and savings from cost complementarities in 1865. These results were obtained holding constant passenger and goods average train-loads and passenger and goods haul lengths. Longer passenger train hauls were associated with absolutely lower total costs, controlling for all other influences. A longer haul for the same load and passenger-miles total implied the use of a smaller number of trains, reducing the need for multiple tracking and lower capital costs per mile.

By a similar argument, the cost coefficients also imply that higher passenger and freight loads per train also lowered total costs, holding haul lengths and total passenger- and ton-miles constant, because fewer trains would have needed to be run. These findings are consistent with Irving's (1978) view that better traffic management, perhaps through enhanced system integration, could have been beneficial. The results in Appendix 2.1, moreover, suggest that the scope for these improvements was common to both small and large companies. In other words, the system as a whole was not cost-effectively organized in 1865 as a consequence of the legacy of the competitive era of expansion.

COMPETITION AND THE EMERGENCE OF PRIVATE GAS AND WATER MONOPOLIES

Though less demanding of the nation's capital resources, the gas and piped water supply industries were hardly less controversial. At the beginning of the century, the demand for gas and water was buoyant, reflecting contemporary industrialization and urbanization and also, in the case of gas, its latent illuminating superiority to candles and oil lamps. Direct ownership or self-generation of supplies by users was common, especially for water, but scale economies from a special supplier drawing from a common source, supported by a distribution network of mains and pipes, from the beginning brought government involvement. The heavy capital requirements of such systems prompted private interests to seek limited liability status, which required the approval of Parliament who, in any case, only granted permission for the breaking-up of streets to incorporated enterprises. The procedures accompanying the private Act of Parliament were geared to checking the financial and engineering soundness of the companies. Other than that, water and gas were treated as ordinary commodities which could be readily provided by private enterprise. (For this and other aspects of gas, see Falkus 1982: 230; Livesey 1894: 646; Chandler and Lacey 1949: 72; Awty 1975: 114–15; Robson 1935: 304–5; Falkus 1977: 146–7. For water, see Select Committee on the Supply of Water 1821: 3–8; Chadwick 1842: 136, 144–5; Commissioners on the State of Large Towns 1844: p. xi, 1845: 46–53; Dakyns 1931: 21–3; Finer 1941: 42, 43, 47; Stern 1954: 998.) Gas production was an innovation in the early decades, and, for such a speculative venture, private enterprise was seen as the proper institutional form. Collective provision of water has a long history in the UK, but the expansion in the early nineteenth century was left to private undertakings. An 1821 Select Committee remarked on the absence of official channels through which customer complaints could be made, and the position had hardly improved by the time of the public health reports of the 1840s.

That both production and distribution were subject to decreasing average costs, at least over some ranges of output, seems to have been recognized. Compared with the small plants operated by consumers, the innovating London-based Gas Light & Coke Company achieved scale economies in the size of retorts and the bulk purchase of inputs. The 1821 Select Committee pointed to the importance of fixed costs in the charging policy of the London water companies, and a later report on Nottingham waterworks showed operating expenses increasing at only one-third the rate of output. All observers were conscious of the extent to which consumers could share the use of the gas and water mains and other parts of the distribution network. The water mains often fed stand-pipes where water was purchased, carried, and stored by the poorer classes, and even a street stand-pipe required a superintendent whose wage bill would not vary a great deal with volume. Moreover, there were certain institutional overheads for large gas- and waterworks, like the costs of obtaining parliamentary Acts and the establishment of a board of directors. Such decreasing costs over relevant output ranges suggest that average unit costs are higher with two or more suppliers than with one. In so far as different areas of water and gas supply are effectively different product markets, then the multi-product exclusive supplier has lower (attributable) costs for each product and product group than has the 'stand-alone' supplier.

If these were the only considerations relevant to market structure, it would be quite reasonable to expect each area to be supplied by only one firm (only one 'in the field'), with profits in the long run constrained to a normal level by the threat of entry (Demsetz 1968). In particular, in the absence of uncertainty and sunk costs, and in the presence of perfect information, firms would compete 'for the whole field', the successful one being that offering the lowest prices to customers and yet able to break even. The first half of the nineteenth century saw competition both in and for the field in gas and water, which led by the middle of the century to a system dominated by exclusive suppliers. Organized water sources had for centuries often been collectively arranged, but the early nineteenth century saw many joint stock companies emerging in response to the growing demands of industrialization and urbanization which enhanced what was, by virtue of the vast range of possible water sources, a relatively competitive environment. Water was often begged or stolen, and private proprietors supplying largely their own needs outnumbered all other forms of suppliers throughout the nineteenth century; springs and other underground sources often meant distribution systems were not needed. In some cases, more than two companies operated the same area. Nottingham and Liverpool were oft-quoted cases. In London at the turn of the century there were three companies—London Bridge, New River, and Chelsea—but in the following decade, the East London, West Middlesex, and Grand Junction Companies were formed, with the encouragement of Parliament that this would promote competition. Direct competition between incorporated undertakings was more widespread in gas, including Birmingham, Brighton, Sheffield, Wolverhampton, Norwich, York, Liverpool, Edinburgh, Tynemouth, and Bristol. In London south of the Thames there were two companies operating in the 1820s; in 1833 the South Metropolitan Gas Company was formed. By 1850, over the whole metropolis, there were fourteen separate companies operating. In Glasgow, a company was incorporated in 1817, but a second company was established in 1843, and a third competitor as late as 1859.

Competition in the field led, by virtue of the replication of plant and mains, to high costs, poor quality service, and low dividends. The 1842 Chadwick Report suggested that the duplication of water facilities in parts of London accounted for the low dividend rates of 4–6 per cent and a general inhibition to the extension of supplies. Chadwick himself felt competition induced 'skimping', and others have attributed the state of pollution of London water supplies and the absence of filtration to competition in the overlapping areas. In Nottingham, where competition was strong, the companies were struggling to declare any dividend. In the case of gas, four or five sets of mains existed at one time in some London streets and such competition has been seen by several observers as leading to the neglect of apparatus, the low pressure of the gas, the inaccuracy of the meters, and enhancing the risk of escaping gas and the incidence of serious accidents.

By the middle of the century, however, competition in the field had virtually ceased in the provinces and Parliament was refusing to sanction new companies if this created competition. We have already noted that the classic concern with a decreasing cost industry is that a single supplier will be able to restrict output, thereby raising prices above average (and marginal) costs, and raising profits above a normal rate of return. The argument was put most explicitly perhaps by Knoop in his review (1912: 20) of the development of municipal trading in the UK in which he singled out gas and water because of their price inelasticity of demand. It clearly also lies behind the description of Falkus (1977: 152–3), Robson (1935: 309–10), Finer (1941: 50), and the Balfour Committee (1928–9: 307–8) of the mid-nineteenth-century concern over monopolistic abuse and the need for price regulation. Given the presence of sunk costs, exclusive suppliers are certainly in a good position to fight price wars, and many observers then and subsequently have pointed to indirect evidence of monopoly power in inflated share prices, in charging policies, and in the fact that, in the large towns area, exclusive suppliers emerged via districting agreements encouraged sometimes by Parliament. Moves towards districting in London started as early as 1815 for water and the 1820s for gas. They also had a long history in Liverpool and thereby enhanced the shares of the two districted companies: Harringtons and Bootle & Liverpool (Falkus 1977: 146–8; Robson 1935: 304–5; Livesey 1894: 677; Dakyns

1931: 22–3; Select Committee on the Supply of Water 1821: 4). Parliament, however, never legalized exclusive franchises and the potential competition continued.

There are, in fact, three types of evidence which support the proposition that monopoly power was curbed by the continuing threat of entry. First, there is the attitude of the companies and investigatory commissions. In the 1840s survey of fifty towns by the Commissioners on the State of Large Towns and Populous Districts, only two had more than one water company (Nottingham and Liverpool, and in the latter case districting had a long history). The Commissioners nevertheless felt 'the exposure to the risk of competition frequently imposes a salutary check on the conduct of the managers of Companies' (Commissioners on the State of Large Towns 1845: 53). In a similar vein, the 1850 General Board of Health Report (p. 297) on the London water supply saw the threat of entry as lowering water charges and company share prices. Potential competition was important in the case of London gas as late as the 1850s, with companies unwilling to come to an agreement on districting which was consolidated only in the 1860 Metropolis Gas Act (Livesey 1894: 647; Finer 1941: 47–8). Secondly, the direct evidence on profit rates provides no support at all for the view that monopoly power was extensive. Comparisons with other sectors of the UK economy may be made, as in Table 2.3, using Edelstein's data (1982: chs. 5 and 6). Unfortunately, this covers the latter part of the nineteenth century and is thereby open to the argument that gas and water were then regulated. In fact, as will be argued later, the regulatory framework proved largely ineffective. The earliest subperiod identified, 1870–6, was one of relatively high rates of return in the economy and especially for gas. Nevertheless, the latter's rate of return on equity was marginally below that for the manufacturing and commerce sectors taken as a whole and even below the railways. Averaging over the whole period 1870–1913, the equity rates in gas and water (roughly 6.7 per cent) exceeded the railways but lay below the rate of return of each and every identified sector within manufacturing and commerce. The pattern is sustained even when allowance is made for the differential riskiness of each sector. The risk-adjusted rate of return in gas (at (−)1.28 per cent) was, moreover, below the average risk-adjusted return on the equity of other companies in the social overhead

TABLE 2.3 Rates of return on gas, water, and other UK securities 1870–1913 (%)

Sector	1870–1913			1870–6	
	Number of securities in sample	Unadjusted rates of return	Risk-adjusted rates of return	Number of securities in sample	Unadjusted rates of return
Gas					
Equity	5	6.69	(−)1.28	3	11.12
Water					
Equity	7 (1870–1903)	6.81		6	7.94
Gas, water, and other social overheads					
Equity[a]	40		(−)0.96	24	7.15
Debentures	26 (1878–1913)	3.47			
Municipals					
Debentures	45	3.49	(−)0.76	4	4.69
Railways					
Equity	19	4.33	(−)4.00	19	11.19
Preference	17	4.52	(−)0.36	4	8.76
Debentures				15	6.01
Preference and debentures	48	3.74			
Manufacturing and commerce					
Equity[b]	131	6.31–13.01	0.23–3.04	49	11.20
Preference	16	5.34	0.89	1	9.38
Preference and debentures	56 (1888–1913)	4.00			

a Unweighted averages of gas, water, telegraph, tramways, omnibus, canals, docks, shipping. The debenture figures include also electricity.

b The building and construction sector data do not start until 1876, food until 1880, retail stores until 1882. These sectors are excluded completely from the risk adjusted rate of return (which also excludes banking at (−)1.10) and from the 1870–6 figure which is an unweighted average.

Source: Edelstein (1982: chs. 5 and 6). The data are geometric means of real rates of return relating to dividends, interest, and capital gains on publicly traded first- and second-class securities.

category, and even below the returns on the debenture of municipal corporations and on the preference shares of companies in manufacturing and commerce. Finally, the (unadjusted) rate of return on the debentures of gas, water, and other utility companies taken as a whole was, at 3.47 per cent, below the average return on debentures and preference shares in manufacturing, commerce, and the railways. Third, there are Matthews's recent findings for the London gas companies (1986: 346–53) which suggest that unit costs declined rapidly from 1830 to 1850, and continued falling, albeit more slowly, through to the 1880s, and that gas prices followed a similar path. This is consistent with competitive threats ensuring that cost reductions were passed on to the customer, but absence of hard data on the trend of rate of profit precludes heavy reliance on this pattern.

CONTESTED GAS AND WATER MARKETS

The continued presence of potential entry in conjunction with the absence of competition in the field might be thought to provide benefits to consumers. However, by the mid-nineteenth century, the volume and quality of gas and water supplies were being heavily criticized. This was the case even for gas where, as Matthews's (1986) London evidence suggests, prices fell throughout the century. Now an important source of this concern lay in public health and safety considerations, which we shall discuss later. But what is particularly striking about the deficiencies in supplies is that the companies appeared to be reluctant to develop into profitable areas and this needs explaining. Thus an 1847 parliamentary report on gas by Surveying Officers was critical of the uncontrolled private enterprise system whatever the degree of competition (Johnes and Clegg 1847: l–lv). They claimed that the growing cheapness of gas had not benefited the poor artisans and shopkeepers. Rather, the companies had preferred to secure a rather limited market favouring lower prices for the main ratepayers, that is, large customers who also benefited from the street lighting made available at charges less than cost, and concentrated on the streets of the wealthy. Street lighting was then accounting for one-sixth of total production and was a major source of leakage losses because of the policy of feeding the mains with gas throughout the night. Winter gas was costly in terms of capacity requirements and this was a demand also coming from the main ratepayers. In the case of water, a primary issue we shall examine is the delay in the introduction of comprehensive integrated pipe systems. But the threat of entry was also felt to be inhibiting more generally an extension of supplies in quantity and quality. A typical characterization of the system was that in many large towns polluted water was transferred from streams and rivers through houses and streets, back to enhance the pollution of the streams and rivers (Stern 1954: 999; Frazer 1970: 50–1; General Board of Health 1850: 312). The Commissioners on the State of Large Towns felt they had 'reason to believe that many instances occur where the want of sufficient security against the introduction of rivals prevents the original establishment of works, or deters the adventurers from hazarding further advances of money, to meet increasing demands upon them' (1845: 53). In 1850, the General Board of Health noted that the London water companies were forced to 'charge for the danger to which they are liable of the intrusion of other capitals into their domain' (p. 296).

Why should there have been these inhibitions in extending supplies? Three reasons emerge from an analysis of the ways in which the markets were contested. First, there are grounds for thinking that production and supply conditions were such that the authorized undertakings did not necessarily have a natural monopoly of their geographical area. A natural monopoly position can be meaningfully defined only in relation to a given technology, a specific product range, and set of output levels, and can then be said to exist when the single firm's costs are lower than for all conceivable partitions into two or more firms. This would require that costs rise not only if the firm is dismembered into a number of smaller-scale versions of itself, or into separate specialist product firms, but for all conceivable product groupings. The companies were clearly not always and everywhere necessarily natural monopolies. For gas, this issue was important in the early stages when industrial users might generate their own supplies at no great disadvantage. In addition, the companies experienced significant 'system' effects when supplies were expanded. Leakage was a very important source of gas wastage. Leakage losses increased as mains became more loaded, a problem particularly severe when multiple mains ran down the same street. Matthews (1986: 250–3) estimates that, on average for the London companies, 45 per cent of gas made was unpaid for, of which leakage was a key cause, a figure that was still at 30 per cent by 1850. The scale economies from expansion were therefore limited by such leakage effects. Finally, it is of note that, through a decline in iron prices, the capital costs of new gas plant and networks fell consistently (Rowlinson 1984: 174; Matthews 1986: 250). This suggests the possibility (and no more) that minimum cost-efficient gas volumes and minimum cost-efficient distribution networks would be lower.

The issue in the case of water was that, depending on the level of technology and size of the market, both domestic and industrial users had cheap access to alternative supplies. Commenting on the water companies' use of the Thames, the General Board of Health in 1850 noted that 'the cost of the pipe-water supply, and the additional expense and inconvenience resulting from the present mode of its distribution, causes the population in some suburban districts to resort for water to open ditches, and in other crowded localities to shallow springs or wells' (p. 313). The city of Bath was in 1845 being supplied by the corporation, plus seven 'companies' or rather property owners supplying their own tenants (Local Government Board 1915: p. xii). Ignoring for the moment the health hazards, here we have examples where a single source is not necessarily the least cost market structure, though under a different technology (an integrated constant pressure system) it might be. Similarly, in Manchester and Salford only 21 per cent of all commercial and industrial enterprises in 1845 were customers of the water company; the rest sank their own wells, installed pumps, and built reservoirs (Hassan 1985: 541).

The second problem relates to the economies of customer contiguity in the running and capital costs of the distribution networks. Such economies were an important source of cost advantages for the single gas or water company who would therefore want to capture, in any given area, as many customers as possible. But in some instances, this involved the customer incurring certain transaction costs (cf. meters, sinks). The company, therefore, faced the risk of some customers being unwilling to incur these costs, thus increasing the uncertainties of the company being able to capture the whole market. Evidence on the importance of contiguity can be seen from the experience of small towns. Even where consumption was itself necessarily collective, as in the case of street lighting, and where the gas companies bid for franchise contracts drawn up by Improvement Commissioners or other local authorities, there remained a problem that supply to the smaller towns was not initially viable. By 1821, only towns with populations of 50,000 or more were lit by gas, and it was not until the late 1840s that connections were made to all towns with a population of at least 2,500 (Falkus 1967: s. ii; Awty 1975: 92). In the case of water, a constant theme of the 1840s reports was the absence of proper supplies in small towns and, within larger towns, the costs of connecting pipes to small subgroups (cf. Commissioners on the State of Large Towns 1844: xi, xii; Dickinson 1954: 102). And when, later, major long-distance water resource projects were involved, as in Manchester, Glasgow, and Liverpool, the importance of capturing all the inhabitants was vital. The Commissioners' Second Report (1845: 48−51), the General Board of Health Report (1850: 296), and the Royal Commission on the Water Supply in 1869 (pp. 246−8), all noted that switching to finance from the rates had the key advantage of automatically enrolling a large number of water users.

In the absence of major differences between rival companies, it is not easy for one company to dominate by its price and service offers; in the early 1850s, the Great Central and Surrey Consumer gas companies were established offering massive price reductions, but not all of the customer promises to switch companies materialized and the financial viability of the new companies was undermined (Livesey 1894: 646−7; Chandler and Lacey 1949: 76). The more the customers had to bear costs, the less could a company be certain of capturing the market. Supplying a customer with gas involved the costs of fittings and of the domestic meter (which significantly was often provided without charge) and customers were in any case apprehensive about the safety of gas in the home. However, customer costs were especially important in the case of water companies wanting to extend piped constant pressure supplies to residents previously reliant on street standpipes and cesspools and now faced with the prospect of outlays on sinks and drains. Integrated systems of piped supplies necessitated the connection of a large population, the poorer members of which were undoubtedly not easy to convert. The investigators of the 1840s were convinced that piped supplies were financially attractive to all parties. For many domestic users, the system of fetching and carrying from stand-pipes was costly in time, and the Chadwick Report felt it was uneconomic for households whose members were earning at least the minimum wage. The First Report (1844) on the State of Large Towns described both financial and other economic benefits which had accrued to households in Preston and Hyde from the provision of piped supplies and the predicted lowering of unit water costs in South-wark and Nottingham. The Commissioners were able to conclude that 'it appears that the practical course of efficient improvement is not incompatible with the reduction of existing pecuniary charges independent of the vast gains in public health, conven-ience and comfort' (p. xiii. See also pp. xi, xii; Chadwick 1842: 143; Commissioners on the State of Large Towns 1845: 46, 52–3; General Board of Health 1850: 295, 340–1). The un-fettered unregulated private companies were very slow in achiev-ing the degree of integration necessary to achieve this standard of service. The outcome in general was that supplies were often limited in quantity and quality with scale and contiguity econ-omies unexploited. Each area then experienced either a vacillating competition in the field or, and increasingly over time, there was collusion on market shares leaving the districted incumbents with some monopoly power to restrict volume and quality.

There is a third reason why the position of a single supplier could be undermined. Production and supply conditions may unambiguously constitute a natural monopoly, and yet a single firm may not be a stable solution; the natural monopoly, in the jargon of the literature, is not sustainable. Take, for example, the simple case, as in Fig. 2.1 (see p. 11), of a firm selling only one product type in one market, and where average costs fall initially, reflecting scale economies, but eventually rise. It is quite possible for the conditions for a natural monopoly to be met even if the chosen output level is in the range where average cost is rising; one firm (at C) could still be cheaper than two firms (D and E, not shown in Fig. 2.1) supplying the market. However, when the partition involves one of the firms supplying more than 50 per cent of the market, such a firm (say D) could clearly have average costs lower than the average costs incurred when a single firm (C) supplied all the market. Of course, the other firm (E), in the duopoly case, would have much higher costs so that the natural monopoly conditions would hold; the total costs of D plus E exceed those that would arise if only C supplied the market. But clearly firm D might try to undermine the monopoly position by cutting prices and offering to supply a more restricted volume, leaving the rest of the market to its own devices. The situation is not one of equilibrium, but the incentive for rival D to undermine C clearly exists, and renders the monopoly position unstable. The above example refers only to a single product and/or market. In the more general case of several submarkets (as, for example, supplying different customers and areas with water), the analogous proposition is that, if the (attributable) cost of a submarket rises when there is an increase in the number of submarkets supplied, the monopolist is vulnerable to an entrant catering for a smaller range.

For the early nineteenth-century gas and water companies, this issue is particularly relevant to the prospect of increased unit costs in the face of demands for increased volume and better quality supplies. The problem was again more important for water than gas. For the water companies, two developments raised the prospect of rising unit costs. First, by the middle of the century, the demand for good quality water was rising as the result of continuing urbanization and industrialization. Increasing usage of existing sources was likely in some cases to lead to higher costs in the sense of a poorer quality of supply. 'After a century of industrial pollution . . .', records Hassan (1985: 541), 'the streams flowing through the northern manufacturing regions had become contaminated sewers, with pronounced increase in hardness between their headwater and lower reaches.' The alternative was to look further afield for water sources and this became the pattern from the mid-nineteenth century, with the schemes for Glasgow, Manchester, and Liverpool even more spectacular. The point concerning these longer-distance supplies is not that, as both Knoop (1912) and Hassan (1985) have argued, the investment and planning horizons were beyond the scope of private enterprise, but rather that it rendered the private monopolist vulnerable to entry by firms supplying more restricted markets. A second key development for the water companies was the demand for comprehensive piped supplies under constant pressure. For much of the first half of the nineteenth century, the supply from incorporated water undertakings was intermittent in the sense that it was made available only at certain times of the day whether this was via piped supplies or, in the case of poor residents, at street stand-pipes. Quite apart from the benefits to public health, it was consistently argued in the 1840s government reports that meeting rising consumption by the use of the existing distribution network would only raise prices and that a constant pressure piped system would be to the economic advantage of all parties. Whilst loss of water from leakage or unauthorized consumption did occur with the constant pressure system, overall it was expected to be significantly less than with intermittent supply. The hesitancy of poorer residents to convert, given the anticipated expenditures on sinks and drains, has earlier been raised as a problem facing the water company needing to get wide market coverage. The additional issue relevant to the present context is that a switch to a comprehensive constant pressure system involved a prospective rise in costs associated with monitoring the company's service pipes for leakage and misuse in households (sometimes involving landlord and tenants) in a more comprehensive system, and with assessing whether supplies would have to be metered or whether the whole financial basis could be shifted to the rates (cf. General Board of Health 1850: 314–17; Stern 1954: 1001).

It is not then surprising that the water companies' performance was criticized for restricting piped supplies to the more easily monitored streets of the wealthy and for the slowness in the introduction of the constant pressure system. The 1852 Water-works Act compelled companies to give constant pressure service, but this obligation could readily be avoided since it was hedged in with stipulations that the household pipes and fittings be in a proper condition to receive such a supply. The London companies were continually pointing to the problem of monitoring domestic arrangements with respect to waste and leakage and the problems were still there when the Royal Commission on the Water Supply reported in 1869 (pp. 238, 241–3). Leakage and waste at various points in the system were major problems also for gas. Initially, in the absence of metering, the system had all the problems which plagued water supply. Gas was supplied by contract at a fee (or 'rent') per burner for so many hours each night and inspectors were appointed to monitor service fittings, ensure that the gas was turned on only in the stipulated periods, and that burner jets had not been opened to enlarge the flame. These problems hastened the introduction of meters, which were common by the middle of the century (Livesey 1894: 648; Awty 1975: 99). Again, however, to the extent that serving the poorer households in the population would require close monitoring of company equipment and with leakage and waste having system-wide effects, it is understandable that the private gas companies were cautious in extending supplies to large parts of the population and that, as for water, a central criticism by the middle of the century was that they catered largely for shops and the streets of the wealthier residents.

THE FAILURE OF THE REGULATION OF THE PRIVATE GAS AND WATER COMPANIES 1820–1870

The prime public interest in exercising control over gas and water supplies to eliminate or reduce the above problems was therefore to define the relevant economic areas of production, arrange that each area was served by only one producer, and ensure this producer's charges approximated the cost of supply. Since gas metering was economic, policy had mainly to ensure that prices corresponded to costs, which had not been inflated. None of this, on the face of it, required public ownership. Incumbent private companies could be confirmed as exclusive suppliers, but with financial rates of return and the level of costs subject to monitoring. Competition for the field would have to be encouraged at regular intervals. Because water metering looked uneconomic, a franchise contract would have to be drawn up by the local authority, specifying the area to be covered and the standard of service; finance would be from the rates, as the Commissioners' Second Report of 1845 proposed (pp. 55–7) and the franchise open for bidding, in terms of fee and service levels, by potential private company suppliers.

Gas and water production and consumption generated external effects so that the public interest extended beyond the issues discussed so far. However, the broad features of the form of public control are not significantly affected by such considerations, though they added to the complexity. In the case of gas, there were three kinds of externality. First were the noxious fumes and safety issues associated with leaking gas which, as already noted, was a major source of the heavy wastage of gas. Second was the increase in public safety accompanying better lighting; comprehensive street lighting was, from the mid-nineteenth century, added to the set of urban improvements which local authorities were expected to implement, embracing sewers, paving, water supply, lighting, policing. Again, on the face of it, these requirements could be incorporated in the franchise contract, or in whatever legal measure was used to confer the private monopoly. Similarly, all public utilities caused street disruptions through the laying and repair of mains, and some co-ordination between the various users was clearly needed. This does not necessarily require public ownership as, for example, Kellett implies (1978: 42). Once supply is restricted to one firm it is not obvious that co-ordination between gas, water, tramway, and electric companies required that they be publicly owned. There is some evidence, in fact, that the private gas companies were less disruptive than the municipal companies. There was, however, the question of whether the requirements laid on the gas companies arising from all the above issues would be consistent with the earning of a normal financial rate of return. Then the regulatory body is faced on the one hand with a desire to subsidize some activities, by appropriate subventions to the company, whilst at the same time monitoring overall rates of return to prevent the exploitation of a monopoly position.

In the case of water supply there were additional spillovers of great significance (Commissioners on the State of Large Towns 1844: pp. xi, xii, 1845: 48–51; Chadwick 1842: 341; General Board of Health 1850: 2, 284, 312–23). The social costs of inadequately monitored, policed, and regulated water companies were strikingly demonstrated in Newcastle upon Tyne during 1853 and 1854. A cholera epidemic most probably was caused by contaminated river water supplied by the private water company, even though the company had been established to supply pure water from another source. Then a fire, that might have been contained had the company made water more readily available, destroyed 800 homes and killed 53 people. Yet little statutory action was elicited (Rennison 1978).

In summary, first a more extensive and better quality supply would directly reduce disease and the associated financial demands on sick charges and Poor Law relief. Secondly, a water supply piped under constant high pressure was required for fire-fighting and would reduce the health hazards exacerbated by stagnant water in cisterns and wells under the current arrangements of intermittent supply. Thirdly there was the recognition that water supply needed to be considered in conjunction with drainage and sewage, and that integrated operations were therefore important. What Chadwick and others in the public health movement had stressed was that the link between health and the general condition of urban life was a matter not so much of the quality and size of the buildings as of the deficient services to them, drainage, sewage, and water supplies in particular. The exclusion of poor streets and poor residents from piped water supplies was significant, precisely because on health grounds these were the areas in most need. However, on the face of it, the specific requirements could, again as the 1845 report spelt out, be incorporated into the franchise contract. Many contemporaries and subsequent observers nevertheless doubted whether the private companies were fit or equipped to deal with the public health problem (cf. Stern 1954: 1001–2). Similar views exist on the more narrow market structure problems. Joseph Chamberlain's statement of 1874 that all monopolies sustained by the state should be in the hands of representatives of the people may, as Falkus (1977: 152) argues, have been reflecting public opinion, but this cannot be explained simply in terms of market structure problems. The decisive factor was the unsatisfactory experience with arm's length regulation of the private companies, and to this matter we now turn.

Certain obligations and limits were imposed on the companies from the very beginning, especially where Parliament was encouraging amalgamation or districting (Select Committee on the Supply of Water 1821: 8–9, 1828: 5; Commissioners on the State of Large Towns 1844: p. xx, 1845, 50–5; Dakyns 1931: 21). Thus controls on prices and dividends were written into some of the early Gas Acts for Nottingham, Oxford, Worcester, and Bristol in 1818–19 for example. Following the 1821 Select Committee's revelation that the districting agreement in London had been followed by a 25 per cent rise in water rates, and the 1828 Select Committee's finding that prices were still rising, all special Acts between 1822 and 1845 incorporating water companies included clauses relating to charges, with maximum prices linked to the value of property. The companies had to make supply available to everyone living on a street where a water main was laid. Finally, in recognition of at least one external effect, the companies had to provide fire plugs on the mains and to supply at will in such an emergency. But the main thrust towards regulation came in the official reports of the 1840s which called for controls on supply and profit rates, which Parliament were soon to impose in the face of the emergence of *de facto* monopolies in, for example, Sheffield gas, and water supply in Hartlepool and Sunderland. Competition was abandoned as a policy. The 1847 Surveying Officers' report on gas supplies emphasized the need for the remaining single producer, whether publicly or privately owned, to be accountable to local interests and that price and dividend controls and other limitations needed to be supplemented by the appointment of Inspection Officers (Johnes and Clegg 1847: pp. v, vi). The 1832 Lighting and Watching Act had given relevant enabling powers to local authorities to secure adequate gas lighting, but in water even such a discretionary power was not in the hands of the local authorities. The 1840s health reports demanded, therefore, from the start the imposition of an obligation on local authorities to secure adequate water supplies. In addition, they pressed for franchise contracts financed through rates and for the overall integrated management of water supply, drainage, and sewage to be in the hands of an independent disinterested body (Select Committee on the Health of Towns 1840: p. xx; Chadwick 1842: 148–50, 422–5; Commissioners on the State of Large Towns 1844: p. xx, 1845: 50–5; Dakyns 1931: 21).

In practice, the new legislation was weak and monitoring procedures were almost non-existent. The reasons lie outside our scope but perhaps more than anything else there was a fear of the central authority undermining local interests which, though themselves in some disagreement (cf. Water Commissioners, Highway Surveyors, Poor Law Commissioners), were united in opposing central interference (cf. Lubenow 1971: 85, 100; Frazer 1973: 60–4). The central feature of the legislation was its permissive nature. The Gas Works and Water Works Clauses Acts of 1847 provided that dividends were to be limited to 10 per cent, though this was to be interpreted as taking one year with another, and in addition a reserve fund of up to one-tenth of the nominal capital could be accumulated to provide for exceptional circumstances. In the case of water, maximum charges were set in relation to the rateable values of property; maximum prices were also laid down for gas which could vary with local conditions. The Acts also contained regulations for the laying of mains, the conditions of meters and pipes, and the prevention of public nuisances, as well as authorizing local authorities to issue ordinances safeguarding public interests. But this was only enabling legislation in that it specified clauses which should be inserted in any new bills, and even this was at the discretion of the Private Bills Committee. Similarly, the 1848 Public Health Act authorized the establishment of local boards of health, but only if this was recommended by the General Board of Health and if at least 10 per cent of ratepayers petitioned for them. The local boards had enabling powers to secure adequate water supply, but again this was not mandatory (Lubenow 1971: 80–1; Robson 1935: 307, 315; Falkus 1977: 144–5; Williams 1981: 41; Maltbie 1900: 542–3; Frazer 1973: 65; Finer 1941: 44; Dakyns 1931: 25–6).

Regulation of the companies, at least for the period up to the 1870s, was therefore largely ineffective. Even where the 1847 provisions were subsequently incorporated into specific legal measures, there was no strong enforcement mechanism. Prior to the 1840s, controls on prices and dividends were not common; in the case of water, dividend restrictions have been recorded only in the Acts for Chester and Leeds. But the early experience with other obligations is instructive. The requirement on water companies relating to the provision of fire plugs excluded any references to minimum distances between them, and to continuity of water supply, so the fire hazard remained a serious problem. The obligation to make supply available to all residents of an area only applied to streets where mains were laid so that the streets with poorer residents never benefited from this provision, and in any case the obligations on a water company only held as long as this did not affect its own customers. The maximum prices inserted into the local Water Acts from the 1820s seem to have been set at such a level as to leave plenty of scope for the companies (Commissioners on the State of Large Towns 1845: 47–8, 52–3; Dakyns 1931: 22–4). Matters were not changed by the 1840s legislation since there were no formal procedures for reviewing prices. In the case of gas, where technical change was rapid and costs falling, the price ceilings rapidly lost any significance (Maltbie 1900: 544–6, 549–50; Williams 1981: 41–4; Falkus

1977: 150–1). In any case, evasion was possible by altering meter rents, on which the legislation had initially nothing to say. Matters did not improve significantly until the sliding-scale system spread from the middle 1870s; in so far as company dividends were restrained by the legal provisions, the sliding scale provided a relief to the extent that the company reduced prices, thereby giving an incentive to meet the intentions of the legislation. By 1900, half the private gas companies were, however, still on the maximum price system.

In any case, it was the control of dividends that proved especially difficult. Experience up to the 1870s led to measures to plug certain regulatory gaps, but even by the turn of the century the ability to 'water' the capital base remained a significant problem. The experience of gas, where private companies remained important, has been recorded in detail (Maltbie 1900: 544–7; Williams 1981: 41–7; Falkus 1977: 150–1). Parliament had initially prohibited the payment of the maximum dividend on shares not fully paid up. The ceiling of 10 per cent was a fairly liberal figure and over time lower ceilings had to be set; in the Acts of the 1870s, a figure of 7 per cent was often used, and in 1896 a lower rate was generalized and set at 4 per cent. But other methods of evasion of the ceilings were possible. Loan capital could be converted to share capital; this spreading of profits over a nominally bigger base of share capital became illegal only after the early 1870s. In addition, when the yield on gas stocks exceeded other yields, gas companies made new issues which existing shareholders were able to obtain at par value and immediately thereafter they would make a capital gain. Hence, from 1870, the Acts passing through Parliament came to stipulate that new stock issues should be publicly auctioned, a practice which became mandatory in 1872. The stock might then sell above par but the company was not allowed to pay dividends on the premiums. The ability to take profits one year with another and the lack of standardized accounts compounded the problem in effectively restraining profits. Even though from 1871 the former provision was no longer included and companies were obliged to provide standardized accounts, it was to take some time for an effect to be felt. In 1880, a House of Commons Select Committee was still noting the ease with which the dividend limit could be evaded by the water companies being able to take one year with another (Select Committee on London Water Supply 1880: v). It was always difficult, moreover, to monitor the case where gas companies established subsidiary construction companies from whom new plant was purchased at inflated prices, thereby undermining the significance of the quoted profit rate. Finally, in so far as a company's declining cash flow in an activity is due to ageing assets, its real rate of return may not be falling. Unless the company writes off capital or creates renewals funds, the declared profit rate will be falling, and as late as 1900 the American observer M. R. Maltbie (1900: 544–7) still felt this was a problem in monitoring the dividends of the British gas companies.

The obligation on companies to provide supplies of good quality also took considerable time to become entrenched. The 1847 Gas Works Act contained nothing on the obligations to supply, nor did it include controls on gas quality. These were introduced on an *ad hoc* basis so that by 1870 the legal obligation to supply was widespread, as were the procedures for testing gas and setting illuminating standards, and both issues were enshrined in the 1871 Gas Works Clauses Act (Falkus 1977: 15). In the case of water, we have already noted that the 1848 Public Health Act had not mandated the local health boards to secure adequate supplies, and the 1852 Waterworks Act had qualified the requirement that companies provide constant pressure service with the proviso that households' pipes and fittings were already in a proper condition. Dissatisfaction with the water supplies of private companies was still widespread at the end of the 1860s, especially in London where progress towards an improved and integrated service was slow, and where the companies were explicitly criticized by the 1869 Royal Commission for their neglect in complying with the law with respect to water quality. The 1871 Royal Sanitary Commission noted that promoters of water bills were still being allowed to escape the obligation to provide a constant supply. Not till the 1875 Public Health Act did the country have local sanitary authorities obliged to secure an adequate water supply, and where the adequacy of private company supplies could be tested by arbitration (cf. Royal Commission on Water Supply 1869: paras. 238, 241–3; Royal Sanitary Commission 1871: 41; Falkus 1977: 143–6; Robson 1935: 316; Finer 1941: 44–5).

TELEGRAPHS: COMPETITION AND CO-OPERATION

While gas, water, and railways ended the period subject to arm's length state regulation, the initially private telegraph system was nationalized in 1868, after twenty-four years, because of public concern about the service. Nationalization was supported by most newspapers, which resented the telegraph companies' monopoly of the news, and by chambers of commerce, which felt the service was too expensive, inaccurate, and insufficiently widespread geographically. The Post Office saw an opportunity to remedy this last defect (and perhaps also to grow larger) by employing existing sub-post offices as telegraph stations in a Post Office-owned system (Kieve 1973; Brock 1981; British Parliamentary Papers 1867–8).

Whereas the American industry by the late 1860s came to be dominated by one firm, Western Union, British market concentration declined almost continually throughout the private enterprise period. The lack of integration noted in the preceding industries was also apparent in telegraphy. The first patent was granted in 1837 and by 1844 there were 550 miles of telegraph line. In 1846 the Electric Telegraph Company was founded and purchased the initial inventions. By 1850 there were over 2,000 miles of telegraph line running alongside railway tracks. As new firms entered the industry, the Herfindhal index of British telegraph concentration fell from 1 in 1849 to 0.56 in 1855, reaching a nadir of 0.27 in 1861, rising again to 0.41 in 1865, and ending in 1868 at 0.47 (calculated from British Parliamentary Papers 1867–8). The strategy of the incumbent British firm, by then the Electric & International Telegraph Company (the 'Electric' or EITC), was to establish a profitable *modus vivendi* with other firms in the industry, even if that meant losing market share. By contrast, Western Union absorbed and rationalized rival enterprises. The greater role of mergers and concentration in American industrial organization is often attributed to the 1890 Sherman Act. Since the legislation had not then been passed, it cannot explain the divergent courses of telegraph concentration in the two countries before 1868.

In response to new entry, the Electric's tariff reductions in 1852, 1854, 1862, and 1864–5 were significant sources of sales growth for the company itself and for the industry (Table 2.4). The

EITC's profitability suffered most with the tariff reductions of 1854. Thereafter, price stability appears to have been maintained until the entry of the United Kingdom Telegraph Co. (UKTC). Although the London & District made inroads into the EITC's apparent market share, in fact the service offered was probably not directly competitive. After an agreement had been reached with the entrants in 1856, the Electric doubled the London–Birminghan tariff and increased the rates on the Manchester–Leeds routes by 50 per cent (British Parliamentary Papers 1867–8: appendix). The Electric reduced the number of stations by one-fifth between 1850 and 1852 and then almost doubled the number of offices open to the public in the following two years (Table 2.4). The year 1859 saw a reduction in the number of offices but the advent of the UKTC caused a massive expansion in 1861; again offices open to the public nearly doubled in two years. Entry of the UKTC with a uniform one shilling tariff was met by Electric tariff cuts at nearly 200 places, but only where the Electric faced competition.

The established companies owned the rights of way for tele-graph lines along railway routes, yet this was not an insurmount-able entry barrier. The UKTC put up lines instead alongside public roads, a policy which the incumbent firms bitterly resisted by legal proceedings. 'Men therefore were employed to traverse the roads, suggesting opposition and making the grossest misrep-resentations; counsel's opinions of an adverse character were ob-tained and circulated, suggesting how this company's poles should be cut down' (Directors' Report, Weaver 1867: 39). Profitability of the Electric reached a trough in 1862, as the company's price cut restored most of the market share lost in 1861. Rapid sales growth and an expansion of offices was, however, insufficient to prevent a reversal of the gain over the following three years. The company lost money on the one shilling tariff on the London to Liverpool and London to Manchester routes and was obliged to put up more wires to cope with the traffic generated (British Parliamentary Papers 1867–8). However, the Electric possessed the resources to survive the price war and therefore was able ultimately to dictate peace terms. In September 1864, the con-ditions were agreed; the UKTC was to make no further extensions for two years in return for the EIT maintaining prices (Weaver 1867: 39). Almost one year later, in June 1865, the UKTC pro-

TABLE 2.4 *The Electric Telegraph Company in the British market 1849–1868*

Year	Event	% Growth of EITC paid public messages	EITC average tariff (revenue per message)	EITC % market share	EITC stations	EITC profit to turnover ratio
1849	ETC pays first dividend 30 June. The rival British Electric Telegraph Co. (BETC) formed and incorporated by an act of July 1850, opposed by the ETC.	n/a	n/a	100	n/a	
1850	ETC's wires on only 2,215 miles of railway out of 7,231. 64,734 messages sent. In the USA over 12,000 miles of telegraph and 20 telegraph cos.	n/a	0.50	n/a	257	
1851	English & Irish Magnetic Telegraph Co. (EIM) incorporated. Numbers of messages transmitted accelerate, 20 words less than 100 miles, 2s. 6d., over 100 miles 5s.	53	0.50	n/a	224	0.38
1852		113	0.32	n/a	207	0.35
1853		16	0.42	n/a	338	0.30
1854	Rates further reduced	133	0.21	n/a	420	0.25
1855	ETC and International Telegraph Co. merged to create the EITC. Permitted by the Electric Telegraph Act which placed a 10% dividend limit. Within London 1s., up to 50 miles 1s. 6d., up to 100 miles 2s.	25	0.20	70	404	0.30

Year	Event					
1856		7	0.21	68	423	0.33
1857	BETC and EIM amalgamate to form 'The Magnetic' under the Joint Stock Companies Act of 1856	10	0.21	68	460	0.33
1858		3	0.20	66	517	0.32
1859	London and District Telegraph Company formed. Offers service at 4d. for 10 words, 6d. for 15 words.	18	0.20	63	428	0.34
1860	UK Telegraph Company formed with a uniform 1s. rate.	9	0.19	60	476	0.32
1861	Ricardo, former direct or of Electric Telegraph Co., writes memo advocating nationalization.	7	0.19	45	772	0.33
1862	London & South of Ireland Telegraph Co. formed.	28	0.14	57	900	0.30
1863	Telegraph Act retricts the sale of telegraph companies without the consent of the Board of Trade.	19	0.14	56	1,022	0.35
1864		29	0.11	50	1,022	0.36
1865	The three companies introduce a new tariff as the UK abandons the 1s. rate. National Assoc. of Chambers of Commerce Committee reports on poor telegraph service.	26	0.11	47	1,180	0.40
1866	Snow brings down many miles of line.	6	0.11	n/a	1,249	0.39
1867		6	0.10	n/a	1,249	0.39
1868	Act authorizing state purchase of telegraph companies.	12	n/a	57	n/a	0.44

posed that the rate for inland messages be increased for up to 100 miles to 1s., up to 200 miles to 1s. 6d. and over 200 miles, to 2s. The Electric accepted the proposal on the condition that the UKTC publicly announce in each town where they operated a station that the uniform one shilling rate had proved a failure.

The price agreement of 1865 ushered in a period of slower sales growth, greater market share, and profitability rising to unprecedented levels. A portion of the greater profitability is attributable to the reduction of maintenance expenditure and the ending of expansion after 1866, when the nationalization debate began. Investment in expansion of the system was typically charged to current expenditure. The response to the first entry was then price cuts and reduction of offices and to all subsequent new entrants a price cut and an expansion of offices. In all cases, the ultimate aim of the tactic was to form a cartel which fixed prices.

British management only appreciated the possibilities of merger, rather than a cartel, as a result of a visit by Western Union's Cyrus Field in 1864. The secretary to the Electric, Weaver, was impressed by Field's account of combining American telegraph companies to maintain profit rates and yet at the same time offering cheap tariffs. Weaver was particularly interested in the techniques for amalgamations; how prices were agreed for shares (such as those of some of his rivals) trading at a 50 per cent discount, and whether amalgamated companies worked as an integrated system or maintained all their old offices. Ultimately, in response to the nationalization threat, the principal British companies did try to rationalize after a fashion. In December 1867 they held a special meeting about the transfer of the telegraphs to the state and discussed a traffic working agreement between the three companies. Before then, working arrangements had been restricted to companies whose interests were clearly complementary. The British Electric Telegraph Co., incorporated in 1850, early boasted a connection with the Submarine Telegraph Co. The successor, Magnetic Telegraph Co., reached an agreement with the London & District in 1859. Very differently, the dominant firm, the Electric, seems to have found problems achieving co-operative working, in contrast to co-operative pricing, with almost anybody, even the Submarine. Difficulties between these two companies were the subject of unsuccessful negotiations in 1856, 1858, and 1860. On the last occasion, the Electric was urging the Submarine to maintain charges for Continental messages while in Paris asking for a concession on another line at a greatly reduced tariff (Submarine Telegraph Co. 1861). Aggression towards rivals combined with timidity where technological advances were concerned. The Electric's chairman, Grimston, declined to support the cause of Atlantic telegraphy in 1866 by buying shares, on the grounds that they were 'speculative' (Weaver 1867: 39); and this despite the recognition of the key importance for business of international connections. Perhaps the Electric's only successful co-operation in working was the agreement with the Universal Private Telegraph Co., which supplied private line services and therefore did not compete in public traffic. A more co-operative or creative dominant firm could have constructed a rather different industry.

GOVERNMENT TELEGRAPH POLICY

These problems were not unique but they took different forms elsewhere because, outside the United Kingdom and the United States, geopolitical considerations in the nineteenth century generally elevated defence to the first objective of state policy. The new communications technologies, the railway and the telegraph, were vital contributors to the internal and external security of continental European states. As such, most states carefully planned, regulated, and, when possible, administered these networks. Later nineteenth-century European governments were also concerned with national economic development. Their control of national telecommunications networks, originating in security policy, allowed them some influence over the competitiveness especially of fast-growing communication-intensive national industries, such as commerce and financial services. The speed, accuracy, price, and spread of the telegraph could make a considerable difference to the development of these industries, just as more complex telecommunications facilities today are regarded as a key element in European competitiveness (Commission of the European Communities 1987).

Through their concern for security and their desire to maintain a monopoly of communications infrastructure, the major European powers could help or hinder the emergence of the new networks on their territory. Policy differed markedly between states in the early days. Once established, the greatest value of electronic communications was over long distances, as precocious North American telegraph growth demonstrated. In Europe, long-distance communications required an unprecedented degree of intergovernmental co-operations because of the numbers of frontiers over which messages had to be transmitted. Despite the nationalism of the time, co-operation was quite successful in achieving the standardization that facilitated communication. Traffic volumes could not match those of pre-Civil War North America though, except perhaps for the small European states which subsidized internal telegrams with the proceeds of transit and international traffic.

Morse's successful transmission in 1844 post-dated a number of European systems, but the American networks immediately grew far more rapidly. During the first year of operation, 1847, 33,000 messages were sent between Toronto and Quebec (Preece and Fischer 1896: 473). By contrast, as may be seen in Table 2.5, four years later the largest entire European network, that of Britain, transmitted only three times as many telegrams in total. The great distances between major American population centres, which already had large numbers of economic connections, were major contributors to the quick success of the American telegraph. Even with the coming of the railway, personal contact or the postal service took far longer than electrical communication.

Within European nation states, distances were shorter and therefore the commercial advantage of the telegraph was reduced. But governmental needs for rapid news of insurrection or invasion were sufficient to warrant the construction of visual telegraph systems. The British Admiralty in London communicated with the navy at Portsmouth by such a system, unless the signals were obscured by fog. The French Chappe visual telegraph was offic-ially regarded as satisfactory for many years after the electric telegraph had been proved viable because each signalling tower could be protected against subversive action, unlike telegraph wires (Attali and Stourdze 1977). Sixty-one Prussian semaphore telegraph stations in 1833 connected Berlin, Magdeburg, Paderborn, Cologne and Koblenz (O'Meara 1913: 2). Instead of encouraging an interest in the electric telegraph, the state visual telegraph at best promoted indifference (the British case) and, at worst,

TABLE 2.5 *European telegraph and postal development 1851*

	Telegrams	Telegrams per thousand persons	Mail items per head
Austria-Hungary	56,164	1.8	1.15
Baden	4,148	—	n/a
Belgium	14,025[a]	3.2	n/a
France	9,014	0.2	5.56[b]
Germany (North)	40,065	1.5[c]	2.57[b]
United Kingdom	99,266	3.6	20.20
The Netherlands	0	0.0	3.60
Switzerland	0	0.0	6.80
Sweden	0	0.0	1.15[b]

[a] From 1 Sept. 1850 to end 1851.
[b] Excludes newspapers.
[c] Includes Baden and Bavaria.

Sources: Telegrams: Anderson (1872: 306); UK: Kieve (1973); Belgium: *UK Abstract of Foreign Statistics*; Mail items: Mitchell (1980).

obstructed the innovation. The French, Prussians, and later the Austro-Hungarians were not at first inclined to let their subjects utilize or experiment with the new communications media. Nor was the indifference of the British authorities fertile soil for the electric telegraph. Not until 1849 did the British Electric Telegraph Company pay its first dividend. Yet judging by postal traffic, the UK clearly had by far the strongest European demand for communications and indeed telegraph traffic per head is shown in Table 2.5 to exceed that of any European country in 1851.

The attitude of the state to communications was clearly not the only reason for the slow early European development of the electric telegraph, as British experience showed. The Cooke–Wheatstone patent had been granted in 1837 and a message successfully sent between Euston and Camden Town in London, but seven years later the patentees owned, as we have already noted, only about 550 miles of line. The Admiralty by then had decided the electric telegraph was superior to the visual telegraph and had authorized a Portsmouth–London link. By 1850 wires ran along only 2,215 of a total of 7,231 miles of British railway lines. In comparison, there were over 12,000 miles of telegraph line and 20 telegraph companies in the United States (Kieve 1973: 51). Possibly patents slowed development under British private enterprise in a way that was not permitted on the Continent. Excessive payments for patents kept prices high and retarded development by the company that held the rights, which the existence of a patent prevented any competitors entering the industry with that technology. When founded in 1846, the Electric Telegraph Company paid £30,000 for the Cooke and Wheatstone inventions. By the beginning of the next decade, this sum had increased by more than five times (Directors' Report, Post Office 1861). In the interim, the company had made profits of more than £190,000, mainly from railways. Some believed the company's profits were only maintained by the purchase and 'smothering' of patents, such as Davey's, to prevent competition (Fahie 1984: 43). The telegraph inventor Bain was given a position in the company to silence allegations that Wheatstone had copied his work (Marland 1964). The company's costs (and prices) were therefore raised, but an asset for competitors was taken off the market.

In marked contrast to Britain, the Belgian government adopted a positive policy towards the telegraph for economic development, as they had for railways. As with railways, policy was directed towards exploiting through traffic. Belgian telegraph development was, therefore, dependent upon some degree of adoption of the telegraph around her. Cooke and Wheatstone's Brussels to Antwerp line of 1846 at first had little traffic, but once the line was sold to the Belgian state in 1850 and the Dover–Calais (1851) and Dover–Ostend (1853) cables were in place, Belgium could take advantage of her position on the most direct telegraphic route from the United Kingdom to the Rhine and central Germany. As Table 2.5 shows, Belgium in 1851 was one of the most extensive users of the telegraph as a proportion of the population and should have ranked third to Britain on the basis of mail traffic. Other small open economies with considerable communications demands but less forceful governments, The Netherlands and Switzerland, still possessed no networks at that date.

The French state only reluctantly allowed the public access to the telegraph in November 1850, having constructed a line for its own use in 1845. Highton in 1852 described the restrictions on the public telegraph in France and Prussia, where governmental permission had to be asked to send messages, as providing 'more a weapon in the hands of government that a means of promoting social and commercial communications for the community' (Highton 1852). Consequently, even by November 1853, only seventy-eight telegraph stations were open in France compared with 257 three years earlier in the United Kingdom (Lardner 1866). Mail items indicate the extent to which the telegraph demand was suppressed.

Prussia at first showed only slightly less inertia than France. Despite interest from the (semaphore) Telegraph Corps and financial support for experiments in 1840, satisfactory trials were not completed in Prussia until 1846. An application by an American, William Robinson, to build a line between Hamburg and Berlin was turned down in 1847 by the Prussian government, who themselves opened a line on that route eighteen months later, using the Morse system that Robinson had originally proposed. Not until June 1848 was the construction authorized of electric telegraph lines between Berlin and Frankfurt, from Berlin to Cologne, and on to the Belgium frontier (O'Meara 1913: 6–7). Prussian railways recognized the value of the electric telegraph by 1845 when four applied for permission to introduce private line telegraphs, but the government could not reach a decision for two years. When the authorities eventually make up their minds, the sixteen conditions that had to be fulfilled if railways were to operate telegraphs were extraordinarily restrictive, including the necessity for government control of the railway's service by state telegraph officials at the railway stations.

Commercial telegraphs developed earlier elsewhere in Germany, where bureaucracy was less stifling and economic liberalism more acceptable. Lines were constructed in 1844 between Kassel and Wiesbaden along the Taunus railway, the following year between Dresden and Radeberg along the Saxony and Silesia railway, and in 1846 between Bremen and Bremerhaven. Though private enterprise could introduce the electric telegraph in Germany, outside Prussia it could not develop a network because of the political fragmentation of the country. One government's refusal of permission could scupper a scheme involving the crossing of many boundaries and in any event the time consumed by negotiations would cut the profitability of the capital invested in the system.

The Prussian line from Berlin to the Belgian frontier required negotiations with twelve separate governments.

Austria-Hungary's telegraphic precocity in 1851 (cf. Table 2.5) is largely explicable by the perceived security needs of a large and disparate empire. Telegraph use was much greater than mail demand would have suggested relative to other nations. The first Austrian electric telegraph was put into service in 1847 by a private railway company between Vienna and Brünn (Bauer and Latzer 1988). Shortly before the line was completed, Metternich persuaded the Emperor that national security required a state monopoly of electric telegraphy. Under the 1847 decree, which still forms the basis of the Austrian state telecommunications monopoly, telegraphy was restricted to the railways and the state. Private messages were forbidden. State security none the less supplied a motive to expand the system rapidly. At the end of 1847, nearly 500 miles of line were in operation. Two years after the 1848 revolution, the new Emperor Franz Joseph opened the State Telegraph to the public.

The state in Sweden played an even more positive role in telegraph development. Not only was Sweden well behind France, Germany, and Austria-Hungary in the absorption of new technology (railways did not arrive until 1850) but she was also believed to be well behind her Scandinavian neighbours in national product per head (O'Meara 1915). Yet the military impetus behind the Swedish telegraph in 1853 gave Sweden a service before Denmark or Norway.

The government, then, was by no means always a brake upon the adoption of the electric telegraph. At the international level, where the European telegraph could be most effective, each government recognized that its neighbours could retard their electronic communication. The Austro-German Telegraphic Union, established at the Vienna Telegraphic Congress of 1851, therefore aimed to avoid the difficulties inherent in communicating between countries with different regulations, instruments, and signals. A major achievement was standardization on Morse's Telegraphy which had early been adopted by the Prussians (Lardner 1866: 267). The prices at which the new service could be used were as important as availability and quality of service. International communications were therefore facilitated when at the Paris Telegraphic Congress of 1853 France, Belgium, Prussia, Austria-

Hungary, and the smaller German state agreed a tariff for all messages sent to or from these states. Each telegraph region was divided into zones measured from the Belgian frontier according to the air-line distance. France was divided into six zones from Belgium, and Germany and Austria-Hungary were organized into eight zones which extended to north-eastern Italy.

Technical progress combined with public pressure to reduce both the level of telegraph tariffs and their increase with distance. In Britain, we have seen, tariff cuts occurred whenever a new firm entered the market. During the early 1860s the rate was thereby reduced to a uniform one shilling for some years. Eventually the entrant had to admit that tariff was unprofitable and a four-zone rate (including one zone for London) was re-established. On the Continent, where there was no threat of competition and dividends were not a policy objective, different, less cost-related tariff structures could be enforced. There, the uniform national tariff made headway earlier, but first the tendency for the tariff to increase with distance was reduced. The Austro-German rates were cut by 65 per cent in the first zone in 1858 and in 1859 telegrams sent within any state of the Telegraph Union were reduced a further 17 per cent. In 1863, zones were reduced to three, the third covering all distances over 208 miles, and the rate in the first zone was cut again, this time by 5 per cent (O'Meara 1913: 28–9). On 1 January 1862 the French tariff was reduced to one franc between two places in any department, an average of fifty miles, or two francs between any points in different departments (Lardner 1866: 266).

Belgium's internal tariff corresponded entirely to the first zone of France—the rate was a uniform one franc from 1862. Three years later it was halved. This pricing policy was only possible because of the profits earned on the high volume of international and transit messages. Even so, the financial position of the Belgian telegraph system began to deteriorate. In the mean time, though, the example encouraged emulation in Britain and America. Continental European tariffs in the 1860s were sufficiently low and telegraph usage sufficiently high in the smaller states, Belgium, the Netherlands, Denmark, and Switzerland, to provide ammunition for those who wanted to nationalize the private British and American networks. But as we show later, different service quality and subsidies underlay these low charges.

CONCLUSION

Free enterprise behaved similarly in all network industries. The principal difference stemmed from the gas and water companies being more concerned with distribution from a central node (the gas- or waterworks) whereas railways and telegraphs carried traffic over more complex networks with many nodes (stations or offices). The area of supply was thus limited in the first pair of industries. In the second, there was a tendency to over-supply stations and offices.

Early railway competition gave way to revenue-sharing agreements and some amalgamation. But even by 1865, the evidence from the study of forty-six companies with over ten miles of railway showed that unit costs, and therefore rates, could be brought down by more co-ordinated company operations that raised average freight and passenger loads, and increased passenger train hauls. Integration had not proceeded far by the time public pressure for effective regulation became strong. As the area supplied by gas and water companies extended from the central distribution point, average costs were driven up by the greater transmission distance. Competitors could therefore choose to supply only a portion of the area at lower unit costs. As with railways and telegraphs, facilities were duplicated and prices were higher than necessary. There was less reason in the telegraph industry why such duplication should have taken place and why high prices and limited geographical coverage should have been maintained because there was a dominant firm that could have organized a more integrated industry. Yet only under the threat of nationalization did the Electric and International Telegraph Company begin discussing working agreements, by which time it was too late.

Regulation, even for safety, was largely ineffective. How great was the railway's ability to prevent any form of regulation in these years is shown by the frequency of changes in regulatory bodies and their reduction to collecting statistics. The contrast in railway and telegraph policy with continental Europe was striking. Security considerations (or, in Belgium's cases, national commercial strategy) gave many governments an interest in integrated networks which they themselves often controlled. By the late 1860s adverse comparisons were being drawn between the outcomes of Britain's *laissez-faire* regime and the greater planning on the Continent. In the next few decades, criticism was to become more vociferous and to trigger institutional change.

APPENDIX 2.1
Cost Functions for Railways in Britain in 1865

Data for 1865 on the forty-six UK railway companies referred to in Chapter 2 are used to estimate logarithmic total cost functions. In Table A.2.1 equation (2) regresses the log of total costs on the logs of the independant variables. Equations (4) and (5) present estimates for companies of different sizes. Equation (1) is a restricted form of the general translog function (see also Appendices 6.2 and 6.3). Increases in passenger and freight volumes raise total costs whilst increases in trainloads and length of train haul lower total costs. A more detailed interpretation is given in the fourth section of Chapter 2 and in Foreman-Peck (1987*b*). The role of the Hausman test is explained below.

Typically the profit-maximizing firm chooses outputs and costs simultaneously. The error term, e, in a cost function of the form

$$C = Qa + e,$$

will then be correlated with the output variables (Q), and ordinary least squares (OLS) estimates of the output coefficients (a) may be biased. In that case the inferences drawn from them in the main text could be wrong. But railways were not typical firms, for they were obliged to run regular passenger schedules and to carry what freight was offered largely at prices laid down in their rate books. A good approximation may therefore have been that they behaved as if their output levels were beyond their control; railways minimized their costs taking outputs as given.

That proposition can be tested by a two-stage method proposed by Hausman (1978). The principle is that the first stage generates a variable set satisfying the OLS assumption by eliminating from the independent output variables that part which is correlated with the disturbance term. If the fit is not improved by this correction, we may infer that the absence of two-way causation made it unnecessary. In practical terms the first stage is to save the predicted values and the residuals from the regression of the output vector on a set of variables that railways must have taken as given in 1865—in this case the 1860 values of the output vector. The second stage is to regress railway costs in 1865 on both predicted values of the output variables and the residuals. If outputs were not taken as given in railway cost decisions then the second stage equation ((3) in the table) should fit significantly better than one estimated by OLS (eqn. (2) estimated on a smaller sample for comparability with (3)). Pairs of the two sets of coefficients should be roughly equal if there is no two-way causation. Goods load and ton-miles are, but the rest diverge considerably. However the test is on the two groups not on the pairs and the resulting likelihood ratio is 7.3876 compared with a critical value of $X^2_{0.05}(6)$ = 12.6. The hypothesis that the Q vector was not exogenous may be rejected. Similar findings were obtained when only the goods output vector was treated as potentially endogenous.

TABLE A.2.1 Total cost functions for British railways in 1865

	(1) Restricted translog	(2) Log–log	(3) Hausman test	(4) Log–log railways under 100 miles	(5) Log–log railways over 99 miles
SSR	6.326	9.1221	5.5287	3.9739	2.9438
n	46	46	34	25	21
$\bar{R}^2$	0.9519	0.9395	0.9264	0.8427	0.8296
Constant	1.6656[a] (0.66)	0.3473 (0.47)	—	-1.1310 (-0.98)	0.5001 (0.26)
Goods train-load	-1.8950[a] (-3.61)	-0.4587[a] (3.53)	[-0.7727] (-1.23)	-0.1403 (-0.70)	0.6741[a] (3.05)
Passenger train-load	-1.8222[a] (-1.73)	-0.2761[a] (-1.92)	[0.2851] (0.14)	-0.6266[a] (-2.28)	-0.1412 (0.60)
Goods train haul	-0.0990 (-0.7223)	0.0472 (0.35)	[-0.1246] (-0.42)	-0.2497 (-1.15)	-0.1335 (0.50)
Passenger train haul	-0.0011 (-0.0011)	-0.3948[a] (3.67)	[-0.7215][a] (2.62)	0.0774 (0.34)	-0.6361[a] (3.32)
Max. ton-miles	0.7710[a] (4.57)	0.3475[a] (5.34)	[0.4930][a] (2.5)	0.2724[a] (3.14)	0.3151[a] (2.89)
Max. passenger-miles	0.7428[a] (9.27)	0.6094[a] (7.95)	[0.1069] (0.08)	0.7533[a] (5.71)	0.6713[a] (3.80)
(Passenger load)^2	-0.1883 (-1.50)	—	—	—	—

Ton-miles × passenger load	(0.3318)(1.64)	—	—
Passenger haul × goods load	0.750 (0.45)	—	—
Passenger haul × ton-miles	−0.1779[a] (−2.88)	—	—
Passenger haul × passenger load	0.5242[a] (2.8891)	—	—
Passenger miles[b]	—	0.9679[a] (3.01)	—
Passenger load[b]	—	−0.2193 (−0.96)	—
Ton-miles[b]	—	0.4102 (1.31)	—
Goods load[b]	—	−0.5168 (1.75)	—
Passenger haul[b]	—	1.4538 (0.25)	—
Goods haul[b]	—	−0.7319 (−0.23)	—

Note: Square brackets denote predicted values.

[a] Indicates significance at 5% level, *t* statistics in parentheses. All variables in logs.

[b] Residuals.

3

The Political Response to Market Failure: Railways and Other National Communications Networks 1870–1914

INTRODUCTION: THE POST OFFICE MODEL

Since competition was apparently less than wholly successful in the network industries and unregulated private monopoly was unacceptable, state ownership began to look an attractive policy option in the 1860s. For national networks the state response to the perceived failure of competition was influenced by the costs, of nationalization. The telegraph seemed a fairly low cost acquisition but the vast capital of the railway system and the influence that accorded the railways encouraged an arm's length regulatory response to public dissatisfaction. Judged by productivity growth, capital costs, and continuing controversies over freight rates, railway policy was none too effective. Telephone policy fell between telegraphs and railways for, when state policy became a live issue, the Treasury was very conscious of the expense of a subsidized telegraph system. At the same time telephones competed with the established state telegraph business. British telephony therefore failed to take full advantage of the technology, with adverse effects for industry as a whole. The other side of the coin was a large, effective, and integrated telegraph network, albeit one that was subsidized by postal users.

As we have seen in Chapter 2, the long-established state-owned Post Office offered a model for some would-be reformers of the transport and communications industries. But state industry prestige was not universally high in the 1860s. Management of supplies to the armed forces was notoriously incompetent for instance. Having sold a former naval vessel, the *Medway*, in Burma, the requisitioning authority then paid the buyer for the stores on the ship a sum double the *Medway*'s purchase price (Jevons 1874). However the evidence in favour of state industry from Post Office reform associated with Rowland Hill far out-weighed such inefficiencies in the judgement of many Victorians.

Originating with an Elizabethan statutory monopoly (Post Office 1911: 7), the Post Office was an implausible candidate to become a paragon of industrial efficiency. Postmasters-General (PMGs) jealously protected their source of revenue rather than promoting innovation. Henry Bishop, the Restoration PMG who introduced the penny post stamp, was something of an exception. When William Dockwra, a merchant, improved upon Bishop and began a London penny post in 1680, employing a franking machine, he was allowed to continue for two years until the service showed profits, at which point it was taken over (Crutchley 1938; Robinson 1948: 70, *passim*). A century later mail coaches were introduced, raising the speed of letter delivery from three to ten miles an hour. The Post Office rapidly took advantage of railway transport for the mails on the Liverpool & Manchester run in November 1830. 'Remailing' or 'bypassing' the official long-distance post, and using only the local penny post, was widespread because of high charges unrelated to costs. Postage was payable on delivery rather than by the sender, which reduced the incentive to accept post and cut Post Office revenue.

In his 1837 pamphlet, Hill showed that costs varied so little with distance that the administrative simplification of a single rate was worthwhile, although it encouraged other proposals for similar pricing in industries with different distance–cost relations. What mattered more was the volume of letters between two points; there were great economies of density. Under the old regime demand, and therefore utilization of economies, was constrained by inland letter rates, for one sheet of paper, ranging upwards from the minimum non-local 4*d*. for under fifteen miles. From Edinburgh to Glasgow a sheet cost 16.5*d*. (Post Office 1887). As a result half of the letters delivered in London were posted within twelve miles of St Paul's and among the campaigners for Hill's proposal was the Mercantile Committee in London, which included a member of Baring Brothers, the merchant bankers. Even so the policy change was a matter of political chance, arising from Lord Melbourne needing support from independent radical MPs, who exacted postal reform as their price. (The chance role of politics here resembles the role of the Falklands War in allowing the Thatcher government another term of office to proceed with

privatization during the 1980s. Then once the ball is rolling everything that follows is different. In this sense the evolution of
British network industries over the last century and a half has
been path dependent.)

Hill's idea of the 'adhesive label' or postage stamp to allow
prepayment was introduced with the 'Penny Black' of May 1840.
This paid for the much lower uniform letter rate established across
the kingdom. Daunton (1985) notes that Rowland Hill's penny
post proposal was not original and that he miscalculated the
effects of the 1840 price cut. Not until the 1860s was Post Office
profitability restored to the level attained before the introduction
of the penny post. Hill's 'inverse square law' (demand equals the
reciprocal of price squared), on which he based his unsuccessful
projection of revenues from the 1840 price cut, was an assumption that the price elasticity of demand was -2. The persistence of
reduced revenue for thirteen years suggests the price elasticity for
postal services was, instead, well below one, and the short run
(year-to-year elasticity) was nearer one-half.

None the less Rowland Hill and the Post Office were held in
such high regard by the 1860s that nationalization was quite
widely considered a desirable treatment for allegedly poorly performing private network industries. Essentially this was because
the post had been transformed from a means of taxation, or
monopoly exploitation, into an efficient and pervasive public service. Letter traffic grew at an annual average rate of 7.2 per cent
in the 1840s and 4.8 per cent in the 1850s, far greater than the
expansion of economic activity. Victorian industry and life-styles
required increasing long-distance exchanges of information, a phenomenon common to other European countries as well, where the
evidence is that the income elasticity of demand for postal services
was around three (calculated from Crafts 1983).

Unit costs in 1853 were less than one-third those of 1839. These
reductions were stimulated in part by economies of scale, broadly
defined, and in part by innovations like that of the novelist and
Post Office official Anthony Trollope (deputy surveyor of rural
letter deliveries in the South-West, and ultimately aspirant under-
secretary), to whom is attributed the post-box. Trollope made the
proposal, based on French experience, in an 1851 letter from
Guernsey to his Post Office superior (Booth 1951: 13–14; Pollard
1978: 5; we are grateful to John Treble for these references).

Again these cost reductions were a godsend for putative reformers of other network industries. Even taking into account the reduction of illegal postal arrangements, by cutting costs and prices, Post Office reform massively increased consumers' surplus (the excess of willingness to pay over actual payment for service), the conventional measure of benefit from a policy change (Crew and Kleindorfer 1991).

Frank Scudamore's success with the Post Office Savings Bank after 1861 further enhanced Post Office prestige. The Post Office already remitted low value savings by money orders. With the passage of Gladstone's bill of 1861 the Bank began operations in September, paying 2.5 per cent interest. By 1872 the number of Post Office savings accounts exceeded those of the (higher average value) trustee savings banks, and generated a surplus for the department of over £300,000. Between 1880 and 1900 the number of Post Office savings accounts rose from 2.8 million to 8.4 million. The state Post Office had become an integral part of provident working-class life, holding more deposits than building societies and friendly societies together. Life insurance was introduced in 1865 and postal orders in 1881. In short the Victorian Post Office continually responded to social needs and made money out of doing so, despite the absence of a profit motive.

NATIONALIZATION OF THE TELEGRAPH AND THE EFFECT ON COSTS

Contrasting the behaviour of the telegraph companies with the Post Office was detrimental to 'private enterprise', which was accused of restricting services and charging excessive prices. They were able to do so, a number of contemporaries thought, because the technical characteristics of telegraphy were such that one firm could supply services more cheaply than two or more (which was not to say that any one firm would); there were economies of scale or scope or both. (See for example Anderson's 1872 calculation assuming costs do not increase proportionately with messages. Brock (1981) believes scale economies were quickly exhausted but his discussion does not include all the overheads or system effects.) Many believed the fixed costs of the industry, such as the poles or trenches which carried the wire or the telegraph offices, were sufficient to lower the average costs of a firm as it grew bigger, by spreading the overheads over a larger volume of output. The biggest firm could therefore temporarily charge prices that new entrants to the industry were unable to match in the long run and thereby ultimately insist on price leadership, a cartel, or a monopoly.

Alternatively or in addition, the costs of sending a telegram along one route may have been reduced by the possession of a network that supplied a number of related routes, again because of the sharing of fixed costs. In this case working arrangements between companies could in principle equalize the unit costs of a multiple firm industry with those of a monopoly. In so far as this technical feature was important, the costs of agreeing working arrangements relative to the private benefits appear to have been too high for the British industry. The 1863 Telegraph Act, which required the consent of the Board of Trade to the sale of any telegraph company, might have proved a stumbling block for mergers in view of the presumption in favour of competition, but there is no sign that the dominant Electric saw it as such.

In contrast to the later telephone, pricing for access to, rather than use of, the telegraph network was difficult. The telegraph office was a type of public good. It was available to all who lived in the neighbourhood even though only regular users paid. Moreover senders of telegrams could not easily be charged marginal cost prices since total revenues were unlikely to cover the costs of the offices. Yet with price competition from new entrants, prices were likely to be forced down to marginal costs. (This is the 'Bertrand conjecture', that firms choose their prices on the assumption that other firms will not change theirs in response.) For the whole market then competition would ultimately prove unsustainable, and either a monopoly or a cartel would emerge.

In the process firms would locate offices to steal each others' business so that they clustered in town centres and left outlying regions unserved (Hotelling 1929). Tables 3.1 and 3.2 present some evidence of this type of behaviour in the private British industry of 1868. The number of messages per office was small compared to most other national systems. That might be interpreted as an indication that competition was successful in spreading telegraph facilities into outlying regions where demand was less strong, were it not that total telegrams sent per head were also

TABLE 3.1 *National telegraph systems and income c.1868*

		Telegraph messages per head	National product per head 1870	Telegraph wires per line	Telegrams (000) per office	Telegrams (000) per mile of line	Telegrams (000) per mile of wire
United Kingdom	(1868)	0.203	904	4.742	1.904	0.381	0.080
United States (Western Union)	(1868)	0.166	791	1.945	1.990	0.128	0.065
France	(1869)	0.148	567	2.826	1.924	0.209	0.073
Belgium	(1869)	0.339	738	3.177	3.934	0.659	0.207
Switzerland[a]	(1868)	0.432	589	2.163	2.512	0.406	0.187
Holland[a]	(1868)	0.418	591	2.784	18.024	1.222	0.438
Italy	(1870)	0.082	467	2.882	1.761	0.198	0.068
Austria	(1870)	0.166	446	3.188	2.800	0.294	0.092
Hungary	(1870)	0.096	345	2.738	3.057	0.248	0.090
Spain	(1868)	0.047	391	2.017	6.434	0.175	0.086
Germany	(1868)	0.146	579	3.292	3.099	0.407	0.123
Denmark	(1870)	0.288	563	2.598	6.853	0.422	0.162
Sweden	(1868)	0.121	351	1.967	5.409	0.127	0.064
Norway	(1870)	0.257	441	1.454	4.667	0.126	0.087
Russia	(1868)	0.027	252	1.906	3.585	0.082	0.042

Notes: Cols. 2–6 refer to 1869 for Switzerland, 1867 for Germany, 1866 for Sweden, 1860 for Spain.

[a] State system only.

Sources: Crafts (1983); *UK Abstract of Foreign Statistics*; Brown (1870); Anon. (1871).

TABLE 3.2 *Telegraph network labour productivity c.1868*

		Messages sent (000)	Employment	Messages per employee
United Kingdom	(1868)	6,438	5,339	1,206
France	(1869)	5,346	3,709	1,441
Belgium	(1869)	1,723	982	1,754
Switzerland	(1869)	1,369	607	2,255
Italy	(1870)	2,189	2,676	818
Germany (excluding Württemberg and Bavaria)	(1870)	4,380	2,934	1,493
Russia	(1868)	2,029	3,453	587
Sweden	(1866)	419	375	1,117
Denmark	(1870)	514	191	2,691

Sources: UK *Abstract of Foreign Statistics*; Brown (1870); Anon. (1871).

quite low by international standards. Low labour productivity supports the judgement that the industry was not behaving in an ideal fashion.

A caveat is that the output measure in this comparison fails to take into account variations in the quality of service between national systems. Speed of delivery and accuracy were vital attributes in determining the advantage of the telegram over the post for certain types of message. Although the Post Office complaints of the two-hour or more waiting time for its own telegrams were part of the evidence accumulated to support nationalization, in international comparisons the British system, both before and after the transfer to the state, was almost certainly well above average, judged by these criteria. The cheap Belgian telegraph rate offered a poor service. The Director-General of the Belgian Telegraphs pointed out that the low half-franc tariff had been forced upon Belgium by the terms of the 1865 International Telegraph Convention (Chapter 2) (British Parliamentary Papers 1867–8: app. 1). A great number of telegrams were sent but without either speed or accuracy; the half-franc messages were forwarded by post. If speed was required, a tariff three times that rate was charged, and for really urgent telegrams the fee was two francs. In view of the central role played by the Belgian service in the case for nationalization of the British telegraph system, this qualification is of considerable importance. It should be noted however that the companies in the United Kingdom charged porterage for messages sent to destinations further than half a mile from the telegraph office. Possibly the relatively low number of messages per employee in the United Kingdom was a consequence of the need to maintain capacity to send messages quickly even during the busy hours (10 a.m.–1 p.m.).

A similar argument cannot be applied to the messages to offices ratio though. Inspection of the pattern of telegraph offices in the large towns at the time of the transfer to the state does not offer support for an efficient private industry. Typically large areas were unserved and offices of rival companies were grouped together. In Edinburgh the majority of the nine stations were in two clusters at Leith and Princes Street/Hanover Street. Glasgow, with thirteen stations, was better served but again they fell into two groups and four of the offices belonged to the Universal Private Telegraph Company (British Parliamentary Papers 1871: 22–3). A simple index of spatial dispersion sums the ratio (the distance of each office to the nearest)/(the distance of each office from the nearest office of the same company). The index tends to zero as competitive clustering increases. For Glasgow the index was 0.5 and for Edinburgh 0.39.

A private monopoly was likely to be able and willing to offer lower prices and costs than a cartel which exercised the same market power but did not attain the economies of scale or scope of the monopoly. On that reckoning the British pattern before 1870 was the worst of both worlds. Nationalization under Acts of 1868 and 1869 at least created an integrated monopoly. The state industry may also have avoided exploitation. On the other hand state ownership and legal entry barriers may have removed pressures for internal efficiency of the organization. Costs may have risen so that price exploitation would have occurred, except that the Post Office telegraph received subsidies, so that other customers (postal users) instead were unfairly treated.

As a justification for state ownership the Post Office could show clear examples of system integration. The Magnetic owned a circuit from Bristol through Gloucester to Birmingham and London and the competitor UKTC owned a virtually useless Gloucester to Uxbridge circuit. The Post Office joined the lines at

Gloucester and extended the circuit from Uxbridge to London. In so doing three high-traffic routes were created; London–Birmingham, London–Bristol, and Bristol–Gloucester, with three intermediate stations (British Parliamentary Papers 1871: 45–6). By introducing a switch into the central telegraph office in London, the Post Office established direct connection with a greater number of branch offices, so reducing delivery time. Another device to the same end was the extension of the city pneumatic tube delivery systems, investment in which became more desirable with a unitary organization (Routledge 1891; the more extensive French system is described in Brown 1870).

Under the companies in 1868 there were 2,155 public telegraph offices and 1,226 railway offices which the public might use. By 1872, Post Office telegraph stations totalled 3,444. Railway offices were a good deal more abundant in the mid-1870s as well but thereafter their numbers declined until the end of the decade. The volume of telegraph traffic leaped upwards. In the year ending March 1871, 9.8 million messages were sent, compared with 6.4 million in the calendar year 1868. During the financial year 1872, traffic volume was almost twice the 1868 total (Table 3.3). Both the number of instruments and employment approximately doubled between the transfer and August 1870. Traffic was responding not merely to the reduction of long-distance tariffs to the uniform one shilling rate but to more free porterage for messages, more free words for names and addresses on the telegrams, and a more convenient arrangement of offices.

The downside was that transfer of telegraphs to the state proved far more expensive than had been expected. Economies of scale and scope were not realized sufficiently to counter other increased costs such as porterage. Negotiations with the railways to buy out their rights proved a lengthy and expensive business. Assimilation of the work-force to civil service pay and conditions inflated costs further. Telegraph employees took advantage of the new regime, obtaining backdated pay awards in 1872 after a strike, and showing a higher propensity to join a union than under the companies (Clinton 1984: 119–21; Kieve 1973: 185–7). Hours of work were reduced from ten or twelve to eight and a supervisory class which did not operate was introduced. In the Engineering division, 248 established officers in 1875 supervised 350 established linesmen and mechanics. Rapid expansion after the transfer accounted for the inflated numbers of the supervisory class but did

TABLE 3.3 *The telegraph service under the Post Office: fiscal years 1871–1894*

	Telegraph messages forwarded (000)	Working expenses (£000)
1871	9,850	394
1872	12,474	592
1873	15,536	875
1874	17,821	968
1875	19,253	1,077
1876	20,973	1,031
1877	21,726	1,124
1878	22,172	1,164
1879	24,460	1,089
1880	26,547	1,111
1881	29,412	1,242
1882	31,346	1,366
1883	32,092	1,504
1884	32,843	1,709
1885	33,278	1,731
1886	39,146	1,733
1887	50,244	1,940
1888	55,183	1,928
1889	59,559	1,969
1890	64,103	2,180
1891	68,622	2,265
1892	72,154	2,507
1893	72,303	2,567
1894	73,300	2,641

Note: Minor changes in coverage are included in these series.

Source: Postmaster-General's reports and Annual Abstracts of Statistics.

not justify their continuing employment. Variation in work-forces between offices and overtime indicated overmanning in some places. Edinburgh central office sent 50,000 more messages than Dublin, yet cost £7,092 less. Between 1872 and 1873 Edinburgh increased the volume of messages sent by 50 per cent with no increase in clerks. Dublin transmitted almost half as many telegrams again in 1876 as in 1872, yet managed to reduce the number of clerks employed from 401 to 286 (Select Committee on the Post Office 1876: paras. 7, 40, 43, Evidence, qs. 1596, 160218).

Ten years after the transfer of the telegraphs to the state, the

Postmaster-General boasted of the doubling of the number of telegraph offices and an approximately fourfold expansion of messages sent and instruments in use. Employment had increased less than proportionately with messages; telegraphists roughly doubled their numbers and messengers tripled (Postmaster-General 1880: 16–17). These figures did appear to vindicate earlier claims that there were economies of scale, of scope, or of integration.

Political lobbying imposed new burdens on the state industry. In 1883 the government acquiesced in a House of Commons resolution that the charge for a telegram be reduced to 6*d*. Introduced in October 1885, the tariff cut expanded messages from 33 million in 1884/5 to 50 million in 1886/7. Until the implementation of this tariff, revenue had exceeded expenditure to meet at least some of the interest on the stock created for the acquisition of the telegraphs. Pay awards in August 1881 and in July 1890 pushed the telegraphs further into the red. In this last round, telegraphist wages were raised to a level about 20 per cent above that of 1875. Low-grade engineering staff achieved very little until the end of the 1890s but high-grade engineers were earning 65 per cent more than their mid-1870s pay by the early 1890s (Post Office 1911: 77; Kieve 1971: 193–5; Clinton 1984: 129–30; Routh 1954: 216, 222).

The 1875 Treasury Committee commented that the very low tariff for newspapers was a source of loss to the service. Yet the power of the press was such that no action was taken before the outbreak of the First World War, even when it had been established that the concession was costing around £200,000 a year (Post Office 1911: 69, 77; Kieve 1971: ch. 11). Free railway messages negotiated under the 1868 Act were also a source of loss for the telegraph service. Between 1871 and 1890 the volume of this traffic in England and Wales increased more than twelve-fold to just over 1.2 million. Unlike the press, the railways were persuaded to accept a curtailment of their 1868 privileges in the form of an upper limit on the number of words and messages that they were permitted without charge.

Under state as under private ownership, the industry maintained price stability for long periods, with an occasional concession to customers. In contrast to the private industry, the principal goal of the state telegraph service was not earning profits but extending the service, subsidized by the post. The pressure to do so, operating through Parliament, was far stronger than for the private industry. Among the few countervailing forces was the greater tendency for wage costs to rise.

System integration under the Post Office reduced the costs of supplying a given volume of industry services but the nationalized industry brought higher costs in other respects which might have more than offset increased utilization of economies of scope. In order to test that proposition a simple cost comparison between the Electric and the Post Office telegraph is presented. Details are in Appendix 3.1. Ideally a comparison with the entire private industry would be undertaken. Lack of data precludes that option and the test is therefore biased against the state regime. The output of the dominant firm is likely to have been produced at lower costs than that of the smaller firms in the industry that were less profitable.

Formulations of cost functions must take into consideration the tendency for both the companies and the Post Office to charge investment in the extension of the telegraph system to current costs. A second property the functions should possess is an allowance for the pace of expansion, and changes in factor prices, upon costs, as the account of the growth of the Post Office system indicated. Maintenance outlays were conventionally included in current costs even though the traffic which had imposed the necessity for that expenditure had been carried in the past.

All variables in the Electric equation have the expected signs. The coefficients on lagged telegrams and costs imply very strong increasing returns to scale. A 1 per cent increase in messages sent raised costs by only 0.33 per cent. This result includes the effects of technical progress on costs, as well as output. The Post Office equation is less satisfactory, with the lagged price index showing the wrong sign. The long-run scale coefficient, at 0.47, is almost half as high again as the Electric's. That may be because of a slower intrinsic rate of technical progress in the later stages of telegraph development, but it does not bear out grandiose claims for the superiority of a unitary state organization over a private firm. Not surprisingly, the equations allow a rejection of the hypothesis that the EITC costs behaved similarly to the Post Office's.

More interesting is the Post Office equation with the wage index replacing the wholesale price index. The explanatory power of the equation is improved and all the coefficients are statistically significant with the correct signs. The long-run scale coefficient remains virtually the same (0.48) and the estimate of the long-run wage elasticity is greater than one. This last probably reflects the tendency for wage awards to be backdated. Although how an Electric equation with a wage index would compare cannot be known, the two Post Office equations are consistent with a change in the employment and wage-bargaining regime under the Post Office that the qualitative sources indicate. Equally it is possible that the later nineteenth-century evolution of the national labour market would have altered Electric cost behaviour in the absence of a state take-over. Yet company secretary Weaver's response in 1866 to circulars promoting the Telegraph Clerk's Association, that no one associated should find employment in any telegraph company in Great Britain, was not likely to encourage unionization, by contrast with the more accommodating Post Office approach (Weaver 1867: 132). The conclusion that Post Office telegraph costs were greater than the Electric's would have been is not proved, but seems highly likely.

AN INTERNATIONAL COMPARISON OF TELEGRAPH USE

During the nationalization debate, Belgium and Switzerland were often held up as countries with telegraph administrations of the type to which the United Kingdom should aspire. The Post Office need not have behaved in the way it did, nor need the private industry. Alternative models of organization and behaviour were available on the Continent. An international comparison of telegraph usage at the time the Nationalization Act was passed can provide further insights into what was possible. For details see Appendix 3.2. In such a comparison competitive duplication of facilities is taken into account, which it was not in the cost function comparison. The basic principle is to estimate a relationship which includes both demand and cost influences (Fig. 3.1). The method has the advantage of eliminating the need to compare international price or cost structures for telegrams of different lengths or being sent different distances, by substituting these terms out.

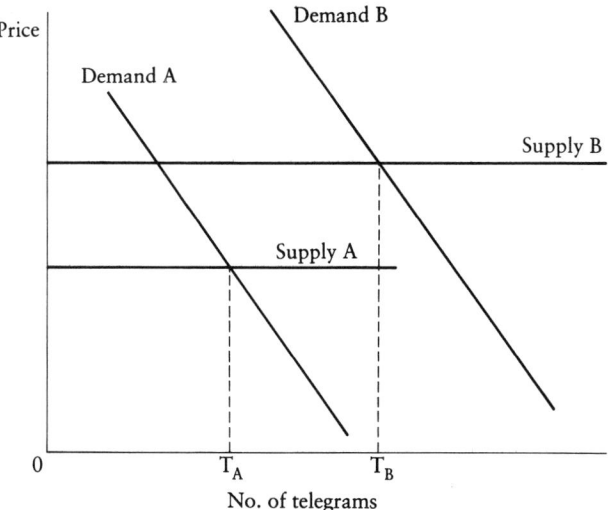

Note: System A is more efficient than system B but, facing a lower demand, sends fewer telegrams.

FIG. 3.1 Telegraph supply and demand

Richer people are likely to require to communicate more, both because household demand is responsive to income and because communication-intensive services become more important with economic development. For a given level of efficiency of a telegraph network, higher income countries will therefore have sent more telegrams, and at similar income levels, countries with more efficient telegraph networks would have also sent more messages. Table 3.1 shows that, despite the highest income per head of the sample, the United Kingdom did not use the telegraph most intensively. Other factors influenced demand and supply apart from income but the joint impact of these cannot be inferred easily from the table.

In all cases the models predict a higher telegraph penetration for Britain than was actually attained in 1868. On the other hand in no case can the hypothesis that (the American and) the British system behaved similarly to those of other countries be rejected. Table 3.1 and Appendix 3.2 indicate that the two free enterprise systems were performing worse than predicted from the state network sample. In the American case, both the after-effects of the

Civil War and the exclusion of non-Western Union networks suggest true US performance may have been close to average. The telegraph network in the United Kingdom can be excused on the grounds that the quality of service was generally superior in the UK, or on the grounds of the cheapness and speed of the competing postal service, or that investment in the system had been virtually stopped after 1866 when the nationalization debate began in earnest, or by a possible overstatement of UK income relative to other countries. (The Crafts measure of income per head appears to be bigger than that in Maddison 1982: table A2.) The earlier comparison with Belgium shows that the quality of service may explain at least some of the underprediction. Perhaps what is of most interest is that the differences in performance between Victorian state and private enterprise were small enough to be statistically insignificant. Each had their distinctive inefficiencies but the net effects were not so dissimilar.

The private industry did not perform ideally because the technology required some form of co-operation. The clustering of offices and the small number of messages per office indicate adverse effects of competition. Compared with a merger or with working arrangements, the form of co-operation chosen, the price cartel, was inefficient. A better-organized private industry could have been achieved by a regulatory body which insisted on working arrangements between companies for traffic management. These arrangements would have offered incentives to eliminate excess capacity in populous areas and spread service to outlying regions. If companies could have used other firms' trunk lines at little more than cost, they would have been more inclined to develop facilities in areas where there were no competitors. They would have linked such areas into the national network and charged the appropriate price (generally higher than for routes joining large population centres). That solution is more historically implausible than a merger, the barrier to which was initially agreeing a value for the shares or property to be acquired.

Given the behaviour of the private telegraph industry, those with an interest in nationalization could present a case that seemed disinterested. There were economies of scope to be gained from linking the post offices with the telegraph (Chapter 4). There were economies of integration that could be achieved by unitary control. The tariff issue was in principle entirely separate. The uniform tariff and the favourable terms for press traffic were in retrospect major arguments against nationalization as it was undertaken. They were redistributions of income in favour of particular groups by means of pricing, an archetypal case of regulatory capture. If these manipulations, and the upwards pressure on wage costs, could have been resisted, then the massive expansion of traffic in the first few years of the Post Office regime shows that the state organization might have offered a service that was more efficient than that of the private industry in the form adopted until 1868.

In fact the cost function evidence suggests the dominant private firm was more efficient than the later Post Office telegraph department in the sense that costs were driven down further as output expanded. A private (integrated) monopoly, without statutory barriers to entry, therefore was likely to have been socially preferable, on conventional cost–benefit analysis criteria, to the actual Post Office regime. As it was, telegraph users were subsidized by postal users, which almost certainly involved a transfer from the poorer to the better off. If income distribution effects are ignored, then a case on efficiency grounds for the cross-subsidy may exist, but there seems to be no good reason to make that leap.

International comparison of the 1868 industry shows the hypothesis cannot be rejected that the private British industry performed neither better nor worse than other, mainly state and often subsidized, industries. To modify and make more plausible Hamlet's maxim, 'Nothing's good or bad but comparison makes it so.' Both the private British industry and the Post Office telegraph were inefficient in comparison with theoretical ideal types. When they are compared with each other, or with how they might have been on the basis of the experience of other countries, warts and all, the difficulties of picking the better are enormous.

RAILWAY TARIFFS, SERVICES, AND COSTS

Far more important to the economy than telegraph businesses, private railway companies sank in public esteem in the four decades before the First World War, as the telegraph companies had earlier. Most historians have reached the conclusion that the public attitude was justified. While Aldcroft (1968) emphasized managerial incompetence as an explanation for excessive increases in capital costs, Cain (1972) argued that competition on the basis of quality rather than price was responsible, and Irving (1978) pointed out that political pressures became inimical to efficient management until 1899. Again it is worth emphasizing that no actual system was likely to approximate the efficiency of ideal types.

It is much easier to describe the characteristics of railway operations in these years than to explain them, but a causal account is necessary to reach conclusions about the regulatory system and railway business organization. So for example the high speed and frequency of British trains could have been an efficient response to high British incomes (relative to continental Europe) rather than wasteful non-price competition. Highly urbanized and densely populated Britain may have imposed altogether different costs and working patterns from other national railway systems so often used as comparisons, instead of those costs being higher in Britain primarily because of the regulatory system or the nature of British railway competition. Aggressive unions might have pushed up operating costs, while political manipulation by traders forced down and constrained revenue. On the other hand the regulatory system could have been a response to the railways' unsatisfactory performance and political insensitivity, while labour unrest may have been caused by management trying to raise output by increasing the intensity of work, rather than by improving working methods.

At first sight, the statistical indicators seem to show a satisfactory performance by this massive industry. Nominal fares halved between 1870 and 1914 and freight rates per ton-mile fell by perhaps one quarter (Cain 1988). Between 1872 and 1907, when the total rail mileage in England increased from 11,136 to 15,987, concentration continued to rise gently from sixteen companies owning 85 per cent of the mileage to thirteen companies owning 88 per cent (Departmental Committee 1911: app. 1). Traffic carried grew continuously. On the other hand profitability was less satisfactory, as indicated by the 30 per cent fall in stock prices of the leading railway companies between 1896 and 1911. As the railway system expanded by virtually 50 per cent in rail miles, capital per mile almost doubled. Above all, international comparisons often suggested that British railways were no longer on the best practice frontiers. When combined with railway labour unrest, these adverse tendencies proved sufficient in 1914 for a Royal Commission to be appointed with a brief to consider railway nationalization as a solution, and the formation in 1908 of a Parliamentary Railway Nationalization Society (Eldon Barry 1965: 100).

Agitation over railway rates led in 1881 to the appointment of a Parliamentary Committee to consider the matter. Railway management showed themselves conservative and arrogant (Clapham 1963: ii. 196) but, as long as the general price level was falling, so also were their costs and they could maintain their nominal rates comfortably. Political pressure was particularly focused on the levying of 'terminals' or multi-part tariffs that in principle were wholly justified, but which seemed to introduce elements of arbitrariness into payments for the non-transport-related component, to cover loading and storage and such like (Chapter 2). Though Parliament could not bring itself to recognize terminals the courts eventually did in 1885. Distance was not the only determinant of a cost-related tariff and therefore the observation that the relationship between haul length and ton-mile charges was weak proves little (Freeman 1988). As discussed under costs below, the density of traffic on a route must also be included.

In the 1892 Railway Rates and Charges Act small shippers obtained an advantage relative to a cost-based tariff and the Act removed an incentive for railways to identify their true costs. When the Act came into force in January 1893 the railways, claiming insufficient time to work out new rates, adopted all the maximum rates specified in the Act. This pushed up the general level of rates substantially and triggered a burst of public outrage. The political response was an Act the following year that allowed customers to appeal to the Railway Commissioners against rate changes. Fear of litigation thereafter discouraged tariff movement in either direction. Railways also held wages constant, provoking, in the face of a rising cost of living, labour troubles in 1910–11. They were at last allowed to raise prices by an Act of 1913.

At the beginning of the 1890s British freight rates found their most vigorous defender (in particular against Jeans 1887) in Acworth. Refuting detrimental comparisons with Continental rates, he pointed out that delivery dates abroad were longer, station availability and location were worse, and that extra charges had to be paid for loading. Express delivery attracted higher charges on the Continent. He showed that a random selection of German rates compared adversely with charges for similar British traffic (Acworth 1891: 181–200; in his enthusiasm for the defence Acworth sometimes overstepped the mark. Discussing allegations that English charges were high because of the enormous railway capital expenditure, Acworth maintained that must be incorrect because railway managers aimed to maximize net revenue and did not fix rates in relation to track costs. His contention however neglects the long-run requirement that railways needed to charge prices sufficient to break even if they were to survive). By the turn of the century Acworth was on the defensive. Although British trains still tended to run faster on average than those elsewhere in the world, the fastest performances had deteriorated and been overtaken by those abroad. Leeds–Kings Cross, about the same distance as Paris–Calais, took three hours fifty minutes in 1899 compared with three hours fifteen minutes on the French run, a reversal of the position a decade earlier. The US Philadelphia–Atlantic City trains averaged 69–70 m.p.h. on the fifty-five-mile daily run in 1897, compared with London–Brighton's fifty-one miles in sixty minutes (Johnston 1949: 278–80). In the new century some speed laurels returned to Britain. The 'City of Truro' held 102.3 m.p.h. for one-quarter of a mile through Somerset on a public service train hauling 148 tons in 1903 and a special train on the London–Brighton run cut the time to forty-eight minutes forty-one seconds. Twenty-five minutes were clipped off the Paddington–Birmingham run. Whether this speed and service competition was as desirable as the price competition it displaced is debatable. Money saved from price cuts can be spent on whatever the customer chooses. To a lesser extent this is also true of time saved in faster travel, but not of other service competition. Passenger rates were clearly above those on the Continent by 1908 and probably were earlier, despite Acworth's defences. That might be excused by higher British wage rates. Moreover the great majority of British passengers travelled third class by the turn of the century, and perhaps obtained service quality comparable with higher classes elsewhere (Johnston 1949: 245–6, 250; Royal Economic Society 1912: 78; Sherrington 1934: 265, 286, 295–6).

Tariffs ultimately needed to generate enough revenue to cover costs, and railways presented acute problems for pricing in relation to costs while keeping the number of rates low. In any case as mentioned in Chapter 2 there is a case to be made for charging prices related to what the market will bear in an industry with such high fixed costs. A rule of thumb was that about half of total costs were fixed. Railway output that influences costs has a number of dimensions. Customers generally prefer a shorter time in transit to a longer, but additional speed used more resources, especially coal. The commonly accepted measure of work done by a railway is freight ton-miles and passenger-miles. Yet even ignoring the time dimension, shorter hauls or trips are likely to cost more because of the fixed costs associated with each individual load. Ideally each dimension of output, average speed, haul and trip length, and total freight and passengers carried, would be taken into account in costing exercises. The foregoing refers to useful work done. The railways however had to schedule trains, subject to regulatory restrictions, to best satisfy customer requirements while minimizing the resources needed. As far as they were concerned their output was the number of trains run, the total train mileage, and what was carried. Hence output measures obtainable from the official railway returns for this period are of passenger and freight train-miles and passengers and freight carried. The relations between all these concepts is as follows:

- passenger- or ton-miles = no. of passengers or tons of freight × average haul or trip;
- Train-miles = no. of trains run × average route length;
- Train capacity utilization = average trip or haul length/ average route length;
- Average train-load = no. of passengers or volume of freight/ trains run.

Therefore train-miles are measures of 'work done', passenger- or ton-miles, so long as haul length, average train-load, and train capacity utilization remain unaltered since train-mile per passenger or freight ton equals average trip or haul length/(average load × train capacity utilization).

Most railway systems elsewhere in the world collected and published more informative accounting information than did the British. French railway company accounts detailed costs by section and branches, showing main lines with heavier traffic could charge lower rates yet earn high profits, while branch lines with light traffic often made losses even with higher tariffs (Acworth 1905: 54). Costs were not merely determined by ton-miles but by the volume of traffic. In England the South Western Railway before the Court of the Railway and Canal Commissioners in the *Southampton Docks* case showed that through traffic to the docks over seventy-eight miles earned more profit at lower rates than uneven local traffic. With rising import competition the matter was obviously sensitive. Not only were costs dependent on a number of traffic characteristics but it was difficult to divide costs between passenger and goods. From the Buenos Aires Western Railway in 1903, a British-managed company not subject to the weight of tradition and regulation of British railways, less than 5 per cent of expenditure could be so allocated (Acworth 1905: 42).

George Paish, editor of the *Statist*, visited the USA in 1899 and became convinced of the advantages of heavy train loading practised there. He did not expect British railways to match US train-loads, but the US figures had increased markedly over the preceding twenty years whereas there was no such trend in Britain. He suggested the legality of pooling arrangements in the UK allowed British railways to remain small and to compete on speed of delivery (which necessitated small wagons and loadings) instead of on price. The Great Northern in 1883 boasted twenty-three express journeys daily over each mile of its system. In the USA greater competition provoked rate-cutting and merger. G. S. Gibb of the North Eastern noted the custom of British trade was against heavy loading, and the longer waits and greater stock holding this entailed. The obvious policy which he did not mention was to offer traders a discount commensurate with the savings to encourage them to change their ways. British corporate refusal to collect ton-mile and passenger-mile statistics appalled even friendly observers and Paish attributed the poor performance to this lack of information. Indian railways with in some respect similar managerial traditions were obliged by the government to collect these statistics over the preceding generation and increased their train loadings by one-third in twenty years.

Paish (1902) obtained the co-operation of the London & North Western in estimating their ton-mile and haul length statistics so as to allow a comparison with the US Pennsylvanian Railway, and to examine performance over time. On the British line, passengers carried increased by 94.9 per cent 1880–1900 and passenger receipts rose 56 per cent, but average haul fell, from 14.5 to 12.8 miles, and the number of passengers per train was up from 45.6 to only 49.4. With goods traffic the average train-load rose a mere 4.5 per cent to 68.6 tons, compared with 484.6 tons on the Pennsylvanian and 196 tons on the East Indian Railway. Whereas the cost of moving one ton a mile fell by 33 per cent between 1880 and 1900 on the Pennsylvanian, it rose 24 per cent on the London & North Western over the same period. There seemed to be a great potential for cost reduction on the London & North Western.

AMALGAMATIONS, REGULATION, AND RAILWAYS AS BUSINESSES

Railway mergers that almost certainly would have cut costs created sufficient public concern in 1872 that they were forbidden by Parliament. The following year railway regulation took legal form, but outside the courts, with the appointment of the Railway Commissioners. This judicial body dealt with as many cases as had been considered between 1854 and 1873. They were primarily concerned with complaints brought by traders against companies for charging excessive rates. The Commission was an unsatisfactory form of regulation for it was unable to offer railway companies anything in return for lowering rates. The companies therefore had an incentive to fight cases rather than improve operating techniques. By contrast Gladstone's earlier suggestion, trading lower rates for guarantees of freedom from competition, would probably have saved resources and been more satisfactory for customers. But that would have required a departure from *laissez-faire* and the legal tradition. The Board of Trade could have used its powers under the 1888 Railways and Canal Traffic Act to require collection and publication of ton-mile and passenger-mile statistics, but chose not to (Acworth 1891: 179; Cleveland-Stevens 1915: 269–70; Parris 1965).

Where safety was concerned, the Board of Trade pursued a more proactive policy, pressing for interlocking signals, block telegraph, and continuous brakes. The first two were conditions for new lines and the Board required progress of existing lines to be published in the hope this would shame companies into compliance. Not until the Armagh accident in 1888, caused by the train lacking continuous brakes, did an Act require them to be fitted. And even then there was no standardization of brakes. Safety regulations under the 1889 Act, nominal additions to capital, and the debiting of capital account with expenditure that should have been paid out of revenue all raised costs, as did the widespread provision of track and sidings and the general enlarging of the capacity of the system. Yet railways elsewhere in the world also were obliged to respond to the demands of expanding traffic and did so at lower costs.

Competition could not be counted on to regulate railways, indeed competition may have made safety regulation more necessary. By 1911, new entry to railways was improbable because no competitive schemes approved in the preceding twenty years were likely to have achieved an adequate return on capital. The market test appeared to be indicating that the industry was a regional natural monopoly at least. In any case competition tended to encourage extension into high-cost, unprofitable areas (Cain 1988: 115). State control of rates and schedules, as well as safety regulations, increased. Labour costs were raised by the limitation of working hours in the interests of safety by an Act of 1893.

Total factor productivity, a weighted average of labour, fuel, and capital productivities, declined continuously after 1870, becoming negative in the Edwardian period (Foreman-Peck 1991a). Dodgson's (1989) finding of a very low rate of technical progress (0.3 per cent p.a.) among the twelve largest companies between 1900 and 1912 is consistent with the result if performance in the rest of the industry was considerably worse. A faster rate of depreciation lowers the growth of the capital stock and therefore slightly improves total factor productivity growth. This observation may be taken as an interpretation of declining long-run productivity growth. Wasteful competition, like Sir Edward Watkin's unnecessary Great Central trunk line to London in the 1890s, required the faster than ideal writing off of capital. Another, not mutually exclusive, explanation for the trend is that output has not been correctly measured to take into account improvements in the quality of service. Speed increases required the rising consumption of coal per train-mile, raised wear and tear, and required higher manning levels to maintain safety. Passenger rolling stock came to be lighted by electricity and gas instead of oil and to run on pairs of four-wheel bogies instead of four rigid wheels. Carriage heating was still by hot water cans in contrast to the North American method of utilizing steam from the locomotive's boiler. Express trains acquired kitchens and toilet facilities. Continuous automatic brakes became obligatory after 1889. Mineral train mileage was reduced by the introduction of wagons capable of carrying double or treble the eight- to ten-ton capacity of the British wagon traditional at the beginning of the period and the average speed of locomotives increased. How much should be attributed to such quality improvements is hard to say, but the observation that United States railway total factor productivity growth (Fishlow 1966) was at least double British between 1870 and 1910, and that the USA usually innovated quality improvements in this period, supports a conclusion of relatively poor British railway performance. In particular the total factor productivity results are not consistent with an Edwardian recovery in railway performance (Cain 1988), any more than are stock prices. Attributing this to labour militancy probably is to identify the wrong direction of causation. Railway management failed to get anywhere near US productivity increases and therefore could not pay the wages that labour expected. Improvements in performance were unlikely to be sustained because of an unwillingness to change working practices very much. Before 1890 the Great Western had experimented with large wagons but could not get the loads except for coal traffic. Until after 1909 they maintained ten tons as standard. The Great Northern announced between 1900 and 1902 reduced train-miles and increasing earnings per mile. They ordered some twenty- and thirty-ton trucks but maintained ten tons as the maximum load for normal working (Grinting 1903: 452–3; Sherrington 1934: 281).

As these examples suggest, although railway companies were prime examples of large-scale British managerial capitalism rather than the more widespread family firm that predominated in manufacturing, they did not always inspire admiration for their efficiency and innovativeness. The divorce of ownership from control concerned a number of railway shareholders (Phillips 1877). Directors ensured continuation of their personal power and policies by proxy voting and by the non-attendance of share-holders at annual meetings. Only the Midland gave shareholders free railway passes to attend. Sir Edward Watkin's election to the Great Eastern board, the exception that proves the rule, was possible only because the incumbent board members were taken by surprise. Shareholders generally only influenced policy when they were induced to do so by rival companies. When the Midland planned extensions to become independent of the surrounding companies, these railways drew Midland shareholders' attention to the expense involved. The Midland conciliated the opposition by establishing a joint committee with shareholders that eventually proposed abandoning the Settle and Carlisle line. Parliament refused permission for this policy shift however. Individual directors might be personally interested in the development of unprofitable branch lines. On the other hand shareholders were not necessarily concerned more with dividends than with railway services to their region (Irving 1976).

Railway companies showed a pattern that was to be repeated in many sectors of British life over the following century. Organization and customs that had been appropriate to one epoch of railway technology persisted when opportunities and challenges changed. Inertia was encouraged by an absence of competition initiated either by regulation or market forces. Mistakes of the past were ossified into the industry structure and management acquired the mental accompaniment of institutional inertia, complacency. It is this that casts doubt on Gourvish's (1972, 1986) claim that railway management were forerunners of those professional managers to whom Chandler (1990) gives such a prominent role in the USA. Although they managed very large enterprises, the way they did so was rarely innovative. They were unwilling to collect the information that would have improved management decision-taking and the pressures on them were not there to improve. Even had they been, the organizations were sufficiently inflexible that there must be some doubt as to whether they would have turned around, or merely declined. A corporate culture that preferred to hold down costs by squeezing wages and working employees such long hours that safety was imperilled, rather than improve working methods, was not conducive to long term survival. The 1891 Select Committee found overwork systematic and widespread (Parris 1965: 226). Wages rose by 5 per cent between 1886 and 1906, much more slowly than in other trades despite demands for greater effort; cotton-manufacturing rates were up 23 per cent and building 18 per cent (Bagwell 1963: 262). Whereas in the expansionary period to 1870 management had to be recruited from outside the industry, thereafter personnel were largely 'home-grown' and the pool of acceptable ideas was thereby reduced, though the North Eastern did begin recruiting university graduates in the new century. Unlike the telegraphs, where railways provided alternative expertise to the telegraph companies, railway companies could claim a monopoly of knowledge about how railways should be run. They were therefore able to dismiss overseas experience as irrelevant to British conditions, and render themselves immune from outside criticism or even from much self-assessment. Equally the Inspectorate could often be disregarded. Sir Edward Watkin in 1873 referred to their 'insolent interference'. Culture is not necessarily a given. Had public opinion tolerated more competition and mergers, more progressive management strategies might have emerged. And had regulation been more effective public opinion might have been more accommodating to the companies. Everything did not have to be as it was: 'Men at some time are masters of their fates.' The ultimate responsibility lies with those charged with changing the 'rules of the game'; the governments of the day failed to find a fully satisfactory framework.

THE COSTS OF RAILWAY SERVICES: AN INTERNATIONAL COMPARISON

Essentially the proposition is that railway organizations became 'scelerotic' and arm's length regulation gradually reduced their freedom of action in the interests of lobbyists, without encouraging any regrouping of railways that could have lowered capital costs. This hypothesis can be tested by comparing British railways to those in other countries. If there were unexploited opportunities for system integration at the national level then comparisons with other countries, where the state almost invariably took a greater hand in positive railway planning, can be expected to show higher costs for the British regime. The empirical question is how to distinguish such avoidable industry costs from those arising from national economic and topographical conditions.

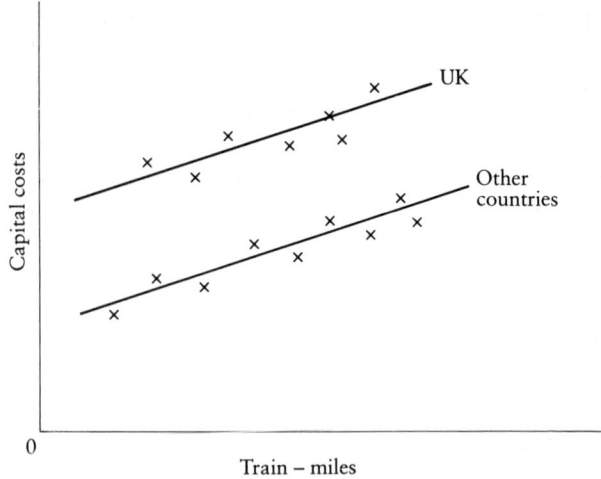

Note: Each x represents a railway system in a particular decade.

FIG. 3.2 Railway capital costs and train-miles

The first data set we employ to confront this issue is a pooled cross-section/time-series sample of countries with observations at generally decadal intervals from 1840 to 1910. Fig. 3.2 shows the cost relationships analytically. Detailed empirical estimates are in Appendix 3.3. What we are trying to explain are the differing capital outlays on railways. Given the integration of the nineteenth-century world capital markets, the costs of borrowing did not vary greatly between national railways, but Britain's systems generally had access to among the lowest costs of capital. British capital costs relative to other nations will therefore be understated and the results of the test biased against the hypothesis of excessive capitalization.

Competition between companies may be expected to change costs with the expansion of systems, but the impact of national economic conditions should be stable. A country with a concentrated population needing expensive multiple tracking in one decade will have had similar requirements relative to more sparsely populated countries in earlier decades. The results in Appendix 3.3 suggest that capital costs per rail mile are strongly linked to the previous decade's capital costs per rail mile. Even controlling for that effect, costs per rail mile in each decade grow proportionately more in the United Kingdom, independently of general improvements accruing to all national rail networks. Belgium is taken as the comparison country for the sample—all other countries with significant country effects have lower capital costs per mile than Belgium and, of course, than the United Kingdom. Capital costs rose on average at about 0.5 per cent per annum because of improvements to the systems.

Railway systems such as the United Kingdom's that ran more train-miles per mile of track than average necessarily required more expensive constructions. However Table 3.4 shows that, around 1906, whereas the United Kingdom's construction costs were two-thirds greater than those of the Belgian railways. United Kingdom train-miles per mile were only 12 per cent higher. From Table 3.4 the United Kingdom can be seen to be almost alone among the industrial nations in abjuring the at least partial state ownership that went along with state planning of the railway system. Only the United States, Greece, and Spain in this sample pursued similar policies. Utilization data are lacking for Greece and Spain leaving only the United States in a similar position to Britain, and Lardner writing in 1850 thought American regulation was more effective than British (Parris 1965: 9). Table 3.5 suggests US performance compares favourably with Romania's and Italy's but unfavourably with India's. Obviously such comparisons are far less convincing than that with Belgium, given the greater differences between national economic environments.

A second cross-national data set analysed in Appendix 3.3 involves the data in Table 3.4 pooled with similar observations for 1895 and offers an alternative means of controlling for the influence of economic conditions on the capital costs of railways. Train-miles run provides a measure of traffic carried (though, as discussed above, a less than perfect one). Urbanization for instance could raise construction costs but it would also enhance the demand for transport as measured by train-miles. Less densely populated countries require more rail miles for given train-miles, thereby incurring different construction costs. Both length of line and train-miles are therefore included as determinants of capital costs. If, having allowed for the effects of these variables, differing national costs are identified, then these may be attributed to the organization of the industry, rather than to the economic envi-

TABLE 3.4 National railway systems c.1906

	Construction costs per mile of railway c.1906 (£)	Length of line open to traffic 1906	Train-miles per mile of line, av. 1902–6	Percentage of lines owned by the state 1906	Gross per mile expenses, annual averages c.1902–6 (£)	Gross receipts per mile, annual averages 1902–6 (£)
United Kingdom	56,000	23,060	17,729	0.0	2,928	4,617
France	28,600	29,270	8,728	5.9	1,341	2,531
Belgium	34,000ª	2,880	15,808	87.8	2,315	3,728
Holland	13,700ª	2,180	11,807	53.2	1,691	2,022
Germany	21,400	34,480	11,212	92.8	2,123	3,415
Sweden	6,570	8,100	3,405	32.2	503	742
Norway	7,660	1,580	3,236	85.4	474	623
Denmark	9,900ª	2,080	n/a	56.2	1,371	1,684
Switzerland	23,900	2,675	9,304	56.0	1,656	2,574
Spain	20,350	9,195	n/a	0.0	654	1,341
Portugal	n/a	1,420	n/a	39.4	n/a	n/a
Italy	21,000	10,110	5,178	77.1	1,240	1,588
Austria-Hungary	18,360	24,479	6,449	64.1	1,138	1,803
Russia in Europe	18,800	32,740	6,392	60.3	1,398	2,144
Bulgaria	8,570	970	n/a	76.3	n/a	n/a
Serbia	12,700	440	n/a	88.6	n/a	n/a
Romania	18,064	1,975	4,221	100.0	740	1,305
Greece	n/a	845	n/a	0.0	n/a	n/a
United States	14,200	222,635	4,885	0.0	1,341	2,011
Argentina	10,800	14,550	2,042	11.8	562	1,034
Japan	9,100	5,010	7,359	35.3	689	1,383
India	8,800	29,100	3,934	74.6	504	1,011
Canada	12,700	22,170	3,281	7.7	808	1,162

ª State-owned lines only.

Source: Webb (1911), citing principally UK Abstract of Foreign Statistics. Also UK Annual Abstract of the British Empire.

ronment. Variable costs and revenues equally may be expected to differ between countries with traffic conditions and network configurations. In turn variations in industry organization could create different relations between train-miles run and these variables; a regulated or state-operated industry could generate less revenue per train-mile than a private monopoly, working expenditure could be raised by competitive 'business stealing' in the same way as with fixed costs, or by labour costs enhanced by measures such as the 1893 Act. By the late nineteenth century, as we have suggested, British regulation was probably sufficiently effective to prevent monopolistic revenues or excessive variable costs. The effects of competition on the railway system should be observable only in the capital costs.

The analysis of the 1895 and 1906 cross-national data in Appendix 3.3 shows that the number of train-miles per mile of track had a significant positive effect on construction costs per mile, on working cost per mile, and on revenue per mile. It also shows that, after allowing for these effects, the UK had significantly higher construction costs per mile but no higher working costs or revenue. For the United Kingdom there was a significant national effect on capital costs that could be attributed to industry organization but no comparable influence was at work on working costs and revenue per mile. Regulation seems to have encouraged behaviour comparable to nationalized enterprises for working costs and earnings, but not for past decisions. The construction cost result implies that, if the UK had had a regime similar to other countries', construction costs per mile in 1902–6 would have been £37,750 instead of £56,000, about 32 per cent lower, and railway usage and social savings would have been accordingly greater.

In contrast to the Averch–Johnson model (Chapter 2), state regulation in the UK exerted direct pressure on prices and services, rather than on rates of return, lowering the return on railway capital and restricting railway expansion. Given that the companies had to pay for the expensive system and could generate the revenue if permitted to do so by government, the alternative policy was to permit a higher UK rate of return. A higher return would also have restricted the use of railways, unless the capital values were written down, an outcome that amalgamations into territorial monopolies were intended to prevent. UK gross working expenses in 1906 were £2,928 per mile and the railways were allowed to earn £4,617 per mile. As a return on previous investment—the £56,000 construction costs per mile—that left £1,689, amounting to a 3 per cent return. Had construction costs been lowered to the levels predicted by the Appendix 3.3 analysis this return would have risen to 4.47 per cent (compared with 4.16 per cent for France).

UK construction costs were a considerable proportion of total railway costs. At 4 per cent, construction costs amounted to 43 per cent of the sum of working expenses and payments on construction outlays, at 5 per cent they were 48.9 per cent. Thus a reduction of UK construction costs to levels predicted for the Continental regimes would probably have lowered total rail costs by between 14 and 16 per cent. Applying the static social saving approach to this figure suggests an increase in GNP of the order of 0.75 per cent. As a static benefit this is a downward biased figure; increased sales encouraged by lower prices and costs would probably have enhanced the figure.

Competition in the railway system had burnt itself out by the end of the nineteenth century because both suppliers and customers found it incompatible with the technical conditions of the industry. National economic and topographical conditions alternatively may have been entirely responsible for high British railway capital costs but two 'experiments' do not support that explanation. Even allowing for general expensive improvements in service between 1840 and 1910, and recognizing that country characteristics could raise the level of capital costs, Britain still showed the greatest increases in capital costs per rail mile. Around the turn of the century British capital costs per train-mile were far more expensive than most other countries', though revenues and variable costs were comparable to those of other national systems.

The most credible inference is that the largely unregulated free enterprise system of railway investment probably raised construction costs by 50 per cent and lowered national income per head by at least 0.75 per cent in 1906. The counterfactual is a more interventionist, but competent, regime in the early years of railway development that planned a national trunk layout and prevented wasteful competition, either by state ownership (the conventional solution) or by effective regulation.

THE TELEPHONE COMPANIES, THE POST OFFICE, AND THE ROAD TO NATIONALIZATION

As a new industry, founded when railways and telegraph had already reached maturity, telephony might have hoped for a fresh start. But instead the telephone became bogged down in the political and institutional mire around the earlier technologies, and urbanization, as well as in the intrinsic problems of network industries. In telephony also, competition was short-lived and private monopoly was regarded as exploitative. Complaints about the privately owned telephone service were widespread and vociferous, and the use of the service was very limited by comparison with other countries, such as the United States or Sweden. Patents played a greater role as an industry entry barrier and as a competitive weapon, in the broadest sense, than in railways.

The regime changes that attempted to grapple with these complexities are summarized in Table 3.5. Phase one, obstruction, gave way to some liberalization in 1884, followed eight years later by the decision to nationalize the trunk system, in response to mergers. That did not improve the anomalous position of telephony, over which the Post Office claimed a statutory monopoly that it (or rather the Treasury) had chosen not to exercise. Private telephone companies were blocked by Post Office regulations and by local authorities refusing rights of way for telephone lines (Baldwin 1938; Kingsbury 1915). Introduction of municipal and Post Office competition from 1899 failed to provide a satisfactory regime, and so complete nationalization was agreed in 1905, though not implemented for another seven years.

The technology of the industry was built on Alexander Graham Bell's invention of 1878, which offered a different form of communication from the Post Office's electric telegraph; conversation at a distance with a potential multitude. The telegraph was far less suited to exchanges between persons, and required a simpler electronic signal. A rival company to Bell's was formed in 1879 to work the Edison patents. Within a year the two companies abandoned competition and combined under the name the United Telephone Company (UTC). Bell then served 400 subscribers at their London exchange and Edison 200.

Waking up to the importance of the telephone, the Crown (the

TABLE 3.5 *A chronology of British public policy and the telephone*
1876–1913

1876	Bell secures British patent rights.
1877	Alexander Graham Bell comes to England to display his telephones. Post Office Engineer in Chief reported against adoption of telephone on the grounds of its very limited use.
1879	First English telephone exchange opened in London, 36 Coleman Street.
1880	Edison and Bell interests merge to form United Telephone Company. Courts declare the telephone is a telegraph and therefore is covered by the Post Office monopoly. Post Office licences issued for restricted areas.
1884	Postmaster-General Fawcett removes 4–5-mile radius restrictions on telephone company operations, substituting the payment of a 10% royalty.
1889	Principal telephone companies merged as National Telephone Company.
1892	Government decides to buy NTC trunk lines for Post Office.
1896	NTC trunk lines transferred.
1899	Local authorities empowered to operate telephone systems.
1901	PMG and NTC agree to develop London area jointly with a view to a Post Office take-over in 1912.
1905	Parliament ratified the agreement that the Post Office should purchase the entire NTC system.
1912	Post Office assumes complete control of telephone system.
1913	Portsmouth municipal undertaking bought by Post Office. Only Hull survives.

Post Office) took action for infringement of its monopoly of telegraphic communication conferred by the earlier nationalization of the telegraph. When the action was successful, the United Telephone Company was granted a licence to establish exchanges in any part of the kingdom on condition the Post Office received 10 per cent of their gross receipts in royalties. The licence was granted for thirty-one years from January 1881, the government reserving the right to purchase at a price to be settled by arbitration in 1890, 1897, or 1904. This condition was included in all licences granted subsequently. A curious oversight with unfortunate consequences was the absence of provision for acquisition of the telephone company when the licence expired at the end of 1911.

The original licences were granted for particular districts only, generally covering a radius of three to five miles. Telephone companies were forbidden to establish trunk wires between towns except on prohibitive conditions. The Post Office demanded a minimum annual payment of ten shillings per mile per subscriber in royalties on trunk lines, which consequently made heavy losses in 1882–3. Longer-distance communication was anyway more difficult by telephone than by telegraph because of greater signal deterioration, but such penal taxation did not encourage attempts to improve telephone transmission. Similarly call offices were scarce because the Post Office claimed 50 per cent of receipts as royalties. In order that the Post Office could circumvent the telephone patents, the licensed company was obliged to supply the Post Office with instruments and the right to manufacture them (Batten 1884).

Stated Post Office policy was to favour one exchange per area because of the desirability of intercommunication between all subscribers. It turned out that there was no automatic right to a licence even when an exchange had been established in anticipation. The Post Office required the UTC to close its Plymouth service on 29 October 1881 and opened its own exchange on 15 December. In July 1882 the Post Office compelled the closure of the Newcastle upon Tyne exchange. Not until ten months later was a licence handed to the telephone company (Wood 1976: 3). Neither this obstructiveness (by 1884 seventy-seven licences had been applied for and eight granted) nor other restrictions encouraged the spread of telephony in Britain.

Blame for slow telephone development in the UK has been placed squarely upon the shoulders of the Post Office, extending the life of telegraph technology relative to long-distance telephony (Brock 1981). Alternatively the Treasury (Perry 1977: 85) or a general misconceived belief in telephone competition (Hazlewood 1953) have been the villains of the piece. Competition, as we have seen, was not a cornerstone of policy although it was often tried without adequate interconnection rules and supervision, essential for network competition to operate. Without the arbitrary decision of the courts that the telephone was covered by the state telegraph monopoly, the Post Office would have had no power to licence the telephone companies, and Post Office officials were not invariably obstructive of the telephone. Repeating Frank Scudamore's earlier judgements on the private telegraph system, Post Office officials pointed out that a number of towns would have been without telephone exchanges had the service been left to the companies. Political manipulation of the telegraph tariff, discussed above, was as much responsible for the overextension of telegraph technology as the Post Office. Had telegraphy been less cheap, demand would have been lower. For budgetary reasons, conscious of the expense of the telegraph system, the Treasury did prevent the Post Office extending their service or supporting officials in their arguments for nationalization.

Once more the Edinburgh Chamber of Commerce was in the forefront of agitation for reform of telecommunications policy. A deputation from Portsmouth in 1884 pointed out to the Postmaster-General (PMG) that their local telephone company objected to the provisions of the licence, specifying they should supply the Post Office with patent phones, on grounds of illegality, and that the Post Office alternative service was offered at rates considerably higher than the company's. The Post Office had obtained only 700 subscribers under the very restrictive regime, and Henry Fawcett, the PMG, conceded telephone development had been checked. In response to the Portsmouth delegation Fawcett announced a policy change; the public were to be allowed to choose between a private company and the Post Office. From 1884 telephone companies were allowed to construct and use trunk lines and the clause requiring the companies to supply instruments to the Post Office was dropped from licences. However companies were unable to acquire compulsory powers for obtaining wayleaves, by contrast with the earlier railways, and their operations continued to be hampered by right of way problems, especially with local government. Some co-operation between the Post Office and the telephone company at last began in the spring of 1885, when subscribers were allowed to receive and send (Post Office) telegrams by telephone through the central telegraph office in St Martins-le-Grand.

Like the American Bell companies, the UTC encouraged rapid growth in the early years of operation by ceding regions to other telephone companies, receiving in return some of their shares. UTC's own territory was limited to the county of Middlesex and those counties within a twelve-mile radius of the General Post Office, with a trunk line to Brighton. This area included London and suburbs. At the prices charged, even with the Post Office licence payments, the telephone was highly profitable. In seven years the UTC's gross revenue exceeded £100,000 and profits were over £62,000.

The regional companies were: National Telephone Co. (incorporated 10 March 1881); Lancashire & Cheshire Co. (21 March 1881); Northern District Co. (13 December 1881); Telephone of Ireland Co. (27 May 1882); Western Counties Co. (17 December 1884); South of England Co. (29 June 1885). High profits tempted the competitor London & Globe Company into the industry, registering in 1882 and receiving a licence in January 1883. Hoping to avoid the Bell patents entry barrier, Globe used a Bell receiver, but with a horseshoe magnet and the Hunnings transmitter. The Globe's tariff was virtually half of the UTC's, but according to the UTC, their competitive methods were destructive. The Globe allegedly tied wires round UTC lines and then connected their wires to the Globe exchange. In consequence the London & Globe sent current through all the bunched UTC lines, setting all the subscribers' bells ringing and effectively destroying their telephone service. When judgement for infringement of patent was given for the UTC, the UTC bought out the Globe at the end of 1884.

Expiry of the Bell British telephone patents in 1890 and 1891 prompted the established companies to amalgamate in 1889 so as better to deter entry. Their profits exceeded their working expenses, prices remained high, and service and usage limited (Bennett 1895). A new company, the Mutual, entered in the Manchester area in 1891. No interconnection with NTC was permitted and therefore subscribers who also wanted NTC access were obliged to pay both charges (£10 plus £6). The Mutual sold out in 1892 to the National Telephone Company (NTC), as did the owners of the other twelve telephone licences issued between 1881 and 1895. The government lacked the powers to prevent monopolization of the industry (and chose not to seek them) (Meyer 1907: 32–7; Anns 1911: 162).

By the beginning of the 1890s it was apparent that private telephony could not just blame Treasury restraint and Post Office expansionism for the slow diffusion of telephony in Britain.

Largely reacting to what they judged were the deficiencies of private provision, local authorities and chambers of commerce in particular pressed for changes in telecommunications policy. The Associated Chambers of Commerce participated in telephone protests in 1888, 1908, 1910, and in 1911. As early as 1884 the Board of Works of Wandsworth District prosecuted the United Telephone Company over their telephone aerial wires, then spreading rapidly in London. Such actions encouraged the telephone companies repeatedly to try to obtain statutory rights of way for underground lines but without success. A Select Committee reported in 1885 that the danger of overhead wires was much exaggerated and recommended the companies should have rights of way, but the government declined to act on the recommendation. Against the NTC's 1891/2 application for statutory wayleaves 170 local authorities, and nearly fifty gas, water, electricity, and railway companies, petitioned. A private NTC was by then too much distrusted to be given such powers.

In 1892 the government decided that the solution to the rights of way problem, now accentuated by telephone interference from electric trams, by the threat to telegraph revenue, and by concern about private monopoly, was for the Post Office to acquire and operate the NTC's trunk lines. State ownership of the trunk lines, by promising trunk interconnection, would encourage new competition (Baldwin 1938: 577; Hazlewood 1953). Even that policy proved contentious with telephone lobbyists. The London County Council (LCC) objected to the bill confirming the agreement eventually reached in 1895 on purchase of the trunk system. Less surprisingly the NTC also proved difficult and disputes over valuation deferred the take-over until 1896.

Nationalization of the trunk system did not silence critics, among whom was counted *The Economist*, of the NTC's 'monopoly profits'. Telephone company concern with profit rather than with service goes some way to explaining municipal attitudes to private telephony. But municipalities also took ideological positions as shown by the statement by the Association of Municipal Corporations: 'The telephone is a system for the benefit of capitalists and the more well to do people and not for the public at large. It is not like gas and water which are a necessity' (Kingston upon Hull Telephones 1954: 9).

By controlling rights of ways over, or under, urban streets

needed for telephone lines, municipalities possessed great powers of obstruction. Their successes as they judged in running water, gas, and other businesses encouraged some to consider supplying telephony as well. Glasgow applied for and was refused a licence in 1893. Its persistence was rewarded with an inquiry in 1897 over the desirability of a council telephone service. The Sheriff concluded that Glasgow's poor service was largely due to local authority obstruction directed to establishing its own service. Local authorities responded by parliamentary lobbying. The Financial Secretary to the Treasury, R. W. Hanbury, with the backing of the National Association of Municipal Corporations, managed to secure the appointment of a Select Committee in 1898 and to ensure that it would recommend the granting of licences to local authorities. Under the 1899 Telegraph Act, which authorized the use of local authority rate funds for telephony, interconnection was required between local authority and NTC systems at terminal charges of between 1d. to 1.5d. for each call until local authority systems reached the same size as the NTC's. At that point interconnection would be free.

Thirteen local authorities took out licences but only six installed telephone exchanges. The most successful of these gained free interconnection despite the larger size of the NTC's system. Hull city council had been strongly urged by the Hull Chamber of Trade in 1899 to appoint a special committee to consider municipal telephony (Kingston upon Hull 1964). Once a licence was granted, Hull achieved free interconnection by threatening the NTC's underground plant with its right of way powers (Anns 1912: 214).

In other municipalities where rival systems were opened, competition was savage and inconvenient to subscribers without interconnection, or where the service was made unreliable by artificial difficulties in interconnecting calls. There were even mutual allegations of plant sabotage. As a national company the NTC was in a strong position to conduct local price wars. The NTC cut rates in response to Glasgow Corporation's entry, primarily by the introduction of party lines, which it found unexpectedly successful. For single parties the Glasgow municipal rate remained well below the NTC's, in contrast to Hull, where only the exclusive business line was cheaper. But Hull offered interconnection and Glasgow did not.

Inappropriate choices of exchange further hampered municipal competition. Glasgow adopted a call wire system instead of a central battery exchange (Kingston upon Hull Telephones 1954; Meyer 1907: 323–6). One subscriber wire called the exchange and was permanently attached to the head telephone of the operator. The subcriber needed to state own number as well as destination and then ask for disconnection when the call was completed. Many wrong numbers and inappropriate engaged signals were generated by this system. Hull also adopted the call wire system but rectified the mistake more quickly. The lives of the municipal exchanges were generally short: Glasgow's lasted from 1901 to 1906, Tunbridge Wells's from 1901 to 1902, and Swansea's and Brighton's from 1903 to 1906. Apart from Hull only Portsmouth outlived the NTC (by one year). Municipal and Post Office competition did encourage the spread of telephony though. Glasgow overtook Hamburg in numbers of telephones and in 1909 possessed more than Manchester and Birmingham combined, even though the municipality had abandoned the field by then. There were more phones in Hull than in the much larger Leeds and about the same number as in the administrative capital of Scotland, Edinburgh. Post Office efforts, when combined with the NTC, in London achieved a growth in subscribers almost as spectacular as Hull's (Table 3.6).

At the same time that municipal telephony was sanctioned the Post Office was also given the opportunity to try its hand at local networks. The Post Office objected to statutory powers being granted to its licensees and therefore successfully blocked any private bills to ease the company's task of obtaining rights of way. Until 1899 the Post Office lacked the money to do much other than obstruct local networks. But under the Telegraph Act of 1899, the Post Office was voted £2 million to compete against its licensees, on whom it levied a royalty of 10 per cent of receipts. The £2 million enabled the Post Office to develop a London telephone service in 1899. London inevitably dominated telephone traffic and the telephone controversy. By the outbreak of the First World War London originated 35 per cent of all UK traffic, a measure of the economic importance of the city even at the time when the staple industries of 'outer Britain' are believed to have been pre-eminent in economic activity and exports. The Post Office achieved interconnection with the NTC in the vital London

TABLE 3.6 *The effects of municipal and state enterprise on urban telephony 1893–1909*

	% growth in subscribers/lines 1893–1909	Numbers 1909
London	2,350	164,208
Glasgow	1,373	43,928
Edinburgh	1,210	10,889
Leeds	698	9,072
Manchester	922	21,209
Birmingham	1,123	13,479
Hull	2,700	10,800

Note: 1909: NTC, PO, and municipalities.

Sources: Calculated from Post Office (1893); *National Telephone Journal* (July 1910), 75.

network by threatening a denial of rights of way in 1901 (Anns 1912: 215). The Post Office agreed to buy the NTC's London system at the end of 1911. Meanwhile full interconnection was to be allowed and both systems would charge equal rates.

There were other players in the game of London telephone politics though. The London County Council objected to their exclusion from negotiations, to the rates charged (in particular the proposed message rate), and to the failure to introduce what they regarded as effective competition. Together with other local authorities in the London area they maintained that the agreement between the company and the PMG was illegal. But in a 1902 vote in the House of Commons Post Office policy was upheld. As a result of the agreement between the NTC and the Post Office, London became the first city with a substantially underground system of telephone distribution. West London was given to the Post Office and the NTC was left the East. How high the political temperature had risen is suggested by *Punch*'s apprehension (see dust-jacket illustration), but the graph of London telephones shows the genuine benefits to Londoners (Fig. 3.3). The central exchange for 14,000 lines opened in 1902. When the systems were amalgamated in 1912 NTC were responsible for 131,506 phones and the Post Office for 77,315.

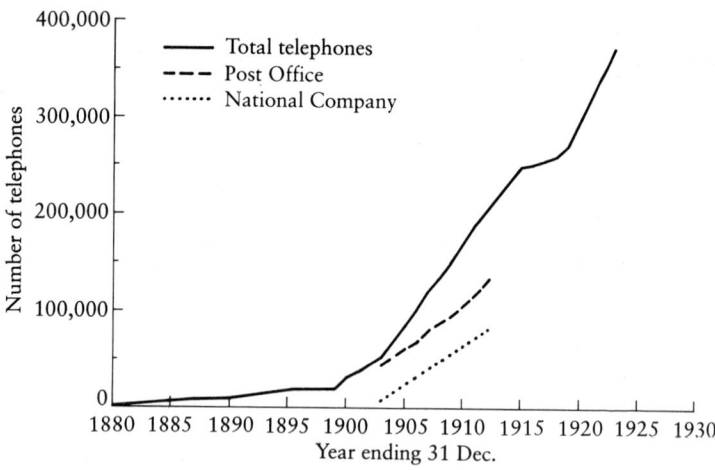

FIG. 3.3 London telephone growth 1880–1914

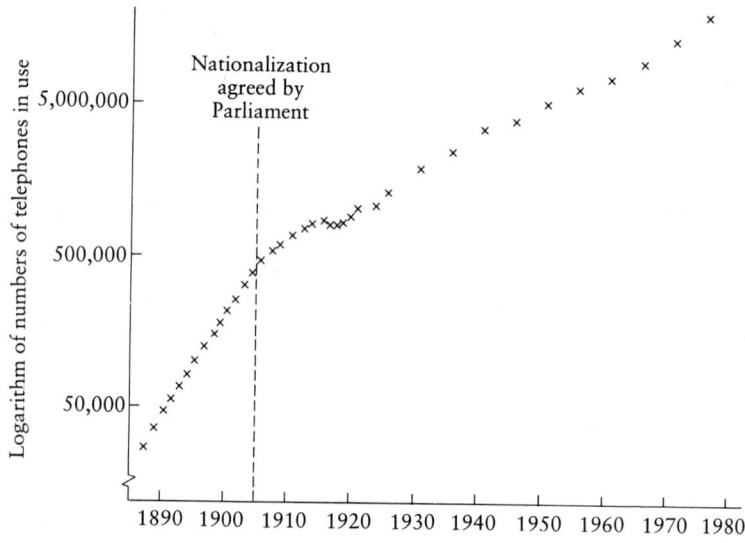

Note: Southern Ireland excluded after 1922.

FIG. 3.4 The spread of telephone usage in the UK 1890–1980

Lobbyists for nationalization generally expected to obtain more favourable rates and service under state ownership. In February 1905 an agreement for voluntary purchase was reached and ratified by Parliament in August. Unfortunately it was not well thought out. Three years later the president of the NTC warned the Postmaster-General that the company would not be investing further in works whose profitability required a longer life than that remaining until the expiry of the licence unless interim compensation arrangements were made. No agreement was reached and telephone development slowed down (Fig. 3.4). Ultimately lobbyists probably received a worse service than if they had devoted their efforts entirely to their businesses.

Meanwhile a small number of large users was active in resisting charges that varied with the number of outgoing calls (measured rates). For telephone companies in the early days of the telephone, the attraction of charging subscribers a fixed annual rental for an unlimited number of calls was the guaranteed income generated. Later, subscribers began to crowd lines with traffic to avoid the cost of a new line. New York's experience of measured rates was influential. Telephones rose from 17,600 in 1905 to nearly 22,000 in 1906 and more than doubled by the end of 1909 (Anns 1911: 182). Hostility to a proposal for measured rates in Sheffield had caused the NTC to retreat from the policy in 1892. The result was that at the beginning of 1907 24 per cent of London calls were met with an engaged signal (*National Telephone Journal* (1907), 232; (1908), 108). Measured rates introduced for the provinces in 1907 were greeted with widespread protests from chambers of commerce but these were resisted (Anns 1912: 221). Charges for each call over a certain minimum reduced the number of calls per subscriber and allowed each operator to take more lines. But since calls had to be recorded on tickets for billing, the increase in lines was not proportional to the reduction of calls per line by 1907. By raising the number of telephones and lines in use, measured rates increased effective calls, the purpose of the telephone system. The introduction of this volume-related charging system is therefore one indication of the extent to which the NTC resisted or reduced the political manipulation of the telephone system. Conscious of the political emotions attached to telephone rates, the company waited until after nationalization was agreed before introducing the new tariff.

AN INTERNATIONAL COMPARISON OF
PERFORMANCE IN TELEPHONES

Inevitably confusion over telephone policy carried implications for the development of the service, but there were other, more important retarding influences. At first sight, if similar engineering techniques were employed in Britain and the United States from where the innovation and the majority of improvements originated, then British telephone service should have been cheaper than an exactly comparable service in the United States because British labour in the twentieth century could be paid lower wages. Demand for telephone services was lower, also because of lower wages, so the net effect on telephone usage could well have been what is shown in Table 3.7, even with no differences in the efficiency of supply. American observers before complete nationalization were convinced that telephone technology was not employed efficiently by British organizations, however. For AT & T., H. Lawes Webb commented on the National Telephone Company in 1895 that they had never studied operating or efficiency tests. 'Such questions never seem to have occurred to NTC officials.' Rules were hung everywhere except in the operating rooms. Waiting times for connections were very long; the shortest that Webb found was fifty-three seconds for a local call in the City. A trunk connection from the City to Westminster took six minutes. The NTC maintained no organized force of instrument inspectors or of trouble-shooters. Construction linesmen were detailed when necessary, with the same lack of management and supervision (Webb 1895).

Webb accused the NTC management of paying more attention to revenue and expenditure than to services. All matters of accounting were carefully considered but little attention was given to telephony. Much later than in the USA, research into traffic was begun, in 1902, and two years later an investigation department for engineering research was established. The department then quickly paid its way by showing how transmission efficiency could be trebled by loading cables. Earlier in the field in personnel training, the NTC claimed to establish the first organized tuition in the world for operators in 1899 (Anns 1912: 216–17).

The Post Office scarcely presented a better picture of British telephony. A Postmaster-General who could say in 1895, 'the

TABLE 3.7 *Telephone systems on 1 January 1913*

	GNP per head (1960$)	Exclusive government ownership	Telegrams sent (×10³)	Telephone conversations (×10³)	Telephones per 100 population	Number of telephones	Proportion of government telephones
Austria-Hungary	498	1	37,845	567,940	0.5	236,940	1.000
Belgium	894	1	9,460	138,030	0.8	58,640	1.000
Bulgaria	263	1	2,300	7,500	0.07	3,200	1.000
Denmark	862	0	3,878	226,670	4.2	118,400	0.012
France	689	1	67,120	396,100	0.7	293,200	1.000
Germany	743	1	64,309	2,324,900	1.9	1,302,700	1.000
Great Britian	965	1	88,494	1,098,400	1.6	738,740	1.000
Greece	322	1	1,970	3,000	0.1	3,097	1.000
Italy	441	0	25,315	230,000	0.2	89,166	0.647
The Netherlands	754	0	7,077	169,710	1.3	77,195	0.707
Norway	749	0	4,000	170,000	3.1	75,000	0.507
Portugal	292	0	5,000	7,000	0.1	8,040	0.146
Romania	336	1	4,300	20,000	0.3	21,000	1.000
Russia and Finland	326	0	45,000	900,000	0.2	282,480	0.382
Serbia	284	1	2,385	5,927	0.1	3,606	1.000
Spain	367	0	6,600	35,000	0.2	34,000	0.050
Sweden	680	0	4,996	434,160	3.9	217,550	0.680
Switzerland	964	1	6,494	68,569	2.3	90,573	1.000
Australia	1,397	1	14,000	168,460	2.6	121,020	1.000
Canada	1,120	0	9,253	770,530	5.6	431,050	0.248
USA	1,388	0	112,660	15,600,000	9.1	8,729,600	0.000
Japan	363	1	33,757	857,400	0.4	198,440	1.000

Sources: GNP: Bairoch (1976); Maddison (1982: tables A2, A3, B2, and the US GNP deflator). Other variables: AT & T., *Telephone and Telegraph Statistics of the World* (1913), bulletin no. 2. Canadian telephone conversations interpolated from Urquhart and Buckley (1965), and US data.

telephone could not and never would be an advantage which could be enjoyed by the mass of the people', and then went on to add that, if it was, the system would prove unmanageable, was not an ideal supervisor of a national telephone system. Internal efficiency was no more exceptional than regulation. The report of the Select Committee on Post Office Servants of 1907 stated that, through parliamentary pressure, the government was obliged to tolerate a degree of inefficiency which in private employment would lead to dismissal of the employee.

Despite this rather discouraging picture, British, and European, telephone charges were at first generally much lower than in the USA, not only because of lower labour costs but also because of a lower European willingness to pay; European demand was weaker and that was one reason for lower use. In 1912 the Post Office charged £17 for unlimited service in London. In New York the comparable figure was £48 and in Chicago £32 (giving access to far more subscribers than London). Large cities were more expensive to supply with telephone services because, given the constraints upon maximum exchange sizes, they needed a hierarchical network which raised switching costs more than transmission costs were reduced.

Even though British average income per head was higher, under a state-owned and -operated system from the beginning Germany attained more telephones per head early on. Yet even Germany did not always efficiently utilize its substantial investments in telephony. After several years a large new telephone exchange in Hamburg was still only being employed for two overflow switchboards in 1907. This heavy investment did not create major differences in prices charged customers in the two countries in that year. At the bottom end of the tariff structure German rates were identical to those of the NTC (Webb 1908).

A more systematic analysis of international comparative data can be offered using a model similar to that employed for telegraphs. The year 1913 offers a greater range of experience than later years (e.g. Littlechild 1983a); for example then Russia operated a private telephone system. The results shown in Appendix 3.4, and in Foreman-Peck (1985), suggest that exclusively state-owned systems allowed greater telephone usage at lower levels of income per head, but increased telephone penetration among higher-income countries was less when they operated exclusively state systems. A poorer performance of state, compared with mixed or private, systems only emerged and increased among wealthier nations on the eve of the First World War. The British road appears to have followed the opposite direction for greatest efficiency, if the experience of other countries is anything to go by. That in turn may be explained by the failure to achieve a politically acceptable framework in which the industry could operate.

The Crown monopoly, and the relatively new local authorities, blocked access to wayleaves and wayleave rights, an essential requirement for a network industry and one that earlier turnpikes, railways, and canals had had far less difficulty obtaining. Competition proved as unsustainable in telephony as it had in those other networks, but public policy became more interventionist in an *ad hoc* fashion. If competition was to be maintained restrictions on mergers were essential, and interconnection and pricing regulation had to be enforced. Unwilling to restrict private enterprise to this extent, governments were eventually persuaded to nationalize. Pressure groups and politicians favouring nationalization would have done well to apply Macbeth's principle 'If it were done when 'tis done then 'twere well it were done quickly', for delay held back telephone development, already retarded by political uncertainties, for another five years.

CONCLUSION

State ownership was increasingly popular as a solution to the problems posed by network industries solely on the basis of limited experience with municipal enterprise and with the Post Office. Public discussion was more a struggle of opposed interests than a detailed consideration of the best way in which these industries should be run. Special interest groups saw state ownership as a means of achieving sectional advantage. These industries were of great importance to other employers and to government, providing services for which on occasion the consumers' surplus (the maximum that would be paid over what actually is paid) was enormous. They supplied the rapid information and transport that are central to business activities. If they did so less than well, or absorbed excessive amounts of capital in doing so, there were domino effects throughout the economy.

An expanding economy will always require institutional change if the framework of economic activity is to be appropriate to new technologies and life-styles. What seems to be distinctive about the British approach in these years is the lack of consensus and consultation which led to frequent national policy changes and contributed to poor business performance. That in turn may be a reflection of a deeper crisis in British society, deriving from an unacceptable distribution of power, income, and security, of the form identified by Dangerfield (1935).

After a detailed discussion of the British economy in the years 1870–1914, Pollard (1989) absolves the economy from charges of failure. The above analysis allows the indictments to be framed more precisely and thus raises the chances of conviction. In long-established railways, productivity growth and innovation declined, although advances were still being made at a greater pace elsewhere in the world. Even new industries could become entangled in webs woven by established industries. The picture that emerges for the key transport and communications sector contains elements that are common to Olson's *Rise and Decline of Nations*, and to Lazonick's account (1986) of the cotton industry. Established organizations and approaches became outmoded but, instead of radical economic adjustment, optimizing behaviour directed use of the political system to erect defences. Creating new institutions and replacing or modifying old are costly processes, and adjustment to these costs shaped future British economic development.

APPENDIX 3.1
Cost Functions for Telegraphs in Britain 1851–1894

The basic function is assumed to be

$$C = a_0 + a_1 Q + a_2 W + a_3 T,$$

where C is working cost as conventionally defined, Q is messages sent, W is a factor price index, T is a measure of technical progress, and a_i are parameters, $a_0, a_1, a_2 > 0$, $a_3 < 0$. Expansion and adjustment costs are

$$EC = a_4(Q - Q_{-1}) + a_5(W - W_{-1})$$

where the subscript -1 indicates a one period lag and $a_4, a_5 > 0$. Some portion of current maintenance expenditures will have been incurred because of traffic and traffic growth in earlier periods. Measured costs TC will therefore include the term $a_6 TC - 1$ ($a_6 > 0$) to reflect maintenance costs.

$$TC = a_0 + a_1 Q + a_2 W + a_3 T + a_4(Q - Q_{-1}) \\ + a_5(W - W_{-1}) + a_6 TC_{-1}$$

To improve the parameter estimates, the first difference of measured working costs is the dependent variable in the first order error correction estimating equation.

$$\Delta TC = a_0 + (a_1 + a_4)\Delta Q + (a_2 + a_5)\Delta W + a_1 Q_{-1} + a_2 W_{-1} \\ + a_3 T + (a_6 - 1)TC_{-1}$$

The long-run equilibrium elasticities are found when rates of change of the TC, Q, and W variables are zero. The above equation then solves to the long-run relation:

$$TC = a_0/(1 - a_6) + a_1/(1 - a_6)Q + a_2/(1 - a_6)W + a_3/(1 - a_6)T.$$

Telegraph organizations had to respond to the demand for telegrams at their offices and that determined their costs. Causation did not also run from costs to messages and therefore OLS estimation is appropriate. The principal difficulty in obtaining data for the variables of the estimating equation arises for the factor price and technology variables. For technology the best that can be done is a time trend. For factor prices, under the EITC only a general wholesale price index is available, but for the Post Office, wage indices could be obtained. EITC working costs and messages are summarized by Price Williams and for the Post Office these

TABLE A.3.1 *EITC and Post Office telegraph cost functions 1851–1894* (dependent variable, change in working costs)

	(1) EITC 1851–68 (calendar years)	(2) PO 1871–94 (fiscal years)	(3) PO 1871–94 (fiscal years)
Const.	0.6544	2.0478	−2.7630
	(0.7474)	(0.7500)	2.265
ΔQ	0.0682	0.1984	0.3799
	(1.0507)	(0.6379)	(2.3390)
ΔP	0.8862	0.4708	—
	(3.4547)	(1.3469)	
Q_{-1}	0.1436	0.1972	0.3309
	(2.9970)	(1.2788)	(4.7911)
P_{-1}	0.1049	−0.2086	—
	(0.4946)	(0.5655)	
TC_{-1}	−0.4317	−0.4223	0.6869
	(4.2710)	(4.2506)	(5.9424)
ΔW	—	—	0.8579
			(3.0293)
W_{-1}	—	—	0.9333
			(2.728)
R^2	0.8942	0.6706	0.7202
DW	1.89	1.36	1.51
SSR	0.02116	0.07174	0.0609

Notes: All variables in logs. White heteroscedastic consistent t statistics in parentheses. P and W are respectively the wholesale price index and the Routh wage index. Δ indicates a first difference operator.

The long-run scale elasticities (dlog TC/dlog Q) for the three equations are EITC 0.1436/0.4317, PO (*a*) 0.1972/0.4223, PO (*b*) 0.3309/0.6869.

variables are recorded in the Postmaster-General's reports and the Annual Abstracts of Statistics.

The equations in Table A.3.1 are estimated in logarithms and with T excluded since it contributed nothing to the explanation of the change in costs.

APPENDIX 3.2

International Comparisons of Telephone Usage c.1868

In the cross-national telegraph analysis a regression model of the following form was estimated:

$$Q/PP = b_0 + b_1 Y + b_2 P + b_3 A + b_4 S$$

where Q/PP is telegrams sent per head of population, Y is national product, A is area of the country, and S is the subsidy or profit per message. Larger countries almost certainly had a longer average haul of messages, which would have been more expensive; a negative coefficient on the area variable is predicted. Systems serving larger populations for given areas and incomes required more infrastructure which must have raised costs; a negative effect on messages sent is expected. A subsidy, which does not lead to offsetting reductions in efficiency, may be anticipated to increase telegraph use. The subsidy was measured by the ratio of revenue to expenditure for each national system: the higher the subsidy the lower the ratio of income to spending. Since the subsidy coefficient had the incorrect sign and was statistically significant (suggesting subsidies did cause offsetting inefficiency), the variable is not included in the reported equations.

Equation (1) in Table A.3.2 is estimated from the countries with state systems and then predicts telegrams sent per head on the assumption that the same relationship held for the United States (the only other major private enterprise system) and the United Kingdom. The F statistic tests for structural change between the samples including and excluding these two countries. Equation (2) is estimated including the USA in the sample.

Measurement errors for telegrams per head are a source of the error term on which the regression model depends and do not bias the parameter estimates. Errors in the measurement of national product are likely to be larger and, because they cannot be included in the error term of the OLS model, they can bias all the coefficients. To correct for this possibility, rail miles was used as an instrumental variable for national product in equation (3). The coefficients and the prediction change little.

TABLE A.3.2 Regression analysis of telegraph use across nations c.1868 (dependent variable, messages per head of population)

	Estimation method	Constant	National product	Population	Area	$\bar{R}^2$	SSR	Prediction USA	Prediction UK	F-Test for structural change
(1)	OLS	-8.50 [5.36]	1.63 [9.42]	-1.95 [10.94]	-0.05 [-0.64]	0.842	1.0046	0.200	0.300	0.16
(2)	OLS	-7.88 [9.18]	1.56 [10.73]	-1.87 [-12.84]	-0.07 [-1.98]	0.845	1.0043	0.170	0.284	0.73
(3)	IV	-7.43 [7.72]	1.49 [9.49]	-1.80 [0.16]	-0.07 [2.08]		1.0099	0.164	0.272	0.70
Actual								0.170 (Western Union only)	0.200	

Notes: Equation (1) excludes both the USA and the UK, equations (2) and (3) exclude only the UK t statistics based on heteroscedastic-consistent (White) standard errors in parentheses. Equation (3) uses rail miles as an instrument for national product. All variables in logarithms. $F_c^{0.05}$ (4, 10) = 5.96.

APPENDIX 3.3
International Railway Cost Functions 1840–1910

Data on capital costs averaged for each decade 1840–1910 are available for the various countries listed in Table A.3.3. Capital costs were regressed on railway mileage and lagged capital costs with dummies used for the various countries and with Belgium the country used as benchmark. The results are discussed in Chapter 3. Additional insights arise from the more detailed data available for the years 1895 and 1906 for the countries listed in Table 3.4. Table A.3.4 shows three regression equations with train-miles per rail mile as the independant variable and with the dependant variables as construction costs per mile, working costs per mile, and revenue per mile. The Table A.3.4 results imply that the number of train-miles per mile of track had, across the sample of countries, a significant effect on construction costs, working costs, and revenue per mile. After allowing for these effects, it is clear that the UK had significantly higher construction costs but no higher working costs or revenue per mile.

TABLE A.3.3 *Cross-national comparison of railway capital costs 1840–1910*

Constant	-4.7045^a
	(1.1490)
Log rail mileage	0.9486^a
	(0.0389)
Time	0.0046^a
	(0.0013)
Log capital cost	0.7013^a
$t-1$	(0.0908)
Log rail mileage	-0.7090^a
$t-1$	(0.0873)
United Kingdom	0.3007^a
	(0.0777)
France	0.1080
	(0.06322)
Germany	0.0422
	(0.0750)
Switzerland	-0.1278^a
	(0.0549)
Sweden	-0.4081^a
	(0.1443)
United States	0.0147
	(0.1386)
Canada	-0.1887^a
	(0.0910)
India	-0.2629^a
	(0.1170)
Australia	-0.2943^a
	(0.1129)
Russia	-0.0256
	(0.0745)
Austria	-0.0299
	(0.0622)
Italy	-0.0439
	(0.0596)
$\bar{R}^2$	0.9974
USSR	0.3667

[a] Significant at the 5% level.

Sources: *UK Abstract of Foreign Statistics* (various); Mulhall (1892); Webb (1911).

TABLE A.3.4 *OLS analysis of pooled cross-national railway cost and revenue: Data for c.1895 and c.1906*

Dependent variable	Constant	Train-miles rail per mile	$D \times$ train miles	SSR	$\bar{R}^2$
Construction cost per mile	$5,190.57^a$ (1,959.70)	1.8361^a (0.2566)	1.1015^a (0.2596)	0.6309×10^9	0.828
Working expenses per mile	160.247 (102.24)	0.1436^a (0.0134)	0.0112 (0.0135)	0.1717×10^7	0.854
Revenue per mile	274.233 (162.74)	0.2238^a (0.0213)	0.0265 (0.0215)	0.4351×10^7	0.865

Notes: The restrictions imposed in the above equations were tested and found consistent with the data; 32 observations for each equation. D is the United Kingdom dummy variable.

[a] Significant at the 5% level.

APPENDIX 3.4
Telephone Usage in Private and Public Telephone Systems in 1913

An explanation of cross-national differences in telephone usage is possible by exploiting the data from Table 3.7. Table A.3.5 reports regressions of national income and population on the number of telephone conversations, using slope dummies to explore the role of institutional effects. The results are discussed in Chapter 3.

TABLE A.3.5 *Performance of private and public telephone systems in 1913*

	Constant	GNP	GNP per head	Population	Exclusive government ownership	G × telegrams	G × GNP	G × population	G × GNP/ population	R^2
(1)	-7.1227	1.0774	—	—	-8.1372	—	0.4086	—	—	0.8048
	(-1.6079)	(4.4391)			(-1.3944)		(1.2737)			F = 24.7
(2)	-19.181	—	3.2028	0.9420	+3.1735	—	—	0.4776	-1.4754	0.9386
	(-5.7350)		(8.1959)	(6.4435)	(0.7655)			(2.2783)	(-2.8857)	F = 48.9
(3)	-19.611	—	3.2189	0.9697	7.2882	0.4387	—	—	-1.8953	0.9348
	(-5.7153)		(7.9963)	(6.5003)	(2.0956)	(1.9876)			(3.3678)	F = 45.9
(4)	-22.833	—	3.4433	1.1174	8.8817[a]	—	—	—	-1.4561[a]	0.8960
	(-5.5146)		(5.9294)	(8.6096)	(1.8557)				(1.9670)	F = 36.6
(5)	-22.786	—	3.3380	1.1742	8.9707	—	—	—	-1.5018	0.9187
	(-6.9254)		(7.7405)	(10.037)	(2.4551)				(-2.6316)	F = 48.0
(6)	-19.971	—	3.0747	1.0271	5.8589	—	—	—	-0.9944	0.9471
	(-8.1768)		(9.6046)	(11.826)	(2.1599)				(2.3474)	F = 76.0

Notes: Dependent variable is 'Telephone conversations', except for equation (6) which has 'Telephones' as dependent variable. All variables except for 'Government ownership' in logarithms.

[a] = Government stations/total stations; 22 countries in sample; t statistics in parentheses: $t(0.01, 17) = 2.898$. $t(0.05, 17) = 2.110$.

4
Prices, Profits, and Government: Gas and Telegraph in the Late Nineteenth Century

INTRODUCTION

The political importance of the twentieth-century consumer and taxpayer is such that firms, whatever their ownership forms, tread a narrow line between high prices, high profits, and 'exploitation' on the one hand and low prices, deficits, and 'inefficiency' on the other. Whereas British observers of the post-1945 period tend to associate the second type of behaviour with state industry, public ownership has in fact yielded many examples of the alternative scene. US municipal governments have been accused, on occasions, of using their local utilities as a tax base, that is setting local monopoly prices so that profits may be creamed off into municipal finances. Private coal companies in the inter-war period in both the USA and the UK struggled to avoid financial losses and thereby attracted subsidies, accusations of incompetence, and invidious comparisons with well-managed German collieries.

In this chapter we examine the experience of certain network industries to throw light on how their profit levels and pricing policies have been affected by links with government. If government subsidizes state industry, does this raise output and if not why not? If profits are siphoned off does this imply that prices are higher? Would public firms charge prices different from private firms? Two sectors are examined in detail. The first is the local utilities sector in late nineteenth-century Britain, which embraced electricity, tramways, water supply, as well as gas supply, which will be a special focus of attention. The second is the electric telegraph in the same period, comparing the experience of European and US governments in their interventions.

THE OBJECTIVES OF LOCAL UTILITIES: SIZE, PROFITS, VOTES?

The second half of the nineteenth century witnessed a large expansion of both private utilities and municipal enterprises in activities like electricity, tramways, gas, water supply. This was the period of the massive expansion of the local infrastructure responding to the pressures of industrialization and we shall analyse this in more detail in the next chapter. The existing literature on these utilities has been dominated by the case-studies of particular towns with few generalizations possible about pricing policy, the interests of town councils, the costs of services, the effectiveness of parliamentary regulation. By looking at significant samples of undertaking we shall in this chapter be able to shed light on these issues. In addition it is of interest to assess whether the behaviour of municipal enterprises was different from that of the companies. Matthews (1986: 269) argues that in the gas industry both types of undertaking were run on commercial lines for profit. Waller (1983: 328) maintained that the municipalities 'pursued philanthropic policies as regards prices to consumers and wages to employees, this social aim taking precedence over business practice'. Was profit-making, in the words of the 1928 Balfour Committee, 'a subsidiary consideration to that of giving the best possible service at the lowest cost compatible with the avoidance of financial loss and thereby securing the largest possible utilisation of the service by the public' (1928–9: 308)? In this context, Knoop (1912: 41, 180), echoing some contemporary thought, viewed the local authorities in their provision of water, gas, and tramways as a society of consumers uniting to provide the necessities of life directed especially to those classes of the community deemed to be in need of assistance. Finer was even more specific: 'Quite consciously they are adopting the policy of serving as many consumers as possible, at prices as near to the cost of production as can possibly be estimated.' This, he felt, reflected both 'a charitable principle where special allowances are made not so much for small as for poor consumers' and also the fact that one 'must be unjust to the commandment of the cost of production in order that the small consumers who are the largest number may not grouse' (1941: 299–302). Here are very different hypotheses from those which stress commercial factors. Indeed, yet another possibility, reflecting the interests of the managers of the undertakings, would be the motive to expand, to generate large empires. Hassan, (1985: 545) has speculated that municipal water undertakings had sales-maximizing goals.

What role was played by the transfer of some of the municipals' trading profits to local authority accounts in relief of rates? Most writers have seen this as one of the important motives for municipalization and in some cases, Birmingham being the classic case, power to make such transfers was specifically written into their parliamentary Acts (cf. Finer 1941: 146; Robson 1935: 310; Falkus 1977: 152; Balfour Committee 1928–9: 308). Waller (1983) has observed that some contemporaries saw it as a 'malversation' (p. 308). Williams (1981: 43) records that customers who were not ratepaying beneficiaries protested at being 'overcharged'. Finer described the practice as 'mulcting the undertakings' (1941: 158). What effect did it have? Did it affect prices or the amount of ploughed back profits?

THE GAS INDUSTRY 1870–1914

To answer these questions we look at the gas industry in some detail and first of all, in this section, spell out the main features of its prices, profits, and markets. In the period 1873–1913 gas sales were growing at about 3.7 per cent per annum with the net capital stock, according to Feinstein's recent estimates (Feinstein and Pollard 1988: table 13.1), at 2.2 per cent per annum. As Table 4.1 shows, the average size of companies in terms of sales or consumers grew over the period as the number of mergers increased and by 1913 the difference from the municipally owned undertakings in this respect had diminished. Consumption per customer was less for the municipals. Some writers have attributed this characteristic, as well as the larger number of consumers per undertaking, to lower prices charged by municipalities. 'Owing to the cheapness of price and better service' argued Maltbie (1900: 559), 'under municipal operation, a larger number of the poorer classes used gas'. From the Board of Trade returns on all authorized undertakings, on sales receipts and production levels, he calculated an average price for 1898 of 36.5*d*. per 1,000 cubic feet

TABLE 4.1 *Number and size of gas undertakings in Great Britain 1882–1912*

	Number of undertakings	Sales (m. cu. ft.)	Sales per undertaking (m. cu. ft.)	Number of consumers (000)	Consumption per consumer (000 cu. ft.)	Consumers per undertakings
Companies						
1882	352	45,485	129	1,055	43	2,997
1897/8	436	77,773	178	1,549	50	3,552
1911/12	520	126,002	242	3,906	32	7,511
Municipal						
1882	148	21,129	143	916	23	6,189
1897/8	212	44,447	210	1,475	30	6,957
1911/12	306	72,921	238	2,743	27	8,964

Source: Board of Trade, *Return Relating to all Authorised Gas Undertakings* (annual).

in the municipals and 42*d*. in the companies. Donald (1903: 92) has the same figure for companies for 1899 and 40*d*. for municipals. For 1903/4 Howe (1906: 35) put the municipal figure 10 per cent lower than the company figure and a similar differential for 1913 was noted by the Balfour Committee (1928–9: 312). However, none of this necessarily implies that municipal policy was different from that of the companies. Many of the towns in the South were served by the companies whilst the gasworks of the industrial towns of the North were often, though not always, municipally owned. Only by explicit allowance for potentially different market characteristics in different regions could one conclude that policy was different and this will be part of the analysis of later sections. Indeed the rate of profit on turnover or on the value of fixed assets seems to have been little different in the two sectors, varying from 5 per cent to 9 per cent depending on the specific years chosen (Matthews 1986: 262; Howe 1906: 40; Maltbie 1900; Donald 1903: 72).

The general characteristics of the sample of undertakings analysed in this paper are shown in Table 4.2 and the accompanying notes. The selection of undertakings was based partly on the quality of data available in *Gas World*, a key source, and on the need to include many of the large undertakings in order to get a good coverage of the industry's activities. In aggregate, the undertakings in the sample in 1897/8 sold 64,000 million cubic feet of gas or some 50 per cent of the industry total. They also accounted for 48 per cent of the industry's gas consumers. Consumption per consumer is, like the national pattern, significantly higher in the company sector. The number of consumers per undertaking would also be lower but for the inclusion of the London companies. There are sixteen companies in the sample and, notwithstanding Sheffield, Newcastle, and Dublin, the majority are in the South of England. This is typical of the industry as a whole, with Scotland and the North of England populated more by municipals. Clearly, with the inclusion of the very large London companies and municipal undertakings like Glasgow, Nottingham, Manchester, and several other large northern industrial towns, the sample includes only a small proportion of the *number* of undertakings. The very small undertakings are therefore under-represented. However, since the sample does include undertakings like Barnet, Dunfermline, and Hastings, the

TABLE 4.2 *General characteristics of 1897/8 sample of gas undertakings*

	Companies[a]	Municipal[b]
Size and consumption[c]		
Gas sold per undertaking (m. cu. ft.)	2,492	1,027
No. of consumers per undertaking	47,036	36,712
Consumption per consumer (ooo cu. ft.)	53	28
Prices and costs (£)[c]		
Gas sales revenue per ooo cu. ft.	0.142	0.127
By-product revenue per ooo cu. ft.	0.031	0.025
Meter rent per customer p.a.	0.323	0.044
Cost per ooo cu. ft. of gas made[d]	0.169	0.147
Profits and transfers (£000)[c]		
Gross aggregate trading profits	2,104	672
As % turnover	27.9	24.5
As % rate of return on capital	7.5	6.8
Loan charges[e]	236	422
Dividends	1,864	—
Transfer to rate accounts[f]	—	135
Balance to reserves		114

[a] The sixteen companies in the sample were Alliance & Dublin, Barnet, Brentford, Brighton & Hove, Bristol, Bromley, Commercial, Croydon, Crystal Palace, Gas Light & Coke, Harrow & Stanmore, Hastings & St Leonards, Newcastle upon Tyne & Gateshead, Sheffield, South Metropolitan, Tottenham & Edmonton.

[b] The nineteen municipals included in the sample were Blackburn, Bolton, Bradford Carlisle, Darwen, Dundee, Dunfermline, Edinburgh and Leith, Glasgow, Lancaster, Manchester, Nottingham, Oldham, Salford, Stafford, Stoke, West Bromwich, Widnes, Wigan.

[c] The raw data used to calculate the figures in the table were as follows: Gas revenue; gas sold in ooo cu. ft.; number of customers; income from rental of meters and stoves and miscellaneous receipts; income from residuals (i.e. by-products); gross cost of gas; gross profit; capital value of works; loan charges comprise sinking fund contributions plus interest paid, less interest received; dividend; transfers to rates and other municipal accounts are recorded in the footnotes to the *Gas World* accounts and were supplemented by data in the parliamentary return; balance to reserves is the residual.

[d] The entry for cost per ooo cu. ft. of gas made is taken from previous work (Millward and Ward 1987).

[e] The loan charges figure excludes Barnet, which is a joint gas and water undertaking whose financial charges are not attributed to separate sections.

[f] Transfers to rate accounts could not be identified for four municipal corporations—Bradford, Oldham, Stoke, and Edinburgh. If all surpluses after paying loan charges had been transferred to rate accounts rather than to reserves, then the former figure would rise by some 42,000 and transfers to reserves would be smaller by the same amount.

Sources: *Gas World* (1898, 1899) and Board of Trade (1898). Most of the data were taken from the annual accounts reported in *Gas World*. There were some discrepancies with the parliamentary returns. Details may be obtained from the author.

cost and demand characteristics of small-scale undertakings are picked up.

Average gas prices and meter rents in the sample were lower in the municipal sector, as were rates of profit, though the latter difference was not statistically significant. Costs are analysed in Chapter 5, and the lower level in the municipals was largely accounted for by lower wage rates, coal prices, and interest rates. Of more immediate concern is that Table 4.2 also provides some guide to the size of the transfers from municipal trading to local authority rates and other municipal accounts. In the municipal gas undertakings it is relevant to view such transfers as one of the ways in which gross trading profits were allocated alongside loan charges and ploughed back profits, important data for the debate on whether local authorities municipalized gasworks in order to get access to their profits. Gross trading profits here comprise revenue from gas, by-products, meter and stove rentals, less operating costs including repair and maintenance. In the sample, transfers to municipal accounts accounted for up to 25 per cent of gross trading profits. In some towns like Manchester, Nottingham, and Bolton, the transfers were even more substantial. The retentions for reserves were nevertheless much bigger than the companies' after loan charges and dividend payments had been met.

To obtain some idea of the aggregate transfers to rates and other municipal accounts, Table 4.3 uses data from the annual local taxation returns to calculate, for certain sample years over the period 1893 to 1908, the relevant components for all gas undertakings owned by the different kinds of local authorities in England and Wales. Taking 1907/8 as a benchmark, the transfers were only some 3 per cent of the county boroughs' income from rates and even less for other boroughs. This may represent an underestimate of the significance of the transferred surpluses during the late nineteenth century for three reasons. First is that by 1907/8 there was increasing awareness, apprehension, and possibly restrictions of the transfers following some very detailed parliamentary returns for all the trading activities of all boroughs for the period 1893 to 1902 (Local Government Board 1899*b*, 1902) and detailed evidence collected by a Joint Select Committee on Municipal Trading which reported in 1903. Secondly, rate income in the 1890s was much smaller relative to trading profits,

TABLE 4.3 Annual profits and transfers to rate accounts in municipal gas undertakings 1893–1908 (£000)

	County boroughs					Other boroughs					Urban district councils				
	Gross trading profits	Loan charges	Net transfer to rate accounts	Balance to reserves	Rate income	Gross trading profits	Loan charges	Net transfer to rate accounts	Balance to reserves	Rate income	Gross trading profits	Loan charges	Net transfer to rate accounts	Balance to reserves	Rate income
1893/4–1897/8	883	561	322[a]		8,136	298	248	50[b]		2,734	477	n/a	n/a	n/a	3,436
1907/8	1,362	903	404	53	14,250	407	290	69	48	4,879	292	245	n/a	n/a	6,026

Notes: Profits consist of trading income (including Exchequer grants but excluding any local authority subsidies) less working expenses, maintenance, and depreciation. Loan charges include interest and sinking fund payments. Net transfer to rate accounts covers surpluses transferred in aid of rates and other local authority accounts, net of subsidies. The composition of the local authorities has changed over time. Entries in the first row for rate income and UDC profits relate to 1897/8 only.
[a] Includes balance transferred to revenues.
[b] Includes balance transferred to reserves.

Sources: Local Government Board (1899a, 1899b).

as the table shows. Thirdly, prior to the 1900s the annual local taxation returns did not clearly separate the accounts of the municipal trading enterprises from other accounts; indeed the annual returns did not fully attribute loan charges and Table 4.3 for the 1890s uses data from the special parliamentary returns for all boroughs. Since gross trading profits have tended to be some 20–30 per cent of turnover, that is total revenue, then the gas undertakings' revenue in the 1890s was on a par to the local authorities' income from rates. How far this affected matters like the pricing policy of the enterprises is considered later. In the mean time, it should be noted that the transfers became much less important after the war. Indeed, provisions against such transfers appeared in many of the Gas Acts for England and Wales from 1920, matching what had been an old provision in Scottish Acts (Chantler 1938: 80–3).

Before analysing the demand for gas in detail, several general features of the market should be mentioned and this section also indicates how gas prices and other revenue items are to be measured. Gas had several uses and the market should ideally be segregated for purposes of analysis. Up to the latter part of the nineteenth century, the gas load was largely one for lighting. From its wide use in public lighting at the beginning of the century it spread to commercial premises and aristocratic households, reaching middle-class living rooms in the period 1840–70 (cf. Matthews 1986: 246). In the next twenty years gas cooking and heating were making inroads into middle-class kitchens. The 1890s saw a further decline in the price of gas which, together with the use of the incandescent mantle, hiring of cookers, fires, and geysers, and the introduction of coin slot meters, enhanced the use of lighting and cooking in working-class homes. Finally gas was being introduced for many heating processes in industry. Electricity was, by 1910, eroding the lighting load, though mainly for large users like hotels. By 1919 lighting accounted for only 35 per cent of gas sold (Chantler 1938: 108–9; Matthews 1986: 262; Knoop 1912: 205, 213).

The charge for gas for power, heating, and cooking tended to be less than for lighting and larger users, including public lighting, benefited from discounts. Unfortunately, the available data do not distinguish between the various uses of gas and hence it is not possible in the demand analysis to disaggregate gas consumption in each town into the various submarkets. The Census of Population 1901 was used however to get a measure of the population of each of the towns in the sample and an index of industrialization in the form of a measure for each town of the proportion of the male working population in industrial work (i.e. paper, textiles, metal, precious metals, gas, electricity, water, and sanitation— orders IV–VIII, XII, XVI, XXI). This was used in the demand analysis as a variable reflecting in each town the size of the industrial demand for gas.

Prices and dividends had both been regulated from the mid-century if not earlier but with rather weak enforcement mechanisms. A 10 per cent limit on dividends was established by the 1847 Gas Clauses Act but the medium for monitoring and appeal was the County Quarter Sessions. In subsequent private Acts the percentage ceiling was lowered to reflect the lower general level of returns. Maximum prices were also specified in private Acts but with no regular machinery for revision. The sliding-scale system was introduced first in London and then from the 1870s extended to other areas. A benchmark price was established (usually at the old maximum price) as well as a standard percentage dividend which could be exceeded if prices fell in specified amounts below the benchmark. This system was restricted to the company sector with the municipals still on maximum prices though both fell under the regulatory control of the Board of Trade from the 1880s.

This pattern of tariffs is reflected in the sample with most municipals carrying maximum prices and most companies on a sliding scale. Similarly many municipals in the sample provided meters free, matching the pattern which others have observed throughout this period. Companies often charged meter rent, though in our subsequent analysis we could not unscramble this from stove rentals and other miscellaneous receipts. Finally we should not forget the by-products—coke, ammoniacal liquor, tar—which accounted for 15–25 per cent of the total revenue of the undertakings in the sample including even the tiny ones like Barnet and Dunfermline (Chantler 1938: 33–6; Knoop 1912: 215–22).

A household's demand for gas and a factory's demand for gas would vary with gas prices and the availability and prices of substitutes like electricity. We estimate here the demand for gas by looking at a cross-section of the sales of the thirty-five undertakings in the sample for 1897/8. This yields estimates of demand elasticities which are used in the later parts of the chapter to form estimates of marginal revenue and profit for the undertakings. Since the consumption of gas requires fittings and pipes, the quantity of gas sold at any point in time is a product of the number of connected customers and the amount of consumption per consumer. In the case of domestic users, consumption per consumer, that is household consumption, is likely to vary across the country according to the price of gas, household income, and the availability and cost of substitutes like electricity, coal, and paraffin. Information on household incomes at the level of towns is not available. The proxy measure which was used was the wage rate of engineering turners which is available at a local level (see Appendix 6.3). The measure of the gas price is affected by the fact that the total quantity of gas sold and the number of consumers cannot be divided into household consumption and industrial usage. Thus the price of gas is measured for each town simply as gas revenue per thousand cubic feet of gas sold. In so far as consumption per consumer is different for industrial users, it is hoped that this effect will be picked up, as indicated earlier, by the industrialization index calculated for each town.

Turning to substitutes, it is fortunate that data on the variation

TABLE 4.4 *Gas demand and cost elasticities 1897/8*

	Mean	Range
Consumer demand for gas with respect to gas price	(−)1.80	(−)1.51−(−)1.95
Gas demand price with respect to number of customers	0.66	0.60−0.72
Income elasticity of demand for gas	0.90	0.37−1.56
Consumer demand for gas with respect to price of electricity	0.46	0.29−0.61
Total cost with respect to number of customers	0.14	0.11−0.18
Total cost with respect to quantity of gas produced	0.81	0.81−0.81

Note: The elasticity values vary with the level of quantity sold, number of customers, etc. The range is from the 1st to the 3rd quartile.

in electricity prices across towns may be obtained from the special parliamentary returns which were made in 1899 and 1901 (see Board of Trade 1901–2). The sample of gas undertakings includes thirty-two provincial towns for each of which there was often a corresponding electricity undertaking. For the exceptions, the price of neighbouring electricity undertakings was used, whilst the London gas companies were matched to the appropriate clusters of electricity undertakings (Millward 1991*b*: n. 36). An average revenue per British electricity unit sold was then calculated for each area as total receipts for 'energy and public lighting' divided by total units sold and this showed considerable variation from 2*s.* 7*d.* to 8*s.* 9*d.* Electricity may have still been out of the range of many households. Coal would be an important substitute, at least for cooking and heating for domestic and industrial users. Coal prices for each town were estimated from the gasworks' own usage of coal. Paraffin may still have been an important alternative to gas but no data on the variation of its inland prices are available.

Detailed analysis of the demand function is in Appendix 4.1 but the more important results are listed here in Table 4.4. The first row shows the elasticity of the demand for gas with respect to the gas price in the range (−)1.51 to (−)1.95. This estimate holds the prices of substitutes and income levels constant and by also holding the number of consumers fixed it effectively reflects the price elasticity of consumption per consumer. Contrary to what some have thought about this period (cf. Knoop 1912: 20), the demand for gas is highly sensitive to the gas price. It was not sensitive at all to the price of coal, whose role as a cost item may have confused matters. The result for electricity prices in Table 4.4 implies that shifting to areas where electricity prices were 10 per cent lower would reduce the demand for gas by 4.6 per cent on average though this was not statistically significant. It looks as though, subject to the earlier qualifications about paraffin, at least for the 1890s the prices of substitutes were nowhere near as important as the price of gas itself. Income levels proved to be an important influence and the range for the elasticity in Table 4.4 of 0.37–1.56 indicates that it rose with income levels. Finally, it should be noted that the relationship between the gas demand price and the number of customers is estimated with the quantity of gas sold held fixed. A larger number of customers in these circumstances may be expected to 'bid up' the demand price and this is borne out by the mean elasticity value of 0.66. Undertakings with 10 per cent more customers, all other things equal, will experience their customers' marginal gas demand price bid up by 6.6 per cent on average. Table 4.4 for completeness also includes the cost elasticities which are drawn from the cost function results discussed in Chapter 6 below. That chapter analyses how the annual total costs of an undertaking (including capital costs) varied with number of customers, quantity produced, wage rates, and the prices of other inputs. The results indicate, as Table 4.4 shows, that increases in quantity produced or number of customers, when observed separately, involve increasing returns to scale. When combined, however, a 10 per cent increase in both customers and quantity produced involves a rise in total costs of very nearly 10 per cent and for undertakings with a very large number of customers (like the London companies) decreasing returns to scale apply.

RESULTS AND CONCLUSIONS OF THE GAS INDUSTRY CASE-STUDY

We are now in a position to assess the objectives of the gas undertakings—whether they included profits or sales maximization or perhaps advancing the interests of consumers. As explained in the introduction, the way this is approached is by observing certain variables over which the undertakings had clear control and considering whether the observed levels are basically consistent with one or more of the hypotheses. The key choice variables are taken to be the number of customers and the volume of gas sales. In this section we indicate what would characterize the undertakings' choices under different objectives and also indicate how some of the relevant concepts, like marginal revenue, are to be measured using the demand and cost elasticities reported in the previous section. A formal model and detailed results are in Appendix 4.1.

How would an undertaking behave if it were solely interested in profit? It would extend its sale of gas to the point where marginal profit was zero, that is marginal revenue from extra gas sales equalled marginal cost. Analogously it would enlarge the number of customers to the point where the marginal revenue from an extra customer equalled marginal cost. Can we calculate marginal revenue and marginal cost and test this? Marginal revenue from increasing gas sales depends for each undertaking on its gas price, demand elasticity, and by-product revenue. All of this information is available and the precise method of calculating marginal revenues is explained in detail in Appendix 4.1. Marginal cost may be calculated from data on cost per unit of output (cf. Table 4.2) and the data on cost elasticities—since cost elasticity is precisely equal to marginal cost divided by average cost. This done we could then examine whether across the sample of undertakings marginal profit is significantly different from zero.

The above relates to profit maximization. What would be the implications under price regulation or for undertakings geared to pursue the interests of consumers or managers? Consider first the case where a management interest promoted the objective of size. At the point where profits are maximized total revenue might still be rising if either gas sales or the number of customers is increased. In these circumstances the firm geared to maximize revenue would increase the volume of sales and thereby total revenue incurring a marginal deficit on output. The same applies to increasing the number of customers. Moreover, the firm will increase sales rather than customers if the marginal revenue per pound of marginal profit on extra output exceeds that on extra customers. A limit to this process will exist if the firm is constrained to earn a minimum total profit. Although there is no way of knowing what the size of this minimum profit is, the logic of the above is that the firm's equilibrium position would be where the relative marginal revenues would equal the relative marginal profit on output and consumers. Firms with greater relative marginal revenues should have bigger relative marginal profits. This can therefore be tested in our sample of undertakings. Of course if the profit constraint is not binding, the firm will expand its sales until the marginal revenue of output is zero and its customers until the marginal revenue from customers is zero. This can also be tested. Finally, if the firm focused more on the sheer volume of its gas sales then the number of customers would presumably be kept at the profit-maximizing level while the volume of gas sales would be extended beyond that. Thus marginal profit on customers would be zero but marginal profit on sales would be negative. This again can be tested.

The above reasoning gives a guide to how one might test for the presence of price regulation for a firm which is basically maximizing profits. Suppose that price regulation constitutes an effective constraint in that the profit-maximising number of customers and gas sales involves a gas price higher than is permitted. Clearly then an increase in gas sales, with the associated reduction in the gas demand price, would reduce the danger of breaking the pricing limit. Conversely since an increase in the number of customers, with gas sold fixed, bids up the gas demand price then such extra customers push the gas price further above the maximum allowed. It follows that a profit-maximizing firm for whom price regulation is an effective binding constraint will be characterized by a marginal deficit on output and a positive marginal profit on customers. This can be tested. Furthermore, the relative impacts of gas sales and customer numbers on gas prices would tend to reflect the relative profitability of the two choice variables.

Consider now the alternative hypothesis that the firms are geared to promoting the interest of consumers. If this simply involves maximizing the number of customers subject to a break-even constraint then the implications are straightforward. The number of customers would be extended beyond the profit-maximizing point but the firm would not want to extend its level of sales. Hence such a firm would be characterized by a zero marginal profit on output but a negative marginal profit on customers. A less crude version of this would allow the firm to promote economic benefits to consumers; that is to maximize the value to consumers of their access to gas and the value to them of the size of their gas consumption. This again only makes sense in the context of a minimum profit constraint. Intuitively, in the simple case where a firm produces a single dimension to output (e.g. volume of sales) then the outcome would be that where price equalled average cost. In the present context the economic benefits would consist of what consumers are prepared to pay for access to gas and for different levels of gas consumption. The reader is referred to Appendix 4.1 because the issues are more complex and in any case the tests rejected this hypothesis, as we shall now see.

The first stage in the testing involves ascertaining whether marginal profit and marginal revenue variables tended to zero. The results set out in Appendix 4.1 indicate that the marginal revenue variables were significantly positive as was the marginal profit for customers. The marginal profit on output was significantly negative for both private and public firms. It was also found in a regression exercise that the relative impact of output and customer numbers on the gas price is strongly correlated, across the sample of undertakings, with the relative marginal profit on sales and customers.

What conclusions can be drawn? The main one we believe is that all undertakings had profit as a strong objective but price ceilings were an effective constraint. The reasons are as follows. The idea that the enterprises were geared to maximizing the interest of consumers finds no support even for the municipals. One would expect the marginal profit on consumers to be negative rather than positive and no correlation was found between the relative profitability of output and consumer numbers and the relative marginal benefits. Similarly it seems unlikely that firms are revenue maximizers, since there is no correlation between relative marginal revenue and relative marginal profits; neither is there support for the possibility that the profit constraint is not binding since the marginal revenues would then be zero whereas for both sales and consumer numbers they are both significantly positive.

It is true that empire builders who are maximizing the volume of sales would have a negative marginal profit on output. But there is no reason to expect such firms to have a distinctly positive surplus on marginal consumers. In fact the coexistence of these phenomena is quite consistent with such firms maximizing profits subject to a ceiling on prices and the above regression result supports that conclusion. As compared to the profit-maximizing position extra sales require lower prices and hence relax the price constraint but extra consumers tighten it since the gas demand price is 'bid up'. The private companies were under a weaker form of price ceiling which may therefore go some way to explain the larger spread of their results.

Finally it is worth stressing that some of the observed differences between companies and municipals arise not from different objectives but rather from the particular economic characteristics of the towns in which public and private happen to be located. Thus consumption per consumer is much lower in municipals but there is no evidence that this reflects a conscious policy of connecting more customers irrespective of commercial considerations. The average consumption of the customers of the private companies is higher but so also is the general level of gas prices. They are serving populations (often in the South) which have higher incomes and higher gas expenditure per household and their demand curve is 'to the right' of that for municipals. Both types of undertaking were strongly motivated by profit and this similarity of objectives is reflected in the fact that there is no statistically significant difference between the two sectors' rates of return for 1897/8. Nor can we discern any effect on prices from the particular way in which profits were used. Apart from what was added to the reserves of the undertakings, the companies distributed their profit as dividends, the municipals to their 'owner', but there is no evidence that this affected the level of prices.

In summary, then, during the period 1880–1912 there was considerable variation, across the towns examined in this study, in the pace of industrialization, income levels, gas prices, coal prices, and other cost factors. In so far as the data on consumption per customer reflect the household sector well, then household demand for gas appears to be sensitive both to the price of gas and is the level of household income. The price elasticity ranged round a mean value of $(-)1.8$ whilst the mean income elasticity of demand was 0.90. The number of customers was responsive to the level of meter rents though the calculated elasticity was less than unity. During the 1890s it does not appear that the local price of electricity had much effect on the demand for gas nor the local price of coal, though it is difficult to unscramble this aspect of coal from its other role as an input in the production of gas.

From their observed behaviour in the market for gas and its by-products, all the gas undertakings seem to have been motivated strongly by considerations of profit; consumer interests and managerial pressures were not apparently influential. Whilst the structure of tariff schedules did differ considerably across the various undertakings (sliding scales, maximum prices, discount), actual prices charged seem, allowing for the local economic context, to have reflected commercial considerations. This confirms the hunches of that group of historians typified by Matthews (1986) who have viewed municipal undertakings as strongly commercial entities like the companies. Price regulation appears to have had some effect on the level of gas prices especially for the municipal undertakings who were not on sliding scales but subject to a control on maximum prices. The danger of hitting price ceilings is less the larger the total gas consumption and the smaller the number of customers. The gas undertakings' behaviour conformed closely to this pattern with the marginal profit on extra customers much higher than the marginal profit on extra gas sales.

The municipal undertakings had lower sales per customer. This does not necessarily reflect any conscious policy to extend supplies to poor consumers. Rather, many municipals were located in areas where the customers had lower income levels and smaller expenditures on gas per household. Municipal gas prices, often lower than those of the private companies, were not immune from commercial considerations and seem in fact, given the presence of price regulation, to be perfectly consistent with profit maximization. Transfers of the trading surpluses of municipal gas undertakings in aid of relief to rates and other municipal accounts were sizeable in some cases and may, certainly in the earlier periods, have appeared to the local governments as attractive revenue sources relative to revenue from rates. Such transfers did not however affect pricing policy or the self-financing of investment. Where private companies distributed profits as dividends, the municipal undertakings transferred them to their 'owners' and may indeed have ploughed more back into the gas business.

GENERAL FEATURES OF TELEGRAPH TARIFF RATES IN EUROPE AND THE USA 1850–1914

We now turn to tariffs and profits in another network, the electric telegraph. Since telegraph networks were national, indeed international, in scope, it was central government rather than local government which was involved. In comparison with American tariffs, European telegraph rates did not look very high when the financial state of European networks was taken into consideration. But the political pressures on state telegraph systems to cut tariffs and extend the service regardless of cost continued to build up, as demonstrated by Dutch and British experience. The intention had been for the Dutch system to break even, yet unproductive extensions of the state network and subsidies to competitor private companies from the late 1850s ensured this goal was not achieved. Between 1858 and 1867 investment in the state network tripled and many new offices were opened, a good proportion of which sent less than an average of eight telegrams a day. Moreover the Dutch Post Office until 1870 remained separate from the Telegraph Service, even in small villages. The state's losses were exacerbated by tariffing of messages which passed over both state and company lines that discriminated against the state. The companies 'skimmed the cream' from the densely trafficked routes, leaving the unprofitable lines to the government, as would be predicted if the companies had successfully influenced state policy (see Anon 1871).

After the nationalization of the British system in 1870, the introduction of a uniform one shilling tariff was more consistent with 'regulatory capture' than with welfare maximization. The network was greatly expanded, telegraph numbers increased, but profits were quickly eliminated. Ministers bemoaned their inability to act as if the telegraph service was a private concern and bemoaned the tendency to extend the network to distant and unprofitable locations. Wages and salaries rose as a proportion of total costs from 39 per cent in 1870 to 72 per cent by 1895. Pressure groups petitioned the House of Commons for further tariff reductions. In 1885 a 6*d.* tariff accelerated the growth of the deficit (Kieve 1973: 187, 195). By this time more telegrams per head were being sent in the UK than in any other European country, extending the pattern for 1851 shown earlier in Table 2.5. Table 4.5 also shows continental Europe lagging behind the USA. Telegraph usage by the 1890s had progressed furthest in the

TABLE 4.5 *American and continental European telegraph performance 1873–1890*

	Telegrams per head of population				Western Union's receipts/ expenditure
	France	Germany	Italy	Western Union	
1873	0.24	0.33	0.19	0.35	1.42
1880	0.45	0.38	0.21	0.6	1.84
1890	0.82	0.56	0.27	0.9	1.48

Sources: UK *Abstract of Foreign Statistics*; Preece and Fischer (1877: vol. i).

UK, even further than in the USA, but Western Union Co. of the USA continued to maintain that the Americans provided a better service and that the high British telegraph use was due to the considerable subsidy from the post. When allowance was made for differences between the United States and the United Kingdom in the words allowed in each tariff interval, average message charges to the sender were similar. Long-distance rates between the United Kingdom and the Continent were higher than for similar distances in the United States (see AT & T. Archives, Box 1350).

European costs tended to be higher than those of America, a fact which was only partly concealed by the tariffs (compare the telegrams per head of Table 4.5). The consequence of holding tariffs down was losses, even on such potentially profitable services as the French international telegraph from 1866. Unconstrained by international agreements, but limited by actual and potential competition, American internal tariffs over comparable distances were more closely linked to costs. The analysis in Appendix 4.2 suggests that in 1870 they were both lower than the French and increased less with distance. The French levied a frontier tax on international messages but this was inadequate to restore the financial position and caused a divergence of prices from costs.

With cost and tariff differentials of this magnitude, it is no surprise that European international telegraphy was less developed than American long-distance traffic. The reasons for higher European tariffs and telegraph costs were principally bureaucratic and cultural. American technology was possibly slightly superior since the British gradually introduced the American Morse system. In 1896 there were 5,478 Morse instruments in the British service out of a total of 30,644. During the 1890s the American system was unique in operating telegraph lines from a dynamo current. The only European technology that the Americans adopted was the English Wheatstone instrument that worked some of the American long circuits. Even so 96.7 per cent of Western Union's instruments were Morse in 1896 (*Journal télégraphique* (1897), 245–7). Unlike the Americans, the French and the Italians were obliged to send government telegrams free; these therefore had to be paid for by private messages. An estimate for 1869 was that 600,000 of a total of 5.3 million telegrams transmitted in France were government messages (Brown 1870: 6). Twenty years later the Italian Ministry of Posts and Telegraphs was expressing concern about a similar number of official telegrams from a total of 19.2 million (Foreign Office Miscellan. Series No. 22 1891: 6–7).

The organization of Western Union, the principal American carrier, offered some distinctive cost advantages over British and therefore also over other European networks. Telegraphists in the New York central office dealt with twice as many messages per head in 1877 as did their opposite numbers in London. Admittedly, London conditions were less conducive to a high throughput; the peak of the daily load was more pronounced, slower, foreign-language traffic constituted a considerable proportion of London's business but a negligible portion of New York's, and daily hours of work in New York were 25 per cent more than the eight in London (Preece and Fischer 1877: 166–202). Even granted these handicaps, the American system's greater efficiency seems to have been enhanced by a high wage, high skill, and high responsibility strategy. A male clerk's average annual wage at the central telegraph office in New York was £200 compared with £80 in London and average female wages were respectively £112 and £48. Only a small component of the wage differential could be accounted for by higher New York living costs. The ultimate cause was the motivation and the incentives of the American staff. In contrast to the telegraphists of the British state network, the Americans knew they were likely to be dismissed or suffer a wage reduction if they did not exert themselves and that exceptional performance would be rewarded by promotion—possibly almost to the top of the company. All of the top officials of Western Union, with the exception of the president, had been operators. A subsidiary factor was that the Wheatstone system of the UK encouraged overmanning in off-peak hours. Moreover the Wheatstone was operated by three or four clerks on alternate messages so that individual responsibility for the working of a particular instrument was not so apparent as in the Morse system. On the Continent, where Morse systems were much more common, this problem was reduced. Work discipline may also have been tighter than in the United Kingdom under state ownership. Discipline in the French system was maintained by office heads empowered to impose fines to the amount of four days' salary per month for mistakes or misconduct (Brown 1870: 5). Efficiency was encouraged among the German staff by the introduction of a system of premiums linked with telegraphists' performance (O'-Meara 1913: 29–30). The overall effect, other than on costs and prices, was that Continental systems generally provided greater accuracy than the British but the British network transmitted messages more quickly (Preece 1875).

In part a telegraph organization's cost conditions, which underlay the supply of services, varied with country characteristics. The costs of sending a given number of telegrams a given distance may have varied with the size of the population among which communication was taking place. A larger population required a greater number of offices, delivery boys, and a larger network for a given number of messages. The telegraph infrastructure was therefore less fully utilized. An ability to use the Post Office facilities obviously helped telegraph organizations in some respects. Both for reasons of security and to satisfy the public, European state telecommunications authorities extended their networks beyond the size to which commercial organizations of comparable efficiency would have aspired. The German Telegraph Directorate therefore reached an agreement with the Postal Department for telegraph work to be undertaken by postal officials in Post Office buildings. The postal administration provided the accommodation free of charge and the telegraph administration contributed towards the wages of the postal officials according to the volume of telegraph traffic with which they dealt. A delivery charge was also paid for each message transmitted to 'combined' telegraph offices. The first of these offices opened in 1854 and by 1869 14 per cent (662) of the Post Offices dealt with telegraph work (O'Meara 1913: 28). Since a telegraph office had one of the attributes of a public good—making a line available to two or three people in a locality made it available to all—there was some justification for support of offices by local authorities. When they were prepared to guarantee any deficit from telegraph offices, local authorities could arrange for facilities to be extended to their area. By 1863 fifty-six offices had been opened under such guarantees. The Swiss operated a similar arrangement (Brown 1870: 23–4). In Italy by 1890 about 1,000 of the 5,511 offices of the postal and telegraph services were jointly administered. About one-third of British post offices had by then acquired telegraph facilities.

In another respect the opportunity for continuous cross-subsidy from the postal service was not necessarily desirable. That a subsidy *per se* was not harmful, and indeed was helpful to industry development when used as 'start-up' support, was demonstrated by the United States Congress's $30,000 grant to Morse for the Washington–Baltimore line in 1844. On the other hand the annual British subsidy to the Red Sea and India Telegraph Company did not achieve a successful link. A once and for all commitment was apparently more productive than continuing support. The opportunity to 'milk' the postal service equally was no incentive to keep costs to a minimum and even when, in any case, costs were minimized, the subsidy may have encouraged over-expansion of the telegraph system.

Three theoretical justifications might be offered for a postal subsidy to the telegraph. The first is that the industry was subject to increasing returns and therefore, in the absence of multi-part tariffs, socially efficient marginal cost prices could not be charged and industry costs covered (cf. Brown and Sibley 1986). A subsidy on each telegram to finance the excess of average cost over price was therefore warranted. The second justification is that if there were common costs, such as offices shared between the post and the telegraph services, and if, as was the case, the telegraph service faced a more elastic demand than did the post, then welfare was maximized when the post marked prices up on marginal cost by more than the telegraph in order to generate the revenue to cover fixed costs. In either case a subsidy could both increase output and enhance social welfare (defined to ignore or abstract from questions of distribution). If returns to scale in the telegraph industry were constant or decreasing, then a subsidy might still increase output, but from society's viewpoint the extra resources would have yielded a higher return elsewhere. The third justification is that the telegraph conferred direct benefits to society over and above those to the user. The state had long recognized the value of the option demand for access to the network during security crises, especially in 1848.

TESTING THE JUSTIFICATION FOR SUBSIDIES IN EUROPEAN TELEGRAPH SYSTEMS

A minimal test of these justifications for subsidies is whether in fact they did increase telegraph output. The test is minimal because an increase may have been such as to reduce social welfare, but if the test is failed then certainly subsidies were mistaken. Whether telegrams increased or not can only be ascertained in a model that specifies all the determinants of telegraph output. Telegraph usage was determined by the level of economic development of the country and dependence on communication-intensive services, especially finance and commerce. The level of development influenced both the business and household demand to send and receive telegraph messages. How much the customer had to pay and the accuracy, availability, and speed of the service determined how many telegrams would be sent. This second group of factors was partly under the control of the supplying organization.

The precise model and its testing are discussed in Appendix 4.3. It develops a framework for analysing the demand for telegraphs and a cost function. Demand is deemed to be a function of national income levels, the telegraph tariff relative to other prices and population. Costs are expressed as a function of the number of telegrams, the average length of travel, the prices of labour, and other factors of production and population. The sample was limited first to European countries for which national income estimates were available. Portugal therefore had to be omitted despite readily available telegraph data. Second, and more important, in order to compute the effects of subsidy, separate telegraph accounts had to be available. Despite the use of Post Office postal facilities, such accounts were generally kept in the early years. Inspection of Table 4.6 shows that the number of countries maintaining separate accounts diminished with the passage of time, the most notable absences by 1880 being France, Germany, and Italy. Telegraph accounts included maintenance expenditure, which was a substantial capital cost since telegraph equipment was not long-lived and, until the later 1870s, the lines were vulnerable to storms such as those of 1876. Working expenses, principally labour, were also included but typically no allowance was made for the opportunity cost of capital. In the British case that opportunity cost included the interest charges on the bonds issued to buy the private telegraph company assets under the Act of 1868. Only in 1870–1 and 1880–3 did net profits cover this interest (Kieve 1973: 181) but in part that was because excessive prices had been paid for the private companies.

TABLE 4.6 *European telegraph development data 1873–1890*

	(1) Telegrams per head of population	(2) Ratio of telegraph receipts to expenses	(3) Postal items per head of population	(4) GNP per head (1970 $US)
1873				
Germany	0.334	0.926	13.71	579
Austria	0.243	0.903	13.09	466
Hungary	0.169	0.808	4.40	345
Belgium	0.696	0.871	27.25	738
Denmark	0.357	1.091	9.52	563
France	0.243	1.166	18.64	567
UK	0.629	1.107	38.98	904
Italy	0.191	1.391	8.73	467
Norway	0.388	1.131	4.22	441
Netherlands	0.567	0.679	21.23	591
Russia	0.040	1.238	1.41	252
Sweden	0.242	1.262	3.96	351
Switzerland	0.925	1.091	25.89	589
1880				
Austria	0.278	1.083	14.63	556
Hungary	0.191	0.851	7.34	435
Belgium	0.634	0.847	46.45	832
UK	0.855	1.286	47.45	979
Netherlands	0.768	0.704	30.65	707
Russia	0.069	1.360	2.10	253
Sweden	0.222	1.034	9.23	419
Switzerland	0.972	1.309	27.97	715
Spain	0.137	0.851	5.68	410
1890				
Belgium	0.875	0.911	53.22	932
UK	1.753	1.068	68.06	1,130
Norway	0.727	0.959	15.39	548
The Netherlands	0.950	0.804	41.91	768
Russia	0.088	1.516	3.29	276
Sweden	0.369	1.063	15.13	469
Switzerland	1.260	1.077	40.91	750
Spain	0.255	1.023	9.29	464

Note: The last Russian figure refers to 1886.

Sources: Telegrams, receipts, expenses, and population (occasionally interpolated): *UK Abstract of Foreign Statistics*, 23 and 8; *Journal télégraphique*. Postal items: Mitchell (1980). GNP per head: Crafts (1984: 438–58).

The American Western Union receipts to expenses ratio was 1.42 in 1873 (Table 4.5). In the European sample only Russia in 1890 exceeded this value. So far as possible all postal items, not just letters and post cards, are included in column 3 of (Table 4.6).

The years chosen were the heyday of the European state telegraph but the British network was only taken over in 1870. Some time had to elapse before the effects of state control could be identified. The year 1870 was equally not a good one to study the normal working of the French telegraph system and therefore 1873 was chosen as the nearest year to the beginning of the decade free from exceptional disturbances to the telegraphs. The end of the period is marked by the coming of the telephone. Already by 1890 some telegraph administration accounts included telephone expenditures and receipts, although these were typically a small proportion of the total.

The results suggest, first, that diminishing returns were present in the sense that an increase in population was associated with a more than proportionate increase in telegraph costs. On the other hand the link with postal business was good; a 10 per cent bigger postal output, on average, cut telegraph costs by 4 per cent. Finally and central to our investigation bigger subsidies had no statistically significant impact on the volume of telegraphs per head—holding that is population, income, and volume of postal business constant. Thus co-operation with national Post Offices had favourable cost effects but there were marked disadvantages from subsidies which that co-operation permitted; output fell or at least did not rise as the subsidy was increased. Political price cuts in the telegraph network may have necessitated these subsidies and then investment may have been rationed. But that does not offer any additional support for the subsidy policy. Contrary to the views of many contemporaries, who conflated technical progress with economies of scale, European telegraph networks apparently supplied under conditions of decreasing returns. Even efficient subsidies to improve resource allocation on scale grounds were therefore not justified.

CONCLUSIONS ON TELEGRAPH
FINANCIAL POLICY

European states had a distinctly mixed record of managing their telegraph networks. For most, it was proving an expensive business by the 1890s without any sound justification. Subsidies did not even increase output. On average governments did not hold back the introduction of the telegraph very much, with the exception of France, and in some cases they accelerated adoption. Patents may have slowed early British *laissez-faire* development. The principal cause of the delay relative to North America however was the pre-existing political division of Europe which had brought with it economic fragmentation that greatly reduced the demand for long-distance communication. Even so international tariffs remained high and must have inhibited traffic growth. Costs also remained above those of North America for bureaucratic and cultural reasons.

The advantages of being able to use existing postal facilities without bearing the full costs were very valuable. What never seems to have been discussed was opening this option to private organizations. The indications that large networks had higher unit costs than small suggests some form of 'control loss' that may have been limited by more commercially oriented organizations. The objection to privately owned networks on security grounds seems unwarranted since the British government found no difficulty using the private network against the Chartists in 1848 or later against the Fenians. Both American and British newspapers objected to private monopoly control of telegraphic news but the state-owned systems of continental Europe were not always noticeably more liberal. Finally the concern that private organizations charged excessive prices could be tested from time to time, and indeed was in Britain and America, by the entry of competitors. Most European telegraph networks excluded this option by conferring statutory monopolies upon themselves. Brock's contention in general seems to be correct for the nineteenth-century European telegraph industry; subject to the very important proviso of an adequate regulatory framework to facilitate international communications and to oversee national competition, most European states could have gained more from the electric telegraph than their state organizations permitted.

The Gas Pricing Model and the Demand Function for Gas in the 1890s

It proved more convenient to estimate demand functions in the form of demand price as a function of quantities. Two equations were used, one for gas price (P_g) and one for the access price or meter rent (P_n). These are therefore to be viewed as demand prices and the functions in general form are

$$P_g = f(Y_d, N, W, P_e, P_t, IE) \qquad (1)$$

$$P_n = F(Y_d, N, W, P_e, P_t, H), \qquad (2)$$

where N is the number of customers, W income levels, Y_d quantity of gas consumed, P_e the price of electricity, P_t the price of coal, H population of the town, IE the industrialization index; measurement of these variables is discussed in the text. Each enterprise's total annual costs (C) are deemed to be a function of gas produced (Y_q), the number of customers, and factor prices. The revenue of an enterprise is

$$R = P_g Y_d + R_b + P_n N, \qquad (3)$$

where R_b is by-product revenue.

Consider now an enterprise geared to *maximizing profits*. Its choice variables are the number of customers and the level of gas sales. The enterprise is in equilibrium when marginal profits in each line are equal to zero. That is:

$$\partial(R - C)/\partial Y_d = \partial(R - C)/\partial N = 0 \qquad (4)$$

This may be tested by estimating marginal revenue, marginal cost, and hence marginal profit using elasticities calculated from the demand and cost functions. Since the elasticity of cost with respect to the number of customers (E_n) is equal to marginal cost divided by average cost, we have that marginal cost of customers is:

$$MC_n = E_n C/N \qquad (5)$$

Analogously, if the elasticity of cost with respect to gas produced is E_q and the elasticity of gas produced with respect to gas sold is E_{qd}, the marginal cost of gas sales is:

$$MC_y = E_q E_{qd} C/Y_d \qquad (6)$$

Marginal revenue from an increase in gas sales $\partial R/\partial Y_d$ is, bearing in mind equations (1)–(3):

$$MR_y = P_g + Y_d(\partial P_g/\partial Y_d) + R_b/Y_d + N(\partial P_n/\partial Y_d) \qquad (7)$$

where by-products are assumed to be produced in strict unvarying proportion to gas and each enterprise is a price taker. If the elasticity of the gas demand price with respect to quantity sold is written as E_{gg} and that between the meter price and quantity of gas sold as E_{ng} then

$$MR_y = P_g(1 + E_{gg}) + (R_b/Y_d) + E_{ng}P_nN/Y_d \qquad (8)$$

Analogously, the extra revenue from an extra customer, $\partial R/\partial N$, is

$$MR_n = P_n(1 + E_{nn}) + E_{gn}P_gY_d/N \qquad (9)$$

where E_{nn} is the elasticity of the meter rent with respect to number of customers and E_{gn} is the elasticity of the gas price.

Consider now the possibility that the enterprises face *price regulation* in the form that P_g is not to exceed a prescribed level (say x). The firm may then be viewed as maximizing the following Lagrangean:

$$L = R - C + \varphi(S + P_g - x), \qquad (10)$$

where S is a slack variable. The Kuhn–Tucker conditions for the case where the constraint is binding (in situations other than the unconstrained profit-maximizing position) involves $S = 0$, $\varphi < 0$, and

$$(-)\varphi = \frac{\partial(R - C)/\partial Y_d}{\partial P_g/\partial Y_d} = \frac{\partial(R - C)/\partial N}{\partial P_g/\partial N} \qquad (11)$$

In so far as we expect $\partial P_g/\partial Y_d$ to be negative and $\partial P_g/\partial N$ to be positive, we have the implications of price regulation:

$$\partial(R - C)/\partial Y_d < 0 < \partial(R - C)/\partial N \qquad (12)$$

Bearing in mind also the elasticity definitions given above, we have

$$\frac{\partial(R - C)/\partial Y_d}{\partial(R - C)/\partial N} = \frac{E_{gg}/Y_d}{E_{gn}/N} \qquad (13)$$

where the right-hand side is labelled RIMGAS in the regression results. When firms are *revenue maximizers* the relevant Lagrangean is:

$$L = R + \lambda(R - C - S) \qquad (14)$$

In the case where the constraint is not binding we have

$$\partial R/\partial Y_d = 0 = \partial R/\partial N \qquad (15)$$

Otherwise with $S = 0$ and $\lambda > 0$ we have

$$(-)\lambda = \frac{\partial R/\partial Y_d}{\partial(R - C)/\partial Y_d} = \frac{\partial R/\partial N}{\partial(R - C)/\partial N} \tag{16}$$

Relative marginal profits equal relative marginal revenues. If instead firms are maximizing the volume of sales the relevant Lagrangean is:

$$L = Y_d + \lambda(R - C - S) \tag{17}$$

and the first-order conditions are

$$1 + (\lambda\partial(R - C)/\partial Y_d) = 0 = \lambda\partial(R - C)/\partial N \tag{18}$$

It makes no economic sense for the constraint here not to be binding so that with $\lambda > 0$ we have the result that the marginal profit on output is negative and on customers is zero.

Turning now to the analysis of firms motivated to promote *customer interests*, consider first the firm maximizing the number of customers subject to a break-even or profit constraint. By analogy with the above we have

$$1 + (\lambda\partial(R - C)/\partial N) = 0 = \lambda\partial(R - C)/\partial Y_d \tag{19}$$

Hence the marginal profit on customers is negative and on output is zero. Alternatively, we may think of firms maximizing gross consumer economic benefits subject to a break-even or profit constraint. We need a concept (V) analogous to the area under the standard demand curve such that the firm could be viewed as maximizing

$$L = V + \lambda(R - C - S) \tag{20}$$

In the present context:

$$V = \int P_g(\ )dY_d + R_b + \int P_n(\ )dN \tag{21}$$

where $P_g(\ )$ and $P_n(\ )$ are the price functions in equations (1) and (2). If the constraint were not binding, prices would be approaching zero even though the enterprise was breaking even. It seems more realistic therefore to take the case where the constraint is binding and $\lambda > 0$ where

$$(-)\lambda = \frac{\partial V/\partial Y_d}{\partial(R - C)/\partial Y_d} = \frac{\partial V/\partial N}{\partial(R - C)\partial N} \tag{22}$$

Thus relative marginal profits equals relative marginal consumer benefits. Note

$$\begin{aligned}\partial V/\partial Y_d &= P_g + (R_b/Y_d) + \partial[\int(P_n(\ )dN]/\partial Y_d \\ &= P_g + (R_b/Y_d) + (E_{ng}NP_n/Y_d)\end{aligned} \tag{23}$$

where the last term, additional meter income from a rise in gas sales, is a rough proxy to the correct measure. Analogously

$$\partial V/\partial N = P_n + \partial(\textstyle\int P_g(\ )dY_d)/\partial N = P_n + (E_{gn}Y_dP_g/N) \qquad (24)$$

In the regressions which follow the term RELVAL is equal to

$$\frac{\partial V/\partial Y_d}{\partial V/\partial N}.$$

Testing the various hypotheses outlined above requires knowledge of demand and cost elasticities and these were estimated from cross-section data for the sample of thirty-five undertakings for the financial year 1897/8. The demand functions, equations (1) and (2), were estimated in logs and in such a way to allow that the elasticities of each variable might vary with the level of the variable itself. In the case of gas sold, for example, both $\log Y_d$ and $0.5(\log Y_d)^2$ were independent variables and thus the estimating form for the gas price equation (1) was:

$$\log P_g = A + a_y \log Y_d + a_{yy}0.5(\log Y_d)^2 + a_n \log N$$
$$+ 0.5(\log N)^2 + \ldots + \varepsilon_g \qquad (25)$$

TABLE A.4.1 *Gas demand and cost functions: Ordinary least squares 1897/8*

Independent variable	Dependent variables					
	Log total cost		Log gas price		Log meter price	
	(a)	(b)	(a)	(b)	(a)	(b)
Intercept	−0.553	−0.058	53.92	109.63*	−397.4	−51.2*
Ln Y_q	1.085*	0.894*				
0.5 (Ln Y_q)²	−0.015					
Ln Y_d			−1.350*	−1.472*	20.307*	−17.710*
0.5 (Ln Y_d)²			0.087*	0.085*	1.580*	1.380*
Ln N	−0.461	−0.313*	0.979	1.298*	21.732*	21.026*
0.5 (Ln N)²	0.055	0.039*	−0.085	−0.100*	−2.303*	−2.234*
Ln W			−28.85	−61.42*	217.4	19.021*
0.5 (Ln W)²			8.187	17.494*	−56.28	
Ln IE			0.162			
0.5 (Ln IE)²			0.172*	0.147*		
Ln H					1.360	
0.5 (Ln H)²					−0.120	
Ln P_t			−0.564		12.274*	13.419*
0.5 (Ln P_t)²			−1.366*		16.194*	18.362
Ln P_e			−0.708		2.319	
0.5 (Ln P_e)²			0.487		−1.103	
Ln I	0.137	0.167*				
0.5 (Ln I)²	0.013					
D	−0.015					
R^2Adj	99.3%	99.4%	66.3%	61.7%	75.0%	78.2%

Notes: (a) is the full list of variables, (b) is the best. An asterisk (*) indicates the coefficient is significant at the 5% level.

A similar procedure was used for the meter rent equation (2). The results using OLS are shown in Table A.4.1. In the case of costs, reliance was placed on a previous study (Millward and Ward 1987) where a translog form of the cost function was estimated from the cross-section of undertakings. The coefficients related to factor prices were estimated from cost share equations. Coefficients related to output were then estimated from an equation of the form:

$$\log C = X + c_q \log Y_q + c_{qq}(\log Y_q)^2 0.5 + c_n \log N$$
$$+ c_{nn}(\log N)^2 0.5 + c_i \log I + c_d D + \varepsilon_c \quad (26)$$

where I is a variable reflecting the vintage of plant, D is a dummy for public firms, and where X represents a known variable for each undertaking reflecting the factor prices and associated coefficients already estimated. OLS estimates of the above are in Table A.4.1.

Since the cost and demand functions for each undertaking involve a simultaneous equation system then several independent variables like Y_d

TABLE A.4.2 *Gas demand and cost functions: Three-stage least squares 1897/8*

Independent variables	Dependent variables					
	Log total cost		Log gas price		Log meter rent	
	(a)	(b)	(a)	(b)	(a)	(b)
Intercept	1.487	0.330	38.681	48.383	−128.749	−55.311*
Ln Y_q	0.317	0.808*				
0.5 (Ln Y_q)^2	0.036					
Ln Y_d			(−)0.637	−1.556	−30.988	−18.341*
0.5 (Ln Y_d)^2			0.003	0.073	2.182	1.487*
Ln N	0.245	−0.229	0.158	1.353	34.752	22.769*
0.5 (Ln N)^2	(−)0.009	0.038	0.049	(−)0.071	−3.775	−2.518*
Ln W			−22.093	−26.918	36.451	18.587*
0.5 (Ln W)^2			6.352	7.706	0.012	
Ln IE			−0.165			
0.5 (Ln IE)^2			0.797	0.204*		
Ln H					7.580	
0.5 (Ln H)^2					−0.403	
Ln P_t			−0.349		13.779	9.092*
0.5 (Ln P_t)^2			−0.703		20.481	12.252*
Ln P_e			1.745	0.800	3.915	
0.5 (Ln P_e)^2			0.947	−0.370	−4.640	
Ln I	0.115	0.167*				
0.5 (Ln I)^2	0.011					
D	(−)0.091	−0.070				

Notes: (a) columns are full models, (b) columns are best results. An asterisk (*) indicates coefficient significant at the 5% level. The exogenous variables were taken to be W, IE, H, P_t, P_e, and I.

are in fact endogenous and correlated with the disturbance terms. This would suggest using 2SLS. However, there is also the possibility of contemporaneous correlation between the disturbances in different equations (demand, cost) for the same undertaking. Thus 3SLS was used and the results reported in Table A.4.2. Note finally that not all gas produced is sold. As part of the above estimates the two output variables were regressed on each other to yield

$$\log Y_q = 0.456 + 0.946 \log Y_d + 0.004(0.5)(\log Y_d)^2 \qquad (27)$$

where the last term was not significant. Hence the elasticity between the two, E_{qd}, was taken as 0.95 and used in the calculation of the marginal cost of gas sales.

In the estimates of marginal profit and related concepts, the elasticities were taken from the (*b*) columns of the 3SLS regressions in Table A.4.2. They vary with the level of the independent variables and elasticity values for the quartile range are reported in the text.

The final element in the statistical work involved ascertaining whether marginal profits and marginal revenue were significantly different from zero. The results are shown in Table A.4.3 where MPROFOT is the shorthand for marginal profit on output, MPROCUS for marginal profit on customers. All variables therefore were positive and significantly different

TABLE A.4.3 *Tests of profitability 1897/8*
(*t* test of mu = 0 vs. mu N. E. 0)

	Number of observations	Mean	St Dev.	SE mean	T	P value
Full sample						
MPROFOT	35	(−)0.049	0.035	0.006	(−)8.15	0.000
MPROCUS	35	2.440	2.159	0.365	6.68	0.001
MR_y	35	0.089	0.021	0.003	24.74	0.000
MR_n	35	3.408	2.180	0.369	9.25	0.000
Municipal						
MPROFOT	19	(−)0.049	0.023	0.005	(−)9.14	0.000
MPROCUS	19	1.715	0.904	0.207	8.27	0.000
MR_y	19	0.077	0.011	0.003	29.56	0.000
MR_n	19	2.319	0.833	0.191	12.13	0.000
Private						
MPROFOT	16	(−)0.048	0.046	0.012	−4.11	0.001
MPROCUS	16	3.300	2.852	2.852	4.63	0.000
MR_y	16	0.104	0.021	0.005	20.21	0.000
MR_n	16	4.702	2.579	0.645	7.29	0.000

from zero except the marginal profit on output, which was significantly less than zero. Hence the conclusion drawn in the text. A sensitivity exercise on these results may be found in Millward (1991*b*). This also includes a regression of relative marginal profitability (as defined above) on the relative impact of sales and customer numbers. A significant association between the two was found suggesting, as mentioned in the text, that price regulation was a binding constraint. Other regressions of relative marginal profitability on relative marginal revenues and RELVAL (cf. above) suggested there were no statistically significant relations.

APPENDIX 4.2
Tariff–Distance Functions for Telegraphs in France and the USA 1870

Data were assembled for telegraph tariff rates in the USA in 1870 and for French international telegraph rates in the same year. These rates varied with distances and the results of regressing telegraph rates with distance are shown in Table A.4.4. The first row shows the constant terms whilst the coefficient relating the telegraph rate to distance is shown in the second row. In the USA the rate rises with each mile but the change in the rate (0.19) is less than for France (0.20) and by virtue of the constants the average rate is consistently lower. The log linear functions show a similar result except that the elasticity of the tariff with respect to distance is higher in the USA (0.88) than in France (0.29).

TABLE A.4.4 *OLS regression estimates of telegraph tariff–distance functions for France and the United States 1870*

	Linear functions		Log linear function	
	USA	France (international)	USA	France (international)
	−9.50 (0.9)	52.64 (6.37)	−1.03 (−2.31)	3.02 (8.59)
	0.192 (14.63)	0.204 (6.66)	0.88 (12.12)	0.29 (4.14)
$\bar{R}^2$	0.85	0.65	0.80	0.41
DW	0.45	2.02	1.02	2.29
n	37	24	37	24

Note: US data in depreciated 1870 cents. French data converted into gold cents. Distances are air-line miles in both cases. *t*-statistics in parentheses.

Source: Government Telegraphs (1870), AT & T. Archives, Col. Orton's testimony.

APPENDIX 4.3
A Model of European Telegraph Costs and Development

The principal purpose of the three equation model is to estimate the impact of subsidies on telegraph usage. Equation (1) is a log linear cost function:

$$\ln C_1 = \ln \alpha_0 + \alpha_1 \ln Q_1 + \alpha_2 \ln Q_2 + \alpha_3 \ln A + \alpha_4 \ln w \\ + \alpha_5 E + \alpha_6 \text{POP} \tag{1}$$

where C_1 is the costs of the telegraph network, Q_1 is number of telegrams sent, Q_2 is postal output, A is average telegram haul, w is an index of factor prices, E is efficiency of the organization, POP is number of persons in the national market, and α_i are parameters, with $\alpha_1, \alpha_3, \alpha_4, \alpha_6 > 0$, α_2, $\alpha_5 < 0$.

Equation (2) is a price equation:

$$P_1 = m\partial C_1/\partial Q_1 = m\alpha_1 C_1/Q_1 \tag{2}$$

where P_1 is the price of a telegram and m is the mark-up on marginal costs. Whether a particular value of m implies a subsidy depends upon returns to scale in the industry. Under constant returns, $m < 1$ indicates a subsidy.

Equation (3) represents market demand:

$$\ln Q_1 = \ln\beta_0 + \beta_1 \ln P_1 + \beta_2 \ln Y + \beta_3 \ln \text{POP} + \beta_4 \ln P_0 \tag{3}$$

where Y is an index of real income per head, P_0 is an index of the price of all other goods and services, and β_i are parameters with

$$\beta_1 < 0, \ \beta_2, \ \beta_3, \ \beta_4 > 0.$$

The hypothesis that a subsidy discourages efficiency is represented by

$$E = \gamma \ln m \tag{4}$$

and $\gamma > 0$. For a firm that exercised substantial monopoly power, $m > 1$ and quite possibly there would be less incentive to minimize costs as m increased if m rose high enough. In this case the function should be quadratic with $\partial E/\partial m < 0$ once profits exceeded a certain level. However, such points are not included in the European sample examined here and so for simplicity we restrict the function to $\partial E/\partial m > 0$.

From (2)

$$\ln m = \ln(R/C_1) - \ln\alpha_1 \tag{5}$$

where $R = P_1 Q_1$ or telegraph revenue. Taking logs of (2), substituting for C from (1) and for m from (5), yields

$$\ln P_1 = \ln(R/C_1) + \ln\alpha_0 - \ln\alpha_1 + (\alpha_1 - 1)\ln Q_1 - \alpha_2 \ln Q_2$$
$$+ \alpha_3 \ln A + \alpha_4 \ln w + \alpha_5 E + \alpha_6 \ln \text{POP} \tag{6}$$

Substituting into (6) from (4), then into the demand function (3) and rearranging;

$$\ln Q_1 = (1 - \beta_1(\alpha_1 - 1))^{-1}\{\ln\beta_0 + \beta_1[(\ln(R/C_1) + \ln\alpha_0 - \ln\alpha_1$$
$$+ \alpha_2 \ln Q_2 + \alpha_3 \ln A + \alpha_4 \ln w + \alpha_5\gamma(\ln(R/C_1) - \ln\alpha_1)$$
$$+ \alpha_6 \ln \text{POP}] + \beta_2 \ln Y + \beta_3 \ln \text{POP} + \beta_4 \ln P_0\} \tag{7}$$

$(1 - \beta_1(\alpha_1 - 1)) > 0$, therefore $\partial\ln Q_1/\partial\ln Y$, $\partial\ln Q_1/\partial\ln P_0 > 0$
$\partial\ln Q_1/\partial\ln Q_2 > 0$, $\partial\ln Q_1/\partial\ln A < 0$, $\partial\ln Q_1/\partial\ln w < 0$,
$\partial\ln Q_1/\partial\ln(R/C_1) \gtrless 0$ as $\alpha_5\gamma \gtrless -1$, $\partial\ln Q_1/\partial\ln \text{POP} \gtrless 0$ as $\beta_3 \gtrless |\beta_1\alpha_6|$.

Equation (7) is a reduced form of the model with only exogenous variables determining the equilibrium number of telegrams sent. As expected, telegraph usage increases with income and population but the true income elasticity, β_2, cannot be identified from the income coefficient, $\beta_2/(1 - \beta_1(\alpha_1 - 1))$. With increasing returns to scale, $\alpha_1 < 1$. Since $\beta_1 < 0$, the effect of a given increase in income is magnified: the estimated income coefficient overstates the income demand elasticity. The converse is true for decreasing returns. The coefficient on the subsidy variable (R/C_1) may be positive or negative. On the one hand a subsidy allows lower prices to be charged or facilities to be extended into unprofitable areas (a higher subsidy, a lower R/C_1, with an elasticity of $\beta_1/(1 - \beta_1(\alpha_1 - 1))$). On the other hand a subsidy may either encourage inefficiency or be paid as a means of offsetting increasing inefficiency, $\alpha_5\gamma/(1 - \beta_1(\alpha_1 - 1)) > 0$. If the coefficient is positive the subsidy fails the minimal test set earlier. A more extensive postal service increased telegraph usage by providing more facilities which telegraph authorities could utilize without paying the full cost; $\alpha_2\beta_1/(1 - \beta_1(\alpha_1 - 1)) > 0$ since α_2, $\beta_1 < 0$.

Although equation (7) is a very simple representation of the European telegraph industry's operation, it still needs rather more variables than are available for the last quarter of the nineteenth century. Estimation therefore requires further simplification. The net influences of factor prices w (< 0) and of other goods and service prices, p_0 (> 0), are assumed to offset each other in any one year through the process of international trade. With the passage of time, any tendency for their movements to exercise a net effect on telegram penetration is captured by dummy variables. Average haul of a telegram (A) is itself only a proxy for a number of other characteristics of the output of the industry not captured by the volume of telegrams. Number of words per telegram for instance influenced costs by increasing the duration of the message. In turn this was influenced by the pricing system. The average English message in the 1870s contained 29 words compared with 20 for Belgium, 19 for Austria, 18.4 for France, and 17 for Germany (Preece 1875: app. A). Unfortunately more data were not available for this information to be employed in a systematic fashion. As an alternative for average haul we employ area of the country. The assumption is that, since most messages were internal, the average message travelled a shorter distance in a country the size of Belgium than in one the size of France or Russia.

In the estimating equation the dependent variable is deflated by population so that heteroscedascity is not introduced by the different country sizes. The estimating equation therefore becomes

$$\ln(Q_1/\text{POP}) = \phi_0 + \phi_1 \ln(R/C_1) + \phi_2 \ln Q_2 + \phi_3 \ln A + \phi_4 \ln Y \atop + \phi_5 \ln \text{POP} + \phi_6 D_1 + \phi_7 D_2 \tag{8}$$

where A is now area, D_1 and D_2 are period dummy variables, and all other variables are as previously defined. $\phi_1 = \beta_1(1 + \alpha_5\gamma)/(1 - \beta_1(\alpha_1 - 1))$ from (7) and similarly for the other parameters on previously defined variables, with the exception of $\phi_5 = \{(\beta_3 + \beta_1\alpha_6)/(1 - \beta_1(\alpha_1 - 1))\} - 1$. Thus although the original population coefficient (the term in the braces) was positive, ϕ_5 is not necessarily. The most plausible value for β_3 is unity but if $\alpha_1 > 1$ because of diminishing returns, $(1 - \beta_1(\alpha_1 - 1))^{-1} < 1$, (and since any way $\alpha_6\beta_1 < 0$) $\{(\beta_3 + \beta_1\alpha_6)/(1 - \beta_1(\alpha_1 - 1))\} - 1 < 1$ and $\phi_5 < 0$. This is one indication of returns to scale in the industry. A second is to compare the estimate of ϕ_4 with direct estimates of income elasticities. A time-series estimate for France 1860–80 found the income elasticity for internal telegrams to be about two and rather more for international messages. By the same reasoning as for the population coefficient $\phi_4 > 2$ would therefore be consistent with scale economies in the telegraph network. The data are discussed in the text and the regression results shown in Table A.4.5.

Table A.4.5 shows that the ϕ_4 coefficient on GNP per head variable is invariably positive and significantly different from zero at the 5 per cent level, with a range between specifications of 0.94–1.17. This is well below 2 and therefore is suggestive of diminishing rather than increasing returns in the industry. The population coefficient ϕ_5 supports that view: ϕ_5 ranges from -1.17 to -1.47 and is always significantly different from zero at the 5 per cent level. If β_3 were unity then $(1 + \beta_1\alpha_6)/(1 - \beta_1(\alpha_1 - 1)) = 0.17$ to 0.47. Assuming β_1 is about -2 then the coefficients of equation (1) imply $\alpha_6 = 0.32$ (since $a_1 = 1.56$ from ϕ_4). The relationship between the reduced form and the structural parameters is:

TABLE A.4.5 *OLS regression analysis of European telegraph use, 1873–1890*

	ϕ_0 Constant	ϕ_1 Telegraph receipts/ expenditure	ϕ_4 GNP per head	ϕ_5 Population	ϕ_2 Postal items per head	ϕ_3 Area	ϕ_6 Dummy 1 1873 = 1	ϕ_7 Dummy 2 1873 and 1880 = 1	$\bar{R}^2$
1.	−3.10 (−0.84) [−0.83]	0.39 (1.52) [2.18]	0.94 (2.03) [1.99]	−1.17 (−2.53) [−2.49]	0.38 (2.12) [2.17]	—	—	—	0.924
2.	−3.87 (−1.08) [−1.07]	0.16 (0.55) [0.76]	1.12 (2.44) [2.45]	−1.45 (3.03) [−3.13]	0.43 (2.42) [2.56]	0.12 (1.67) [1.95]	—	—	0.929
3.	−4.37 (−1.17) [−1.12]	0.15 (0.54) [0.74]	1.17 (2.48) [2.44]	−1.47 (−3.06) [−3.15]	0.38 (1.88) [1.83]	0.10 (1.13) [1.45]	0.10 (0.95) [1.18]	−0.17 (−1.33) [−1.52]	0.929
4.	−4.55 (−1.21) [−1.12]	0.32 (1.25) [1.16]	1.12 (2.38) [2.20]	1.36 (−2.86) [−2.66]	0.29 (1.55) [1.47]	—	0.07 (0.68) [0.85]	−0.23 (−1.87) [−2.10]	0.928

Notes: T statistics in parentheses. White heteroscedastic robust t statistics in square brackets. One tailed $t_{0.05}$ (25) = 1.708, $t_{0.05}$ (22) = 1.717, $t_{0.01}$ (25) = 2.48, $t_{0.01}$ (22) = 2.51 for ϕ_3, ϕ_4, ϕ_2. Two tailed test for ϕ_1, ϕ_5, ϕ_6, ϕ_7, $t_{0.05}$ (25) = 2.06, $t_{0.05}$ (22) = 2.07, $t_{0.01}$ (25) = 2.79, $t_{0.01}$ (22) = 2.82. All variables in logarithms except dummies. Dependent variable telegrams per head. Data in Table 4.6. Total number of observations 30.

Coefficients from
equation(1)

$$\frac{\beta_1\alpha_2}{1 - \beta_1(\alpha_1 - 1)} \quad = \phi_2 = \quad 0.38$$

$$\frac{\beta_1(1 + \alpha_5\gamma)}{1 - \beta_1(\alpha_1 - 1)} \quad = \phi_1 = \quad 0.39$$

$$\frac{\beta_2}{1 - \beta_1(\alpha_1 - 1)} \quad = \phi_4 = \quad 0.94$$

$$\frac{\beta_3 + \beta_1\alpha_6}{1 - \beta_1(\alpha_1 - 1)} - 1 \quad = \phi_5 = \quad -1.17$$

A 10 per cent larger population served by a telegraph network typically raised costs by 32 per cent for the same number of messages. From ϕ_2, α_2 = −0.4; a 10 per cent larger postal output cut telegraph costs by 4 per cent. Finally from ϕ_1, $\alpha_5\gamma$ = −1.41, but of more interest is ϕ_1 itself, which shows that a reduced subsidy increased telegraph output. The coefficient is not significantly different from zero however and the most plausible inference is therefore that a subsidy neither increased nor decreased output.

Although the above structural coefficients are obtained from the reduced form equation on apparently rather arbitrary price and income elasticity assumptions, the results are not changed by a credible range of alternative values.

5

Explaining the Shift to Public Ownership at the Local Level: The Halcyon Days of Municipal Ownership 1870–1920

INTRODUCTION

The last quarter of the nineteenth century and the years of the new century up to 1914 saw a massive expansion of the local infrastructure and related services, with an increasing share provided by local government. Public health facilities, roads, police, and education were growing and so also were the local network industries, where electricity and tramways now joined gas and water supply. Real national output in Britain was growing at 1.8 per cent per annum on average but the figure for gas, electricity, and water was 5 per cent (Matthews, Feinstein, and Odling-Smee 1982: 240–1). A particularly dynamic period was the eight years 1898–1905 when electric lighting spread rapidly, tramways electrified, and large-scale water schemes were planned. Annual capital expenditure on gas, electricity, water, and tramways averaged £20 million, that is about 10 per cent of national gross fixed capital formation. In 1896/7 local authority debt over all its activities accounted for 40 per cent of the National Debt.

By this stage the developing pattern of ownership of the local networks was as follows. Municipally owned gas undertakings, which, as we saw in Chapter 4, accounted for 30 per cent of all statutory gas undertakings in 1882 in Great Britain, by 1912 had acquired a 37 per cent share. By that last date 80 per cent of statutory water undertakings were in municipal hands. Tramways had been developing from horse-drawn buses to horse-drawn tramways by the middle of the nineteenth century. Initially, as we shall see, local authority involvement was limited to the provision of the track (rather than the ownership and operation of trams) and by 1883 they owned one-third of the track mileage. The 1890s saw a rapid growth of electric tramways in which the municipalities were heavily involved; by 1906 they owned the track and operated the trams in the majority of large towns in Britain, 123 towns in total. In a further fifty-two towns they owned but leased out the track, leaving 137 mainly small towns where private companies owned the track and the operations (Bussel 1988: 4). Finally electricity supply was also booming in the 1890s and especially in the early 1900s. In 1895 there were thirty-four companies and sixteen municipal enterprises, mainly concerned with lighting. They supplied to the tramways, but were less committed to the railways, who generated their own electricity. They also supplied industry, which regarded electricity as a very flexible power source, and the off-peak demands of industry were very attractive to the electricity undertakings for 'smoothing' their load profiles (Hannah 1979: 19). The data are patchy before 1920 but the increasing dominance of municipal enterprises is not in doubt and by 1925/6 they accounted for 64 per cent of units sold and 60 per cent of total undertakings (Balfour Committee 1928–9: 326–7).

The main purpose of this chapter is to explain this shift to public ownership at the local level. We shall argue that there were two fundamental causes. First, market failure arising from economies of scale and externalities provided the initial impetus for public intervention. Second, the form of intervention was affected by the unsatisfactory experience with arm's length regulation and by the sectional interests of ratepayers who used the opportunity of intervention to further their own ends. Before any of these issues can be addressed, it is necessary to sketch out some of the background of the new utilities.

THE NEW NETWORKS IN ELECTRICITY AND TRAMWAYS

The increased interest of local government in many aspects of the local infrastructure and related services was facilitated by the parliamentary legislation of the 1870s and 1880s. This legislation was in turn a product of the ineffectiveness of the regulation of the private gas and water companies in the period 1840–70 and of what were perceived as unsatisfactory services. Since electricity and tramways were in embryonic form in the 1870s and 1880s there was scope for more intervention than there had been in the gas and water supply industries. In the latter, as we saw in Chapter 2, private companies were, by the middle of the century, ensconced with *de facto* monopolies 'in the field'. The ability of a local board of health to monitor and secure adequate supplies was possible under the 1848 Public Health Act but it was not mandatory. To set up gas or water supply on its own account, a local authority needed the consent of the local private company. The 1870 Gas and Water Facilities Act eased matters only by allowing the process of consultation and approval to be expedited by a provisional order of the Board of Trade rather than a full parliamentary bill. But the writing was then on the wall. The 1872 Public Health Act divided the country up into sanitary districts and the 1875 Act *required* the relevant local authority to secure adequate supplies in its district. Whilst the private companies could still dispute the question of adequacy of supplies the matter had, as we noted in Chapter 2, to be decided by arbitration. Knox (1901: 501–2) argued that the greater importance of health matters for water supply led in practice to private water companies being taken over quite readily under the 1875 legislation whereas a local authority could well be unsuccessful in the case of gas if the local company put up a fight.

Given this experience it is not surprising that in legislative provisions for the new utilities in electricity and tramways, Parliament put the interests of local authorities from the start on a par with private enterprise. In an engineering sense trams were especially favoured in towns with very wide streets, like Paris boulevards, or where the road surface was so terrible (as in New York) that digging it up could only improve matters. London fell into neither category and in the middle of the nineteenth century was not deemed attractive for tramway development. English streets and roads in general were narrow and winding and tramways were therefore liable to be very disruptive of existing traffic and buildings. The first proposal for a public tramway was the 1868 Liverpool Tramways Act which granted a franchise to a private company (Ochojna 1978: 134). The Secretary of the Board of Trade in the late 1860s felt local authorities were the best bodies to construct and develop the tramlines, given their disruptive nature, but thereafter they should be leased out to private operators. The 1870 Tramways Act did limit local authorities in this way, at the same time allowing private companies to build track and/or operate and without any ceilings on dividends. There is no doubt however that the legislation recognized the interests of local authorities in the potential monopoly power of the local utility as well as in its environmental effects. The environmental impact required that track construction be reconciled with the interests of the local authority as well as with those of 'frontagers' and the road authority. The tramway undertaking needed parliamentary authority to lay track, if only because trams were in law a public nuisance. The 1870 Act made provision for the use of a Board of Trade provisional order to speed up the process but this procedure could not be used if compulsory land purchase were involved or if there were objections from frontagers, local authority, or road authority for any significant stretch of the track. (Cf. Knox 1901: 497–8, who felt the scope for objections was too wide and promoted engineering devices to circumvent the law—narrower gauges, single track.) Moreover local authorities could pass by-laws on the speed and frequency of traffic. The companies were subject to maximum fares and obliged to offer workmen's concessions. Finally, local authorities were granted powers under the 1870 Act to purchase the track and company after twenty-one years; most revolutionary, at a price which effectively excluded goodwill and/or prospective earning power. The method of valuation, as afterwards interpreted by the House of Lords, was that price should equal the cost of the initial construction of the track plus the amounts paid for street widening and road improvements, less allowances for wear and tear; the precise value was to be fixed by a referee (Knox 1901: 503).

A similar purchase clause for electricity supply undertakings was put into the 1882 Lighting Act which gave municipal authorities a clear mandate to set up plant if they wished and which set maximum prices for all undertakings. Some have again seen, in this legislation, the shadow of the earlier experiences with gas and water; the Balfour Committee argued that the 1882 Act was drafted to secure the safety of the public from 'exploitation by commercial monopolies' (1928–9: 315). Indeed for both tramways and electricity there is a school of thought which sees the legislation as inhibiting development and especially private development (Knox 1901; Garcke 1907; Byatt 1978). The evidence is far from clear. The 1870s saw a large number of applications for private tramway developments, often from syndicates of ex-railway engineers, financiers, and parliamentary agents. Obtaining parliamentary approval was itself a specialized art and many syndicates were awarded a concession, set up the company, and then floated it for others to operate. Similarly in electricity the 1882 Act was followed by a large number of applications from private companies; the purchase clause never applied to power companies and for lighting it was extended to forty-two years by an Act of 1888. Initial supplies were very primitive (cables laid on streets or slung on wooden poles) but by the end of the decade many companies recognized that towns needed fully fledged distribution systems. The USA was moving ahead more quickly but whether this was due to the British legislation is debatable. The USA was growing faster in most areas of economic activity. Moreover gas was cheaper in Britain. It is true that in 1890 most generating stations had only 0.1 megawatt capacity but sales rose from fifty-two gigawatt hours in 1896 to 1,896 (*sic*) gigawatt hours in 1912/13, by which date new stations were of two-megawatt capacity (Hannah 1979: 12).

Most concern seems to have been directed to the electrification of tramways, where Britain was way behind the USA, 90 per cent of whose trams were electric by 1897. In part this might have been a product of the 1870 Tramways Act whose twenty-one-year purchase clauses were in the 1890s approaching their end for companies set up in the 1870s. The large investment needed for electrification may then have appeared a very risky proposition (Hannah 1979: 16). The lag with the USA was actually only very short term because the municipalities took up the initiative. Some of them in the 1880s had obtained parliamentary approval to operate trams where private development had not been forthcoming (Huddersfield, Halifax, Doncaster) or had flopped, as in Plymouth. By 1896 Parliament had given general powers to municipal undertakings to operate trams as well as to lay track. Electric tram mileage rose from forty-five in 1895 to 2,195 in 1905/6, at which point 90 per cent of Britain's trams were electric (Hannah 1979: 15–16). These municipal developments were reflected in the pattern of ownership; as we have earlier recorded, most large towns were, by this date, being served by municipal tramway undertakings. By 1925 municipalities owned the track in 73 per cent of the towns and owned 83 per cent of the tramcars; there were 170 municipal undertakings as compared to seventy-one companies serving either small towns or inter-town traffic. Some towns gained great fame for their initiatives. The Glasgow system was municipalized in 1894, electrified by 1901, and showed good financial rates of return. In this, as in its other municipal ventures, Glasgow was for a while a model for the USA, whose burgeoning, immigrant-congested cities with corrupt political machines were threatening the American dream of democracy. As Aspinall says (1977: 66, 74–5), Glasgow was seen by some as a city with a strong sense of purpose, reflected in its municipal services. Some went so far as to characterize it as a 'practical Christianity'; a city run neither by corrupt political machines nor by 'gentlemen'! (See also Shaw 1890; McKay 1976.) Others, with the benefit of hind-sight, might have preferred 'Red Clydeside before the Bolsheviks' as a more suitable description.

GENERAL FACTORS IN MUNICIPALIZATION

What explains the eagerness of many local councils to operate these local network industries? We shall approach this issue in two ways. First is to identify some of the main factors which occasioned the shift from private to public. In this we will be essentially synthesizing much of the existing secondary literature. However that literature has not fully confronted the very complex pattern of private and public ownership, in which many towns resisted municipalization. Hence the latter half of this chapter presents a detailed quantitative analysis of the issue for the gas industry which, since municipal enterprises never accounted for more than 50 per cent of the undertakings or total output, displays the conflicts and choices in a clear form.

The acquisition by municipalities of local private utilities certainly had more than minority appeal. The *Birmingham Daily Post* in 1882 claimed to be capturing a popular mood in discerning, in the context of electricity supply, 'a general feeling that for the purpose of preventing the creation of a new monopoly in private hands, to ensure the control of the streets, and then to promote public convenience, and also to limit as far as possible injurious competition with Corporation gas lighting, the supply of electric light ought to be in the hands of the local governing authority' (Jones 1980: 19). The existing literature stresses the problems of natural monopoly and environmental issues as important causes of public control and ownership. In so far as the nineteenth-century technology of many utilities involved some economies of scale over a limited area, efficient operation would appear to point to single undertakings in each town but this raised the prospect of monopoly profits. Environmental spillovers arose from the problems of leakage of gas as well as the disruption to streets from the laying and repair of mains. Falkus (1977: 151) and Robson (1935: 1309–10) emphasized these matters in explaining the shift to public ownership. There were two other issues of which they were aware but which have been stressed perhaps rather more by other writers (Rowlinson 1984: ch. 6; Balfour Committee 1928–9: 307–8; Hennock 1973: 117–21; Waller 1983: 298–305; Finer 1941: 50). One was the desire by local government to use the profits of the network industries to finance urban improvements. Transfer of profits 'in relief of rates', urged by Joseph Chamberlain, is deemed to have proved sufficiently attractive to induce the acquisition of some private undertakings by the local authorities. And finally some have stressed 'civic pride', prompting councillors to build large town halls and operate their own utilities.

There are several problems with our current understanding of these matters. First is that on the face of it there were alternatives to public ownership; many towns left the undertakings in private ownership and relied on arm's length regulation based on parliamentary legislation. Which towns were in this category and why? The second and closely related point is that the above arguments have not been confronted with the perplexing pattern of private and municipal ownership. If the relief of rates was important for Birmingham and Salford why was it not for say Newcastle and Norwich, where private undertakings flourished? Why should considerations of natural monopoly and public safety be more important, if indeed they were, in Wolverhampton (public) than in Sheffield (private)? As Matthews has said: 'Geographically most municipal gas works were located in the industrial midlands, the north and Scotland, though why some councils decided to take over their gasworks while others did not is not immediately obvious and the answer must await more detailed examination' (1986: 261). It does not appear to be due to any particular ideological proclivities. Students of these matters have emphasized the pragmatic policy of many civic leaders—a 'structural problem' of economic organization in the words of Sutcliffe (1982), rather than ideological or purely technical, and involving public intervention to fill the gap between actual and desired performance; municipal capitalism rather than socialism in Waller's terminology (1983: 300); municipal enterprise in a search for efficiency and economy unfettered by doctrinaire considerations in Kellett's words (1978; 44). Later in the chapter we demonstrate that there was no clear general tendency for Conservatives to go one way and Liberals another. Moreover, if civic pride is relevant, why are we to expect it to be stronger in, say, Oldham than in Exeter? The recourse to 'each town was different' is unsatisfactory unless the general patterns have been exhaustively analysed. Finally it is important to know whether the main causes acted independently of each other or whether any one on its own could be decisive. Were towns like Aylesbury, Cardiff, and Whitby homogeneous in lacking all the features to be found in the municipalizers like Dewsbury, West Bromwich, and Yeovil?

CASE-STUDY OF GAS: THE BASIC DATA

From 1882 the Board of Trade collected data annually on gas undertakings. Prior to that their returns were less frequent and reliable and for the earlier period we have made use of trade journals like *Gas World* and the *Journal of Gas Lighting*. It was decided to exclude Scotland and Ireland from all detailed analysis since the data for these countries before 1882 are not abundant. Large private undertakings had to seek joint stock status from Parliament, which also stipulated certain supply conditions. Such undertakings together with municipal enterprises constitute the statutory sector. During the nineteenth century there was a very large number of non-statutory undertakings which obtained permission to open up the streets from local authorities. Detail on such enterprises may be obtained in Millward and Ward (1993), which reports results for a slightly different sample from the one used here. Fig. 5.1 shows the results for the statutory undertakings which rose in number continuously up to the First World War, increasingly at the expense of the non-statutory sector. There were clearly large increases in statutory undertakings in the 1870s and a

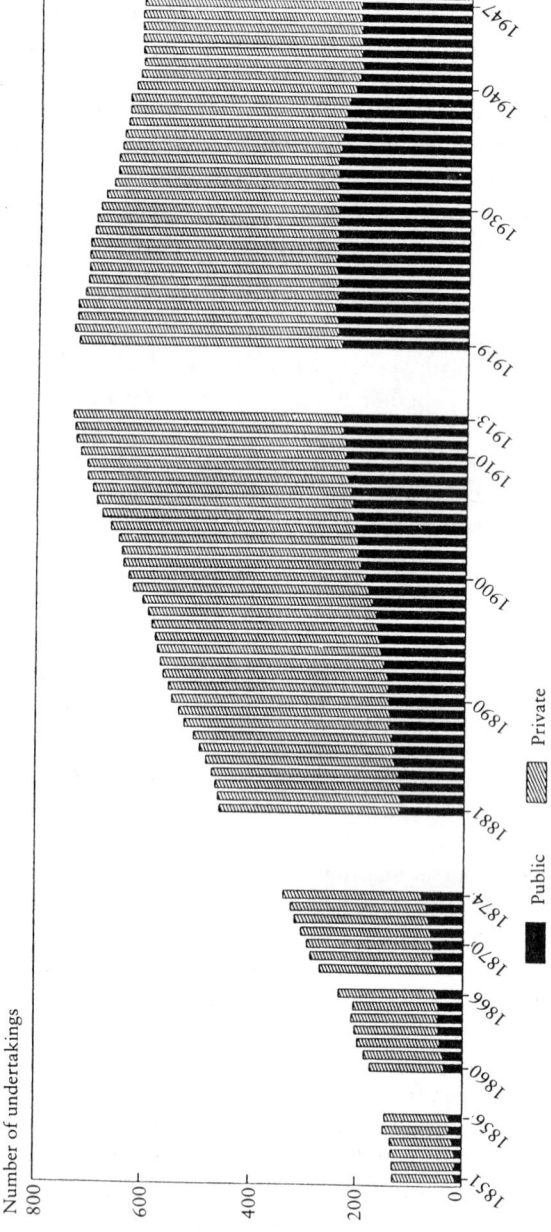

FIG. 5.1 Statutory gas undertakings, England and Wales 1851–1947

further surge of private statutory undertakings in the late 1880s and of municipal undertakings in the years from 1890 to the First World War.

Municipal undertakings accounted for only 10 per cent of the total of statutory undertakings in 1851, but this share rose to 26 per cent in 1881 and 31 per cent by 1913. Some undertakings were set up from scratch by public bodies as in Manchester, Bollington, and Blackpool, for example. In other cases the emergence of a publicly owned undertaking meant the acquisition by public authorities of gasworks previously operated by an individual or private company, authorized or unauthorized. In attempting to portray the process of municipalization, there are complications arising from the fact that public bodies disappear sometimes into larger governmental units and the identity of the stock of private companies changes through merger and the advent of new firms. For detailed analysis it was therefore decided to focus on the 1939 Board of Trade return. This records a total of 634 undertakings for England and Wales and this group is henceforth to be called the 1939 Board of Trade sample. These undertakings are analysed in subsequent sections in terms of the economic and social development in the nineteenth and twentieth centuries of the towns in which they were located, as well as by the financing, organization, and history of the local government units. For the moment we may note that use of the sources already mentioned allows the ascertainment of the 'date of birth' of the municipal undertakings. There were 228 such concerns in the 1939 sample and Fig. 5.2 shows the year, or rather five-year period, in which they first appear as municipal undertakings. It confirms the surge in the period 1870–1905 with a lull in the late 1880s possibly because of a temporary fear of competition from electricity. The dating of the surge from the 1870s corresponds to the observations earlier in this chapter and in Chapter 2 that for both gas and water Parliament and local authorities had become more sympathetic to municipalization. They were not in England and Wales to go so far as in Scotland, where, from 1876, local authorities were given the power to buy out any gas company not incorporated by provisional order or Act of Parliament (Maltbie 1900: 551–2; Wilson 1991*a*: 135). Since few undertakings in Scotland had been so established, the demand for municipalization was unimpeded so that by 1900 all but three gas undertakings

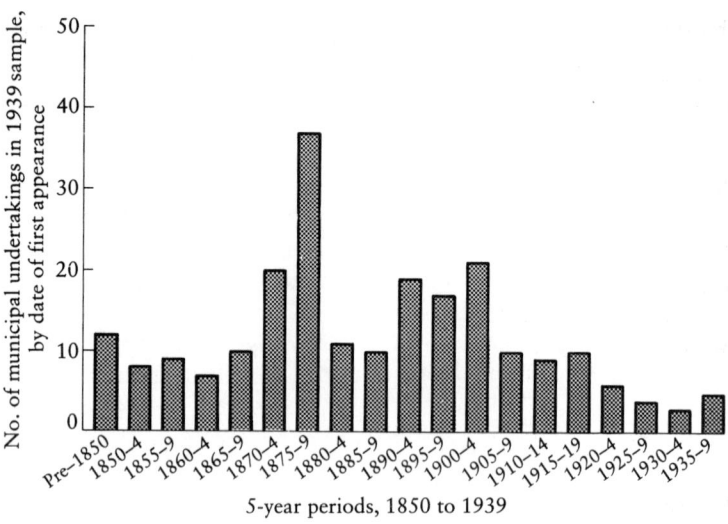

FIG. 5.2 Progress of gas municipalization in England and Wales 1850–1939

were municipally owned. In England and Wales the number of municipal undertakings and their share of the total continued to rise in the inter-war period, which saw an increase in the average size of private statutory undertakings and an absolute decline in numbers in the face of bankruptcies and mergers.

It is well-known that more municipalization occurred in the North rather than South of England. Identifying a regional pattern does not necessarily tell us much about causes unless we know precisely what economic or social factors are intrinsic to the geographic areas identified. Nevertheless it is one way of categorizing the gas undertakings which we should be aware of in case, at the end, there are aspects of the incidence of municipalization which cannot be explained by basic economic and social factors. The details, including the definition of boundaries, are shown in Table 5.1, where the sample has, for reasons discussed in the next section, been reduced to 556 undertakings. The lowest proportion of undertakings municipalized is to be found in the 'South' region, which covers the area to the south of a line from the Wash to the Seven Estuary and skirting southwards of the

TABLE 5.1 *Regional incidence of municipal ownership of gas under-*
takings in England and Wales in 1939

Region name	Definition	No. of undertakings	No. public	% public
North	Cumberland, Durham Northumberland and Westmorland	32	16	50
Lancs. and Yorks.	Lancashire and Yorkshire	139	85	61
W. Midlands	Cheshire, Herefordshire, Shropshire, Staffordshire, Warwickshire, Worcestershire	78	35	45
E. Midlands	Derbyshire, Leicestershire, Lincolnshire, Nottinghamshire, Northamptonshire, Rutland	61	26	43
Wales	All Welsh counties including Monmouthshire	67	28	42
South	Rest of England	179	30	17
England and Wales		556	220	40

Midlands. In fact it could as easily have included South Wales
since the works at Cardiff, Swansea, Newport, and Merthyr Tydfil
remained private. Lancashire and Yorkshire of course dominate
the picture and the time profile of their acquisitions corresponds
closely to that shown in Fig. 5.2 for the national pattern with
peaks in the 1870s and 1890–1910. This is also true of the
Northern and East Midlands regions. The West Midlands peaks in
the 1880s. For Wales and the South there is less of a surge in the
1870s and with relatively more acquired from 1890 onwards.

Finally, the basic data include information on the local government units in which the gas undertakings were located. The period
of study coincides with one when local authorities took on in-

creasing powers and whose organization went through several changes. Several writers have indeed seen the move to municipalization of gas companies as reflecting 'civic pride', a desire to provide a good urban environment and one which compared well with other authorities. The kind of governmental unit in which a gasworks was located is therefore important because the size and geographical boundaries of the government unit might not be appropriate for the operation of a gas undertaking and in addition it is possible that some governmental units were more prone than others to want to take over the gasworks. A large number of gas undertakings did not 'match' any obvious governmental unit. By the middle of the nineteenth century each town in Britain usually received its gas supply from a single undertaking. Competition in the form of overlapping areas of supply had all but disappeared, certainly outside London. The scope for economies of scale seems to have matched the compact provincial towns; a wider efficient span of operations did not occur until the inter-war period if not later (cf. Millward and Ward 1987). A large proportion of the 634 undertakings in our sample supplied an area which coincided with a single unit of local government. There were however several large companies which extended beyond local government boundaries. This was obviously the case for the large London gas companies for much of the nineteenth century and even after the establishment of the London County Council and metropolitan boroughs in the 1890s they retained their private ownership. In addition there were other companies which though not so large in terms of volume of sales were spread over several local government units— North Cheshire Gas Company, South Staffordshire Gas Company, etc.—so that counting in the four London companies there were seventeen large companies who were not municipalized in part because there was no comparably sized governmental unit which would have been their obvious home. Since moreover our analysis of the motives for municipalization will include financial data relating to the governmental units then the above companies have to be excluded from further analysis of the sample. This is also the case for some fifty-four very small gas companies—like Ascot Gas & Coke, Llynvi Valley Gas Co., Titchfield District Gas—which did not correspond to any obvious area of local government. To those seventy-one companies have to be added a further seven undertakings excluded on the grounds of inadequate data.

This brings the sample down to 556 undertakings. The governmental status of the towns in which they were located may be extracted from the Population Censuses and other parliamentary returns. In 1939 the largest number of undertakings, 251, were in areas governed by urban district councils, 167 were in municipal boroughs, seventy-five in county boroughs, thirty-two in rural district councils, and thirty-one in areas which, like Oakham, have both a rural and urban council component. This sample accounts for a high proportion of local authorities especially in terms of population coverage outside London. There were only nine county boroughs not included. By the 1930s also the number of ordinary municipal boroughs was some 260, of which therefore 64 per cent are in the sample and likely to account for an even larger proportion of the population living under the aegis of this type of local authority, since the excluded towns will tend to be those like Beaumaris or Hythe which obtained their borough status a long time ago and which, by 1939, had a relatively small population served by companies like East Kent or Mid Kent Gas, East Anglesey Gas, covering large rural areas.

The extent to which towns obtained borough or county borough status during the latter part of the nineteenth century partly reflects the dynamism of their leaders as well as, of course, their increase in size. Thus the large number of towns which had their borough status confirmed or granted by the 1835 Municipal Corporation Act included many old but small towns like Faversham, Lichfield, Ruthin, Tamworth, or Tenby, which seem to have been less prone to take over their local gasworks. In contrast the towns which did not get their borough status till later included several who progressed so rapidly that they obtained county borough status by the 1888 Local Government Act and these towns— like Blackburn, Huddersfield, West Bromwich—seemed especially liable to municipalize. Table 5.2 confirms these general tendencies for the 556 undertakings in the sample. Taking undertakings in urban district councils as a benchmark it is clear on the one hand that the rural areas tended to remain private, as did the towns which obtained their borough status in 1835 or earlier. More than two-thirds of the '1835 boroughs' kept their gasworks in private ownership. The most significant feature of Table 5.2 is that the later in the period the town gets its borough status, the greater the propensity of boroughs to municipalize.

TABLE 5.2 *Classification of gas undertakings by location in local authorities in 1939*

Local authority category	No. of undertaking	No. public	% public
Mixed urban/rural district councils	31	0	0
Rural district councils	32	8	26
Urban district councils	251	104	41
Municipal boroughs:			
By 1835 Act or earlier	105	34	32
Created 1836–87	33	15	45
Created 1888–1939	29	21	72
County boroughs:			
Borough status 1835 or earlier[a]	38	10	26
Borough status 1836–87	32	25	78
Borough status 1888–1939[b]	5	3	60
Total	556	220	40

[a] Includes five towns which did not get their county borough status until after the turn of the century: Grimsby, Oxford, Newport (Mon.), together with Carlisle and Doncaster, both of which municipalized their gasworks.
[b] Consists of Bournemouth and Merthyr Tydfil (private) and Southend, Smethwick, and Wallasey (public).

Sources: 1939 *Board of Trade Returns* plus Registrar-General (1852, 1866); Census Office (1851–1952); Home Office (1884–5, 1902); Local Government Board (1893–4, 1899, 1910, 1913); Waller (1983; 248); Ministry of Health (1929); Chancellor of the Exchequer (1947–8).

URBANIZATION, FISCAL REVENUE, AND MUNICIPALIZATION

Whilst there is something of a North–South split in the propensity to municipalize and also a similar tendency in the more dynamic local authority units there are many exceptions and clearly there are more fundamental factors at work. Three of the main factors which prompted public control, if not ownership, of gas supplies were the fear of monopoly, the environmental costs of gas production and distribution (disruption to streets from laying mains, safety of leaky pipes), and the general environmental benefits of clean gas and good street lighting. Attempts to deal with these matters during the early and middle parts of the nineteenth century were not particularly effective, as we saw in Chapter 2, and this certainly contributed to the local authorities taking operations into their own hands (cf. Rowlinson 1984: 193). To this should be added the rising electoral rolls of ratepayers demanding both urban improvements and the use of alternative income sources to finance such improvements (Hennock 1963: 218–23; Waller 1983: 255–83). Since grants from central govenment did not materialize until the turn of the century and there was no prospect of local taxes on profits or income, gas profits and similar trading income looked an attractive source provided the costs of acquisition and borrowing were not too high. In summary the potential gain from municipalization for local councils arose from lack of instruments to tax local profits, the limited access to central govenment tax revenue, and the ineffectiveness of parliamentary regulation of the prices, profits, and supply conditions of private companies.

A key part of our work has been to analyse how the above tendencies would manifest themselves and hence how they can be measured. Whilst controlling local monopoly was an important issue it is convenient first of all to consider the problems arising in the finance of urban expansion. Problems of environmental spillover were more severe the more rapid was urbanization and we suggest this may be proxied by the rate of population growth. In fact population growth is also relevant to financing expansion in that the expenditure plans of a local authority were likely to be larger with large urbanization problems. The second half of the nineteenth century is the crucial period and we have therefore used the population censuses of 1851 and 1911 to calculate the average annual percentage growth rate of population for the sixty-year period. The earlier one goes back in assembling data the less easy it is to match the population enumeration districts with the geographical areas identified in our sample and the analysis in Table 5.3 relates to 417 gas undertakings. For those located in areas where population was growing at over 2 per cent per annum, nearly a half were in public ownership. The other rows show that the lower the population growth rate is the smaller the share of undertakings in public ownership. For those with population growth less than 1.2 per cent per annum only 33 per cent of undertakings were publicly owned. The differences are not large however and there are obvious examples which do not fit the

TABLE 5.3 *Population growth in England and Wales 1851–1911*

Annual average population growth 1851–1911 (%)	No. of areas	No. with municipally owned gas supply	% public
Less than 0.46	88	29	33
0.46–1.20	121	40	33
1.21–2.07	103	42	41
2.08 and higher	105	49	46
	417	160	38

Sources: Census Office (1851: tables of the Population and Housing, 1852: tables v and vii, 1911: vol. i); Board of Trade (1939).

pattern. Hull and Sheffield had high population growth but their gasworks remained private. The population of others did not grow (Congleton) or grew only modestly (Wantage 0.40 per cent p.a., Leek 1 per cent) and yet the respective local authority took over the gasworks. This does not mean that population growth is irrelevant. It simply means that it is not the only factor at work and the interrelation between different factors is the essence of the statistical analysis.

   Chapter 4 suggests that the undertakings were run largely on commercial lines and that any apparent differences, in tariff policy for example, as between public and private were due more to the economic conditions (like income levels) in the area where they were located. Municipalization did not change prices. What it did was channel profits to town councils, to holders of fixed interest stock, or to reinvestment in the industry, profits which might otherwise have been paid as dividends. That element of the municipalities' profits (after loan charges) which was not reinvested was siphoned off to the municipal accounts and thereby 'relieved the rates'. It is an old theme that such possibilities were attractive to the expanding local authorities and that this was an important cause of municipalization (Hennock 1973: 117–21; Finer 1941: ch. 8). Certainly there are some classic instances of substantial amounts being transferred and Joseph Chamberlain quite openly contrasted this motive for municipalization with the public health issues relevant to water supply. A sample of municipally owned undertakings for the financial year 1897/8 for example indicates that the Manchester Gas Corporation transferred £50,700 in aid of rates or other municipal accounts—a sizeable sum in a period when the average income from rates per county borough was only some £60,000 (*Gas World* (1897, 1898)). Other notable transfers in that sample were Nottingham £24,000, Salford £13,600, Carlisle £6,147, Bolton £26,466, Wigan £10,300. We have argued in Chapter 4 from an inspection of the aggregate accounts of all local authorities that in the nineteenth century, that is before rate income really expanded, gas revenues may have looked a sizeable revenue source.

What has not so far been established is the extent to which this phenomenon can be shown to contribute to the incidence of municipalization in different local authorities. If Wigan why not Bristol? A direct implication is that the temptation to municipalize would be less the bigger was a local authority's income from other sources in relation to its expenditure plans. Two key sources of income we examine are property income and of course the level of rates. The example of Bristol is instructive for property income since the local authorities in many ports had significant income from their assets in dockland property. Joseph Chamberlain indeed restricted his support for gas municipalization to towns which possessed no extensive estates (Waller 1983: 304). The local taxation returns for two sample financial years in the interwar period record that of all the eighty-four county boroughs the following had a significant income from 'estate profits' which were often transferred in aid of rates: Bristol, Grimsby, Hull, Ipswich, Liverpool, Newcastle, Southampton, Swansea. In none of these cases was the gasworks municipalized—there was some municipal activity in Hull but small beer compared to the private companies operating there, British Gas Light Co. and East Hull Gas. The income from estate profits as a proportion of all trading and estate profits (markets, harbours, cemeteries, electricity, water if municipal, etc.) was 60 per cent for Bristol in 1926/7 and 30 per cent in 1933/4; for Great Yarmouth 63 per cent and 27 per cent, Grimsby 71 per cent and 11 per cent, Hull 17 per cent and 14 per cent, Ipswich 87 per cent and 1 per cent, Liverpool 35 per cent and 56 per cent, Newcastle 51 per cent in both years, Southampton 11 per cent and 13 per cent, Swansea 40 per cent and 6 per cent.

Indeed there were towns, other than ports, with a significant income from property and where the gasworks remained private. Oxford, Brighton, and Bath were county boroughs in this category. Then there were many small towns whose income from estates, when expressed per head of the population, was sizeable— Arundel, Conway, Harrogate, Weston-super-Mare, for example. In order to examine systematically in our sample the links between this income and the continuance of private gas ownership, it is appropriate to use data for an earlier period when most of the municipalization occurred. Unfortunately there is not enough detail on property income in the nineteenth-century sources for our sample of 556 undertakings and we have therefore used the local taxation returns for the financial year 1907/8. These returns itemize for all local authorities various components of revenue including rates, grants, trading profits transferred, and various components of expenditure, education, police, sewage, etc. It is from these accounts that we have extracted the data on rates, to be considered shortly, and that on property income. The latter is taken to be the revenue component identified for urban district councils, county boroughs, and other boroughs as 'rents, profits and sales of property: receipts not elsewhere included'. In the case of rural district councils it is 'Other Receipts'. For Hull for example the figure was £22,252 whilst income from transferred profits of trading enterprises was £21,000; Cardiff and Swansea together recorded £30,000 property income and nothing from trading profits; for Birmingham the figures were £8,246 and £76,564 respectively.

The results have two features. First some 348 local authorities had only a tiny income from this source, less than £500, in many cases zero. Moreover in 65 per cent of these local authorities the gasworks were still private, a figure which was greater than that of the remaining groups and therefore inconsistent with our hypothesis. The latter however is supported by the fact that within the remaining group there is a tendency for the share of undertakings which were privately owned to be larger the greater the income per head of the population. Overall the income from this source seems to be important for perhaps a small number of local authorities but with the general tendency less marked, though we have yet to test whether the relationship holds better for towns with the same rate of urbanization—a matter examined in the statistical analysis.

TABLE 5.4 *Receipts from rates per head of the population in England and Wales 1907/8*

Rates per head	No. of undertakings in sample	No. private	% private
Less than £0.5	149	96	64
£0.5–£0.65	122	83	68
£0.66–£0.99	129	69	54
£1 and over	156	88	56
Total £0.86	556	336	60

Sources: Census Office (1911: vol. i; 1912: table 8); Board of Trade (1939).

Turning now to a larger income source, rates, this had become by 1907/8 a major source of revenue. For example for the county boroughs in aggregate, total receipts from all sources were £25 million, of which rates were £14 million and Exchequer grants for education were £4 million. Across the local authorities the amount of rate income varied enormously even when expressed per head of the population. The relevant entries in the Local Taxation Returns are 'receipts from public rates' or, in the case of rural district councils, 'contributions from overseers'. In only 30 per cent of the local authorities, as Table 5.4 shows, was rate income equivalent to £1 or more per head of the population, and there were certainly several towns in this group which kept to private ownership of the gasworks, many of them with rapidly grow- ing populations—Bournemouth, Eastbourne, Hastings, Reading, Sheffield, York. Table 5.4 shows no general tendency for the share of privately owned undertakings to rise with the rate base but this might be because we have not controlled systematically for population growth, an issue explored later on.

LEGISLATION, FINANCE, AND IDEOLOGY

We turn now to the problem of monopoly power and the legisla- tive and financial problems of municipalization. A private com- pany with an effective monopoly of a town's gas supply may be expected to have higher profits and prices than in a competitive environment and/or to inflate costs by wasteful expenditures. How significant this was for a local authority would depend on two things. To the extent that it wished to get access to gas profits as a source of finance for other municipal activities (as opposed to lowering gas prices), the attraction of municipalization would be higher the more pressing were its revenue needs—an issue already considered. The second factor is that the potential surplus to be expropriated either as lower prices or as rate relief is bigger the larger are monopoly profits and, for a town of any given size, these are bigger the lower the cost of production. Evidence on economies of scale in gas production and distribution in the late nineteenth century suggests that costs would be lower and, *ceteris paribus*, monopoly profits higher the greater the population density (Millward and Ward 1987).

Both population and acreage data are available in the censuses. The implication is that, the larger the population of a town, relative to its acreage, the more attractive would municipalization be, other things being equal. The last qualification is particularly important here. Whilst there are plenty of towns with a population greater than twenty-five per acre (in 1911 for example) which did municipalize their gasworks (Birkenhead, Middlesbrough, Smethwick, for example), it was clearly not the only factor at work so that others remained private, like Penzance, Sunderland, because additional factors were at work—perhaps in these cases because of a significant municipal income from other sources. In general there is no close correlation between population density and the propensity to municipalize, though once we control for other factors, as in the later analysis, both population and acreage do have the effects expected.

There is a further complication arising from questions about the sheer size of a town. Rowlinson has already suggested that the size of population itself shows no obvious link, in his 1882 data, with the number of local authorities who took over the gasworks (1984: ch. 6). The same is true with respect to the 1911 Census data for our sample of 556 towns. No reasons have in fact been so far advanced to suggest such a relationship. However size might be expected to play some role once one looks at the problems faced by a local authority which, perhaps on the basis of some of the considerations already raised, had decided to municipalize. It is quite possible to imagine some minimum critical size below which a town would find the legal and financial costs a significant burden.

From the beginning a town government wishing to set up gas-works had to get the permission of Parliament to engage in 'trade'. This was what, amongst other things, the 1824 Act did for the first publicly owned gas undertaking; the Act empowered the Manchester Police Commissioners to 'trade'. If there were an existing company this would make permission even more difficult, at least by the mid-nineteenth century when Parliament was more persuaded to the idea of just one undertaking for one area. Whilst matters were different with the new utilities at the end of the nineteenth century (electricity, tramways) local authorities never had the right compulsorily to purchase a gas company (Maltbie 1900: 551–3; Finer 1941: 152–3; Wilson 1991a: ch. 5). All of which suggests that the business of obtaining parliamentary permission would involve some irreducible minimum transaction cost, in cash or kind, which would be easier for the larger authorities. Later legislation in the nineteenth century hardly changed this. The 1848 Public Health Act allowed local inhabitants to set up local boards of health but this at most facilitated the establishment of a governmental unit which was capable of then seeking permission to municipalize—as several later did. The 1870 Gas and Water Facilities Act enabled a local authority to buy gas companies by mutual agreement subject to the consent of the Local Government Board and thereby gave general approval to 'trading'. It was also enabled to set up plant but only if no private undertaking existed in the town (as had the 1848 Public Health Act for Local Boards). The 1875 Public Health Act simply confirmed these changes. Moreover the 1872 Borough Funds Act which made provision for central government subventions to local authorities in their urban improvement programmes specifically precluded the use of such funds to finance the promotion of a parliamentary bill for municipalizing gasworks.

When one turns to the financial arrangements associated with the buying out of a company, this reinforces the suggestion that small towns would be at a disadvantage. A local authority might need cash if the existing owner were to be bought out in this way or indeed if a local authority were initiating new works. Finance for this would have to come from an authority's reserves or from loans including stock issued by the municipality. In some cases the existing owners would be issued with annuities which could be financed directly out of the expected profits of the municipalized undertaking. Many municipalities, certainly the growing number with borough status, were issuing their own stock and were able thereby to borrow at relatively low interest (Hennock 1973: 117–21; Wilson 1990, 1991*a*). All in all, a small town with few reserves and no facility for issuing stock would not be in a strong enough financial position to buy out. In summary we might expect to find that population size was important in relation to acreage but also that it would play some role in its own right. It will be seen in the later analysis that this is borne out. In fact the role of minimum size is already confirmed, one suspects, by virtue of the data in Table 5.2. The rural district councils covered areas with significantly lower population than the boroughs and county boroughs and they had a lower proportion of their gasworks in public ownership.

It was suggested earlier that the propensity to municipalize was not limited by the colour of the local political party. At least that is the theme in the existing literature. There could none the less still be occasions when, despite the objective circumstances, a gasworks goes public or keeps private simply because of the ideological proclivities of the local political leaders. Ascertaining the party composition of the 600 or so towns in our sample would be a mammoth exercise in its own right. What one can do is examine the political colour of an area in terms of its voting behaviour in general elections. *McCalmont's Parliamentary Poll Book* (1971) provides information on the political party of Members of Parliament at each General Election, and by 1910 the franchise was sufficiently wide to give a good indication of grass-roots feelings. Of course it is not always possible exactly to match parliamentary constituencies with the gas undertakings' areas and at most 217 areas could be satisfactorily identified. For each we recorded whether the MP (or majority of MPs when a town had several) was Liberal or Labour or Conservative (including Unionist) or Liberal/Labour in equal numbers. The results are shown in Table 5.5 classifying the areas according to whether the gasworks was municipally owned.

The proportion of gasworks in municipal ownership is clearly therefore lowest in Conservative seats, higher in Liberal and in Labour seats like Barrow, Rhondda, and Stoke. But there are

TABLE 5.5 *Sample of parliamentary constituencies in January 1910*

Gasworks	Liberal	Equal Liberal/Labour	Labour	Conservative	Total
Public	40	10	4	34	88
Private	45	5	5	74	129
Total	85	15	9	108	217
% public	47	66	44	31	41

clearly many that do not fit into the categorization. Not only did many mixed Liberal/Labour seats stay private (Derby, Merthyr, Newcastle, Newark) but so also did several Labour seats (Barnard Castle, Gowerton, Normanton, Westhoughton). Many Conservative seats had municipally owned works (Birmingham, Chorley, Chelmsford, for example). Previous commentators have therefore been right to say there is no general tendency. There were nevertheless several towns whose economic and social characteristics might have prompted municipalization but which, for no other reason which we can identify than political commitment, kept the gasworks private. And the same process might have operated in reverse in Labour seats; thus Carlisle, Brigg, Macclesfield, and Newcastle under Lyme had population growth less than 1 per cent, rates per acre more than £10,000, and yet the gasworks was municipalized; the one factor, other than it being a Labour seat, which might help to explain this is a high population density. At the other end of the scale there were several Conservative seats where the gasworks remained private despite the local authority receiving a relatively small amount of rates per acre (less than £5,000) and population growth in excess of 1.5 per cent per annum; Chertsey, Cirencester, Harwich, Malden, Petersfield, Rugby, Thirsk, all of which except Malden being run by rural district councils. Whether political complexion does in the end add anything is explored in the next section.

THE DURATION AND INCIDENCE OF MUNICIPAL OWNERSHIP

The argument of the previous section is that the propensity to municipalize is expected to be greater the larger the potential private gas monopoly profits, the smaller the fiscal revenues available to the local council, and the larger the expenditure programme of the local authority. These variables are to be measured by proxies for each town in the form of population density (for monopoly profits), rates, and property rents per head or per acre for fiscal revenue, whilst the expenditure programmes per head are to be proxied by the rate of population growth and the size of the town taken as an indicator of how the costs of municipalization varied.

The aim of the analysis is to establish how far each variable on its own affects the tendency to municipalization. For example, how far revenue from rates affects the tendency across the sample for gasworks to be municipalized when all other factors (like size and growth of population, region, government group) are held constant. The 'tendency' is itself here measured in two ways. For each municipal undertaking in the 1939 sample we know the date of municipalization and hence can calculate the length of time over which an undertaking had been under municipal ownership, with those not municipalized carrying a zero value. (This variable is labelled MUNYRS.) Alternatively one might treat, for any group of undertakings, the percentage of undertakings municipalized by 1939 as a probability of being municipalized and examine how the fiscal revenue and population variables affect that probability. Both these approaches have been used. A detailed list of variables together with the results of the statistical analysis are shown in Appendix 5.1, but an intuitive, non-technical, explanation may be given as follows.

Population growth (denoted as GRP5111 and measured as indicated earlier) comes through consistently as a strong positive influence both on the probability of the gasworks being publicly owned and on the length of time over which, by 1939, it had been municipalized. The level of rates had as expected the reverse effect. Its role has to be viewed relative to some measure of the size of the local authority in question and the best measure proved to be rates per acre (RTACRE measured in pounds). Property income also had, in some regressions, a similar effect to rates but was never statistically significant, confirming the earlier suggestion that it may have been important for certain towns (like the ports, spas, and holiday resorts) without having a general impact on all areas. So far as size and density are concerned, the geographical size of each area (ACRES measured in thousands) proved to have a consistently strong influence and the best results emerged by treating this and population (POP measured in thousand persons) as separate variables. We are thus hypothesizing that some of the variation across the sample in the length of time over which the town gasworks had been municipalized can be explained by GRP5III, RTACRE, POP, and ACRES. The results reported in Appendix 5.1 do indeed suggest that each of these four variables is statistically significant. This implies then that, for example, for undertakings located in areas of the same size (i.e. given ACRES) the propensity to municipalization was higher the faster the population growth, the smaller the rates per acre, the larger the population, and hence the larger the population density.

An illustration of the results is given in Figs. 5.3 and 5.4. Each dot in Fig. 5.3 represents a town and records its population growth rate (GRP5III) and number of years under municipal ownership (MUNYRS). A number like 2 or 3 means that there is more than one town with these values. For convenience and without detracting from the point at hand, Fig. 5.3 excludes all towns with zero value for MUNYRS (i.e. all private companies). There seems therefore to be a tendency for higher population growth rates to be associated with a longer period under muni-

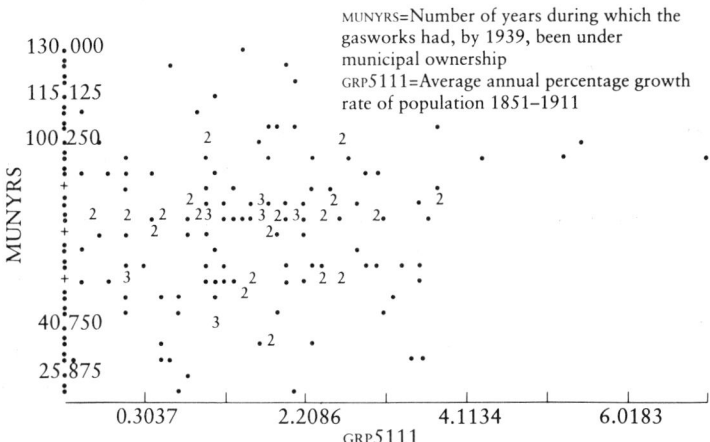

FIG. 5.3 Scatter diagram of population growth and period under municipal ownership 1850–1939

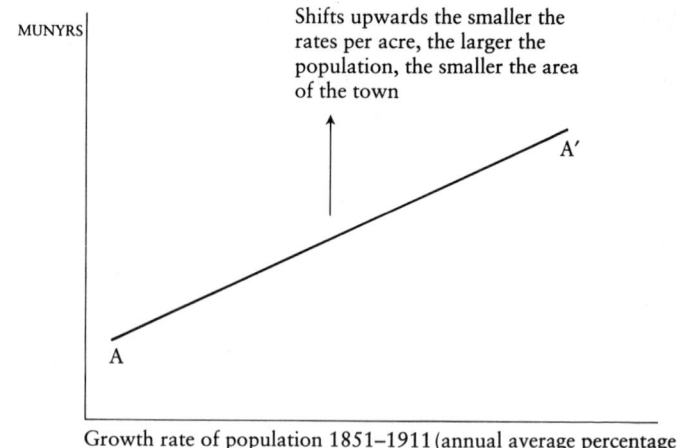

Growth rate of population 1851–1911 (annual average percentage)

FIG. 5.4 The determinants of municipalization

cipal ownership. This possible relationship is sketched out in the AA' line in Fig. 5.4. But clearly there are other variables at work and many towns with the same population growth have different values for MUNYRS. In effect then, as the note to Fig. 5.4 suggests, the link between MUNYRS and population growth shown by AA' reflects given levels of all the other variables; if they change the whole line shifts upwards.

Whilst the fiscal revenue, population growth, and size variables do contribute to our understanding of the shift from private to municipal ownership they do not explain everything. It is clear from the results reported in Appendix 5.1 for example that those towns attaining their borough status between 1836 and 1887 had a stronger propensity to municipalization independent of population size, acreage, population growth, and rates base. It seems plausible to interpret this result as picking up what we might call 'government entrepreneurship'. Towns which were rural district councils (or mixed rural/urban) also seem to be in a separate category; they had a clearly smaller propensity to municipalization than other towns, again independently of the population and rates bases. This result seems to be reinforcing the roles of POP and ACRES in confirming that size mattered and was an indicator of the costs of municipalization.

What finally of the political ideology and regional effects? Towns which had a Conservative Member of Parliament did show a smaller propensity to municipalization, independent of the economic issues. However this factor seemed to be inextricably intertwined with the population and revenue variables whose role, statistically, is thereby reduced. This political ideology variable is therefore adding something but its precise role is not very clear. A similar point applies to regional groupings. As compared to the region identified earlier as the 'South', the Northern and Midlands regions had a clearly greater propensity to municipalize independent of population growth, rates per acre, acreage, or population size. The regional dimension therefore does still add something even after allowance is made for the population and revenue variables. Precisely what this is has not been identified. The issue is especially complicated by virtue of the fact that in an analysis of the towns in the South on their own the population and revenue variables lose their significance; this is true for each and every region and suggests that the variation in population growth, rates per acre, etc. across England and Wales has itself a strong regional dimension. That this is true for most of the government categories— as the results in Appendix 5.1 demonstrate—is perhaps not surprising since such categories were designed, in the local government legislation, to reflect such dimensions. (The exception which proves the rule is the group of 1835 boroughs which were untouched by the nineteenth-century reclassifications and contain a rich mixture of fast- and slow-growing towns.) Hence further research work on the regional dimension is clearly warranted.

SUMMARY AND CONCLUSIONS

That some element of public control was needed over electricity supply, tramways, gas, and water was not significantly disputed in Britain at least from the middle of the nineteenth century. As 'utilities' there were problems which we would now describe as arising from environmental spillovers and natural monopoly. The regulatory activities of central government, stemming from initiatives in Parliament, are explained largely by such matters. Whether that would also involve public ownership and operation of the industry was affected by a number of factors. The arm's length regulation of prices, profit, and supply conditions in gas and water in the period from the 1840s to the 1870s was not especially effective. We have here argued that two fundamental factors affected the shift to public ownership: the severity of the above economic issues, and the extent to which the local government authorities were attracted to these industries as a source of municipal revenue. Whether they could overcome the legal and financial problems of taking over the companies was an additional matter which would be especially difficult for small towns.

The latter part of this chapter has reported in detail on an analysis of these issues for the gas industry. Although detailed work has not yet been done on the same lines for electricity and tramways it seems likely that similar issues were involved. For water, environmental effects together with very complex issues about 'water rights' made for a wholesale transfer to municipal ownership. In the other local utilities it would seem market structure problems and the attraction of utility profits were more important. By the 1920s, as in gas, the larger town councils (even including London) owned their electricity supply and tramway undertakings whereas the smaller towns and rural areas stayed private. It is therefore finally instructive to return to the gas case-study to spell out some of the implications for individual towns. Towns with a good revenue base and low population growth tended to remain private especially if they were not developing as dynamic boroughs. This would account for many of the 'old' boroughs with these economic characteristics—Cambridge, Chichester, Maidstone, Marlborough, Salisbury, Shrewsbury, Windsor, Tenby—as well as some which got county borough status: Canterbury, Chester, Exeter, Norwich, Preston, York. Towns with similar characteristics which were also small in population or population density would have additional reasons for staying private and this therefore embraced the well-heeled small provincial towns, often but not always in the South—Aylesbury, Barry, Bognor, Broadstairs, Mirfield, Swanage, Romford—often run by district councils.

At the other end of the scale are towns with relatively high population growth but not an especially strong revenue base, embracing many of the municipally owned undertakings in the sample and especially the classic industrializing towns of the Midlands and North. The ones which were earliest to shift to public ownership were those striving for borough status in the fifty years following the 1835 Municipal Corporation Act—Bangor, Bolton, Darlington, Darwen, Dewsbury, East Retford, Ilkeston, Middleton, Rotherham, St Helens. Several towns which never achieved borough status and municipalized the gasworks at a later date nevertheless had the key characteristic of low revenue base and considerable population growth—Horsham, Driffield, Bourne, Cheadle, Masham. Some towns with significant urbanization problems which acquired their local gasworks were not always low in revenue—the county boroughs of Doncaster, Leicester, Halifax, Blackburn, for example, as well as some urban district councils, Llandudno, Rhyl, Skegness. When the revenue level became substantial however the desire to go public seems to have been reduced, despite high population growth. Of the county Boroughs this included those with a good rates base like Bournemouth and Eastbourne, those with good property income (Hull, Bristol, and the other ports), and some with good revenue from both sources (Sheffield).

Clearly however the high revenue/high population growth group cannot always be allocated to public or private, even when government category can be invoked, and future work would have to address this problem. The same issue arises for those with low revenue and low population growth though in this case their small size would have worked against municipalization. Some urban district councils like Bollington, Cockermouth, Sandwich, and Wells (Norfolk) went public whilst others with the same low revenue base stayed private and it is the case that several of these— Berkhamsted, Grantham, Bodmin, Bromford—were rural district councils or 'old' boroughs. All these cases where the population and revenue effects work against each other have to be distinguished from the small number of cases we identified where political ideology may have been important such that the towns seemed to have taken decisions about gas independently of the substantive economic issues: Carlisle, Brigg, Macclesfield going public whilst some with better reasons for doing that stayed private—Chertsey, Petersfield, Thirsk, for example.

APPENDIX 5.1
Statistical Analysis of Municipalization of Gas in England and Wales Using 1939 Data

The list of variables, their definition, and measurement are shown in Table A.5.1. Regression results using the number of years under municipal ownership as the dependent variable (MUNYRS) are shown in Table A.5.2. In each case these are simply linear regressions but they use TOBIT.

TABLE A.5.1 *List of variables 1851–1948*

GRP5111	Average annual growth rate of population 1851–1911
POP	Population in 000 persons in 1911
AREA	Area in 000 acres 1911
RATES	Local authority receipts in £000 from public rates in 1907/8 (for rural district councils, contributions from overseers)
RTACRE	RATES/AREA
MUNYRS	1948 minus the estimated year of municipalization but with all 1939 companies counted as zero.

Dummy variables (counts 1 if town is in this category, 0 otherwise)

PUBGAS	Gasworks municipally owned in 1939
BOR1835	Borough status confirmed or granted by 1835 Municipal Corporation Act
BOR3687	Borough status granted between 1836 and 1887
BORC068	BOR3687 and county borough status attained in 1888
BOR8839	Borough status granted between 1888 and 1939
UDC	Urban district council in 1939
RUB	Rural district council in 1939 or town with both a RD council and a UD council
LY	Lancashire and Yorkshire counties
NORTH	Counties of Cumberland, Northumberland, Westmorland, and Durham
WALES	All Welsh counties including Monmouthshire
WMIDS	Counties of Cheshire, Herefordshire, Shropshire, Staffordshire, Warwickshire, Worecestershire
EMIDS	Counties of Derbyshire, Leicestershire, Lincolnshire, Nottinghamshire, Northamptonshire, Rutland
SOUTH	Rest of England
CU1910	Member of Parliament (or majority of members in large towns) was Conservative in 1910 General Election

Table A.5.3 involves a PROBIT regression using as the dependent variable PUBGAS which takes a value of one if a town's gasworks is municipally owned in 1939, zero otherwise. Tables A.5.4 and A.5.5 involve regressions for subsamples related to regional or government categories.

TABLE A.5.2 *TOBIT results for England and Wales 1851–1948*

	(a)	(b)	(c)	(d)	(e)	(f)
Constant	−26.21 (−3.03)*	−20.98 (−2.63)*	−49.28 (−4.30)*	−19.25 (−2.21)*	−52.02 (−4.20)*	−19.32 (−2.57)*
GRP5111	10.11 (2.42)*	11.95 (2.70)*	4.75 (1.37)	10.89 (2.42)*	5.70 (1.51)	12.87 (2.85)*
RTACRE		−1.21 (−1.80)	−0.98 (−1.65)	−1.77 (−2.47)*	−1.63 (−2.41)*	−1.83 (−2.59)*
POP	0.18 (0.81)	0.24 (2.83)*	0.14 (2.07)*	0.21 (2.66)*	0.13 (1.93)	0.21 (2.65)*
ACRES	−1.09 (−3.61)*	−1.31 (−4.05)*	−1.13 (−3.83)*	−0.61 (−2.11)*	−0.49 (−1.53)	−0.63 (−2.15)*
RATES	−0.04 (−0.25)					
RENTS	0.02 (0.04)					
BORI835				−1.28 (−0.13)	12.75 (1.24)	
BOR3687				51.17 (3.08)*	45.57 (2.87)*	48.02 (3.18)*
BOR8839				34.99 (1.64)	32.57 (1.86)	
RUB				−65.19 (−3.27)*	−53.89 (−2.55)*	−70.14 (−3.51)*
LY			86.39 (5.00)*		75.30 (4.85)*	
WALES			28.34 (1.96)*		25.55 (1.90)	
NORTH			57.15 (3.17)*		65.47 (3.74)*	
EMIDS			52.06 (3.01)*		50.91 (3.09)*	
WMIDS			56.44 (3.99)*		52.76 (4.09)*	

Note: There are 417 observations and the dependent variable is MUNYRS calculated as 1948 minus the estimated date of municipalization with 1939 private companies counted as zero. T ratios are in brackets and an asterisk indicates the coefficient is significant at the 5% level.

TABLE A.5.3 *PROBIT results for England and Wales 1851–1948*

	(a)	(b)	(c)	(d)	(e)	(f)
Constant	−0.44	−0.34	−0.83	−0.30	−0.95	−0.36
	(−4.40)*	(−3.84)*	(−5.91)*	(−2.41)*	(−5.61)*	(−3.51)*
GRP5111	0.14	0.17	0.09	0.20	0.12	0.21
	(2.60)*	(3.24)*	(1.52)	(3.25)*	(1.83)	(3.63)*
RTACRE		−0.02	−0.02	−0.03	−0.03	−0.03
		(−2.60)*	(−2.27)*	(−3.09)*	(−3.16)*	(−3.47)*
POP	0.002	0.003	0.002	0.002	0.002	0.003
	(0.54)	(2.80)*	(1.60)	(1.82)	(1.54)	(2.50)*
ACRES	−0.01	−0.02	−0.02	−0.008	−0.008	−0.009
	(−2.91)*	(−3.50)*	(−3.22)	(−1.41)	(−1.31)	(−1.60)
RATES	−0.0004					
	(−0.17)					
RENTS	−0.002					
	(−0.22)					
BOR1835				−0.11	0.22	
				(−0.68)	(1.20)	
BOR3687					0.78	0.71
					(3.15)*	(3.45)*
BORCO68				1.20		
				(3.13)*		
BOR8839				0.50	0.62	
				(1.65)	(1.94)	
RUB				−1.06	−0.83	−1.00
				(−3.58)*	(−2.54)*	(−3.42)*
LY			1.36		1.28	
			(7.12)*		(6.28)*	
WALES			0.41		0.37	
			(1.70)*		(1.52)	
NORTH			0.85		1.02	
			(2.99)*		(3.47)*	
EMIDS			0.87		0.91	
			(3.73)*		(3.76)*	
WMIDS			0.78		0.77	
			(3.84)*		(3.69)*	
% correctly predicted	63	61	71	69	71	67

Note: There are 417 observations and the dependent variable is PUBGAS which carries a value of one for municipally owned gasworks, zero otherwise. T ratios are in brackets and an asterisk indicates the coefficient is significant at the 5% level.

TABLE A.5.4 *TOBIT results for Regions and government categories 1851–1948*

	(a)	(b)	(c)	(d)	(e)
Category	UDC	BOR1835	LY	SOUTH	England and Wales
No. of observations	149	143	93	154	200
Constant	−20.27	−28.16	22.16	−38.80	−13.51
	(−1.44)	(−1.37)	(2.28)*	(−1.64)	(−0.94)
GRP5111	5.35	21.25	7.48	−5.68	14.70
	(0.72)	(1.40)	(1.70)	(−0.44)	(2.33)*
RTACRE	−1.18	−3.50	−0.70	−1.88	−1.47
	(−0.45)	(−1.69)	(−1.22)	(−0.60)	(−1.73)
POP	0.51	0.21	0.03	−1.20	0.11
	(0.50)	(0.81)	(0.52)	(−0.62)	(1.10)
ACRES	0.29	0.92	−0.07	−0.65	0.43
	(0.25)	(0.22)	(−0.11)	(−0.79)	(0.62)
CUI910					−21.93
					(−1.78)
BOR3687			46.19		48.57
			(3.13)*		(2.67)*
RUB			−81.69		−139.50
			(−2.76)*		(−1.32)
R^2(OLS; adjusted) (%)	0	3	3	2	26

Note: The dependent variable is MUNYRS in each case. T ratios are in brackets and an asterisk indicates the coefficient is significant at the 5% level.

TABLE A.5.5 PROBIT *results for Regions and government categories 1851–1948*

	(a)	(b)	(c)	(d)	(e)
Category	UDC	BOR1835	LY	SOUTH	England and Wales
No. of observations	149	143	93	154	200
Constant	−0.42 (−2.33)*	−0.39 (−1.73)	0.13 (0.47)	−0.50 (−2.58)*	−0.28 (−1.36)
GRP5111	0.12 (1.13)	0.27 (1.89)	0.23 (1.99)*	−0.06 (−0.39)	0.26 (2.78)*
RTACRE	−0.01 (−0.39)	−0.05 (−2.59)*	−0.02 (−1.37)	−0.02 (−0.75)	−0.03 (−2.50)*
POP	0.004 (0.22)	0.002 (0.91)	−0.001 (−0.02)	−0.01 (−0.93)	0.001 (1.17)
ACRES	0.01 (0.68)	0.02 (0.35)	0.001 (0.07)	−0.006 (−0.58)	0.02 (1.07)
CUI910					−0.38 (−1.92)
BOR3687			1.09 (2.68)*		0.79 (3.02)*
RUB			−1.70 (−2.23)*		−2.12 (−2.14)*
% correctly predicted	58	70	76	83[a]	73

Note: The dependent variable is PUBGAS is each case.

[a] It predicted zero municipals whereas there were 26.

6
Ownership and Cost Effectiveness: Evidence from the Early Twentieth Century

INTRODUCTION

Efficiency in the use of resources has been a theme in all public debates on proposals for industrial reform. It is true that, in the case of municipalization in the late nineteenth century, expropriation of trading profits was a key driving force, as we saw in the last chapter. But cost effectiveness certainly figured prominently in the way local councillors presented the case. It is also true that in the UK during the 1980s privatisation of many public firms reflected in part a desire to widen the share ownership of private companies and also to reduce the central government's borrowing requirement by eliminating the financial deficits of nationalized industries. But there is no doubt that efficiency was a central issue and that ownership was seen as just as important, possibly even more so, than a competitive market structure; So also was efficiency a key element in the 1940s proposals for nationalization. As we shall argue in more detail in Chapter 8, nationalization was expected to reap advantages from a more efficient size of business organization whilst the parliamentary Acts of nationalization contained provisions requiring that services be efficiently provided and financial clauses to facilitate monitoring of performance.

Ownership has to be distinguished from the question of market structure. Both can affect efficiency. To evaluate the effect of ownership on efficiency one would ideally like to examine the performance of public and private firms in the same industry, in the same country, in the same period. This is possible in the utilities sector in the USA, where some cities have municipally owned electricity supply, refuse collection, etc. whilst others allow private companies to operate freely or contract for services, sometimes on the basis of tenders for franchises. In the UK since 1945 sectors like railways, coal, and electricity have been public monopolies, thereby precluding the kind of detailed comparisons characteristic of the North American literature on that period. Furthermore in the UK in the early nineteenth century private enterprise dominated, as we have seen, in the provision of railways, water supply, and gas, so again a public/private comparison is not easy. By the end of the nineteenth century and the first forty years of the twentieth century private companies coexisted with municipally owned enterprises in electricity, tramways, water, and gas and it is this structure that allows meaningful efficiency comparisons of UK data. The issue was a live concern by the end of the nineteenth century in Britain and in the USA, where the experience of municipalization in Britain was watched with great interest. There was much concern by British observers about the rise in local authority debt and the efficiency of municipal enterprises. The American R. P. Porter felt that 'with the exception of two or three well managed municipal gas plants, the British Corporation plants are neither so well nor so economically managed as the private plants, nor do they serve the public so advantageously' (1902: 111). Statistical support for the arguments was enhanced by the growing body of Board of Trade returns on public utilities. The debate was in part about prices and profits, but also about costs, where, however, the focus became average unit costs so that there were no serious attempts to examine how costs varied systematically with output, factor prices, or plant vintages.

Since then, interest in statistical comparisons seems to have waned. Indeed Herman Finer in his authoritative 1941 study of municipal trading avoided 'comparisons of the success of municipal and private enterprises . . . for the reason that they are practically impossible. Comparisons between one municipal utility and another are also practically impossible,' said Finer (p. 35), resting his case on Pigou's dictum 'that attempts to conduct a comparison by reference to statistics are foredoomed to failure'. There is a more up-to-date secondary literature in economic history books and journals on municipal performance. Little of this literature is concerned with detailed determinants of costs or prices or with looking systematically at significant samples of undertakings, so that the observations on performance are either guesses or are closely qualified (Waller 1983: ch. 7). In this chapter we present new findings for this period in the UK. In the next section some general theoretical considerations about performance are considered as well as some of the findings in the current, mainly US, literature. Then we focus on electricity and gas in Britain and start with a summary of the main economic trends and main features of economic organization in the period 1890–1940. The contemporary attempts at comparing municipal enterprises and private companies in this period are reviewed. We then set out the arguments for assessing performance in terms of cost functions, examine the general factors which determine costs, and describe the data to be used for electricity and gas undertakings. The results of the analysis are presented and conclusions drawn. All technical material has been placed in Appendices 6.2 and 6.3.

EFFICIENCY AND OWNERSHIP: SOME GENERAL CONSIDERATIONS

A seminal article on the theory of the public firm is that of Alchian (1965), who argued that managers in private companies are under continuous monitoring from the unilateral ability of shareholders to sell their rights and from the threat of mergers and take-overs. These pressures from the capital market are not present in state-owned enterprises because their 'owners', the electorate, cannot sell their property rights. Nevertheless they can still voice their concern about high prices. The smaller number of 'owners' of a municipal compared with a national undertaking dilutes the interests of the electorate to a smaller extent and political feedbacks may be accordingly stronger. For the large private company, Demsetz (1983: 387) argues that the similar dilution of widely dispersed shareholding will be no bar to shareholders eventually ousting unsatisfactory management because of the concentration of share ownership in financial institutions and in take-over activity. An analogous argument can be made for publicly owned enterprises. In both cases the key issue is how long the homeostatic process takes, a question which would seem to be principally empirical.

Where performance targets are clearly set and widely recognized, the incentive effects provided by managerial labour markets (Fama 1980) might be as effective in the municipal enterprise as in the private corporation. In both types of firm the manager who seeks to maximize the value of his human capital by moving or threatening to move between firms will take decisions, in his managerial capacity, to justify being paid the maximum possible. A monolithic nationalized industry is more likely to internalize managerial labour markets for the relevant skills; the remuneration management can command is less likely to depend upon their efficiency because there is no general external monitoring of their unit's performance. Even the municipal enterprise may succeed in removing the incentive effects of managerial labour markets by imposing certain control and reward systems. Governments and civil servants have no necessary individual acquisitive interest in designing such frameworks to bring about cost minimization or profit maximization by publicly owned firms. Where the external regulation of the firm is concerned, the absence of direct economic interest by politicians and administrators in constructing efficient systems may lead to a variety of distortionary effects, but these may well differ between governmental organizations.

The existing evidence does not however suggest that public firms are less cost-effective than private firms. The point is clear from the utility sectors of countries like the USA where large numbers of both public and private undertakings coexist in the same industry, and where cost and production functions have been estimated.

Both Canada and Australia also offer helpful industries for evaluating ownership-performance differences in the years after 1945. The publicly owned Canadian National and private Canadian Pacific railways, competed over many routes and were subject to less and less rate regulation. The calculated growth rates of productivity in moving from one company to the other showed little annual variation between them when inputs were controlled. In 1967, for example, Canadian National productivity was 4.1 per cent greater. In Australia both the public Trans-Australian Airlines and the private Ansett Transport Industries supplied similar airline services. Operating on interstate routes the Australian government equalized practically every aspect of operations. Freight tonnage per employee was vastly higher in the private firm. But once passengers carried were also taken into account, appropriately weighted, there is no clear evidence of a difference between the two businesses. (Davies 1980; Forsyth and Hocking 1980; Caves and Christensen 1980; Millward and Parker 1983).

Many economists have accepted this evidence and see improvements in cost effectiveness arising not from ownership, but rather from a more active competition (Kay, and Silberston 1984; Shackleton 1984; Wright 1987; Helm, Kay, and Thompson 1988). It is reflected also in the reservations which commentators have expressed over the disinclination of the UK government to break-up British Gas into generating and distributing units.

Unfortunately even with the introduction of effective competition natural monopolies remain a problem. Competition in the field lowers the potential cost advantage of a single firm. Competition for the field is undermined in the presence of sunk costs, leaving regulation as the only alternative. The US experience of regulatory capture and/or overinvestment is clear. Evidence on contestability in the utility sector in Britain is still limited (but see Chapter 2 above). In so far as National Express did enjoy an element of natural cost advantage, its sunk costs allowed both predatory prices and an aggressive policy with respect to its key 'unnatural' monopoly advantage, that is its ownership of passenger terminal facilities (Davis 1984; Jaffer and Thompson 1986).

A shift to private ownership is likely to induce a closer alignment of prices with private costs; deregulation has a similar effect. There is clear evidence from the US electric power industry of the 1960s and 1970s that private utilities, even when regulated, have tariffs more closely reflective of costs than public firms and offer a wider range of rate schedules. The traditional element of cross-subsidy by regime or function in British public enterprise is well known. Once privatized, British Telecom moved away from the subsidy by business users of domestic users. Deregulation of long-distance coach travel in the UK in the 1980s led to a fall in the real level of fares on densely trafficked routes and a rise in the real level of prices on the more costly lightly trafficked routes, where service levels have fallen. Privatization and active competition tend to cut out activities which are privately unprofitable.

ECONOMIC STRUCTURE AND TRENDS IN ELECTRICITY AND GAS 1890–1940

We now consider detailed evidence on the performance of public and private firms in the UK in the pre-nationalization period from 1890. As Table 6.1 shows, this is the period of very rapid growth for electricity supply. The number of consumers expanded continuously, greatly offsetting the decline in average consumption per consumer. Gas saw nothing like the same expansion and lost a lot of its lighting load to electricity. Nevertheless it continued to expand both the total number of consumers as well as total consumption, generating demands for heat and power in industry which offset its losses in domestic lighting. The private companies and the municipal enterprises continued to coexist in large numbers in both electricity and gas, thereby facilitating comparisons of performance. Some background is needed on the structure of the industries in this period, but since the economic organization of the gas industry was discussed in some detail in Chapter 5, the focus in this section is electricity.

The structure of the inter-war electricity supply industry in the twentieth century before nationalization is largely to be explained by nineteenth-century government policy (Byatt 1978; Hannah 1979). In the early days of the industry, as we saw in Chapter 5, companies were granted limited-term franchises, at the end of which municipalities were to have the option of buying up the operation. Maximum prices were also stipulated, but the 'sliding scale', inversely linking prices with dividends, was little used in electricity, though widely employed in the gas industry. In adopting this policy of limited-term franchises, governments were pursuing a line taken earlier with railways to allay public fears of exploitation by 'natural monopolies'. No consideration seems to have been given to franchise competition at the end of the limited period, as now practised in commercial television. By the turn of the century the practice and advocacy (by prominent figures such as G. B. Shaw) of municipal socialism had reached its peak, as local authorities exercised their rights to buy out electricity supply companies.

A disadvantage of municipalization turned out to be the freezing of the structure of the industry. After about 1905 existing municipal operating areas began to prove too small to bring down costs to the minimum permitted by the available technology. Nor was the company sector in any better condition because the company operating areas characteristically were those left between the local authorities—usually of awkward shapes for distribution networks and with low populations. The exception was the

TABLE 6.1 *Trends in consumption of gas and electricity 1895–1939*

	Electricity			Gas		
	1895	1920	1938–9	1897–8	1920	1935
No. of consumers in millions	n/a	1.0	9.3	3.0	7.5	10.5
Average consumption per consumer	n/a	3,600 kWh	2,100 kWh	40,417 cu. ft.	31,600 cu. ft.	28,100 cu. ft.
% of sales to households	n/a	8.0	26.7	n/a	n/a	65[a]
No. of local authority undertakings	16	358[b]	364	212	245	243
No. of statutory companies	34	233[b]	208	436	489	405
Joint boards etc.	n/a	2[b]	9	—	—	—

[a] 'Pre-war' data according to Heyworth Report (1945).
[b] Data refer to 1925.

Sources: Palmer (1943); Balfour Committee (1928–9); Heyworth Report (1945); Hannah (1979: 1); annual Board of Trade returns on gas undertakings.

North East Electricity Supply Co., which, because of Newcastle Corporation's lack of interest in generating electricity and easy access to coalfields among other reasons, became the largest and lowest-cost electricity supplier in the country before the outbreak of war in 1914. Unfortunately this single success story was insufficient to prevent Britain falling behind her industrial competitors in the use of the new electrical technology; fear of private monopoly power had ultimately constrained the introduction of modern techniques and contributed to industrial retardation.

After the war, in recognition of these organizational failings, the Electricity Commissioners were brought into being in an attempt to increase operating areas and station size, largely by voluntary agreement. The decisive step in the reorganization of electricity supply was taken in 1926 when the Central Electricity Board was set up with the objective of establishing a national distribution grid, or rather, a series of interlinked regional grids. The Board selected enterprises which were to supply this grid and used those with the lowest costs to supply the base load, working on a three-shift system, whereas the less technically efficient stations supplied the peak loads. The Board was empowered to direct and defray costs, but not to own plants. To ensure satisfactory co-operation of participating suppliers, the Board did not invariably give priority to cost minimization in generating plans. The prices at which suppliers sold to the grid were regulated by the Electricity Commissioners as were the prices at which electricity could be bought— —although there was room for negotiation in this latter case on the basis of the counterfactual generating costs of the purchasing supplier, which were related to actual costs.

CONTEMPORARY STUDIES OF PERFORMANCE

At the turn of the century the relative performance of public and private undertakings was a matter of keen debate. By this stage the Board of Trade was producing comprehensive returns for all authorized undertakings and in 1905 a large team of officials and experts from the USA investigated, on behalf of the National Civic Federation, several undertakings in great detail, producing a three-volume report in 1907. The broad approach in all these studies was to look at average values for certain performance indicators for samples of public and private firms making informal allowances for other factors which were at work. Thus in the years between 1895 and 1905 gross profits as a proportion of capital employed were for many gas undertakings in the range 4–9 per cent. Calculations using all the Board of Trade data as well as samples of the larger undertakings suggested municipal and private rates of return were broadly similar with, if anything, the private company rate of return slightly higher (Donald 1903: 72; Howe 1906: 35, 40; Maltbie 1900: 563). These profit rates will be reflecting both price and cost factors. For seven large towns in 1905 the National Civic Federation study (1907: 212) found that prices were higher in the municipal firms, as had Porter (1902: 111) for 1901, but much of the other evidence, including the comprehensive data of the Board of Trade, suggested that prices per cubic foot of gas were lower in the publicly owned sector, the importance of which was recognized in the larger average number of consumers in public enterprises (Donald 1903: 72; Howe 1906: 35; Maltbie 1900: 556; Balfour Committee 1928–9: 312). Of course lower prices may be offset by poor quality. One measure of the illuminating power of gas is its candlepower. Whilst available figures suggested this was higher in the municipal firms, there was considerable dispute concerning the accuracy of the data. Lower prices can also be offset by high meter rents, but in this case there seems less dispute that these were lower in the municipal firms: in 1898 for example 12 per cent of the customers supplied by private companies got their meters free whilst for the municipals the figure was 62 per cent (Donald 1903: 72; Maltbie 1900: 553).

Prices and profits may of course be simply reflecting costs, which can clearly vary with output levels, the prices of materials and other inputs, the geographical setting, as well as with institutional factors. Most of the contemporary studies concentrated on identifying differences in unit costs, and hence implicitly allowed only for the level of output. Again the National Civic Federation's study for seven large towns suggested (1907: 207) unit labour costs and unit material costs in gas were higher in the municipals, but the other studies tended to point the other way. Donald (1903: 72) found unit operating costs for 1897 lower in Manchester than in Liverpool (private). The comprehensive Board of Trade data for 1898 suggested that unit operating costs were lower in municipals, whilst for 1903/4 the same source showed

municipal operating costs 10 per cent lower than private, matching the 10 per cent lower figure for the average level of prices
(Maltbie 1900: 569; Howe 1906: 35). The precise source of all
these cost differences was not, however, analysed systematically
and the figures do not include capital costs.

In the case of electricity, the interesting period is 1919–39,
when the industry had come to full maturity. At first glance, the
greater efficiency of the company sector seems to be indicated by
the disproportionate selection by the Central Electricity Board of
companies over municipal suppliers (Hannah 1979: 225). The
average cost of generating electricity in both sectors fell rapidly,
but whereas the local authorities had been on average 8 per cent
more expensive than private firms in 1922/3, by 1937/8 they had
become 25 per cent more when generating under CEB directions,
and more so when the comparison includes non-selected stations.
Disproportionate selection is evidence for comparative efficiencies
only if the CEB selected on the basis of efficiency and if the two
sectors faced comparable economic environments in the circumstances in which they previously operated. For example input
prices, especially coal prices, varied over the country, as did the
scale of operations.

Certainly the single supplier position of many electricity supply
companies appears to have given room for inefficient private
sector policies, such as spending on staff and perquisites in line
with predictions of managerial theories of the firm (e.g. Williamson 1964). In 1922/3 the numbers of administrative staff
used in the generation of a given quantity of electricity were
approximately the same for the two sectors. During the following
fifteen years administrative employment grew much more rapidly
in the private sector, so that by 1937/8 local authorities were
apparently selling almost twice as many units per administrative
employee. About one-third of private sector employees were
administrators by then, compared with one-fifth in the local
authority generating stations. This divergence in part may have
been due to changing optimal factor proportions. However it
could also have been due to the performance of some local authority enterprise administration by municipal servants. In part it
may have reflected overmanning by non-administrative employees
in municipal plants, dictated by electoral considerations in conditions of heavy unemployment. Another explanation might be

found in the inability of large municipal enterprises to pay management at rates comparable to the private sector for fear of upsetting differentials with the Town Hall. This allegedly provided an incentive for the best management to leave and lowered efficiency in the local authority sector (Hannah 1979: 319). No such constraint limited the payment of non-administrative labour.

Similar biases, it has been maintained, were built into the employment of capital. In the earliest comparison of the two sectors —a surprisingly sophisticated study of the industry of 1911— Ashley Baker (1915) claimed to find that the municipalities had lower costs, partly due to those enterprises not having to pay dividends. Because they could offer the local authority rate income as security, they could also borrow at lower interest rates than private companies, encouraging what has come to be known as the Averch–Johnson (1962) effect, an increased capital intensity. During the inter-war conditions of underutilized resources this may have been no bad thing. In any case the magnitudes were probably small. The Balfour Committee on Industry and Trade (1928–9) suggested the difference in the borrowing rates of the two sectors in the second half of the 1920s was about 0.25 per cent. The Electricity Commissioners had to sanction new capital for electricity generation for local authorities and were inclined to constrain excessive capital usage.

Sectoral divergences in coal usage may have occurred because of differences in buying policies caused by the usual multiple objectives of publicly owned industry (Aharoni 1981). An examination of the average prices of coal paid by electricity enterprises does reveal some curious cases. In 1937 Cardiff Corporation apparently paid 47 per cent more than the average net selling value of coal raised in the South Wales colliery district despite substantial bargaining power. The possibility arises that Cardiff was using its buying policy to ease the position of the major local industry. This suggests the need to look further for a general municipal sector difference in coal-buying policy.

The two sectors did not differ only in production. By charging high prices and thereby reducing consumption, a private electricity supplier could be less socially efficient, as Baker (1915) implied. Conversely it is possible that the municipal supplier could be less socially efficient if it charged excessively low prices, thereby diverting excessive resources to the sector. Consistent with

Peltzman's (1976) theory of regulation, there is some evidence of municipal price discrimination for electoral purposes which may have had this effect: municipal domestic electricity supplies were low priced relative to industrial and commercial uses, by comparison with the company supplies (see Table 6.2, which however does not control for the regional differences in demand and cost conditions). The welfare implications of such price discrimination are in general ambiguous, though final consumers undoubtedly benefited.

COST FUNCTIONS AND THE SAMPLE DATA IN
ELECTRICITY

Under competitive conditions the profitability of undertakings may give some indication of their efficiency. In the utility sectors we are looking at here, each undertaking had something of a local monopoly of supplies. Moreover tariffs were regulated, and then rather unevenly, by Parliament. It makes more sense therefore to assess efficiency in terms of the effectiveness with which resources are used. Two possibilities arise. One is to examine how much labour, capital, and materials are used in producing specific output and service levels and within that framework to assess whether public firms use more or less resources than private firms. This 'production function' approach requires data which are not

TABLE 6.2 *Average revenue per unit of electricity sold*

	1921–2		1925–6	
	Local authorities	Companies	Local authorities	Companies
Lighting and domestic	5.47	6.39	3.38	4.95
Public lighting	2.96	2.41	1.94	2.07
Traction	1.76	1.46	1.19	0.92
Power	1.80	1.52	1.01	0.97
Total revenue per unit	2.57	2.33	1.64	1.66

Source: Balfour Committee (1928–9: 320).

always available and this was the case here. An alternative is to use data on costs and examine how they are affected by output and the prices of factors of production. In fact if these latter prices are exogenously determined—outside the control of individual firms—then the results from the 'cost function' approach convey much the same information as the production function. For the gas and electricity industries under consideration here the main factors of production were coal, labour, and capital, and to a large extent coal prices, wage rates, the price of capital goods, and interest rates were all determined by economy-level forces. In fact the level of demand and the prices of electricity and gas were not under the complete control of individual undertakings so that the level of output is also mainly an exogenous vehicle for these undertakings, all of which is convenient for purposes of statistical analysis.

The broad approach is then to assess how costs vary with the ownership of firms having controlled for all the other influences on costs. To do this we estimate a cost function which in the simplest case might be written as $C = f(Q, W)$, where C is total cost, Q is output, and W is factor prices. That is one takes say a cross-section of undertakings—and here we have chosen samples from 1897/8 for gas and 1937 for electricity—and examines across such samples how costs vary with the level of output and factor price. The differences in output, costs, and factor prices across the sample of firms are assumed to indicate the way costs would vary if any one firm experienced such variations in output and factor prices. Finally the effect of whether a firm is public or private is estimated by seeing how the above cost function shifts as one moves from the subsample of private firms to the subsample of public firms. Further explanation of the method used and the data requires that we look at each industry in turn.

Efficient electricity generating stations will minimize the costs of producing any particular output, given factor prices. The impact of the institutional and regulatory framework of the industry, already described, may have been to shift the entire cost function. Particular classes of generating stations—CEB selected or non-selected or private or local authority—may have been absolutely more efficient than others. In addition, biases in factor usage discussed in the preceding section can be regarded as consequences of decision takers' uses of shadow prices that differ from observed prices. If such behaviour was important then a comparison of the cost functions of two sectors, one of which experiences these biases, will yield different estimates for the role of the relevant factor prices. According to the staff and perquisites model, the private sector should have experienced a bigger effect from the administrative salary variable, and a prediction of the use of electricity undertakings as instruments of municipal employment policy is that the effect of increases in wage rates would be larger in the local authority sector.

Turning now to the detailed determinants of costs, in the case of electricity an appropriate general form of the cost function would be $C = f(Q, M, V, W)$, where C represents production costs per period, Q units of electricity generated in that period, M maximum load during the period, V length of production time used in the period, and W factor prices. The three dimensions to output captured in our variables accord approximately with Alchian's (1959) discussion of the multi-dimensional nature of cost, though since his examples all appear to concern discrete-quantity commodities, the parallel is not exact. Thus our output measure (Q, in kilowatt-hours) can be thought of as a volume to be supplied over the year, the precise effect on costs being dependent on the time profile and maximum load variables. The expectation is that increases in volume or maximum load raise total costs. A shorter operation period should reduce total costs of a given maximum load and annual output by allowing the use of generating sets at full capacity, and therefore at maximum efficiency. A longer period of operation entails sets running, during parts of the year, at less than the rate for which they were designed, *ceteris paribus*.

Maximum load and production time per period may be regarded as exogenous variables because the pattern of demand exercised an independent influence on costs before a fully efficient national, rather than regionally linked, grid was established, as recognized by earlier British studies (Baker 1915; Lomax 1952). The difficulty of storage means that, although compared with other commodities electricity is a very homogeneous product, it is nevertheless not completely so, because of the crucial role of the time at which it is to be supplied. At the end of the inter-war years an expert on the industry wrote: 'From a commercial point of view therefore the...cheapness with which an undertaking can afford to supply electricity depends very largely on the magnitude of its load factor' (Parsons 1939: 209). Load factor is defined as units generated (output) divided by maximum load multiplied by the number of hours operated. Our inclusion of a maximum load variable in the cost function alongside output and the output time schedule variable therefore captures the influence of load factor on costs. Finally there is the question of factor prices. American economists from Nerlove (1963) to Pescatrice and Trapani (1980) have emphasized the possibilities of factor substitution in electricity generation in response to factor price changes. By contrast, analysis of the British industry by Johnston (1960) assumed factor prices invariant across the industry at any moment in time, while Hart and Chawla (1970) adopted a Leontief Production function. We prefer to leave open the possibility of factor substitution.

In testing whether there were significant differences in private and public electricity generation cost functions under the inter-war regulatory system one has to choose a period when the effects of the CEB had fully worked through, when the grid was nearing completion. For these reasons the performance was tested on cross-section data for 1937. All observations on plants which could reasonably be said to be appropriate to the predominant technological and institutional framework were included. On this basis the following were excluded:

- all technologies except pure steam generation (oil engines, water power, waste destruction/steam, etc.);
- all stations generating for railway or tramway operations (London Transport, etc.);
- the joint electricity authorities;
- very small output stations, being those with a maximum load of less than 1,000 kilowatts, or generating fewer than 100, 000 kilowatt-hours in the relevant year; most of the very small stations were just disappearing at the time of our sample.

It is likely that differences in technology have been minimized though it was not possible to allow for different vintages of plant because the data are not available. Since ever larger stations were being built scale economy estimates based upon total output

are likely also to incorporate vintage effects, a point which undoubtedly affects some of the other cross-section studies cited
earlier.

The sample, thus delimited, includes both 'selected' and 'non-
selected' stations, both local authority and company stations, both
continuously and intermittently run stations, 171 observations
in all, for 1937. Data sources and methods of construction are
detailed in Appendix 6.1. Working costs of generation broken
down into fuel, wage and salary, and repairs and maintenance
components were readily available. Capital costs were not. Rather
than ignore them entirely we used the nominal value of plant
and machinery as the basis for calculating this variable where
we used it. The price of capital was assumed constant across
all observations, because the small geographical area implies
few differences in construction costs by comparison with the
United States. The price or average value of coal used by each
power station could be inferred from the station fuel bills and
fuel efficiency coefficients. Salaries were determined by national
agreement according to the size of the power station. Wages also
were largely set by national bargaining, which recognized thirteen
districts in which there were usually three rates depending upon
the urban/rural classification of the site. When London is excluded
there was little variation in the hourly rate between regions in
1937. The outdoor labourer's hourly rate ranged from 15.00d. in
district 7 (East Midlands)to 13.05d in district 8 (East Coast)
with a mean of 14.05d. The London district rate was 17.03d.
Employment categories showed different patterns of interregional
variation which increases the difficulty of choosing an average
wage. We therefore merely used a dummy variable for wages to
distinguish the London district, with its 15−20 per cent premium,
from the rest of the country.

METHODS OF ANALYSIS AND BASIC DATA FOR GAS

The total costs of a gas plant are likely to be affected by the
quality of gas produced as well as its quantity; here we include
candlepower as a reflection of its illuminating properties. Other
things being equal technical progress would lower the costs of

producing any given quantity and in this study an attempt is made to reflect this in measures of the age of plant or the number of years since renovation and expansion had taken place. Turning now to distribution costs, each consumer will occasion a certain amount of costs associated with pipes, connections, and repairs. Thus plants of the same vintage and same output may nevertheless be associated with different total costs for the undertakings if the number of consumers varies. The location of consumers will also affect the size of the distribution network and the costs of servicing that network. The mileage of the distribution mains of a gas undertaking will be some reflection of the dispersal of consumers. However undertakings with the same number of consumers and the same mileage of distribution mains may nevertheless have different distribution costs when the gas mains cover a large geographical area rather than being concentrated on two sides of a number of adjacent streets. In addition to the number of consumers a relevant variable would therefore be the distribution mains mileage per square mile of the towns served or alternatively a population density variable. Finally costs will vary with the prices paid for inputs. The levels of wage rates, coal prices, and interest rates paid on loans are taken as the key factor prices likely to influence costs. Thus in a very general form the annual costs of a gas enterprise may be represented as $C = f(Y, N, CP, M, I, Pw, Pt, Pk, D)$, where Y is gas made in cubic feet, N is the number of consumers, CP is the candlepower of the gas, M is population density, I is the age of the plant, Pw the wage rate, Pt the price of coal, Pk the interest rate on loans, and D is a dummy variable which takes a value of one for public firms and zero for private.

Data are therefore required on all cost categories, on the various dimensions of output, and on factor prices. The best source proved to be the Analyses of Gas Accounts in the weekly *Gas World*. For 1897/8 there are detailed financial and operating data on three London companies, thirteen other private companies, and nineteen local authority-owned undertakings. Details are given in Appendix 6.1. It was possible to calculate the annual cost of each of these enterprises and the mean values are shown in Table 6.3. Measured by their annual cost the size of the average London gas company, at nearly £2 million, was some ten times that of the average provincial private gas company, which was of roughly the same size as the average publicly owned enterprise. The raw data

TABLE 6.3 *Costs of a gas enterprise in 1898* (mean values in £)

	London companies	Other private	Public
1. Labour costs	249,009	24,389	22,062
(Wages and salaries)	(12.6%)	(13.9%)	(13.7%)
2. Other operating costs			
Coal	615,865	55,899	54,184
Other	426,290	35,162	32,484
Total	1,042,155	91,061	86,668
	(52.8%)	(51.9%)	(54.0%)
3. Capital costs			
Capital value	6,815,595	599,468	517,194
Annual capital			
cost = 10% value	681,559	59,947	51,719
	(34.6%)	(34.2%)	(32.2%)
Total cost	1,972,723	175,397	160,449
	(100%)	(100%)	(100%)

Source: See text.

on wages and salaries in manufacture, in distribution, and for management and directors were combined to yield the figures for labour costs, which were only one-eighth of total costs. Other operating costs included repair and maintenance of plant and the distribution network, servicing public lamps, rents, rates, other taxes, etc.

Capital costs are a traditionally difficult area. The *Gas World* source included an estimate of the book capital value of the works though we have no way of assessing how far this corresponded to a market valuation of the assets. An annual capital cost figure should ideally incorporate a measure of the annual decline in the market value of assets plus a rate of interest or profit on that used-up capital. In Table 6.3 a rough proxy to this is taken as 10 per cent of the capital value. An alternative is to allow for the differing rates of interest paid by the undertakings for their loan capital and the cost function is estimated later in these two alternative forms. The figure of 10 per cent happens to be double the highest loan rate of interest in the sample and so a crude allowance for the varying interest rates might be to take each undertaking's annual capital costs as $2rk$ where k is the capital value of works and r is the interest rate. This estimate of capital costs improved the statistical fit, so even though the effect was slight this version of the result is quoted in the later sections of the chapter. Either way the mean shares of the three cost categories do not vary greatly between the different categories of enterprises identified in Table 6.3.

The *Gas World* data also include various dimensions of the output of the gas undertakings and the mean values are shown in Table 6.4. In the sample the average public firm, though similar to the provincial private company in the quantity of gas produced and in its total cost, has almost twice the number of consumers, a feature well established in the contemporaneous literature and deemed to reflect the lower average prices charged by the public firms. The annual cost of gas per consumer in the public firms, at £4.3, is therefore well below the figure for provincial gas companies and also below the average for the London companies. The consumer receiving supplies from the private companies on average however acquired considerably larger quantities. Even so, cost per million cubic feet of gas for the private companies, at £1,691, was some 15 per cent higher than for the public firms and the quality of gas as measured by candlepower, or the spread of consumers as indicated by the population density data, do not detract from that.

It is clear from Table 6.4 that some of the reasons for that difference may lie simply in the level of input prices. The *Gas World* figures include estimates for each enterprise of expenditure on coal and tonnage used, from which was deduced a figure for the average coal price per ton for each enterprise and this was used as the factor price corresponding to non-labour operating costs. The price of capital in Table 6.3 refers to the interest rate paid on loans. The Board of Trade returns include figures on various categories of loans outstanding and the interest rate on each. A weighted average was calculated for each enterprise. Wage rates for each enterprise, that is on a town basis, proved the most difficult data problem. The weekly *Gas World* did not include relevant data. From 1893, Board of Trade wage data included figures for 'rates of wages paid to workers in and about gas works'. Unfortunately the regions identified were too large for this study of town gasworks. However the regional variation in these wages is highly correlated with the Board of Trade engineering wage data for fitters and turners, which are available at a more

TABLE 6.4 *Gas unit costs and factor prices in 1898*

	London companies	Other private	All private	Public	All pooled
Annual cost of a gas enterprise in £ million	1.972	0.175	0.512	0.160	0.321
Number of consumers	165,704	19,651	47,036	36,712	41,432
Cost per consumer in £	11.9	8.9	10.9	4.3	7.7
Gas made in million cubic feet	116.02	104.8	302.7	109.3	197.7
Gas made per consumer in thousand cu. ft.	7.0	5.3	6.4	2.9	4.8
Cost per million cubic feet in £	1,700	1,669	1,691	1,465	1,621
Candlepower	16	15.9	15.9	19.4	17.8
Length of distribution					
Mains in miles	1,052	218	375	176	267
Population density (inhabitants per acre)	60.6	19.5	26.9	20.3	23.3
Wage rate (shillings per week)	38.0	36.4	36.7	33.6	35.0
Price of coal in £ per ton	0.56	0.65	0.63	0.49	0.55
Price of capital (% interest rate on loans)	4.11	4.02	4.04	3.44	3.71
Technology vintage of plant (age in years)	33	26.2	27.5	20.9	23.9

Source: See text.

local level. The data for turners were therefore used in this study as a proxy for gasworks wage rates. Full details are given in Appendix 6.1.

The northern industrial cities were often served by municipally owned enterprises. Table 6.4 suggests that the average publicly owned gas undertaking was faced with lower wage rates than the average private company. The public firms were also favoured, in this sense, in terms of the average price they paid for coal and the average interest rate on loans. The precise effect on costs will be examined in the econometric analysis. Similarly another source of the unit cost differences between public and private may be the vintage of plant used. Precise data on this were not available but the proxy measure whose mean values are shown in Table 6.4 is an estimate for each undertaking of the weighted average age of its loan stock. Needless to say these are very rough data indeed. The cost figures in Table 6.3 and 6.4 are consistent with those quoted by Matthews (1986) for 1883 and 1914 for samples of local authorities and private gas undertakings. On their own, however, such data can tell us little about performance unless one controls as precisely as possible for variables, other than ownership, which affect costs. We now do this by estimating the cost function.

RESULTS AND CONCLUSIONS

The adopted approach provides insights on scale economies, substitutability between factors, as well as the role of ownership and related regulatory features. Details of the statistical analysis are given in Appendices 6.2 and 6.3. Here we synthesize the main results and conclusions. Gas is taken first because the issues were in some respects more straightforward.

The technology of gas production towards the turn of the century was such that labour costs in production were less than 15 per cent of total costs. Coal was an important item and the elasticity of total cost with respect to coal prices was upward of 0.3. The evidence supports the expectation that the demand for each factor of production is inversely related to its price—though the effects were sometimes small and in all cases not statistically significant. Similarly there is evidence of substitutability between factors of production. A rise of 10 per cent in the ratio of wage rates to coal prices is associated with a rise of 1.3 per cent in the ratio of coal usage to labour employed. As labour becomes relatively more costly, there is substitution towards technologies which are more capital intensive and more coal intensive, though again the latter effect is small and the former not statistically significant.

The findings with respect to returns to scale and the role of ownership were more clear. For towns with the same population density, the average cost curve was U-shaped, as assumed in many economics texts. That is, as total gas production increased average costs fell initially and these scale economies were quite considerable; but they became exhausted once production approached 130 million cubic feet per annum. As may be seen from Table 6.4 this was just above the mean size of all provincial undertakings. Thus the bigger provincial undertakings, but especially the large London undertakings, were operating in an output range where average costs were rising. However, all this holds only for towns of the same density. The results indicate that a higher density shifts the whole average cost function downwards. Thus large volume production involves lower average costs only if population density is high.

Although the share of capital in total costs was, on average, less in municipally owned enterprises, when account is taken of the level of factor prices, including interest rates, the share is at a statistically significant higher level. Costs per cubic foot of gas were some 15 per cent lower in municipal enterprises but after standardizing for factor prices, and population density, as well as quantity of gas, the municipal enterprises had total costs only 1 per cent lower than private companies. An important element of this appears to be the use of plants of more modern vintage; such plants have a significant impact in lowering total costs and the bias is towards capital saving. The difference in costs between municipal and private is however small and was not in fact statistically significant. The evidence for this industry in this period is therefore that public firms were just as cost effective as private companies.

In the case of the electricity sample, the number of consumers and population density near to the generating plant do not have the same importance since many plants were supplying the CEB grid. In the first attempts at estimating the determinants of costs the focus was operating costs, on the grounds that the capital cost data were less reliable. In fact, under certain stringent conditions the percentage response of total costs to output and factor price changes will be the same as the percentage response of operating costs (cf. Foreman-Peck and Waterson 1984). The results indicate an elasticity of cost with respect to coal prices of the order of 0.36, that is very similar to the gas case. The results also indicate again a U-shaped average cost function—in this case if load factors and period of operation are held constant. That is, average working costs fall initially as total kilowatt-hours produced per annum rise; these economies eventually disappear, though this occurs well beyond the general operating regimes of 1937. For any given annual output average costs are lower the shorter the period of operation since the capacity is being used nearer to its design level. Also any given output and period of operation involved lower average costs the smaller was the maximum load during the year, since the load factor would be so much higher. A 10 per cent reduction in maximum load reduced average costs by 3 per cent. The broad characteristics of the cost functions are illustrated in Fig. 6.1.

There were four institutional categories that could be analysed in electricity supply: selected companies, non-selected companies, selected municipal, non-selected municipal. These different categories showed no significant differences in terms of the effect of wage rates or salaries or coal prices on costs. They do however affect costs in aggregate, that is they do shift the cost function. Stations selected by the CEB had costs some 20 per cent less than the non-selected stations, a piece of evidence against the view that regulation necessarily increases costs. The company stations had costs 20 per cent lower than the municipals. Further analysis revealed that selected municipals had the same costs as selected companies. It was the non-selected municipals which in effect gave a 'longer tail' than the companies. The best municipals were on a par with the best companies and do not appear to show any biases towards the employment of particular factors of production. Nevertheless, in the absence of CEB regulation the local authority sector would have tended to be less efficient than the private sector. The full results are presented in Appendix 6.2; more sophisticated statistical work and some attempts to evaluate total

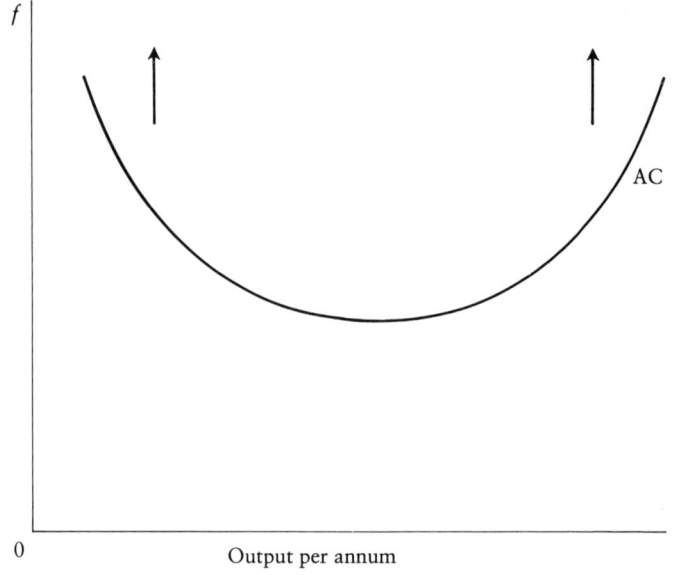

Note: AC function shifts upwards in electricity the longer the period of operation, the bigger the maximum load, and when the sample shifts from CEB-selected to non-selected. AC function shifts upwards in gas the smaller the population density.

FIG. 6.1 Average cost functions in electricity and gas

costs rather than just working costs do not significantly affect the above judgement. There was no systematic tendency for the price paid for coal to vary with the type of generator.

In broad terms then the evidence is consistent with the CEB regulation of the generating system providing efficiency gains. The inter-war regulatory system was probably helpful because it increased contestability relative to the pre-1914 organization of the industry (and indeed relative to the later nationalized industry). If any selected stations could reduce their costs to such an extent that their total costs, paid by the CEB, were less than the marginal costs of an inefficient municipal undertaking in the tail of the distribution, then the CEB had the power to close down the tail undertaking. For new entry the CEB could buy from all kinds of suppliers (authorized undertakings, newly promoted parliamentary companies, aluminium companies, etc.) as well as selling to them. In principle then, new entry with access to the grid was possible. The CEB could, and did, very occasionally organize new entry itself, though usually it preferred to talk to authorized undertakings and persuade them to bid for a new station. This preference seems to have stemmed from the need for a minimum existing expertise and the benefits of technical integration with the existing transmission and distribution network, given the limited number of sites.

The results therefore seem to provide some justification for the liberalization provisions of the later 1983 Energy Act. On the one hand, the similarity of private and municipal cost functions within the regulated system suggests that privatization alone may not confer benefits. On the other hand, the evidence from those undertakings outside the CEB nexus compared with those within may be taken to imply that an increase in contestability, limited private sector competition with a group of public concerns, is beneficial.

APPENDIX 6.1
Data Sources

Electricity Data Sources

Most of the data including units generated, working costs, and maximum load are obtained from the Electricity Commissioners' publications. However it should be noted that definitions differ between the two principal sources. In *Financial and Engineering Statistics*, maximum load on a station is defined to include units 'bought in' from the system for resale, as well as units generated, whereas (the appropriate definition for our purposes) in *The Generation of Electricity of G.B.* units 'bought in' are excluded. Both sources give company data on a calendar year basis, but *Financial and Engineering Statistics* gives local authority data according to the financial year, ending in March. Because the unit cost data and (meaningful) maximum load data are on a calendar year basis, we used calendar year output.

To capture the output scheduling/time profile variable, we used a dummy variable taking the value one when the station operated for more than 6,000 hours per year (based upon the Electricity Commissioners' classification using four categories) and zero otherwise, the idea being that stations working over 6,000 hours per year can be considered as being in more or less continuous operation.

The coal price index is for the financial year, but since coal was bought on long-term contract and there is a nine-month overlap with the calendar year, the likely error is minuscule. The index was constructed from fuel consumption per unit of output (defined differently in the two sources) and fuel bills for each station. The coal price series obtained correlated overall quite closely with an index constructed from area pit-head average values and coal transport costs, although there are some striking discrepancies. As a salaries index we used the Shift Charge Engineer's salary from *Electrical Review* (12 July, 1935), 53, ranging from £242 at the smallest to £576 at the largest station, and power station capacity, taken from maximum load in *The Generation of Electricity in Great Britain*. Capital costs were obtained as indicated in the text from *Financial and Engineering Statistics*. In the case of multi-plant firms, capital costs of individual plants were allocated by dividing plant-generating capacity by total firm capacity and multiplying firm plant and machinery costs by this fraction.

Gas Data

1. The main source was the weekly *Gas World* (*GW*). For the broad period under consideration it was found that the best data coverage for both public and private undertakings was the year 1898. The accounts for the private companies were generally for the year ended June 1898 and for municipal enterprises it was March. Further data on the sample were obtained from the return published by the Board of Trade (BoT 1899).

2. Data definitions were as follows:

(*a*) *Measures of output*: gas made: thousand cubic feet of gas made (i.e. gas sold, gas used on works, and gas unaccounted for) (*GW*).
Candlepower: illuminating power of gas produced, as confirmed by Board of Trade inspectors (*GW* and BoT).
Number of consumers: total number of private customers (*GW* and BoT).
Mains mileage: total recorded mains mileage (*GW* and BoT).
Population density: inhabitants per acre (1901 Census of Population: England and Wales summary table II and Census of Scotland table I).

(*b*) *Factor shares and total cost*: C: total cost measured as the gross cost of gas manufacture plus 10 per cent, or alternative percentages, of the capital value of the works (*GW*).

S_w: the total of all payments to labour (wages, salaries, and directors' fees) for manufacture, distribution, payment collection, and management, as a proportion of total cost (*GW*).

S_k: 10 per cent, or alternative percentages, of the capital value of the works as a proportion of total cost (*GW*).

S_t: the total of all remaining cost headings as a proportion of total cost (*GW*).

(*c*) *Factor prices*: P_w: price of labour. See para. 3 below.

P_k: price of capital. The Board of Trade returns give details of all issued loan stock and the rates of interest payable on each. Weighted averages of these rates were taken, the amounts of each issue being used as the weights (BoT).

P_t: price of other inputs. As the principal other input was coal, the total

TABLE A.6.1 *Comparison of gas and engineering wages 1885–1886*

	R	Rank R	t
Gas workers to fitters	0.800	0.467	1.49
Gas workers to turners	0.877	0.697	2.75

Notes: Critical R (difference from zero, at 0.01 significance level, 8*df*) = 0.765; critical *t* (0.05 significance level, 8*df*) = 2.31.

TABLE A.6.2 *Sources of gas data*

Municipal	Year ended	Wages town
Blackburn Corporation	25 Mar. 1898	Bolton
Bolton Corporation	31 Mar. 1898	Bolton
Bradford Corporation	31 Mar. 1898	Bradford
Carlisle Corporation	30 June 1898	Preston
Darwen Corporation	31 Mar. 1898	Bolton
Dundee Gas Commissioners	30 Apr. 1898	Dundee
Dunfermline Corporation	15 May 1898	Edinburgh
Edinburgh and Leith Corporation	15 May 1898	Edinburgh
Glasgow Corporation	31 May 1898	Glasgow
Lancaster Corporation	25 Mar. 1898	Preston
Manchester Corporation	31 Mar. 1898	Manchester
Nottingham Corporation	31 Mar. 1898	Nottingham
Oldham Corporation	25 Mar. 1898	Oldham
Salford Corporation	31 Mar. 1898	Manchester
Stafford Corporation	31 Mar. 1898	Derby
Stoke-on-Trent Corporation	31 Mar. 1898	Derby
West Bromwich Corporation	31 Mar. 1898	Wolverhampton
Widnes Corporation	31 Mar. 1898	Liverpool
Wigan Corporation	31 Mar. 1898	Wigan
Private		
Alliance & Dublin Consumers Gas Co.	30 June 1898	Dublin
Barnet District Gas & Water Co.	30 June 1898	London
Brighton & Hove General Gas Co.	30 June 1898	Brighton
Brentford Gas Co.	30 June 1898	London
Bristol Gas Co.	30 June 1898	Bristol
Bromley Gas Consumers' Co.	30 June 1898	London
Commercial Gas Co.	30 June 1898	London
Croydon Commercial Gas & Coke Co.	30 June 1898	London
Crystal Palace District Gas Co.	30 June 1898	London
Gas Light & Coke Co.	30 June 1898	London
Harrow & Stanmore Gas Co.	30 June 1898	London
Hastings & St Leonards Gas VCo.	30 June 1898	Brighton
Newcastle-upon-Tyne & Gateshead Gas Co.	31 Dec. 1897	Newcastle
Sheffield United Gas Light Co.	30 June 1898	Sheffield
South Metropolitan Gas Co.	30 June 1898	London
Tottenham & Edmonton Gas Light Coke Co.	30 June 1898	London

amount spent on coal was divided by the tonnage of coal carbonized to arrive at an average cost per ton of coal used (GW).

(d) *Index of technology (I)*: In the absence of any other measure, an attempt was made to estimate the average age of plant by using the issue data of loan stock. A weighted average date was constructed which was then subtracted from 1898 to give an average estimated age of capital.

3. A major data problem was wage rates, since though *Gas World* included figures on outlays on wages and salaries it did not include employment data. In 1892 BoT published *Return of Rates of Wages paid by Local Authorities and Private Companies to Police and Workpeople Employed on Roads, etc. and at Gas and Water Works*. The regions identified were too large to be useful for a study of town gas undertakings. In 1893 the BoT started publishing its annual *Report on Standard Time Rates of Wages*. This included data on fitters' and turners' wages at a local level which closely correlated with the gas wages figures. Comparing 1885 gas wage data and 1886 engineering wage data over regions the results were as shown in Table A.6.1.

There does therefore appear to be a statistically significant correlation and rank correlation between the regional wage distribution of gas workers and engineering turners. The use of time rate of wages data for engineering turners in 1898 as a proxy for the unavailable data on the rate of wages of gas workers in 1898 seems justifiable.

4. The undertakings, the exact financial accounting year in question, and the source of wages data were as shown in Table A.6.2.

APPENDIX 6.2
The Cost Function for Electricity Supply

Estimation of the electricity model in Chapter 6 requires the adoption of some particular form of the cost function. Following Christensen and Greene (1976) and Pescatrice and Trapani (1980), it was decided to use the translog form which is fairly general, including the variable returns to scale generalized Cobb–Douglas form as a special case. A possible alternative, Diewert's (1971) generalized Leontief function, is in some ways attractive, but provides estimation difficulties when scale economies are introduced, which is essential where electricity generation is concerned.

The basic relationship we choose then is the translog unit cost function, modified to incorporate the multidimensional nature of output:

$$c - q = \alpha_o + \alpha_q q + \tfrac{1}{2}\alpha_{qq}q^2 + \beta_m m + \tfrac{1}{2}\beta_{mm}m^2 + \theta_v v + \tfrac{1}{2}\theta_{vv}v^2$$

$$+ \sum_i \alpha_i w_i + \tfrac{1}{2}\sum_i \sum_j \gamma_{ij} w_i w_j + \sum_i \gamma_{qi} q w_i$$

$$+ \sum_i \lambda_{mi} m w_i + \sum_i \eta_{vi} v w_i + \mu_{qm} q m + \mu_{qv} q v$$

$$+ \mu_{mv} m v + D\delta + \varepsilon, \tag{1}$$

where lower-case roman letters denote natural logarithms of the variables defined in Chapter 6, α, β, θ, γ, λ, η, and μ (with subscripts) denote parameters, and ε is the random error term. D is a vector of firm-type dummy variables with parameter vector δ. Homogeneity of degree one in prices implies restrictions on the parameters, but since we lack a price index for one component (repairs and maintenance), the restriction is not imposed in the function we estimate. The translog function is a second-order approximation to any arbitrary cost function and imposes very few restrictions on the data (at the expense of a large number of coefficients). However, if the evidence is consistent with the assumption of homotheticity, the scale coefficient for working costs will not differ from those for total costs (cf. Foreman-Peck and Waterson 1984).

Plant-level cost functions were estimated for the 1937 electricity generating industry first using ordinary least squares regressions with working cost data as dependent variable. If the cost function is homothetic, OLS is an efficient technique and, in addition, the estimates give us considerable insight into the nature of the total cost function. Even if it is not strictly homothetic, OLS has the advantages of simplicity and ease of interpretation. In particular, it is easier to test biases towards particular factors than in more complex forms. We estimated a variable returns to scale homothetic equation. On the basis of an *F* test the hypothesis that the excluded additional terms of the translog equation were non-zero was rejected. Similar tests involving the addition of various subsets of the rejected coefficients also found the additional variables insignificant.

If there were no impact of ownership or regulation on electricity generating costs then, equation (i) of Table A.6.3 would provide a good characterization of the data; it certainly has a statistically good fit for cross-section data. Equation (i) shows that returns to scale diminish as output increases and, in marked contrast to the American studies cited earlier, maximum load is an important influence on costs. The continuous operation of the station also makes a difference, offering a second reason why the time profile of supply matters.

In the case of the company/local authority split, *F* tests establish that we cannot reject the hypothesis of equal slope coefficients and the only

TABLE A.6.3 *Plant cost functions for electricity generation in Britain during 1937* (171 plants)

Dependent variable	(i) OLS log per unit working costs	(ii) OLS log per unit working costs	(iii) GLS log per unit working costs	(iv) OLS log per unit total costs (estimate)[a]
Constant	0.8595	0.1000	8.609[b]	0.0906
	(2.073)	(2.004)	(1.019)	(1.786)
Log output	−0.8572[b]	−0.8568[b]	−0.9052[b]	−1.092[b]
	(0.0754)	(0.0744)	(0.1619)	(0.0663)
(Log output)^2	0.0159[b]	0.0155[b]	0.0188	0.0203[b]
	(0.0039)	(0.0040)	(0.0124)	(0.0035)
Log max. load	0.2989[b]	0.3267[b]	0.0428	0.4080[b]
	(0.0745)	(0.0711)	(0.3125)	(0.0634)
Continuous operation dummy	0.1643[b]	0.1605[b]	0.1706[b]	0.1309[b]
	(0.0508)	(0.0478)	(0.0446)	(0.0426)
Log coal price	0.3859[b]	0.3646[b]	0.1169	0.2119[b]
	(0.0843)	(0.0806)	(0.2642)	(0.0718)
Log salaries	0.1595	0.2933	2.0889	0.6067
	(0.4692)	(0.4436)	(0.2198)	(0.3953)
Log wages (London dummy)	0.1595[b]	0.1375[b]	2.780	0.1197[b]
	(0.0460)	(0.0444)	(1.656)	(0.0395)
CEB-selected dummy		−0.2128[b]	−0.1550[b]	−0.1172[b]
		(0.0507)	(0.0456)	(0.0452)
Company dummy		−0.2396[b]	−0.1885[b]	−0.2170[b]
		(0.0690)	(0.0626)	(0.0615)

TABLE A.6.3 *Continued*

Dependent variable	(i) OLS log per unit working costs	(ii) OLS log per unit working costs	(iii) GLS log per unit working costs	(iv) OLS log per unit total costs (estimate)[a]
Selected company dummy		0.02232[b] (0.0801)	0.01784[b] (0.0723)	0.02379[b] (0.0714)
(Log coal price)²			0.0612 (0.0427)	
(Log coal price × log salaries/wages)			−0.0363[b] (0.0097)	
(Log salaries)²			0.0493[c] (0.0225)	
(Log salaries × log wages)			−0.4113 (0.2824)	
(Log output × log coal price)			0.1013[b] (0.0070)	
(Log output × log salaries/wages)			−0.0349[b] (0.0026)	
(Log max. load × log output)			−0.0098 (0.0350)	
(Log max. load)²			0.0137 (0.0296)	
(Log max. load × log coal price)			−0.0828[b] (0.0111)	
(Log max. load × log salaries/weges)			0.0243[b] (0.0045)	
R^2	0.9330	0.9423	0.9682	0.9667

Notes: Standard errors in parentheses; Col. heads consist 1 equation number and estimation method.

[a] See text.
[b] Significantly different from zero at better than 1% level.
[c] At 5% level.

statistically significant difference is in the intercept term; companies have a significantly lower intercept. In particular, standard tests establish that the partial effect on costs of an increase in wage rates or of an increase in coal prices is no different as between companies and local authorities, which is evidence against apparently plausible hypotheses developed earlier. However, there is weak evidence that the private companies' salary coefficient is significantly higher than that for local authorities, though the position is complicated because this result is sensitive to precise formulation, and because of multicollinearity problems. In the case of the selected/non-selected split, tests show that although the intercept is significantly lower for those selected than for those not selected, there is otherwise no difference between the two groups.

Ownership and grid supply status both influence efficiency as measured in the cost function, and therefore potentially there are four different intercepts. Consequently, in subsequent work we incorporate a 'selected company' dummy as well as a 'selected' dummy and a 'company' dummy, leaving 'unselected corporation' as the base case. Hence we reach the specification in equation (ii). The variables employed in (ii) explain the data very fully. The coefficients on the price and output variables are of expected sign and seem to be about the right magnitude, and all except one are highly significant. They seem pretty robust to specification changes. The elasticity of unit costs with respect to coal price is around 0.36, which is probably about what would be expected given coal's share of working costs. The sign on the wage dummy is correct and, as expected from cost shares, is considerably smaller than the coal price elasticity. The salary variable, which is statistically insignificant, suffers from multicollinearity problems. Its log has a zero order correlation with the log of maximum load of 0.9729, and a high correlation also with output.

The time pattern of output is a significant influence on costs. *For a given output*, a 10 per cent increase in maximum load increases working costs about 3.3 per cent. For a given output, and a given maximum load, continuous operations increase unit working costs by about 16 per cent. Given maximum load and output, imposing continuous operation means the plant finds itself with a greater range of operating conditions whilst supplying electricity.

The output and output squared terms indicate strong scale economies based upon total volume, though again care is needed in interpretation here. We evaluate scale economies on the basis of keeping load factor, as opposed to maximum load, constant, for else a point would come when load factor became impossibly high. On this basis, and using Christensen and Greene's (1976) measure, $SCE = 1 - \partial \ln C / \partial \ln Q$, in equation (ii) scale economies are 0.211 at the mean value of output volume, a figure broadly comparable with Christensen and Greene's results. Scale economies tail off substantially as output volume rises. However, the minimum average cost is reached (according to the point estimates in the table) well beyond 1937 operating regions. It must be remembered that vintage effects may be being picked up as scale economy effects though.

Some improvement in the efficiency of the equations may emerge from estimating the cost share equations *alongside* the cost function. It is possible to identify two cost shares and their corresponding prices from the data: the share of coal and the share of wages and salaries. If we estimate these share equations alongside the cost function, we must take account of two major factors. First, the coefficients on variables in the

share equations obtained by logarithmic differentiation of (1) coincide
with coefficients (on other variables) in the cost function. To take the case
of factor j, using Shepard's lemma and writing input quantity as X_j, share
as S_j, we have:

$$\frac{\partial \ln C}{\partial \ln W_j} = \frac{W_j X_j}{C} = S_j$$

So that from (1):

$$S_j = \alpha_j + \sum_i \gamma_{ij} w_i + \gamma_{qj} q + \lambda_{mj} m + \eta_{vj} v \qquad (2)$$

Secondly, although (2) has no explicit error term (and although the error
term is *not* that on (1)), there is likely to be some association for each
station between the error term in (1) and that in (2) and the other share
equation (call it (3)). Hence in estimating (1)–(3) as a system, OLS is no
longer an efficient technique: GLS is appropriate. A third, minor, point
also emerges: some slight amalgamation of coefficients must occur to
allow for the fact that we have only the share of salaried and waged staff
together.

The resultant estimates are not reported in full: more detail on the
methods is given in Foreman-Peck and Waterson (1984). Groups of
coefficients were tested to examine whether, first, functional form (1) was
sufficient, and secondly (assuming a negative answer), whether all the
various groupings of coefficients were required. It is clear from the tests
that the group of cross-terms between variable V and all others were not
required; they added virtually nothing to the explanation. On the other
hand, both the cross-terms with maximum load and the cross-terms with
output added significantly to the explanatory power. It is in this form that
the results are reported in the table as equation (iii).

Unfortunately, equation (iii) is difficult to interpret, partly because of
multicollinearity problems in the transformed data set. These particularly
affect maximum load, which is highly correlated with several variables,
and combinations of it with itself and output. Hence many of the variables
lose significance. If we estimate scale economies using point estimates on
this formulation (without regard to statistical significance), we obtain a
result close to the earlier values, at 0.214. Taking only statistically significant coefficients into account results in a ridiculously high value (0.917),
which is an indication of the interpretation difficulties.

The most important change in equation (iii) over equation (ii) is in the
price terms. Factor prices do still influence costs. However the equation
shows that the price impacts are not *direct*, but that they are different
for different sized plants. Coal price changes become relatively more
important as output rises (which goes against the maintained assumption

of homotheticity in equation (ii)), for example. This probably arises because larger generating sets do not require proportionately as many operators (so that coal becomes a relatively more important item of expenditure). The effect of a larger maximum load is the reverse; with load *factor* constant, the additional impact of coal price at higher output levels is less marked when load factor is low. The other important interaction is through the cross-price term, suggesting that the higher are wages/salaries, the lesser impact a rise in coal prices has, which is in accord with general theoretical considerations.

Finally, we may note that the firm-type dummy variables are unaffected by the multicollinearity problems, and that they escape unscathed in this more complex estimation. CEB selection appears to be slightly less cost-reducing than previously, as does the effect of being a company. However it remains true that selected companies and selected municipal under-takings exhibit no statistically significant cost differences; the difference is amongst the unselected. Slope dummies on the cross-price terms failed to identify any biases in factor usage according to ownership, as was the case with the more easily interpreted OLS results.

The work so far has been directed towards explaining the working costs of generation. Potentially more relevant from a policy point of view is the behaviour of total costs, including the cost of capital. This is particularly so given the rejection of homotheticity. Unfortunately, there are very severe difficulties because of the paucity of capital data, and the conclusions must be more qualified. The assumption of a fixed price of capital across the whole sample implies that the value of a plant's capital stock provides an index of the magnitude of that stock. Assuming the plant's stock is neither being augmented nor depreciated means the cost of maintaining a plant of that size (i.e. the cost of the capital being used in the course of production) is obtained by finding the interest charges on this capital stock. The capital element of costs is therefore obtained by taking various plausible values for the interest rate and generating interest charges. A range of values was taken from 2 to 6 per cent. (At this time the average dividend of Electricity Supply company debentures was 4.42 per cent, Garcke 1939.) The figures generated were then added to working costs to obtain a total cost figure. The numbers were at least of similar orders of magnitude, but it is difficult to make more detailed checks of accuracy.

A typical example of the estimated equations generated thereby is given as equation (iv) in Table A.6.3 using the structure of equation (ii) and assuming 4 per cent return on capital; different rates of return yielded similar equations. The results appear fairly sensible and generally con-firmatory of our earlier findings. Factor prices have a lesser proportionate effect on total costs than on working costs, but maximum load has a greater influence. Scale economies, if anything, seem to be even more extensive than suggested by earlier results; at the mean output the scale economies index is 0.266. Selected companies again perform no differently (in a statistical sense) from selected corporations, though the gap between selected and non-selected appears slightly narrowed. The fit is extremely good and the similarity of coefficients suggests that though homotheticity is not a completely apt description of the data, the earlier work is soundly based. The results of all these cross-section results are broadly confirmed by further tests, using time-series data reported in Foreman-Peck and Waterson (1984).

APPENDIX 6.3
The Cost Function for Gas Supply

A translog function was used to estimate the determinants of gas costs. In general total costs are assumed to be a function of Y, N, CP, M, I, P_w, P_t, P_k, all variables defined in Chapter 6. The full unrestricted translog cost function is:

$$
\begin{aligned}
\log C = {} & A + a_y \log Y + a_{cp} \log CP + a_n \log N + a_m \log M + a_i \log I + a_d D \\
& + a_w \log P_w + a_t \log P_t + a_k \log P_k + \log I[\tfrac{1}{2} a_{ii} \log I + a_{id} D] \\
& + \log Y[\tfrac{1}{2} a_{yy} \log Y + a_{yw} \log P_w + a_{yt} \log P_t + a_{yk} \log P_k + a_{yi} \log I + a_{yd} D] \\
& + \log CP[\tfrac{1}{2} a_{cpp} \log CP + a_{cpw} \log P_w + a_{cpt} \log P_t + a_{cpk} \log P_k + a_{cpi} \log I + a_{cpd} D] \\
& + \log N[\tfrac{1}{2} a_{nn} \log N + a_{nw} \log P_w + a_{nt} \log P_t + a_{nk} \log P_k + a_{ni} \log I + a_{nd} D] \\
& + \log M[\tfrac{1}{2} a_{mm} \log M + a_{mw} \log P_w + a_{mt} \log P_t + a_{mk} \log P_k + a_{mi} \log I + a_{md} D] \\
& + \log P_w[\tfrac{1}{2} a_{ww} \log P_w + a_{wt} \log P_t + a_{wk} \log P_k + a_{wi} \log I + a_{wd} D] \\
& + \log P_t[\tfrac{1}{2} a_{tt} \log P_t + a_{tk} \log P_k + a_{ti} \log I + a_{td} D] \\
& + \log P_k[\tfrac{1}{2} a_{kk} \log P_k + a_{ki} \log I + a_{kd} D]
\end{aligned}
\tag{1}
$$

Estimation therefore proceeded in two stages. The proportionate change in costs in response to a change in factor price, $\partial \log C / \partial \log P_w$ for example, is equal, whatever the form of the cost function, to that factor's share of total cost. The data available allow costs to be divided into labour, other operating costs (henceforth called the coal share), and capital costs. Data on each share can therefore be used in preliminary regressions to obtain some of the coefficients. In the second stage of estimation the results for these coefficients are fed back into the cost function and a second regression run to estimate the remaining coefficients. This procedure is not without its problems specifically because of the interrelationship between the equations for factor shares.

We start with the equation for labour's share which is:

$$
\begin{aligned}
S_w = {} & a_w + a_{yw} \log Y + a_{cpw} \log CP + a_{nw} \log N \\
& + a_{mw} \log M + a_{ww} \log P_w + a_{wt} \log P_t + a_{wk} \log P_k \\
& + a_{wi} \log I + a_{wd} D + u_w
\end{aligned}
\tag{2}
$$

where u_w is the error term and a_w, a_{yw}, etc. are constant coefficients from the translog cost function.

For the cost function to correspond to a well-behaved production function, it is required that a uniform proportionate rise in all factor prices leads, with output constant, to an equivalent rise in total cost leaving the relative share of each factor unchanged. In the above this implies $a_{wk} = (-)(a_{ww} + a_{wt})$ and the F statistic for this one restriction was 1.340 so that, given twenty-five degrees of freedom, it could not be rejected. Similar procedures were used for the coal share equation, S_t, but this contains a coefficient a_{wt} which symmetry requires should be the same as a_{wt} estimated in (2). There are thus two restrictions in this case but the F statistic was 0.024 so that again the restriction seems valid. Since the three shares must add up to unity, the coefficients for capital's share S_k may be derived, as we show shortly, from the coefficients already estimated for S_w and S_t.

A characteristic of some production functions is homotheticity, which would mean that the proportionate effects of factor prices and output on costs are independent of each other. Thus the proportionate effect of a change in the wage rate on costs would be independent of the level of output implying that in the labour share equation $a_{yw} = 0 = a_{cpw} = a_{nw} = a_{mw}$. Equation (2) was therefore estimated with these four additional restrictions and the F test statistic was 2.444 in a comparison with the regression involving only the factor price homogeneity restriction. Thus production homotheticity seems a valid restriction and the results for this regression were, with t ratios in brackets and with R^2 adjusted for degrees of freedom:

$$S_w = 0.094 + 0.0481 \log(P_w/P_k) - 0.0616 \log(P_t/P_k)$$
$$\quad (0.86) \quad (1.35) \quad\quad\quad\quad\quad (-3.11)^*$$
$$\quad - 0.0525 \log I - 0.0289 D$$
$$\quad (-4.16)^* \quad\quad (-2.92)^*$$
$$R^2 = 0.36 \quad a_{wk} = 0.0135 \quad * \text{Significant at 0.05 level.} \quad\quad (3)$$

The only a priori expectation we have with respect to the sign of the coefficients is that the demand for labour varies inversely with the wage rate. The price elasticity of the demand for labour, with output constant, can be deduced from the above equation (cf. Christensen and Greene 1976; Pescatrice and Trapani 1980) though the key coefficient is not statistically significant. The sample mean labour share, $\bar{S}_w$, is 14 per cent so the elasticity is:

$$\varepsilon_{ww} = \frac{a_{ww}}{\bar{S}_w} - (1 - \bar{S}_w) = (-)0.52 \quad\quad (4)$$

With more than two inputs the signs of the cross-elasticities involve no clear expectations in economic theory and the results will be discussed later as will be those for technical progress and the ownership dummies. In the meantime we may note that with a translog cost function the coal share equation is

$$S_t = a_t + a_{yt} \log Y + a_{cpt} \log CP + a_{nt} \log N + a_{mt} \log M$$
$$+ a_{wt} \log P_w + a_{tt} \log P_t + a_{tk} \log P_k + a_{ti} \log I + a_{td}D + u_t \quad (5)$$

As already noted factor price homogeneity, that is $a_{tk} = (-)(a_{wt} + a_{tt})$, has been found to be a valid restriction of this equation in conjunction with the symmetry restriction that $a_{wt} = a_{wt}$ from the labour share equation. Production homotheticity would require that the output coefficients in (5) are zero. Comparisons with the regression without these four restrictions yielded an F statistic of 2.480 so that homotheticity cannot be rejected and the final form is therefore:

$$S_t - a_{wt} \log(P_w/P_k) = 0.753 + 0.0508 \log(P_t/P_k)$$
$$(5.55) \quad (0.99)$$
$$+ 0.0104 \log I + 0.0053D$$
$$(0.29) \quad (-0.20)$$
$$R^2 = 0.0 \quad a_{wt} = (-)0.0616 \quad a_{tk} = 0.0108 \quad (6)$$

With the low R^2 and t values the coal share varies mainly with the wage rate and is equal to $0.75 - 0.06 \log P_w$. Since the coal share can also be interpreted as measuring the elasticity of total cost with respect to the coal price, then the results imply that a 10 per cent rise in coal prices would increase total costs by 7.5 per cent less an amount that gets bigger with the level of wage rates. The mean elasticity is equal to the mean coal share, 0.55. At that share value the own-price elasticity of demand for coal is $(-)0.36$; it has the right sign but the key coefficient is statistically insignificant. Note that the data on the share of coal in total costs strictly refer to non-labour operating costs so that the above elasticities exaggerate the effects of changes in coal prices.

Finally, the capital share equation in general form is:

$$S_k = a_k + a_{yk} \log Y + a_{cpk} \log CP + a_{nk} \log N$$
$$+ a_{mk} \log M + a_{wk} \log P_w + a_{tk} \log P_t + a_{kk} \log P_k$$
$$+ a_{ki} \log I + a_{kd}D + u_k \quad (7)$$

One approach to estimating the coefficients in (7) is to recognize that the three share equations must add up to unity. Symmetry with the coefficients of the other equations in conjunction with factor price homogeneity implies:

$$a_{kk} = (-)(a_{wk} + a_{tk}) = (-)0.0243 \quad (8)$$

The last result implies an own-price elasticity of demand for capital of $(-)0.77$ but again the constituent coefficients are not statistically significant. Factor price homogeneity also means that for each independent variable the three coefficients across the three equations must sum to zero.

Hence all the output coefficients in the capital share equation must equal zero. Also:

$$a_k = 1 - a_w - a_t = 0.153 \qquad (9)$$

The degree of substitutability in the gas technology may be indicated by the partial elasticity of substitution. This measures the percentage rise in the ratio of, say, labour to capital in response to a given percentage rise in the relative price of capital, with output constant. It can be shown (cf. Christensen and Greene 1976; Pescatrice and Trapani 1980) that at the sample mean this substitution elasticity is measured as

$$\delta_{wk} = 1 + \frac{a_{wk}}{\bar{S}_w \bar{S}_k} \qquad (10)$$

and the cross-price elasticities as:

$$\varepsilon_{wk} = \bar{S}_k \delta_{wk}; \quad \varepsilon_{kw} = \bar{S}_w \delta_{wk} \qquad (11)$$

The results were such that a fall in the price of capital reduces the demand for labour and the ratio of labour to capital; it also reduces the demand for coal and the ratio of coal to capital. But the precise sizes of these effects are not statistically significant. For labour and coal we have the following statistically significant results:

$$\delta_{wt} = 0.12 \quad \varepsilon_{wt} = 0.06 \quad \varepsilon_{tw} = 0.02 \qquad (12)$$

Thus a rise of 10 per cent in the wage rate leads to an increase of 0.2 per cent in the demand for coal and a 10 per cent rise in the relative wage rate is associated with a rise of 1.2 per cent in the ratio of coal to labour. As labour becomes relatively more costly there is substitution towards technologies which are more capital intensive and more coal intensive though the latter effect is small and the former is not statistically significant. The same applies when the price of coal rises and leads to substitution towards technologies involving a lower ratio of coal to capital and a lower ratio of coal to labour.

Finally the deduced results for the capital share equation imply:

$$a_{ki} = (-)(a_{wi} + a_{ti}) = 0.0421$$
$$a_{kd} = (-)(a_{wd} + a_{td}) = 0.0236 \qquad (13)$$

The result for a_{kd} suggests that municipal enterprises have a higher capital share than private firms and, from equations (3) and (6), a lower labour share. Finally, we can note that the lower is I the more modern is the capital equipment assumed to be. The result for a_{ki} suggests that the more modern vintages reduce the share of capital costs in total costs and largely at the expense of a higher labour share. Technical progress appears to be Hicks-type capital saving.

TABLE A.6.4

	Labour	Coal	Capital
ε_{wi}	$(-)0.52$	0.06^a	0.41
δ_{wi}	—	0.12^a	1.31
ε_{ti}	0.02^a	$(-)0.36$	0.32
δ_{ti}	0.12^a	—	1.06
ε_{ki}	0.18	0.58	$(-)0.77$
δ_{ki}	1.31	1.06	—

[a] Significant at 0.05 level.

The full results for the elasticities were as shown in Table A.6.4. The results so calculated may be sensitive to which equation is taken as the residual third. Ideally the three share equations should be estimated simultaneously, with the various constraints imposed, so that the estimation of the set of coefficients would take into account the error sum of squares of all three equations. This has been done with the use of a computer programme involving Gauss-Newton simultaneous non-linear constrained step-wise iterative least squares. The results were as shown in Table A.6.5.

TABLE A.6.5

	Simultaneous	Original
$aw =$	$0.077 \, (0.34)$	$0.094 \, (0.86)$
$at =$	$0.723 \, (4.51)$	$0.753 \, (5.55)$
$ak =$	$0.200 \, (1.08)$	0.153
$aww =$	$0.059 \, (0.81)$	$0.0481 \, (1.35)$
$att =$	$0.043 \, (1.05)$	$0.0508 \, (0.99)$
$akk =$	$-0.004 \, (0.062)$	-0.0243
$awt =$	$-0.053 \, (1.35)$	$-0.0616 \, (3.11)$
$awk =$	$-0.006 \, (0.10)$	0.0135
$atk =$	$0.010 \, (0.273)$	0.0108
$awi =$	$-0.0504 \, (1.91)$	$-0.0525 \, (4.16)$
$ati =$	$0.00965 \, (0.36)$	$0.104 \, (0.29)$
$aki =$	$0.0408 \, (1.53)$	0.0419
$awd =$	$-0.0284 \, (1.36)$	$-0.0289 \, (2.92)$
$atd =$	$0.004 \, (0.02)$	$-0.0053 \, (0.02)$
$akd =$	$0.0244 \, (1.20)$	0.0342
$\bar{R}^2$: S_w	0.313	0.3234
S_t	-0.034	-0.192
S_k	0.212	

As this method is iterative and requires an initial set of parameter estimates, it is possible that any set of final estimates could in fact represent only a locally optimal solution. To test for this, various different sets of initial values were tried. These included a 'neutral' set of initial parameter values (0.33 for the intercepts and zeros for all the slopes) and also the set of values reported in the paper. All these runs yielded the same results. These new results are sufficiently close to the originals for the initial conclusions, in particular the acceptance of the constraints of factor price homogeneity and production homotheticity, still to be accepted. The main differences come in the significance of the coefficients estimated initially in the labour share equation (especially *awt*, *awi*, and *awd*).

The share equations capture the effect of changes in factor prices on costs, including any indirect effects, if they exist, through output and technical change. It remains to estimate from the main translog cost function the direct effect of output and technical progress on costs and this is achieved by treating as the dependent variable an element, G, which is $\log C$ net of the parameters and variables already estimated.

The translog function allows that the effect of output (in all its dimensions) on costs might vary with the level of output and also with the vintage of plants. In fact, the latter effect was found to be insignificant, and given very high correlations between the independent variables this indirect effect of technical progress was eliminated. For similar reasons candlepower and all the dummy slope variables were eliminated. There were problems in capturing the role of consumer numbers and location. As well as the number of consumers, and population density, other variables like the mileage of distribution mains and the area of the territory, were tested. In the end it was found that the effects on costs of output in all its dimensions were best portrayed by the quantity of gas made and population density. The general form of the model is therefore:

$$G = A + a_y \log Y + \tfrac{1}{2}a_{yy}(\log Y)^2 + a_m \log M + \tfrac{1}{2}a_{mm}(\log M)^2$$
$$+ a_i \log I + a_d D, \tag{14}$$

where the coefficients carry the same interpretation as they have in the full translog function. The output coefficients reflect the elasticity of total cost and if the production function is homogeneous the elasticities are constants, implying that the two squared terms in (14) can be eliminated. The F statistic for these two restrictions was 3.44, so there is a high probability that such a restriction would not be valid. The underlying production function is therefore homothetic but not homogeneous. The results for (14) were:

$$G = 1.22 + 0.437 \log Y + (0.0406)\tfrac{1}{2}(\log Y)^2 + 0.146 \log M$$
$$ (0.77) \quad (1.83)^* \qquad (2.33)^* \qquad\qquad (1.67)^*$$
$$ - (0.0803)\tfrac{1}{2}(\log M)^2 + 0.136 \log I + 0.0292 D$$
$$ (-2.23)^* \qquad\qquad (2.62)^* \qquad (0.74)$$

$R^2 = 0.99$ * Significant at 0.05 level.   (15)

In terms of the quantity of gas made there are initially sizeable scale economies with total costs rising at only two-fifths the rate of output. However the elasticity with respect to gas made is $0.44 + 0.04 \log Y$, so that decreasing returns to scale set in at an annual gas production of 1.3 million cubic feet, which is above the sample mean of one million for the provincial gas undertakings. The proportional effect of population density on costs is $0.14 - 0.08 \log M$, so that increases in population density reduce costs once inhabitants per acre are 5.75 or more. Since the sample mean density was 23.34 and all but three companies had densities greater than 5.5, then effectively this variable is one which lowers the level of costs. At any given population density the average cost curve is U-shaped with the base corresponding to a production value greater than the average for the provincial gas undertakings. The lower is population density the higher is the level of that cost curve. The expansion of an undertaking involving equal percentage increases in gas production and in the size of territory served, but with total consumer numbers fixed, would cause average costs to rise if $0.34 + 0.04 \log Y + 0.08 \log M$ exceeded unity. Even at the sample mean for the provincial undertakings this condition is met. The London companies were therefore clearly operating at a point where expansion of this kind would raise average costs.

Finally it would appear that ownership does not play much part, at least in comparing situations where population density and the total quantity produced is the same. Excluding the plant vintage variable I from (14) put the coefficient on the dummy term at $(-)0.01$, implying that costs were some 1 per cent lower in municipal enterprises and that part of the source of the municipals' superiority lies in having more modern capacity. But none of these results was statistically significant. The municipal firms do not have higher costs than private firms but neither do they have statistically significantly lower costs.

7

International Comparisons of Performance in National Networks in the Inter-war Period

INTRODUCTION

During the inter-war years Britain resisted the Continental trend towards state ownership. Instead it founded public-interest monopoly corporations or left industry in the hands of private owners and managers. Nationalization of railways and coal in the aftermath of the First World War was considered and rejected as irrelevant. Self-regulation, legal entry barriers, tariff protection, non-profit corporations were all introduced as alternatives which would not saddle the state with revenue or management obligations. Despite the rise of the Labour Party with its commitment to state ownership, enshrined in clause 4 of the party constitution, inter-war Labour governments found no opportunity to implement this policy. More influential were the new employers' organizations and the businessmen who had worked, none too successfully, in Whitehall during the war.

Policy towards network industries was also directed to reducing 'the costs of an early start'. These industries began competitively and then maintained by non-competitive means an atomized industrial structure no longer appropriate to changed inter-war conditions. Market forces did not, or were not permitted to, promote rationalization and integration that would have lowered costs. The state, often in the form of Montague Norman at the Bank of England, felt obliged to step in to raise the utilization of scale economies and enhance the average level of technological proficiency embodied in industry capital. Part of the legacy of Victorian and Edwardian industrial structure in railways and electricity, as well as cotton and shipbuilding, was abandoned.

None the less state policy in these years has often been regarded as ineffective, even in its own terms. In the absence of quantitative measures of performance, the improvement in policy towards network industries compared with that of the Victorians and Edwardians has often been overlooked. The 1919 Electricity Act was a first attempt to rationalize electricity generation but the Electricity Commissioners were given inadequate powers. The 1926 Act was therefore far more radical. Post-war reorganization under the 1921 Railways Act at last drew together the disparate private networks into four groups and improved efficiency of operations. The 1922 Act establishing the BBC brought the new industry of radio broadcasting to a mass audience within a few years. Subject to heavy criticism immediately after the war (just as the private system had been before), the relatively newly national-ized telephone service (1912) was scrutinized by a Parliamentary Select Committee reporting in 1921.

How necessary and how effective such policies were may be judged by international comparisons. These standards also cast light on continuing concerns such as the efficiency advantages of monopoly or competition in 'natural monopoly' industries and the costs and benefits of private versus state ownership of industry. They point to the role of incentives, technology, and inherited institutions as more fundamental determinants of economic per-formance than ownership and competition.

RAILWAYS

By far the largest of the network industries and undoubtedly their greatest political problem were the railways. Railways alone accounted for more capital than did the entire manufacturing industry. Their operation under state control during the First World War amply demonstrated the benefits of a more unified administration while at the same time running down their assets. Even in the United States, there was a lively political debate as to whether railways should be returned to private ownership or should continue to be operated by the state. Compensation and reorganization at first dominated post-war railway policy but soon road competition challenged railway's transport monopoly and called into question the regulatory framework, predicated on the assumption that no alternative transport facilities were available. The depression in the heavy industries, especially in coal, reduced the demand for rail freight absolutely and, as the centre of industrial activity shifted towards the South and the Midlands, the geographical pattern of demand was transformed. Though productivity improved it did so too slowly to satisfy both wage demands and the need to maintain a satisfactory return on capital.

Under the 1921 Railways Act 120 separate companies were merged into four; the Great Western ('coal and passengers'), the Southern ('passengers'), the LMS and LNER (both 'heavy'). Twenty-seven major companies were amalgamated and ninety-three subsidiary companies were absorbed by 1923. Amalgamation of the Great Western group was comparatively painless because little reorganization was required; the Great Western was also the only company to keep its original name. Regulation of private monopoly power was instituted by the new Railway Rates Tribunal, intended to remove the rigidity of pre-war rates and to acknowledge that higher working costs warranted higher fares and charges. £60 million was agreed in compensation to the railways for depreciation during the war. Though shareholders could be satisfied with the deal, there was no expectation that economies from the new groups would be obtained soon. Eventual savings in rolling stock, depots, buildings, and shops would take a considerable time to organize (Sommerfield 1923).

The general problem the railways faced was that a high proportion of costs were fixed and as traffic stagnated or declined, revenues were often insufficient to cover costs, which were much harder to cut. Between 1913 and 1927 expenditure rose by 211 per cent while revenue only increased by 165 per cent. New, higher railway charges specified by the Act did not come into force until the beginning of 1928 (Wood and Sherrington 1929). Between 1925 and 1927 wage bills were reduced by £2.24 million, materials by £2.16 million, and fuel by £0.689 million despite a greater mileage run, but prices in general were falling. The chairman of the LNER remarked on the goodwill shown by staff of all ranks in economy measures; the satisfactory relations that aided implementation of efficiency schemes might, until recently, not have been present (*The Economist* (1928), 470–1). Contemporary opinion was not however greatly impressed by the savings from the reorganization. Haul lengths seem to have increased a little (Cain 1980). Savings of £20 million, some 10 per cent of railway turnover, were suggested by Acworth in 1923, and by Sir Josiah Stamp in 1931 from LMS experience. But others giving evidence to the Royal Commission on Transport were more sceptical (Acworth 1923; Royal Commission on Transport 1931: 31). The Great Western in South Wales gained little from the reorganization (Channon 1981). An obvious saving was in the clerical labour force of the Railway Clearing House, which almost halved between 1922 and 1939, as 1,600 jobs were shed (Bagwell 1968: 282). The managerial will to integrate operations, or to cut costs by changing procedures, was not very strong. There were notable exceptions, such as Stamp, who, significantly, was not originally a railway man by profession. As general manager and chairman of the LMS from 1927, Stamp's improvement programme cost £20,000 a year, yielding savings purportedly fifty times greater (many of which were unpopular) (Ellis 1959: 329). But even a favourably inclined analyst of the inter-war industry conceded that middle and lower management was of questionable quality and lacking in decisiveness (Bonavia 1981: 31–2). Interests in this long-established industry in preventing rationalization, particularly the trade unions (there were 275,000 members of the National Union of Railwaymen even in 1933), were powerful (Bagwell 1963).

The impact of the reorganization is measured by how much higher railway costs would have been if the 1913 organization had persisted into the inter-war years. Input prices, technology, and demand changes must be allowed to take their actual values, except in so far as they were altered by the reorganization under the 1921 Act, but within an imaginary 1913 system. As Table 7.1 shows, very clearly the big change between 1913 and 1930 was the rise in wage rates, by more than the national average, and the decline in labour productivity, associated with the reduction in the length of the working day. Dividends were squeezed especially during the 1930s but with, say, a 1 per cent a year decline in prices, 3 per cent in the 1930s would be worth 4 per cent in times of a stable price level. By 1937 the wage bill had risen to £102 million from £47 million in 1913, while dividend and loan payments fell from £45 million to £38 million (Short 1946: 39). This does not tell us what the effect of the Act was, only what problems the industry had to face, and presumably would have had to face without the Act. Sources of railway productivity improvement included the replacement of forty-five-feet rails by

TABLE 7.1 *British railway revenue and costs:*
Percentage increases 1913–1930

	%
Change in:	
Wholesale prices	19.5[a]
Freight rates	47.0
Passenger fares	51.0
Gross revenue	52.0
Gross expenditure	89.0
Wage rates	112.0
Wage costs	133.0

[a] 1930 was a year of rapidly falling wholesale prices. Consumers' expenditure average value index had risen by more than 70% 1913–30, but the retail price index, with a different composition, increased by 57%, about the same as the increase in fares.

Source: Douglas Campbell (1932: 70–3).

sixty-footers, more efficient locomotives and better lubricating apparatus enhancing fuel economy, automatic signals saving on signalmen, larger train-loads raising wagon-miles per engine hour, and the reduction of locomotive type variety (but the LMS still maintained around 220 types in 1938!) (*The Economist* (31 Aug. 1938)).

Perhaps the most telling evidence of managerial weakness slowing productivity growth in British railways before and after the grouping is the failure to use ton-mile and passenger-mile statistics and to prefer train-mile data. From 1913 the companies were obliged by law to collect ton-mile and passenger-mile figures but they refused to use or to publicize them. Train-mile statistics presupposed that particular trains should be run, diverting attention from the customer, who would have been better served in other ways; in freight by larger trains and wagons, and, in the passenger service, possibly by electrification and certainly by higher average speeds. The fastest scheduled run in Britain in 1939, 71.9 m.p.h. London to York, was fortieth in the world's list of fast runs. Three trains an hour between New York and Philadelphia averaged over 70 m.p.h. between stops and on other runs trains were exceeding 80 m.p.h. In the percentage of total passenger-miles run at over 60 m.p.h. Britain ranked with Belgium, at 1.3 per cent behind Denmark, France, and Holland (respectively 2 per cent, 3.15 per cent, and 4.55 per cent). Germany with its higher labour productivity operated 1 per cent. Management interviewed later condemned themselves by asserting the ideas and equipment for productivity measurement and improvement were not available (Bonavia 1981: 42, 45–6). In other newer and more dynamic contemporary industries, such as motor vehicles, they were in widespread use (e.g. Foreman-Peck 1981). Attempts to reduce labour costs were devoted more to downgrading posts than to improving operating procedures. A key concept missing from railway management was load factor (Farrar 1931). Careful pricing could have increased the utilization of existing trains, and considered investment could have raised the traffic carried by existing track. Railway advertising was ill directed at visitors to seaside resorts rather than to traders to change their consignment and dispatching habits. And pricing did not motivate traders to lower their shipping costs.

Many Continental systems were improving productivity by electrification to a much greater extent than the British. Reporting in 1930 the Weir Committee on Main Line Electrification estimated a 7 per cent return could be earned. The Chief Electrical Engineer of the LNER in 1934 showed the returns to investment in electrification rose with traffic density and with gradients. With 9.5 million ton-miles, the Manchester–Sheffield heavy gradient route was calculated to yield as much as 15.59 per cent, whereas the King's Cross–Peterborough run with a density of 6.95 million ton-miles returned the lower figure of 10.2 per cent. Despite progress on Southern Railways, only 1 per cent of the route miles in Britain north of the Thames were electrified in 1938 compared with 1.1 per cent in the USA. Overall British track and route electrification figures were similar to Germany's (Table 7.2). Taking into consideration the lack of cheap hydroelectric power and the risk of over-optimistic calculations that could deteriorate further if the economy turned down, the charge of inadequate electrification as a source of productivity improvement is not proven.

A more obvious deficiency was in the freight rolling stock. Freight trains were not automatically braked and so they were constrained to move slowly. Because they moved slowly they

TABLE 7.2 *Percentage of electrified track 1938*

	%
Belgium	0.9
Denmark	1.6
Hungary	3.3
Germany	5.0
Great Britain	5.3
France	7.8
Norway	9.2
Holland	15.1
Italy	28.2
Sweden	42.4
Switzerland	73.8

Source: *Modern Transport* (12 Aug. 1939), cited in Johnston (1949).

congested the track, either requiring more capital tied up in track or limiting the number of other trains that could be run. In contrast since 1917 continuous brakes were fitted on two-thirds of German rolling stock. Small British trucks were underloaded, so that the average freight train had a gross weight less than many passenger express trains. Had Britain increased freight train-loads at the rate the Americans did then many acres of sidings (there were seventy-two goods yards in London alone) could have been sold off to pay for the conversion to larger braked wagons (Aldcroft 1975: 40; Bonavia 1981: 131–3; Johnston 1949). Containerization could have been taken further as a weapon in the battle against road transport (Royal Commission on Transport 1931; Fenelon 1933).

The regulatory system was not particularly helpful, lacking any formal targets for productivity improvement. Quasi-judicial proceedings were unlikely to encourage efficiency, even though the Railway Rates Tribunal bore an obligation to encourage the railways in their economic reforms. In 1939 the Tribunal consisted of three permanent members, the president, a lawyer, assisted by a railway expert and a businessman. They considered whether rates were reasonable and the best available means of raising the revenue. Sometimes a senior barrister supported the railway companies' officials in putting their case. Objections from users were heard at the same time, an arrangement perhaps suitable to decide on fair distributions of the costs of railway transport, but unlikely to alter the organization in which they were incurred.

British railways' challenges were not unique by any means. The French network suffered great damage during the war and was also reorganized in 1921. The introduction of the eight-hour day added to existing financial problems; powerful unions ensured high wages and fringe benefits relative to other sectors. Much of the 1921 reorganization was not carried out because of vested interests and shifting political pressures. Government regulation tended to operate through *fonctionnaires* with powers only to obstruct or carry out pre-established routines. Furthermore, the network had always been and continued to be planned with military purposes in mind. The consequence was that in only three years towards the end of the 1920s were the railways not in deficit, despite the buoyancy of the French economy compared with Britain's. Then came the depression, later but more severe and long-lasting than in Britain. Nationalization in 1937 was widely regarded by then as the only solution (Douglas 1945). Yet French railway labour productivity in 1936/7 was higher than that in the UK system, perhaps helped by a greater proportion of freight traffic (Table 7.3). Even better was labour productivity of the German state-owned and unified Reichsbahn in 1937 (Wohl and Albitreccia 1935: 121). German labour productivity was 74

TABLE 7.3 *British, French, and German railway labour productivity 1937*

	Germany	France
Employment	121	71
Passenger-miles	139	74
Ton-miles	265	113
Output UK weights	210	96
Output other weights	228	102
Labour productivity		
with UK weights	174	135
with named country weights	189	144

Note: Index nos. UK = 100.

Source: Rostas (1948) and calculated from Douglas (1945).

per cent higher with UK revenue weights and 89 per cent higher with German weights. The French advantage was about half of that. Germany's former state railways, including all main lines, were amalgamated in 1920.

Both Continental systems and the USA managed to charge

TABLE 7.4 *Railway fares: International comparisons for the 1930s*
(shillings and pence: *s./d.*)

(a)

Miles	British monthly	British normal	Belgian	French	German
Third class return fares 1934					
6	1/0	1/6	0/6	0/7	0/8
25	4/2	6/3	2/0	2/3	2/8
50	8/4	12/6	3/9	4/0	5/0
150	25/0	37/6	10/6	11/6	14/0
250	41/8	62/6	15/0	18/0	24/0
Six-day workmen's fares 1934					
5		3/0	0/9	1/0	1/4
10		4/9	0/10	1/9	2/3
20		7/3	1/4	2/6	3/0
30		10/6	1/5	3/6	4/6
Monthly third class season tickets 1934					
5		16/6	6/6	6/6	6/6
10		25/0	8/0	8/6	10/6
20		39/0	10/6	12/0	15/0
30		50/0	13/6	15/0	18/0
Inclusive rates per ton of domestic coal 1930[a]					
25		4/3	1/9		
50		7/6	3/0		
100		11/0	5/0		
150		14/0	5/0		

[a] Rates for export and industrial coal are cheaper in both countries.

(b)

Passenger fares in 1938 for 300 km. (186 miles)	Switzerland	Italy	England	Belgium	France	Germany
First class	37/4	31/1	40/8	28/2	30/0	49/5
Second class	18/8	12/4	24/5	11/1	11/0	22/11

Source: Johnston (1949).

generally lower fares and rates and achieve at least as high speeds (Table 7.4). US revenue per passenger-mile fell by about 10 per cent between 1916 and 1938 (1.87 cents) having risen by 40 per cent to 1929 (2.81 cents), less than in the UK. Freight revenue per ton-mile, less subject to road competition, showed a similar rise to 1929 (0.707 to 1.076) but less of a decline in the 1930s (0.983 cents). Despite these handicaps in the United States, at the outbreak of the Second World War British standard third class fares at 1.575*d*. per mile were considerably higher than the equivalent American 'coach' rate of 1.17*d*. International fare comparisons must take into account the discounting of posted fares in all countries; 73 per cent of all revenue passengers travelled at reduced fares in Germany in 1938. Deficits in all European countries were insufficient to account for their relatively low fares, especially when special taxation is taken into consideration. The 1938 German deficit was £9 million but £9.5 millon was paid in transport tax (Johnston 1949). The French deficit of £44 million was more significant but one-half was accounted for by taxes and services rendered to the state. Productivity figures, which tell a similar story, are in any case not open to improvement by subsidy.

RESTRICTING INTERMODAL COMPETITION

Like British railways, all industrial countries' systems were pushed towards reform by road transport competition in the inter-war period. How the state should respond to the new intermodal competition raised important policy issues, for the state built and owned the road system that allowed road transport to compete, whereas the railways invariably both owned their track and managed the operations on it. The terms on which the road system should be made available to commercial freight and passenger service providers was a continuing bone of contention for the railway lobby. Close consultation of the Railway Companies' Association with the new Ministry of Transport in the inter-war years (Alderman 1973) may have contributed to the Road Traffic Acts of 1930 and 1933. These tightly regulated road service providers in the supposed interests of fair competition and transport integration. The 1930 Act restricted and regulated bus and coach services, fares, and timetables, at the same time virtually closing the industry to new entry. Reductions of fares were discouraged, operating costs fell with technical progress in vehicles and with the price level, benefiting existing operators considerably, while protecting railways from further losses of passenger traffic to public road transport. The 1933 Road and Rail Traffic Act almost blocked entry to road haulage and limited the fleets of existing firms to their size before the Act. Only where definite proof could be adduced of increased business and of the unsuitability of other operators or means of transport for undertaking the work was entry permitted. Regulation was undertaken by Traffic Commissioners, who were appointed as licensing authorities. In short the 1933 Act aimed to stabilize relations between road and rail freight as had the 1930 Act for road and rail passenger services.

Restrictions of one part of the transport system stimulated development in another; the effect was probably to encourage the growth of private ownership and operation of transport—to reduce the division of labour. Rising demand for passenger travel in the 1930s was increasingly provided by private cars and bicycles (motor cycle use declined with the requirement for third party insurance). In freight the ancillary user gained in importance. While expenditure on passenger transport and the division between road and rail showed little change between 1931 and 1934, bicycle and car use increased. Cyclists killed on the road and the number of private cars registered rose respectively by over 70 per cent (1930–4) and by over 20 per cent (1931–4). Some, but not all, of higher cyclists' casualties must be attributable to the abolition of the motor vehicle speed limit (Foreman-Peck 1987a). Some must have been due to more cycling. Competition from private motoring in long-distance traffic, which could not be controlled by political lobbying, encouraged the railways to resume high speed timings from the mid-1930s. On the London to Newcastle run in August 1936 a top speed of 113 m.p.h. was reached in ordinary service (of course by steam). In the summer of 1939 over 12,000 miles daily were covered at speeds of 60 m.p.h. or over.

Meanwhile large bus operators absorbed the small, consistent with the existence of scale or density economies, or economies of joint production. Perhaps the most successful institution to emerge from the response to intermodal competition in the 1930s also indicated economies of integration. The London Passenger

Transport Board, formed in 1933, showed rather more growth in operations than elsewhere in the economy, partly because of the drift to the South, partly because of common ownership of all public passenger transport facilities together with co-operation with the main line railways, and partly because the Board's area was exempt from most of the Traffic Commissioners' restrictions.

Such an enormous industry as railways was inevitably a matter of political concern. The state was inclined to protect the industry as a valuable instrument in attempts to alleviate unemployment. When road expenditures were cut during the world depression, railways were encouraged to increase investment by considerably more. An additional element strengthening the ties of the state and the railways was the Treasury-guaranteed loan of £27 million of January 1935 for modernization. Such guarantees removed the necessity to pay stockholders a competitive return if new investment was to be financed externally; the railways' budget constraint became 'softer'. Railway workers and stockholders were rival claimants for increased railway earnings during the upswing of the 1930s, but with government financial support, management could largely ignore stockholders and avoid confrontations with, or more creative responses to, their work-forces. Wages had been cut in 1931 and by 1936 the railways were committed to restoring the third quarter of those cuts. But the unions lodged a claim for complete restoration, and inevitably stockholders' returns were lower than in the 1920s. The Amalgamated Society of Locomotive Engineers and Firemen did not accept the award of the National Railway Wages Tribunal in August 1936, demanding a six-hour day and a thirty-six-hour week with two weeks' paid holiday, estimated to cost £9.7 million in a full year. Rising coal and material prices combined with wage demands to squeeze dividends further and so increase the difficulty of raising fresh capital from the private market (*The Economist* (16 May, 1 Aug., 12 Dec. 1936)).

PRODUCTIVITY COMPARISONS WITH THE USA: TELEPHONES

Though the railway system as a whole was a massive enterprise, in some respects the state-owned Post Office was even larger than any one of the 1921 railway groups. The Post Office that had absorbed the National Telephone Company's local networks in 1912 was by now one of the economy's biggest businesses with well over 200,000 employees. Problems of control and organization should have been no less in the state telephone system than in railways and perhaps greater if private ownership offered greater efficiency incentives. Before the Post Office had time to digest fully the acquisition of the NTC war disrupted operations. Post-war inflation and dislocations added more difficulties and public complaints were so widespread that a Parliamentary Select Committee investigated the service. By and large Post Office management was exonerated but business interests continued to agitate for improvements through the Telephone Development Association. The 1932 Report of the Bridgeman Committee was much less anodyne. Although rejecting the hiving off of telecommunications into a public utility company, the Committee severely criticized the centralization of authority in the Post Office Secretariat, as violating the fundamental principal of separation of policy from practice (Committee of Enquiry on the Post Office 1932). As an alternative structure, the Committee recommended a functional board presided over by the Postmaster-General, on which sat directors of engineering, finance, personnel, and so on. This was consistent with what was regarded as business best practice, as was their proposal for regionalization of the organization. Appropriation of Post Office profits by the Treasury was also condemned as removing incentives for cost reduction. Unfortunately, the substitution of a fixed payment in the second half of the decade did not support their opinion. Wages were increased and telephone rates were cut, with the consequence that the Post Office was obliged to deplete its reserves in order to pay annually to the Exchequer the £10.75 million agreed as a response to the Bridgeman recommendations (Pitt 1980: ch. 4).

That the organization of telecommunications showed scope for improvement is confirmed by data on the spread of telephony. An almost common international telephone technology encouraged international comparisons of telephone diffusion as a means of assessing, or condemning, national telephone service industries. Such comparisons were typically simple in the years with which we are concerned, not correcting for differences in national living standards or income distribution, because these were not generally

TABLE 7.5 *Telephones per hundred inhabitants,*
selected countries 1913 and 1932

	1913	1932
United States	9.1	14.30
Canada	5.6	12.09
New Zealand	4.0	10.10
Denmark	4.2	9.80
Sweden	3.9	9.30
Switzerland	2.3	8.50
Australia	2.6	7.40
Norway	3.1	7.00
Great Britain[a]	1.6	4.63
Germany[a]	1.9	4.57
France	0.7	3.00

[a] 31 Mar. 1933. Boundary changes are not taken into
account.

Source: AT & T., *Telephone and Telegraph Statistics
of the World* (1913), Bulletin no. 2; Gunston
(1933: 56).

known. Britain was usually perceived to be laggardly relative to
the United States from the beginning of telephony. She was not
alone in that respect, as Table 7.5 shows. Surprisingly the international ranking of telephone use changes little over the two
decades after 1913, despite the effects of the final nationalization
of the British telephone service in 1912 which took effect over
that period. North America maintained its position as the most
intensive telephone-using area, obviously helped by the high
incomes enjoyed there. Other regions of recent European settlement for similar reasons were great telephoners. Widespread
Scandinavian telephone use is not so easily explained by high
incomes. Greater income equality may be a contributor. Germany
and Britain were roughly on a par despite a lower German income per head, and France lagged because of well-recognized
deficiencies in state telecommunications policy. Europe narrowed
the gap with the United States in the inter-war years, even though
more hampered by the disruptions of the First World War.

   In view of greater American telephone use, at first sight it is
surprising that in the year of the General Strike (and later in the
year of the Battle of Britain) prices were roughly comparable

in the two countries. But wages of telephone personnel in Britain were much lower than in the USA. Labour productivity was generally less than half, which was true of the whole of manufacturing industry by this date. What is instructive is the detailed British attempt to explain the differential (Post Office 1929). Sometimes higher US productivity was attained because the Americans used more machinery, in erecting poles for instance, or motor vehicles, they employed less durable or more visually intrusive techniques, and were prepared to offer lower service standards, if prices could be cut in that way. Even the installation of a simple telephone took a British engineer two and a half times as long as an American (Table 7.6). US companies were aided by the right of eminent domain (compulsory purchase). Prices of some stores and probably of exchange equipment (helped by long, large, and predictable production runs) were cheaper in the USA (though poles were more expensive). Aerial cable was used extensively and reduced costs of distribution relative to Britain. According to the Post Office, greater density of plant in the USA lowered costs per station, though that was not always true. The lower proportion (less than half) of PBXs, reflecting the higher British proportion of business use, did the same . There were 2.5 million Bell PBX stations in 1928 and 544,000 British but 11.2 million Bell simple telephone stations as against 1,143,000 British. Party lines were more extensively used in the USA, lowering costs of transmission and switching. US poling costs were almost halved by sharing with electric light companies. Motor transport was much cheaper and town layouts simpler. Standardization had been carried further. Yet since a similar productivity gap was to be found in manufacturing industry, some more general causes as well must have been operative. Had management been obliged to pay US higher wages perhaps they would have found more ways of saving labour, or the work-force might have been more willing to support such efforts. In any event it was apparent that virtually sharing telephone engineering technology with the United States was not alone sufficient also to share productivity levels; some fundamental, though unidentified, social influences maintained a massive international gap.

Quality of service is harder to compare. In both Britain and America it deteriorated immediately after the war. Average speed of answer by operators in London during the last six years of

TABLE 7.6 *British and American telephone service prices and wages*

(a) *Wages 1926* (weekly, $)

	London		Chicago		New York Manhattan
	Inner	Outer	Loop	Outer	
At start	7.88	7.45	16.0	15.0	15.0
At end of first year	8.76	7.38	17.5	16.5	18.0
Maximum pay	15.77	14.89	23.0	32.0	34.0

Note: NY operators also received annual bonuses rising to the seventh year of employment which raised average wages about 18%. Overtime in Chicago raised average wages about 11%.

(b) *Local prices 1926* (monthly rates, $)

Individual line	London		New York	Chicago	Philadelphia
	Min.	Max.			
Business					
Incl. 75 calls	3.95	5.47	4.40	4.00	5.00
Incl. 300 calls	8.51	14.60	16.23	12.30	13.5
Residential					
Incl. 60 calls	3.20	4.42	3.85	3.75	4.00

Notes: Minimum charges for London based on calls to exchanges within a five-mile radius. No. of phones: London 432,000; New York 1,217,000; Chicago 742,000; Philadelphia 291,000.

(c) *Long-distance prices 1926* (day rates for initial period, station to station, $)

Distance (miles)	UK	USA
12	0.08	0.10
104	0.73	0.70
404	2.31	2.60

Notes: British rates reduced after 2 p.m. British initial period three minutes, US five minutes, for the shorter distances.

(d) *Prices 1940* ($)

	USA: New York to Stamford[a]	UK: 400 miles from London[b]
Station to station	0.30	0.19
Person to person	0.40	0.28

[a] Both day and night.
[b] 7 p.m. to 5 a.m.

Fig. 7.6. *Continued*

(e) *Construction costs per mile of single wire 1928 (£)*

	USA	UK
Exchange overhead	7.6	25.1
Trunk overhead	19.7	25.7
Exchange underground	3.5	7.8
Trunk underground	7.6	16.2

(f) *Maintenance costs* (man-hours per mile of single wire/year)

| | USA | UK | |
		London	Provinces
Bare wire			
Exchange	3.2	8.3	4.0
Trunk	2.1	2.3	1.0
Aerial cable	0.4	n/a	n/a
Underground	0.09	0.65	0.34

Notes: Installation of simple telephone: USA: 2.5 hours; UK: 5.5 hours. Poling costs: Philadelphia 16,259 man-hours; British equivalent 42,440. Maintenance of panel and director automatics (man-hours per subscriber's line p.a.); Pennsylvania Co. 5.6; Bermondsey 30; Sloane 22.1.

Source: AT & T. Box 58; Post Office (1929).

NTC had fallen from 9.5 seconds to just over 6 (1906–11). Under the Post Office, average answer time fell to 4 seconds in the second half of 1915. War conditions reduced the service to 8 seconds at the Armistice, 10.5 in the first half of 1919, and 7.4 in 1920. Similar war effects were experienced in New York although Bell did not publish quality of service data. One exchange's average answering time was over 8 seconds in December 1919. In technological progressiveness the British were not always lagging behind the Americans. The Post Office automatic installations predated Bell's, and while the Post Office was using 200-pair telephone cables, the USA was unable to produce a satisfactory cable of more than fifty pairs (Anon. (1920–1: 309–23)).

UK plant was apparently much more expensive than the Bell

systems: £77.3 compared with £46.3 prime cost of plant and equipment per subscriber in 1929. Greater use of party lines in the USA kept down costs. More underground plant in the UK, because of greater population density and higher quality service, raised British expenses. With a lower exchange rate the disparity would be less (Medlyn 1929–30). Supposing sterling was 30 per cent overvalued against the dollar as the consumer price index divergences since 1913 indicate, prime costs are much closer to those of the USA at £66.

Some evidence of what might have been achieved with a different organization or policy in the UK is provided by the sole survivor of municipal telephony, Hull. In 1893 before the experiment began in Hull but when there were both Post Office and NTC telephone systems in Newcastle, Hull was relatively poorly served, with 512 inhabitants per exchange subscriber compared with Newcastle's 147.8 (London was worse served than Hull with 636.3 (Post Office 1893)). Under municipal management Hull achieved half as many telephones again as Newcastle upon Tyne in 1937 despite being considerably less wealthy measured by rateable value (£1.75 million compared with £2.5 million) (Chisholm 1937). A more systematic comparison of the performance of Hull's municipal system relative to that of the Post Office can be made by taking rateable value as a measure of wealth and estimating a relationship between wealth and telephone ownership in 1937 across a sample of English towns served by the Post Office. Details are in Appendix 7.1, where the equation predicts that the best estimate for Hull's telephone ownership under a Post Office regime was 7,630, just under half the actual level of 15,339. A plausible (1 per cent) upper bound to the prediction is about 14,300 telephones and therefore Hull's high level of telephone ownership was unlikely to have come about by chance. Had British telephone usage in total doubled, as the regression indicates was possible, then Britain would have achieved densities comparable with the Scandinavians.

Differential urbanization does not explain the international pattern, for with half a million telephones, London achieved 11.8 telephones per 100 inhabitants in 1932, rather more than in Paris (10.5) and Berlin (11.07), but not in the same league as New York (22.2) or Stockholm (31.8). Telephone usage in 1932 was however a considerable relative improvement on 1893, when on average United States towns had three times as many phones as those of the United Kingdom.

PRODUCTIVITY COMPARISONS WITH THE USA: RAILWAYS AND ELECTRICITY GENERATION

In electricity generation and use at the beginning of the inter-war years Britain lagged a long way behind not only the United States, as in telephony, but also Germany and other continental European economies. The state response to the organization of electricity generation is one of the most radical exercises in industrial policy of the period. Whereas distribution remained unreformed, fragmented into many independently owned area networks, generation was rationalized. By determining how much electricity was to be generated at which stations and fixing the payment of generators, the scheme introduced by the Conservative government in 1926 effectively abolished private property rights in the industry. A first attempt at raising the average generating station size so as to take advantage of the well-recognized scale economies in the industry proved a failure because inadequate powers were granted the Electricity Commissioners under the act of 1919. The remedy attempted by the 1926 Act was unusual; the establishing of the non-profit Central Electricity Board (CEB), which, together with the Electricity Commissioners, was responsible for the capital planning of the industry. The principal instrument of the CEB rationalization programme was the construction of the national grid and the selection of stations to supply electricity to this distribution network. Even after the grid was built, a wide range of private enterprises and local authorities' stations still took short-run electricity generation and distribution decisions in the 1930s; holding companies, power companies, joint electrical authorities, small local companies supplying a local authority, county boroughs, and rural district councils. All units within the industry were regulated. Each supply undertaking, including the CEB, was obliged to obtain approval from the Commissioners for raising capital for construction of generating stations and transmission. The CEB guaranteed operating costs, the capital charges on stations within certain limits relating to interest on capital, and when new generating plant was required and installed under CEB direction, the CEB had to guarantee all costs arising from installation. The CEB decided the location of new stations, the extension of existing ones, the design of plant, and planned the operation programme. The Board therefore exercised great influence over 'selected' stations but those stations were responsible for employing their own labour and materials and conditions of operation of personnel.

Non-selected stations also operated under direction of the Board. The original intention of the 1926 Act was that only selected stations would eventually remain in existence but it did not provide for automatic closure. Independent plants could remain in operation when economical, that is when their unit variable costs were less than the unit total cost of grid supply, as were the majority, and many were retained for stand-by against a rental. The CEB could compel owners of generating stations to enter the national scheme. On the one hand this arrangement was criticized for leaving too little discretion to the owner, and on the other for dividing responsibility so much as to remove incentives to efficiency. Holding companies were attacked for failing to integrate their operations and, where they were controlled by an equipment supplier, taking high profits by paying excessive prices for generating machinery. The interests of local authorities were equally conflicting when they also owned gas undertakings, which allegedly restricted electricity development.

Under the 1926 Act the Commissioners, like those for railways, were intended to perform a regulatory and quasi-judicial function, while the CEB, a state industry not responsible to Parliament, was to be the executive and operating body that concentrated generation at the most efficient stations. Capital was obtained by issuing non-voting stock not guaranteed by the Treasury. However, since the Commissioners had been in the field longer, they took responsibility for the initial regional grid plan, the ten-year demand forecasts, and for identifying 'selected' undertakings to supply the grid. Generating stations were selected to supply the grid according to the following criteria:

1. the cost of coal delivered to the station;
2. the abundance of water for condensing purposes;
3. technical characteristics of the station such as type and size of the plant units, steam pressure, etc.;

4. proximity to load;
5. the possibilities of the site for further expansion.

That is, technical efficiency in the economists' sense was only apparently an issue where criterion (3) was involved. In fact selection was influenced by technical efficiency, even though it may have been undiplomatic for the CEB to say so at the time (Ballin 1946; CEB 1930–7; Hannah 1979; Political and Economic Planning 1936; Hammond 1992). Securing the co-operation of selected stations required a great deal of tact if independent-minded generating managers were to be persuaded to co-operate voluntarily as the CEB preferred. One consequence of favouring voluntarism was that concentration of generation, and therefore probably cost reduction, proceeded less far than was originally intended by the Weir Committee (whose report in 1925 had proposed the CEB).

How much the reorganization contributed to lowering costs may be assessed by assuming the 1932 pre-grid size distribution of stations with 1932 maximum loads and hours run to supply actual 1937 output with the 1937 cost function. Much greater capacity was necessary in this counterfactual world because of the loss of scale economies. Factor prices and technical progress measures in 1937 are assumed (at their mean values). Then the costs of generating the 1937 output were reduced by one-third by the CEB, or equivalently, without the CEB costs would have been 50 per cent higher (Foreman-Peck and Hammond 1992).

At the time and later a more common approach to assessing the potential for cost reduction was comparison with the American industry. Probably all British industries were handicapped relative to those in the United States by more expensive natural resources but this appears to be particularly true in electricity, where hydro-generation was far more widely used in America. In contrast, much the greater part of British electricity was generated by steam. A comparison of productivity that controls for natural resource availability must exclude hydroelectric output from the USA. Even doing so, in 1927 US output was more than five times British, about double the British electricity output per head of population (Table 7.7).

British labour in electricity generation put in longer hours per week, about 49, whereas US employees' weekly hours fell from

TABLE 7.7 *Output ratios (USA/GB) 1927 and 1937*

Year	Electricity		Railways		Telecommunications	
	Total	US steam only	Ton-miles	Passenger-miles	Phone calls	Telegraph messages
1927	8.839	5.44	22.92	1.85	26.97	3.09
1937	5.265	3.27	19.73	1.19	15.51	3.06

Notes: Electricity: unweighted bill; kWh. GB railway passenger-miles for 1927 calculated from sum of Feb. and Sept. passenger-miles times six for 1925; 1937 is for main line cos. only for Sept. 1938 to Aug. 1939.

Sources: US Censuses of Production; GB Reports of the Electricity Commissioners; US Statistical Abstract; Aldcroft (1968).

TABLE 7.8 *Labour input (USA/GB) 1927 and 1937*

	Electricity generation	Railways	Telecommunications
1927	3.72	2.60	5.39
1937	1.90	1.82	3.92

Notes: British telecommunications were operated by the Post Office in conjunction with the postal service. Although separate wage and salary figures were provided in the commercial accounts, no figures for telecom. employment seem available. Total postal office employment was therefore multiplied by the share of telecoms. wage and salary in the PO's total wage and salary bill to approximate British telecom. employment.

Sources: GB railway employment, hours, wages from *Ministry of Labour Gazette* (Mar. 1927), 93; (Oct. 1927), 370; (Oct. 1937), 382, 257.

45.8 to 40.3 over the decade (cf. Table 7.8). Manning levels were also higher. Labour productivity in Britain fell relative to America between 1927 and 1937, the years during which the national grid came into operation (Table 7.9), but because electricity generation was not a labour-intensive industry the effects on the rest of the economy were very small. Since both Britain and America suffered from widespread unemployment at the time, it is not obvious why there should have been differential effects. This is especially so since the sectors under consideration were regulated natural monopolies in both countries and therefore the intensity of product market competition cannot be the answer.

TABLE 7.9 *Labour productivity (USA/GB) 1927 and 1937*

	Electricity generation		Railways	Telecommunications
	All sources	Excludes hydroelectricity		
1927	2.37	1.46	4.04	3.38
1937	2.77	1.72	5.81	3.31

Notes: Revenue weights averaged for aggregating railway outputs: USA 1927: 0.17 for passenger, 0.083 freight; 1937: 0.11 passenger; UK 1927: 0.45 passenger; 1937: 0.44. For telecoms. USA 0.85, 0.897 for telephones, for GB 0.79 and 0.891. Geometrical averages employed in this and subsequent tables.

Approximating capital with generating capacity and measuring fuel in coal equivalent tons yields the total productivity indices of Table 7.10. Capacity and fuel ratios by 1937 were much closer to output ratios than was labour input. Consequently the total productivity index for non-hydro-generation in that year was fairly similar for the two countries. Capital and fuel were used more economically relative to the USA over the decade 1927–37 so that the total productivity gap narrowed substantially. In fact we have no reason to suppose that under the pre-1926 regime the USA–GB gap might not have widened further, and therefore the narrowing of the productivity gap would understate the achievement of the CEB regime.

Whereas electricity generation was a rapidly expanding industry in both countries, railways were contracting in the face of road competition. However the decline over the decade in Great Britain was small compared with the substantial contraction in the USA, where passenger-miles fell by more than a quarter and ton-miles by 16 per cent. The pattern of decline reinforced the already striking difference between the outputs of the two systems in 1927: the enormous importance of freight in the USA, generating nearly five times as much revenue as passengers. In Great Britain by contrast, receipts were nearly balanced, with freight accounting for only 22 per cent more revenue than passengers. In 1927 the excess of US telephone calls over those in Great Britain was even more spectacular than the lead in rail freight, and that does not take into account the greater development of long-distance

TABLE 7.10 *Capital, fuel, and total factor productivity (USA/GB) 1927 and 1937*

(a) *Railway capital (USA/GB)*

	Locomotives	Freight cars	Passenger cars	Track miles
1927	2.70	3.31	1.07	8.09
1937	2.34	2.70	0.94	7.55

(b) *Telecommunications capital (USA/GB)*

	No. of exchanges	No. of telegraph offices	Miles of wire
1927	4.68	2.16	8.76
1937	3.35	1.84	6.55

(c) *Capital/capacity ratios (USA/GB)*

	Electricity		Railways	Telecommunications
	All sources	Excludes hydroelectricity		
1927	5.04	3.71	6.70	5.43
1937	4.14	2.95	6.59	4.19

Notes: Assumed weights for railways: track miles 0.85, locomotives 0.1, passenger cars 0.03, freight cars 0.02. For telecoms., 1927, 0.15 for telegraph offices and 0.425 each for exchanges and wire; 1937 telegraph weight reduced to 0.12 and the others adjusted accordingly.

(d) *Fuel* (coal equivalent tons)

	Electricity	Railway
1927	4.67	8.30
1937	3.33	6.45

(e) *Total productivity (USA/GB)*

	Electricity		Railways	Telecommunications
	All sources	Excludes hydroelectricity		
1927	1.98	1.43	2.80	3.37
1937	1.50	1.18	3.57	3.20

Notes: USA telecom. 1927 labour share 0.49, GB 0.71; 1937 GB 0.49, USA 0.46. Railway weights labour 0.62, fuel 0.03, capital 0.35. USA electricity 1927 (1932) labour 0.164, GB 0.167; 1937 USA 0.199, GB 0.165. Capital 1927 USA 0.738, GB 0.695; 1937 USA 0.717, GB 0.698. Country factor shares averaged to form Tornqvist indices.

service in the USA. In telegraphy, an industry whose output unlike telephony was gently declining in both countries, British usage was almost comparable to that of the USA.

US railway employees averaged a 50-hour week (assuming a 52-week year) in 1927 falling to 48.2 in 1937. British hours of work seem to have been similar in the 1920s but without the 3.7 per cent reduction of hours in the 1930s; a comparable divergence to that in electricity but less marked. Weekly hours were 48 but some hours of overtime would normally be worked as well. The US hours' reduction cuts the 1937 labour ratio from 1.89 to 1.82 (Table 7.8). Labour productivity in these industries then shows the pattern of Table 7.9.

Railways were big employers in both countries. Employment in Britain in 1927 was 683,000 compared with 63,000, less than one-tenth the number, in electricity generation. Labour productivity in British railways fell severely relative to American productivity and must have adversely affected the performance of the whole economy. Employment policy is one of the major proximate causes, for the post-war settlement required treating labour as more of a fixed factor of production than before, with a guaranteed working week and comparative security of employment. This is consistent with institutional sclerosis (Olson 1982), though not necessarily with the perjorative implications of that term, or merely a change of attitudes, which was not so obvious in the United States.

Inspection of components of the capital stocks in the two countries (Table 7.10) shows the impact of the much greater area of the USA. Railway track miles and telecommunications wire length was far longer in the USA whereas other components were not so dissimilar, controlling for the differences in population of the two countries. Increasing British telegraph offices in a declining industry enhanced the already greater British intensity here. In railway passenger carriage numbers Britain exceeded America absolutely by 1937, in part because of the slower British diffusion of the motor car.

These calculations are imprecise but the overall picture seems clear. In telecommunications labour productivity in GB only slightly improved relative to the USA, despite a radical increase in capital which enhanced relative total productivity. This last change is however sufficiently small that, given the margin of error in the calculation, it is possible the British state industry merely held its own against the American. In view of the support given to the declining British telegraph industry, the implied performance of the British telephone industry is the more creditable.

In railways capital intensity relative to the USA remained unchanged in Britain but employment increased. Only in British electricity generation was capital used more economically relative to the USA so that the total productivity gap narrowed substantially. Whereas, in the tightly regulated electricity industry, state-sponsored reorganization narrowed the productivity gap between the two countries over the period 1927–37, and in the wholly state-owned telecommunications the gap perhaps slightly closed, in privately owned railways the British productivity lag increased. At least for these three industries, in the (regulated) private sector more than the public there seems to have been a tendency to absorb or maintain excess labour in comparison with the United States for reasons which must be cultural, ideological, or political.

WIRELESS BROADCASTING

The second radical instance of industrial policy widely judged to have been successful in this period was the regulation of wireless broadcasting, with the creation of the British Broadcasting Company/Corporation. Using the ether as a channel for transmission, radio at first sight is freed from the distinctive channels or pathways of network industries. Spectrum and transmission limitations however imposed very similar constraints. These persuaded the government to opt for a state monopoly on the grounds that private industry with fairly free entry, as in the USA, would lead to a deterioration of service quality or the emergence of a private monopoly.

Thanks to the statutory electrical communications monopoly, Marconi's pioneering radio experiments were only possible with the approval of the Postmaster-General. The Post Office withdrew Marconi's licence in 1920, repeating its behaviour over the wire telephone forty years earlier. Marconi, in turn, was persistently criticized by the Post Office and other manufacturers for its restrictive use of patents. As a result of lobbying by Wireless Societies in January 1922 Marconi's licence was reinstated with tight

TABLE 7.11 *Exports of telecommunications and wireless equipment* 1927

	% of 6 countries	Wireless exports only (£m.)
USA	29.8	1.891
UK	29.9	1.005
Germany	29.9	1.873
France	3.1	n/a
Switzerland	0.4	n/a
Belgium	6.9	n/a

Source: *The Electrical Industry of Great Britain* (BEAMA, 1929).

controls; Marconi was allowed half an hour's broadcasting a week. Soon after the BBC was inaugurated and private broadcasting was completely outlawed. The failure of the early British lead in radio to be reflected in exports by 1927 (Table 7.11) probably stemmed from Post Office policy but it was the insistence on freedom of entry to the manufacturing industry, which kept firm size small, that was harmful to continuing innovation, rather than restrictions on Marconi's activities. By 1936 only 9.6 per cent of the world radio trade originated in Britain (Sturmey 1958: 186).

Under John Reith's direction, the BBC's monopoly was not primarily intended to provide listeners with what they wanted but with what was good for them. Correct information and education, broadly interpreted, received a high priority (Briggs 1961: 371). Even during the 1926 General Strike the BBC maintained a considerable degree of neutrality in reporting. Incorporated in 1922, the British Broadcasting Company was guaranteed by Marconi, BTH, GEC, Metropolitan Vickers, RCC, and Western Electric. These ('big six') companies were expected to provide whatever money was necessary to broadcast efficiently until the end of 1924; they were required to act in the public interest in much the same way as the electricity generators under the 1926 Act. Any bona fide British manufacturer could become a member of the company by acquiring at least one share. They agreed to pay a tariff on sets or components they sold equal to fifteen shillings. The early development of radio must have been constrained by the Post Office regarding the receivers' licence partly as a tax, for only half the ten shillings was payable to the company. By May 1923 there were 564 members. When wound up at the end of 1926 there were over 1,700 shareholders. The six companies were responsible for establishing the broadcasting stations (the eight main stations were completed by October 1923) but all comers could sell receiving sets. The industry employed about 40,000 in 1925 with a turnover of £10–12.5 million. By the end of 1924 1.13 million licences were in force. Post Office restrictive policy was not as effective as it might have been for in July 1925 about 3 million sets were in use, as against 1.4 million licences issued. By the end of 1926 the second total had risen to 2.18 million.

On 1 January 1927 all the shareholders were paid off at par and broadcasting vested in the public British Broadcasting Corporation, licensed by the Postmaster-General for ten years. The big six had received only 7.5 per cent per annum for their risk-bearing and no nominal capital appreciation; clearly they had been used by the state rather than 'capturing' the regulatory mechanism. That continued to be true of the BBC as a revenue-raising device for the state. Until 1936 the Corporation received a declining proportion of the licence fee as the number of licences increased. The new Charter granted the BBC a minimum of 75 per cent after Post Office collection expenses were deducted, and the proportion actually increased in the years before the outbreak of war. Other public interest goals were served by the BBC broadcasting weekly forty-four hours of programmes in foreign languages by 1939. But this was not a unique characteristic of non-profit organizations for private enterprise radio in the USA behaved similarly in this respect. The National Broadcasting Corporation broadcast to Latin America from 1932 (Sturmey 1958; Huth 1942).

The British government decided that they did not want the free enterprise pattern of wireless development of the USA, but the same could not be said of the British public. Foreign commercial broadcasting for British listeners began to make an impact in 1930, aided by the International Broadcasting Company, formed in March of that year. At least twenty-one British firms sponsored programmes from foreign stations in 1932. Advertising outlays rose from around £200,000 in 1934 to more than eight times that figure in 1938. Radio Normandy and Radio Luxembourg were the principal stations. Listening was heaviest on Sundays; one-half or more occurred then when the BBC was transmitting. In the rest of the week about half the listening was in the early morning, when the BBC was not transmitting. Thus free enterprise filled a gap in two respects; one by providing less elevated listening on Sunday than the BBC and the other by broadcasting something when the BBC offered nothing (Coase 1950). A more competitive broadcasting industry in Britain would not have left these gaps. Equally a competitive industry would have been less able to encourage the state to attempt the suppression of foreign broadcasts. In the four years 1929–33, perhaps the least auspicious in the twentieth century were it not for the emergence of foreign commercial broadcasting, the number of licences taken out doubled to 6 million. Thereafter expansion to 8.9 million in 1939 was more leisurely.

Inadvertently the monopoly was less repressive in the case of relay wireless. Wire broadcasting began in 1924 when the owner of a Hythe electrical shop ran wires from his radio to speakers in other houses, eventually up to ten miles away. He charged 1s. 6d. a week for the service for which the Southampton Post Office gave permission, providing that his customers also bought receiver licences. When the Post Office headquarters discovered the enterprise they pointed out that it was clearly illegal, but since permission had already been given, they felt unable to ban relay wireless. They merely regulated it so as to raise the risks of entering the industry. The press and the BBC naturally objected to the power of the exchanges to spread foreign programmes and advertising. None the less there were 343 exchanges and 233,554 subscribers by 1935.

United States broadcasting offered a remarkable contrast to the British industry. Any American citizen or society in principle could obtain a licence to broadcast in the 'public interest, convenience and necessity'. The Federal Communication Commission assigned to each station its wavelengths power and broadcasting hours. Licences were granted for only six months and were withdrawn in the event of failure to comply with the requirements of the FCC. By the end of the 1920s the industry employed around 200,000 and operated some 700 broadcasting stations. Finance came primarily from advertising, but in 1940 300 transmitters belonged to or were controlled by newspapers, thirty-five educational stations were the property of universities or colleges, and there

were ten religious stations. As expected from the network technology of the industry competition had resulted in two companies
dominating American broadcasting; the NBC founded in 1926 as
part of RCA was the largest, and CBS, founded in 1927, was
the runner-up. In March 1938 there were 62,000 hours of US
programmes in one week. Commercial programmes paid for by
advertisers took about one-third of the time and 'sustaining'
programmes accounted for the remainder. Programmes rarely
lasted more than fifteen minutes during the day, or half an hour
in the evening, but tastes and techniques developed; the NBC
increased the time devoted to radio drama from 10.8 per cent in
1932 to 20.1 per cent in 1939. Cultural pluralism in the United
States made a pluralist broadcasting policy a more obvious solution, but whether the effective educative power of radio was less

TABLE 7.12 *The international spread of domestic radio/wireless 1928–
1941*

	Sets per 1,000 inhabitants	
	1928/9	1 Jan. 1941
Sweden	60.26	231.87
Denmark	62.88	225.43
USA	60–100	223.26
New Zealand	39.09	212.10
Great Britain	56.48	197.70
Australia	52.45	173.30
Germany	37.69	166.27
Canada	39.13	148.15
France	30.78	122.50
Japan	7.03	77.54
Argentina	52.05	76.16
USSR	1.37	62.07
Chile	7.62	32.02
Italy	6.17	31.11
Mexico	3.49	23.42
Spain	3.45	11.94

Note: All these figures, but the US in particular, are subject to error because of the
difficulty of checking. In countries where licence fees were payable, understate-
ments vary with enforcement procedures and culture. The US figure for 1929 was
'over 8 million sets, some estimates as high as 15 million'.

Sources: Batson (1929); Huth (1942).

than in Britain, as Reith believed, is not the type of question that can be examined here.

The US lead in broadcasting was much less obvious than in other network technology industries. Until 1936 there were more wireless sets per head of the population in Britain than in any other European country, a record not matched in telephony during the twentieth century. (But at the end of the 1920s and the 1930s the Scandinavians achieved similarly high wireless usage as they had maintained in telephony.) That might be taken to support the claim for the BBC's excellence, but more likely the incompleteness of the state monopoly, the availability of foreign commercial broadcasting, and relatively cheap radio/wireless sets were more responsible. At the same time it must be conceded that there is no logical reason why cultural policy should not take precedence over consumerism, and that the cost of doing so might be less consumption. Table 7.12 shows that the gap between the USA and Britain was much narrower in radio than in other, older, industries. There was less institutional inertia to overcome and in radio, although the spectrum capacity was limited with given technology, like other network channels, broadcasting across national boundaries was relatively easy. In the case of commercial radio that could increase the demand for sets despite the BBC monopoly.

CONCLUSION

Both the levels and trends of productivity in comparison with the United States during the 1930s showed British industry in a poor light. Relative to Continental industry the gaps were not always so obvious, but then those economies had caught up in the preceding half-century rather rapidly. Collusion among British firms, encouraged by the lack of an active competition policy (Broadberry and Crafts 1990), and attempts to avoid shedding labour in the face of heavy unemployment, may be a part of the explanation. But productivity comparison of natural monopoly industries in Britain and in the United States allows us to rule out different degrees of intra-industry product market competition and collusion in the two countries as general explanations. Similar or greater productivity gaps are observed in two out of the three cases considered to those in manufacturing where the scope for competition was greater. The three industries showed very different patterns of ownership, regulation, and performance but in none of them was direct product market competition of great importance.

British lag behind the USA was greatest in the oldest network, or 'natural monopoly' industry, railways, as Olson's theory of institutional scelerosis predicts. This was not a matter of technological potential, for productivity continued to rise rapidly in railways abroad. Nor was the lag related to state ownership even though state ownership was associated with policies that could be improved upon in telephony. The poorest performing network industry, railways, was privately owned although it was used as an instrument of government policy in a minor way. The two best performers, electricity generation and radio broadcasting, were the beneficiaries of imaginative state policy, although in the case of radio, state ownership was repressive in the interests of education and culture. At least some of the differences must have been due to the regulatory arrangements. Quasi-judicial control of private railway monopolies did not encourage the growth of efficiency, whereas non-profit central direction of electricity generation clearly did, even if every opportunity was not taken. An adversarial assessment of rates encouraged railways to justify themselves rather than to search for improvements. The CEB by contrast was run by engineers with a clear view about best practice technology and performance that they wished to promote. State ownership of the telephone network was not as efficient as Hull's municipal system but relative to the United States at least productivity did not deteriorate, as it did with railways. In radio broadcasting the network needed no capital. The spread of the service was less constrained by cost or price, and variations between economies with different average incomes should have been less than the diffusion of the other industries.

Would the railways and telecommunications have gained from organizations more comparable with those of radio and electricity generation or were their sizes and different market positions the fundamental causes of their performances? Bridgeman believed telecommunications organization in 1932 could be improved but the financial results of the late 1930s were not encouraging. Bonavia, the railways' most sympathetic critic, acknowledged the rigidity of railway organization, but the likelihood is that the commitment to avoid dismissals where possible and the declining market were the primary determinants of railway performance. Railways were most influential with government because of their size as employers. Regulation of the competing road passenger and freight services in 1930 and 1933 was certainly in the interests of (private) railways, just as earlier restrictions of telephony favoured the (state) telegraphs. Private firms in smaller, newer industries were unashamedly directed to pursue public policy objectives, regardless of their own. The upshot for the interwar economy probably depended primarily on the effectiveness of policy towards the largest and worst-managed industry, railways. A tougher attitude would have been necessary towards unemployment than governments felt politic if labour productivity was to have been raised further. The same was not necessarily true of capital productivity and a 4 per cent improvement would have released 1 per cent of the nation's capital stock for investment elsewhere, with considerable advantage.

APPENDIX 7.1
Regression Model for UK Telephones by Towns 1937

Data on numbers of telephones and rateable values are taken from Chisholm (1937) and London is excluded from the sample, which covers seventy-seven towns. Rateable values are measured in £000. The equation below can be thought of as a reduced form, derived from telephone demand and supply equations with price substituted out. Different supply relations therefore potentially influence both the intercept and the gradient of the reduced form equation. The equation can then be employed to predict telephone ownership in Hull had the town been supplied by the same network and on the same conditions as the seventy-seven towns in the sample. The OLS regression equation estimated is:

$$\ln \text{(telephones)} = 1.3508 + 1.0171 \ln \text{(rateable values)}$$
$$(0.2246) \quad (0.0345)$$

$$R^2 = 0.9205$$

8

The Causes and Content of the 1940s Nationalizations

INTRODUCTION

The performance of the network industries in the inter-war period was an important ingredient of the drive to industrial reform in the 1940s. There were other major factors in what proved to be quite sweeping changes in industrial organization. The industries which were nationalized in the 1940s have been described as 'basic', a loose but commonly used phrase meaning no more than that they were part of the fuel and transport infrastructure or were producers of major capital goods like iron and steel. Nationalization meant that *all* the assets associated with specific products (coal) or services (gas) were brought under public ownership. Many of the existing companies had substantial ancillary activities (hotels for the railways, shipping and brickworks for the coal companies) which were difficult to unscramble from the main line of business; hence whole undertakings were often acquired. The hotel industry was not therefore nationalized though part of it was brought under public ownership. Railways were nationalized and the new Railway Executive had a monopoly of all rail services. Nationalization was thus associated with the sale of certain products and services under monopoly conditions which, as we shall see later, were enshrined in the nationalization statutes.

The industries taken over are shown in Table 8.1, where coal is the first industry of any size. Iron and steel was the last and was denationalized together with the road haulage part of transport after the Conservatives came to power in 1951. Airports and parts of the motor industry (Rolls-Royce, British Leyland) were brought into public ownership in the 1960s and 1970s when iron and steel were renationalized. But the main thrust of nationalization in the twentieth century occurred during the Labour government of 1945–51. It involved a significant shift of resources to the public

TABLE 8.1 *Nationalizations 1940–1951*

Public corporation	Vesting date	Total employees 1950
British Overseas Airways Corporation (BOAC)	1 Apr. 1940	16,000
British European Airways Corporation (BEAC)	1 Aug. 1946	7,000
National Coal Board (NCB)	1 Jan. 1947	730,000[a]
British Transport Commission (BTC)	1 Jan. 1948	890,000
British Electricity Authority (BEA) and area boards	1 Apr. 1984	170,000
Area gas boards and British Gas Council	1 May 1949	140,000
Iron and Steel Corporation of Great Britain	15 Feb. 1951	235,000 (Nov. 1951)

[a] Excluding workers in ancillary activities.

Source: Clegg (1952: 425).

sector. The 2.2 million employees recorded in Table 8.1 for 1950 accounted for 10 per cent of the UK labour force. The nationalized industries were moreover very capital-intensive. Public investment started to account, by the early 1950s, for 50 per cent of national investment. About two-fifths of public investment was undertaken by the nationalized industries, who therefore accounted for 20 per cent of UK investment for much of the post-war period up to 1980.

There is no easy answer to the question of the 'causes' of nationalization and much of the secondary literature is noticeably empty of sustained analysis. Scholars have been content to see the programme as the inevitable outcome of long-standing problems, especially in coal and railways, whilst recording that contemporaries and other observers saw it as the centrepiece of the socialist vision in 1945 (Aldcroft 1968: 105–8, 1986: 224; Alford 1988: 26; Cairncross 1985: 469, 483).

It is mistaken to attribute all the features of nationalization to the Labour Party. The post-war consensus was to the left of centre and the move to public ownership, if not all the details of nationalization, commanded considerable support in other political parties, investigating committees, and professional associations. There were also many strands in the arguments forwarded. They included the promotion of large-scale units of business organization, the rescue of declining industries, and the desire to raise technical performance by increased investment. In addition there were issues more exclusively associated with the Labour Party like the development of co-ordinated policies for fuel and transport, the promotion of economic planning, and the desire to redistribute economic power. What we shall do in this chapter—and Supple (1986; 1987: ch. 15), Chick (1991), and Hannah (1979: ch. 10) have already pointed the way—is to show what role, if any, each of the above issues played in the enhancement of public intervention in industry and in the particular form which that intervention took. Nationalization as an institutional change had many components which we shall aim to unpack and explain. Transport finished up organizationally different from gas and electricity; policy towards iron and steel was rather ambivalent; cotton remained private; arm's length regulation of private companies was rejected in several cases. In the course of defining the institutional characteristics of the new nationalized industries, we shall demonstrate that such features are intrinsic to an understanding of their performance in the post-1945 period, much more than the oft-stressed fact that Ministers and board chairmen came to power in the 1940s with no guidance on the detailed running of such large public enterprises (cf. Gourvish 1986: 27; Thompson and Hunter 1973: 6, 14; Ashworth 1991; Aldcroft 1986: 224).

The thrust of the chapter is that the broad support for public ownership came from the desire to improve industrial organization whilst the outcome in the Nationalization Acts was a set of institutions which in addition gave central government the power to redistribute real income. The next section looks at some background issues in the inter-war period and this is followed by more detailed consideration of the problems of government attempts to improve economic organization in the network industries. In assessing the 1940s shift to public ownership the act of establishing new utilities is distinguished from the public operation of such utilities. Nationalization is then shown to involve yet further features and finally there is a section considering the particular legal and administrative instrument chosen, the public corporation.

GOVERNMENT AND INDUSTRY IN THE
INTER-WAR PERIOD

The development of large-scale units of business organization was an important component albeit not the only one, in the 1940s nationalizations. A relevant starting-point is therefore to outline how that particular concern of government had arisen in the inter-war period and how it related to the broad features of the government's relationship with industry. The inter-war period saw the emergence of industrial problems which were to continue right through to the 1970s. From being in the nineteenth century a country with a relatively low involvement of government with industry, Britain had moved rapidly by the 1940s to one with relatively high commitment (cf. Tolliday 1986: 100). Whilst moreover the manufacturing sector had been little touched by government intervention in the nineteenth century, from the 1920s industrial policy increasingly included this sector as well as the fuel and transport infrastructure.

Inherited from the nineteenth century were four sets of forces which had provoked government involvement in industry. In mining and manufacturing it was safety. This was an issue in the utilities in fuel and transport where, in addition, as we have seen in the earlier chapters, economies of scale, externalities, and rights of way had drawn in the government. Thirdly there were the collective actions increasingly characterizing the wage bargaining of both workers and employers with contingent threats to law and order. Finally the widening of the franchise meant that Members of Parliament were subject to a greater range of political pressures, many of which stemmed from economic, including industrial, issues. In the period 1914–40 three additional factors were at work. The First World War not only brought trade unions into national wage negotiations and introduced central planning in some sectors but it also revealed certain new techniques, technological gaps, and weaknesses on which government action was expected in peacetime—for example airframes, dyestuffs, and-related chemical products leading to government participation in the establishment of ICI in 1926 and the development of the 'ring' of aircraft manufacturers (Fearon 1974; Reader 1977). Secondly the stagnant economic conditions of the inter-war period caused governments to be involved in industrial performance. The most dramatic output losses were in the export trades which had been central to the economy in the late nineteenth century and which were regionally concentrated. Given the now broader electoral base this carried political difficulties and in addition the output losses were seen, then and subsequently, as a manifestation of industrial decline. The third factor was that technological and administrative changes were making for larger-sized industrial undertakings. Political concern with company size stemmed in part from the potential monopoly power of such large business units but also, and (cf. Hannah 1976: 73) perhaps more important, British governments, conscious of the loss of export markets and apparent industrial decline, saw the move to large firms as typical of the USA and Germany, the pace-setters, and indeed of the 'new industries' (non-ferrous metals, telephone apparatus, tyres); hence the green light to push British industry along that path.

A detailed consideration of government policy, in particular for manufacturing, is beyond the scope of this chapter, but some general points need to be made. Policy was as usual coloured by the political and social context. In the 1920s industrialists, politicians, and civil servants clung to the pre-war world, which included an Empire bias (the subsidy to Imperial Airways), whilst the Treasury's classical view on crowding out and wage flexibility helped to erode some of the state intervention surviving from the war (Lowe 1978). Unemployment persisted in certain regions where decline seemed to be reinforced. The establishment view that regional unemployment was essentially a symptom of the world depression and that the depressed areas were a social rather than an economic problem gave way by the 1930s to attempts, albeit half-hearted, to shift industry to the depressed areas (Parsons 1988: chs. 1, 2). A product of this complex of forces was a government policy to industry with two arms. First was a hesitant and often reluctant alleviation of key sectors from the full brunt of market forces. Short-term palliatives to cotton, iron, steel, and other staples came from bank loans and overdrafts which by the end of the 1920s were drawing in the Bank of England, anxious to avoid financial disasters and to avoid embroiling the government (Kirby 1974; Heim 1983, 1986).

The longer-term policy was to support the introduction of price-fixing schemes, whose effectiveness has been much disputed except where foreign competition was excluded by protection as in the 33 per cent steel tariff of the 1930s. In any case such price-fixing came increasingly, as in the coal industry, to be seen as undermining the elimination of excess capacity and promotion of amalgamation. For much of the period such government promotion was hesitant. Contraction and rationalization occurred towards the end of the 1930s for the cotton industry but largely because demand never recovered; rationalization in coal through the 1930 Act was undermined by the lack of compulsory powers which again did not materialize until the end of the 1930s (Kirby 1973*a*, 1973*b*). In the utilities field the major success was the Central Electricity Board, which from 1926 centralized the high-tension transmission of electricity in a national grid and saw the gap with US technical efficiency eliminated by the end of the 1930s (see Chapter 7). Finally the generally protective and anti-competitive attitudes which inter-war governments displayed, especially towards large business units, carried over to transport. In a broad sense the main characteristic of the inter-war years was the emergence of the four railway companies under such tight regulation that they had difficulty in adapting to the new small highly competitive mode of transport. As a result government policy restricted road transport in such a way as to favour both the large railway companies and the larger business units emerging in both road freight and road passenger activities—Pickfords, Carter Paterson, Tilling, Scottish Electric Traction (Savage 1966: chs. 7, 8).

In the next sections we look at the network industries in detail and suggest that the secular movement to larger units observed generally in the inter-war period and with, albeit hesitant, government encouragement had established by the 1940s a wide consensus for public intervention. State action was needed, we shall argue, first because of the apparent slowness with which 'voluntary' or 'natural' amalgamations of companies had proceeded. Secondly an element of public control was believed necessary in markets dominated by large producers and where tariffs or transport costs effectively excluded foreign competition. That the gain from large-scale organization was a central, albeit not the only, ingredient of the enhanced public intervention of the 1940s may be measured by nationalization never getting off the ground in industries with no apparently significant scale economies—

fishing, building, agriculture, to give some obvious examples. The main question we have to ask is what sort of public intervention was warranted by this factor alone—it obviously did not necessarily imply public ownership—and what form of economic organization and public supervision was appropiate for each industry.

THE EMERGENCE OF LARGE BUSINESS UNITS IN ELECTRICITY, GAS, AND WATER 1930–50

The local utilities demonstrate the obstacles to the achievement of what many perceived as economies of scale. As Table 8.2 shows, on the eve of nationalization they were a complex mixture of local authority undertakings, joint stock companies, joint boards, and private companies. In electricity and gas there were well over 500 largely separate undertakings in each industry even ignoring the non-statutory sector. In water supply there was more homogeneity on the surface with local authorities dominant but this, as we shall see, was not the whole story.

A major problem was that voluntary mergers foundered on the mixed public/private character of the industry. This had lain behind the central government initiative to set up in 1926 a national electricity transmission grid run by the publicly owned Central Electricity Board. The pattern of generation in the rest of the inter-war period was determined by the legislative consequences of that initiative. As we saw in Chapters 6 and 7 generation was the business of the companies and local authority

TABLE 8.2 *Number of undertakings in England and Wales in electricity, gas, and water before nationalization*

	Electricity 1946/7	Gas 1947	Water 1954
Local authorities	363	207	906
Companies	191	402	98
Joint boards	11	—	43
Non-statutory	n/a	361	7

Sources: Hassan (1991); Board of Trade returns on gas undertakings (1947); Ministry of Fuel and Power (1948).

undertakings and of these the CEB 'selected stations' for supply to the grid, the rest of the undertakings being involved simply in buying supply from the grid and then distributing it to final consumers together with any electricity they were still generating for themselves. The trend towards large plants and the CEB selection policy meant that, nine years after its inception, of the 148 stations operating under CEB direction only twenty-eight were base load and fifteen were generating more than half the system's requirements (Hannah 1977: 218). With production in non-elected stations dwindling to negligible proportions, the thermal efficiency gap with the USA practically eliminated, the system load factor raised from 25 per cent in 1925 to 37 per cent in 1939, and the Battersea 105-megawatt station the largest in Europe, there were no significant public complaints about the economic organization of generation. With only a small number of generating undertakings facing one transmitter, bilateral monopoly considerations were present and the situation bore some affinity to the post-privatization position of the 1990s. In the inter-war period regulation came through the provisions of the 1926 legislation with respect to the wholesale price of electricity as input to and output of the grid, provisions which bore quite severely on the CEB (Hannah 1979: 100, 128).

Thus the very large number of undertakings recorded in Table 8.2 came to be mainly involved in retail distribution, many with only a small turnover. In 1934 over 400 undertakings accounted for less than 10 per cent of sales (Hannah 1979: 213). The McGowan Committee of 1936 remarked on the high costs of distribution; the multiplicity of boundaries prevented efficient development of networks; there were different voltages in different areas; peak demands might also vary thereby raising, in the absence of interconnection, distribution capacity cost. In 1924/5 distribution accounted for some 44 per cent of the industry's total costs but 60 per cent by 1933/4 as the grid came on stream. Finally the McGowan Committee identified economies which would arise in marketing and finance from large units. Why were they not emerging? A major problem was the local authority sector accounting for 60 per cent of the undertakings. The municipalities did not want to give up their empires nor the profits which accrued. The experience of joint electricity authorities was not encouraging and even Herbert Morrison did not see them as a way forward (Hannah 1979: 331–2). Political conflicts and civic pride militated against collaboration between public sector institutions. The Member of Parliament for Ashton-under-Lyne observed in 1937 that the local council would rather its electricity undertaking were taken over by a new public board than see it fall into the hands of Oldham Borough, the neighbouring authority. Later, when nationalization looked likely, many municipalities were appalled at the prospect that the loss of their undertakings was to be treated largely as a book-keeping entry within the public sector and hence that they would receive as compensation simply the amount of their *net* outstanding debt (Hannah 1979: 337, 351).

In so far as the economies of scale were at a regional (or subnational) level the question was how regional business organizations would emerge. The McGowan Committee proposed that they should be developed from existing undertakings but recognized that legislation and compulsory powers would be necessary. Precisely how this would work out was not clear. Herbert Morrison had seen the solution in regional boards publicly owned on CEB lines. This got support from some civil servants, from the Conservative Minister of Fuel in 1942, and from Liberal Gwillam Lloyd George as Minister in 1943. Many professionals saw it as inescapable. Even E. H. E. Woodward, the general engineer and manager of the North Eastern Electricity Supply Company who wanted larger business units, saw ownership as irrelevant and advocated public boards (Hannah 1979: ch. 10). In the event the legislation of 1947 created twelve such regional distribution boards for England and Wales and two for south Scotland to set alongside the North of Scotland Hydro-Electric Board which had been established in 1943. The legislation did a lot more than that but the additional features, as we shall see later, had no obvious connection with the achievement of scale economies characteristic of the inter-war pressure to larger units of business organization.

A similar issue arises in the case of gas with the simplification that before the advent of natural gas in the 1970s there were no major economies of scale in production or distribution. But there were unexploited economies of scale perceived in marketing and finance. A respected view was the Heyworth Report of 1945 which stressed the need for the development of gas appliances, marketing gas in rural areas, developing new uses of gas, and expanding research, all of which it saw as requiring regional units of business organization. The peak number of undertakings had been 498 for the (statutory) companies in 1913 and 248 for the municipal enterprises in 1930 (cf. Chapter 5). But by the eve of nationalization these numbers were only some 20 per cent lower, as may be seen in Table 8.2. Moreover the distribution of undertakings was, like electricity, highly skewed. As the Heyworth Committee pointed out there were only sixty-five undertakings in 1944 producing more than 5 million therms per annum but they accounted for 70 per cent of total sales; even some of the large private companies were holding companies which the Committee felt had made only modest improvements in efficiency because they always needed the consent of the subsidiaries. As for the local authority sector, the municipal boundaries were not always optimal for production and distribution even in the absence of major economies in these functions and joint boards had not proved successful. The Heyworth Committee makes an interesting contrast 10 years on from the McGowan Committee, rejecting the latter's idea of grouping round existing undertakings. Heyworth went unambiguously for regional public boards and this was taken up in the 1948 Act which established twelve area boards producing and selling gas and reporting separately to Parliament.

Thus in both electricity and gas the 'public board' element arose in part from the problems associated with a 'natural' or 'voluntary' emergence of larger units of business organization. The nationalization programme grafted on to this set of boards certain institutions, objectives, and obligations which cannot be rationalized simply by the pressure to exploit economies of scale (cf. Chick 1991: 107). To this matter we shall turn later. In the mean time it should be noticed that the complex mixture of private and public interests, which constituted in gas and electricity obstacles to the formation of bigger units, is repeated in an even stronger form in the case of water supply. Although the economic organization of this industry has not been well researched the wide range and number of interested parties is clear. In 1915 there were 786 local authority undertakings, some 200 statutory companies, and 1,339 non-statutory companies though the local authorities accounted for 80 per cent of the industry's net output (Millward 1989: 205). Apart from the sheer number of undertakings and the entrenched position of local authorities there were other interested parties. After the First World War the Ministry of Health was given the responsibility for the planning and conservation of water resources. Other Ministries had an interest including the Board of Trade, whose Water Power Resources Committee suggested in 1919 that the wider development of water power schemes was held back by the multiplicity of interests involved. Both Ministries advocated a central water authority. But catchment boards and fishery boards were also able to make their presence felt through the Ministry of Agriculture and Fisheries. The Federation of British Industries had its own Riparian Owners' Committee which was active on the question of the release of 'compensation water' from reservoirs. As Sheail (1983) has shown, the requisite planning of water use and resource development therefore faced considerable obstacles. In 1934 the Committee on Scottish Health Services recorded hundreds of separate undertakings working independently to serve their own areas. In England and Wales a White Paper was drafted to confer on the Minister of Health the role of a central co-ordinating authority empowered to regulate the acquisition of water rights, create joint boards, and revise the areas of supply and distribution. The White Paper never materialized in the 1930s though a Central Advisory Water Committee was established in 1937. As Table 8.2 shows there were still 906 separate local authority undertakings in 1954 and the development of river basin management and national co-ordination had to await the 1973 Act.

AMALGAMATIONS IN RAILWAYS, AIRLINES, AND COAL

Both Aldcroft (1968: 105–8) and Cairncross (1985: 469) treat railway nationalization briefly, seeing it as uncontroversial and inevitable. But the form needs explaining. Regional economies of scale were expected to be realized from the proposals of the 1911 Departmental Committee on Railway Agreements and Amalgamations for regulated co-operation which took its form in the four main line companies established by the 1921 Railways Act. Crompton (1985: 224) has cast doubt on the size of these economies even though they were expected to reconcile rising wage levels with the tight price regulation introduced as a quid pro quo for the companies' protected monopolies. The size of any further economies from national unification was even less clear. In 1918 the Wilson Fox Committee, though not supporting public ownership, had favoured unification. Even the Railway Companies Association, in the course of examining in 1942 the possible form of railway organization after the war, suggested a role for a Central Board and Executive with finances pooled and/or companies merged, albeit with all assets remaining under private ownership.

The problems of shortages and restrictions which they faced after the war might have been overcome, argues Gourvish (1986: 10), by a centralized unified approach. What seems to have been especially persuasive was the apparent success of unified operations during the war, when the government introduced dual control with a Railway Executive Committee of company general managers covering London Transport and the four main line companies. Unable to replace rolling stock, the number of freight wagons in use fell by 8 per cent, and passenger coaches by 12 per cent. Despite this and with only a 2 per cent increase in the number of locomotives, freight traffic rose, as may be seen in Table 8.3, by 27 per cent 1938–46, and passenger-miles by 10 per cent. Aldcroft (1968: 106) attributed this to the streamlining of operations under unified command, especially after 1941, when a Ministry of War Transport was established with power over all forms of transport. What is relevant for our purposes is that the public ownership of railways (let alone its emergence as part of a national transport undertaking) cannot easily be attributed to the problems of securing large units of business organization which were already in existence and in close contact with each other by the end of the inter-war period.

Domestic airlines in the 1930s were in a position somewhat similar to that of the railways before the First World War. Throughout the inter-war period the embryonic domestic air routes were serviced by several British companies free from foreign competition and with financial involvement by companies in competing transport modes like shipbuilding and railways. From 1935 the newly formed British Airways company was servicing Continental destinations, with a government subsidy. Imperial Airways had been doing the same for the Empire from the 1920s. On domestic routes in the 1930s up to twenty companies were operating but by 1938 there were only five important undertakings not in the direct

TABLE 8.3 *Trends in production in the 1940s*
(1948 indexes: 1938 = 100)

Electricity (gigawatt hours)	190.3
Gas sales (therms)	145.4[a]
Coal (tons)	87.5
Manufacturing	120.7[b]
Crude steel (ingot tons)	117.1[c]
Iron ore (tons)	85.9[d]
Railway passenger-miles	110.0[e]
Cars (no.)	100.5
Buses and coaches (no.)	128.3
Rail freight (net ton-miles)	126.9[e]
'A' licence road vehicles (no.)	94.5
'B' licence road vehicles (no.)	118.5
'C' licence road vehicles (no.)	161.9

[a] Annual averages for 1939.
[b] Annual averages for 1936–8.
[c] Annual averages for 1936–40 and 1946–50.
[d] Annual averages for 1937 and 1946.
[e] Annual averages for 1946.
Sources: Pollard (1992: 251); Burn (1958: 268–73); Thompson and Hunter (1973: 223); Aldcroft (1968: 99).

control of the railway companies. Aldcroft (1974: chs. 9, 10), and Lyth (1990) saw no sign of the railway companies promoting coordination for the achievement of scale economies, although of course airline development had barely got off the ground. The Cadman Report of 1938, which was critical of the Ministry of Civil Aviation as well as the airlines, proposed that areas of operation should be streamlined, each to involve only one airline albeit with a subsidy; effectively this was a demand (repeated in the Ministry's own 1945 White Paper) for legislative powers for compulsory amalgamation but retaining private ownership. This did not emerge and therefore the problems of securing gains from rationalization and economies of scale can be advanced as an element in the public ownership which followed. There were obviously other factors at work, as rearmament loomed and the defence potential of aircraft was realized, in the merging of British Airways and Imperial Airways into the new publicly owned British Overseas Aircraft Corporation in 1940 (Eldon Barry 1965:

361; Lyth 1990). But the 1946 Civil Aviation Act did establish British European Airlines as a publicly owned corporation with a monopoly of British scheduled services on domestic and European routes. Also in this context we should note that the manufacture of aircraft raised altogether different issues, including technical progress and the proper location for research and development. Demand in peacetime was uncertain but by the late 1930s a war demand was clearly likely. As Edgerton (1984) has shown the key question came to be whether to keep manufacture private or bring it into the state sector in a form like the naval dockyards or the US Army Corps of Engineers.

Finally developments in coal are especially relevant for a full understanding of the 1940s nationalizations. How far the industry's management and industrial structure were deficient relative to the coal industries of Germany and America and how far large units of business organization were associated with more mechanization and higher productivity have been sources of considerable dispute among historians (Kirby 1973*a*, 1973*b*, 1977; Buxton 1970); the latest analyses suggest that for the interwar period and earlier size, organization and mechanization had positive and quite independent effects on output per head (Fine 1990; Greasley 1990). Whatever the substance of economies of scale in production and marketing, the case for larger business units had been pressed by the Sankey Commission (1919) and the Samuel Commission (1925) and was enshrined in the Coal Mines Act of 1930 which set up the largely unsuccessful Coal Mines Reorganization Commission. Officials in the Mines Department of the Board of Trade were active in keeping the case going (Kirby 1979) and indeed the views of civil servants on rationalization were, during the war, probably more important than those of the Labour Party. Sir Ernest Gowers, the (exasperated) former member of the CMRC, produced within the Board of Trade in 1942 a memorandum arguing that large-scale organization would have to be pressed on the owners probably through the establishment of a public board (Supple 1986: 244). But the biggest push—and bigger than for other industries—came from the Reid Report of 1945. Its critique of the industry was devastating because the Committee was made up of senior mining engineers from the large companies. It stressed the need for a large investment programme to raise the rate of mechanization and the

training of new entrants; for this to be achieved many unprofitable mines would have to be closed and adjacent mines merged.
Changes were needed on a coalfield basis and, in recognition that
progress on a voluntary basis had been slow, the Reid Report
proposed the establishment of a National Authority to enforce
amalgamations. Over the two decades from 1913 the number of
companies and mines had fallen by some 40 per cent. Yet in 1938
of the 1,034 companies 718, that is 70 per cent, still employed
between them less than 6 per cent of the industry's labour force
(Supple 1987: 303). How the necessary amalgamations were to be
achieved, the conflict of interests resolved, and the sovereignty of
private companies protected was not clear from the Reid Report.
A similar gap appeared in the proposals made by the coal owners'
association which envisaged a Central Board raising levies, making loans, and acting as a body by whose decisions every company
would be bound (Kirby 1977: 1940). For many observers it was
but a small step from the Reid Report to public ownership (cf.
Beacham 1945). Immediately after the war in 1945 the then care-
taker Conservative government had clearly accepted the full
implications of the Reid Report (Kirby 1977: 192). A central
point for our purpose is that the optimal scope of business organization was deemed to be regional or coalfield size, certainly
subnational. The fact that the industry was brought under public
ownership can be attributed in part to the lack of success over
the previous twenty-five years in government attempts to enforce
amalgamations. That the National Coal Board established under
the 1946 Act was not simply a collection of regional boards
but a national public board accountable as a national entity to
Parliament cannot therefore be explained in terms of the requirements of business organization.

PUBLIC OWNERSHIP

Informed opinion by the early 1940s was therefore calling for
larger units of business organization in gas supply, electricity retail
distribution, airlines, and coal though on a regional or subnational
scale. At the least this would require legislation to enforce the
amalgamations. Legislation in the inter-war period to promote
amalgamations—coal, cotton, steel—had not been particularly

effective, so that it seemed reasonable to conclude that the expropriation of the private companies in the 1940s was in part
motivated by the desire to create larger business units. But with
this achieved why not sell off the newly created 'regional utilities'
to the private sector, retaining an arm's length regulatory control
of prices, profits, and supply conditions—as in electricity generation and the railways? Such a setting in fact emerged after the
Thatcher privatizations of the 1980s. In the 1940s its rejection can
be laid again at the door of the unhappy experience in the inter-
war period with arm's length regulation—the marketing schemes
for coal, the perilous financial position of the railways, the protection afforded the steel industry all being especially relevant for this
kind of regulation.

Indeed running through both of these aspects of regulation by
legislation was a certain disillusionment, on the part of what
might be called 'middle opinion', with reliance on guidance or
regulation or encouragement of the private companies when they
had proved so reluctant to recognize any of the alleged deficiencies
in their performance. The coal-owners are the more obvious
example. They were discredited publicly as early as the Sankey
investigation of 1919 (Supple 1986: 231–2). During the Second
World War the owners' proposals (cf. above—they were called
the Foot Plan after the chairman of their association) did not help
matters at all by calling for a Central Board, consisting wholly of
people from the management side of the industry (no miners, no
consumers) acting as trustees for the industry in its dealings with
Parliament and the public at large and yet rejecting compulsory
amalgamations. The young Harold Wilson christened the plan a
'scheme of Bourbon self government. Government of the coal
owners, by the coal owners, for the coal owners' (Kirby 1977:
194). Kirby suggested that, coming from technical specialists of
such high standing within the industry, the Reid Report was
interpreted by the public as a strong indictment of the technical
record under private ownership (Kirby 1977: 190). Elsewhere the
1944 report of the Joint Committee of Electricity Supply Associations has been described by that industry's historian as a flabby
compromise (Hannah 1979: 342). In airlines there is a similar
picture. During the war the various shipping and railway companies with financial interests in airlines had put forward a plan
for a national private airline with a protected monopoly whilst

BOAC proposed similar arrangements on the international routes. Lyth (1990: 3) has recently characterized these proposals as attempts by the existing interest groups to obtain cosy working relationships with each other.

The public board, usually of a subnational dimension, was therefore seen as capturing the relevant economies of scale in production and marketing whilst overcoming the problems of the alternative policy instrument, arm's length regulation. It would seem to be these expectations which commended the public board to the wide consensus of politicians and professional groups which the literature has noted (Hanson 1963: 22; Robson 1963: 46–8; Abel 1957: 227–8; Thompson and Hunter 1973: 7–8; Pollard 1983: 259; Hannah 1979: 334); In view of the fact that it was a Liberal government which established the Port of London Authority in 1908 and Conservative governments which legislated for the Central Electricity Board in 1926, the London Passenger Transport Board in 1933, and BOAC in 1940, it would seem that the establishment of regional public boards would not have been a matter of great debate between the political parties in the 1940s, and indeed these arguments for public boards were never seriously challenged by the Conservative Party up to the 1970s (cf. Robson 1963: 44; Thompson and Hunter 1973: 13). Hannah (1979: 334), gauging opinion in the 1930s and 1940s, saw the public boards as being acceptable to middle of the road opinion, willing to examine new solutions within the context of a mixed economy and tired of the debate between capitalism and socialism. To this has to be added the engineers, businessmen, civil servants, and other professional groups, mentioned earlier, who despaired of achieving structural change and modernization within the traditional patterns of ownership and control. The main arguments for nationalizing the aircraft industry came, as Edgerton (1984) has shown, from outside the Labour Party. Perhaps iron and steel proves the point. Large units had emerged on a significant scale and, faced as it was by foreign competition, price control was less important than for the network industries. Even the trade unions and influential members of the Labour Party like Morrison and Greenwood were lukewarm about public ownership since they doubted whether a public board could run the industry better than the present management and owners. Thus in 1947 an Iron and Steel Board was established to promote amalgamations and

BBC

technical developments. Nationalization occurred only at the end of the Labour government's period of office and was quickly reversed by the Conservative government.

NATIONALIZATION

If contemporary notions of efficient business organization had been the sole guide, the infrastructure industries at the end of the 1940s would have therefore consisted of twelve area gas boards, fourteen area electricity boards, the North of Scotland Hydro-Electricity Board, the CEB, a new Board for electricity generation, the London PTB, four railway boards, new regional coalfield boards, and two publicly owned airlines. Support for this kind of outcome came not only from the middle opinion alluded to earlier, but also, when it came to detailed planning in the 1940s, from the Treasury (favouring separate accountability) and some voices in the Labour Party like Gaitskell (Chick 1991: 108). In practice nationalization involved some major additional features. Whatever the role of particular personalities (and Morrison was apparently very influential, Chick 1991: 110) there were three fundamental forces which explain these additions.

First was a consensus that the two large, but declining industries, coal and railways, needed a national rescue act. Both were in long-term structural decline and emerged from the Second World War with, as Ministers said, a 'poor bag of assets' (Cairncross 1985: 471). The large investment needed for modernization together with major policy decisions implied national public ownership rather than a set of regional public boards. The fact that the Conservative Party's 1947 Industrial Charter accepted the need to nationalize coal and railways (as well as the Bank of England) confirms the importance of this factor (Hannah 1979: 352). The position of the railways had so deteriorated by the end of the inter-war period—with the decline of the staple traffic in coal and the advent of road competition—that the companies' demand, in its 'Square Deal', for an end to its legal disabilities was accepted by the government. The war frustrated that, and whilst from 1941 the companies were guaranteed a fixed annual payment (of £43.5 million) the associated regime which continued through to nationalization involved freezing both the level of charges (even though wages and raw material prices were rising) and the replacement of the capital stock (Aldcroft 1968: 90–4). In the period 1945–7 some £17 million was spent on two electrification schemes rather than the £500 million which had been envisaged for post-war reconstruction (Gourvish 1986: 8). Pricing policy was a national issue and any modernization would involve the question of links between regional networks; the national form of public ownership therefore followed.

In coal the situation was similar but exacerbated by severe industrial relations problems. Employment fell in the 1940s in part because the initial mistaken loss of manpower to the military was never fully restored, but what is striking about this period is that output per man fell from 300 tons in 1938 to 248 tons in 1945, so that despite the heavy demands after the war the overall fall in output 1938–48 was 12.5 per cent (cf. Table 8.3). The labour force was ageing but some observers have seen the cause more in the low morale of the work-force (Kirby 1977: 171–4; Pollard 1992: 206). Miners had slipped down the wages league whilst the Essential Work Order of 1941, introducing new disciplinary measures, was interpreted by many as bonding the work-force in a manner reminiscent of the early nineteenth century. Regional boards would involve the potential for inter-district competition in prices and wages against which the miners had long fought. So the industry was in secular decline, the Reid Report was recommending a large-scale modernization programme, and the labour force was resentful. In the view of the industry's recent historian the national form of ownership, the National Coal Board, was necessary to 'buy' the support of labour (Supple 1986; cf. also Beacham 1945).

The second major factor accounting for the difference between a set of regional public boards and the institutional framework that emerged was the Labour Party's commitment to economic planning, an issue which cannot easily be divorced from its distrust of the profit motive and the aim of redistributing economic power. The relevance, for our purposes, of the plan for common ownership of the means of production in clause 4 of the Labour Party's constitution is that it involved the promotion of economic efficiency as well as redistributing income and wealth. There was also a distrust of the use of market forces to achieve these ends. *Hence in broad terms economic planning was to be a means of achieving both justice and efficiency.* How the nationalized industries were to fit into this was perhaps never spelt out. Cairncross (1985: 484) denies they played any role but the Labour Party had in the 1930s announced that public boards would be subject to the control of a central planning board and a National Investment Board (Ostergaard 1954: 217). Moreover some of the remaining features of nationalization stemmed not simply from considerations of economic planning but rather from the way that such considerations affected the third major force we want to raise, that is, the immediate problems facing the Labour government in 1945 in the transport sector and more importantly in an economy in need of reconstruction following the depression and the Second World War.

That transport was a problem area of policy was not in dispute. The Labour Party's approach was to promote co-ordination in the use of resources; as early as 1924 it was promising a systematic reorganization of the whole system of transport and by 1931 the list of basic industries to be brought under public ownership included 'transport'. The co-ordination would be administrative and physical; the Labour members of the 1929 Royal Commission envisaged the use of compulsion. Civil servants with similar inclinations proposed to the Minister of Transport in 1941 a Transport Corporation, the emphasis being that railway unification was not enough (Gourvish 1986: 13–17). It is then this element of economic planning which explains why the various national entities envisaged in transport (docks, railways, etc.) were, in the 1947 Transport Act, not separate public boards but rather divisions (the five Executives for Railways, Road Transport, London Transport, Hotels, Docks and Inland Waterways) of the overarching nationalized entity, the British Transport Commission.

Even more important was how the Labour Party interpreted the general needs of reconstruction in the economy. This was not to be *laissez-faire*. Instead, first of all there was to be an explicit replacement and upgrading of the capital stock and training of the labour force. This is why we find overarching central councils like the British Electricity Authority with responsibilities for promoting research, training, and drawing up investment programmes. The importance of investment planning probably explains also why, in electricity, transmission and generation were merged into the new BEA. The latter's obligations for research, training, and investment are also found in the new Gas Council as well as the Civil Aviation Board, the National Coal Board, and the BTC. The importance of investment planning in all these bodies is reflected in the fact that the relevant Minister had to approve all investment programmes. Thus the 'national' element in the Coal Board stemmed from this factor as well as from the need, discussed above, for a national rescue act. In the case of the BTC there are these two elements as well as the question of transport co-ordination.

The second feature of the Labour Party's interpretation of the needs of reconstruction was that the industries were not expected to behave simply as profit maximizers but to act in the public interest, the manifestation of which in the current context was the requirement in the Nationalization Acts to provide a service throughout the country. The BTC for example was required in its Act to provide 'an efficient, adequate, economic and properly integrated system of public inland transport and port facilities ... [and] to cover costs taking one year with another'. Similar requirements to provide cheap, adequate supplies were laid down for gas, electricity, and coal. This was to prove a key feature of nationalized industry since it seemed to many of the industries' leaders to imply the provision of a service in all parts of the country, whether or not this was profitable (National Economic Development Office 1976).

THE PUBLIC CORPORATION

Whilst the objectives and industrial groupings which emerged under the Nationalization Acts were more contentious than the set of regional boards favoured by middle opinion, the particular organizational solution was less contentious. This was the 'public corporation', a twentieth-century innovation which, granted that nationalization was to take place, also commanded wide support. What explains this chosen legal instrument and how was it likely to affect economic performance?

In the nineteenth century public ownership and nationalization had been invariably associated with an enterprise run by a government department. Where the municipal undertaking was the appropriate form for local government, the Post Office was a model for the nationalized industry. For many outside socialist circles, this had generated a major fear of bureaucratic rigidities and political interference, the naval dockyards often being quoted as a classic example of poor performance (cf. Jevons 1867, 1874). Several observers during the 1920s therefore favoured public boards, taking the operations 'out of politics' (Ostergaard 1954: 206). For some, contemporary changes in the private sector appeared to point the way. The growing dominance of the joint stock company seemed to involve the divorce of ownership and control with top management rewarded by salary rather than profit. As one student of these views said: 'If it was not essential to good management for the directors to own some or all of the capital, could there not be bodies without equity capital, that is without shareholders, but managed by a Board of Directors?' (Chester 1975: 384). On the left there were also leanings towards public boards but for different reasons. Guild socialists and syndicalists envisaged them as boards of management with representatives of labour and hence close to worker co-operatives. In the 1920s the CEB and BBC had of course been established without worker representatives, and some trade unionists—the Union of Postal Workers in particular—opposed the idea of a public corporation right through to the 1940s because it omitted representatives of what they conceived as the democratic elements, Parliament and the unions.

A crucial step in the development of the basis of ownership and control of the public corporation seems to have been a memo drawn up in 1928 in part as a response to the criticisms of the coal industry nationalization proposals which the Labour Party had put to the Samuel Commission. The authors were Shinwell and Strachey, who envisaged a 'public utility corporation' which would be vested with the assets of the industry and which would issue fixed interest stock held by the state in lieu of the compensation it, the state, had paid to former owners (Ostergaard 1954: 209–10). There would be no trade union representatives who would have had conflicting interests and though many subsequently pressed for union representation it never emerged. In practice the CEB stock and the LPTB stock were held by the former owners, a matter of concern to some who saw the industry as thereby reconstructed rather than brought under social ownership.

These reservations disappeared once it had been made clear (by, amongst others, the Trades Union Congress in 1932; cf. Ostergaard 1954: 216) that the stockholders had no voting rights, did not own any equity, and the government was the sole owner. In fact in one or two corporations, including the NCB, the private owners were compensated by government stock and in the 1950s and 1960s this became the general pattern of finance by stock issues. The final strand in the emergence of the public corporation as the administrative instrument was the need to make it answerable to government. This had long been a bone of contention within the Labour Party, which had opposed *ad hoc* boards like the Metropolitan Water Board and the Port of London Authority which were accountable to Parliament but not answerable to the relevant local government authorities. Indeed Morrison broke with Labour Party traditions in promoting the LPTB, which was also *ad hoc* in this sense.

Acquisition of private companies plus the establishment of a public corporation constitute the contents of the 1940s Acts. This legislation set the scene for the performance of the industries over the next forty years. It usually gave each corporation a monopoly of the product or service in question, as in the 1946 Coal Nationalization Act, which charged the NCB with the duty of 'working and getting the coal in Great Britain to the exclusion of any other person' (section 1*a*). Apart from this it is possible to discern in the legislation two major themes. The first was that the corporations were to serve the public interest and have a specific public purpose. We have quoted the public purpose of the BTC earlier. For the NCB it involved 'securing the efficient development of the coal mining industry ... making supplies of coal available, of such qualities and sizes, in such quantities and at such prices, as may seem to them best calculated to serve the public interest in all respects, including the avoidance of any undue or unreasonable preference or advantage ... [and] advancing the skill of persons employed' (section 1 (1) *b*, 1 (1) *c*, 1 (2) (3) of the Coal Act). Whatever subsequent observers have felt about the imprecision of these public purposes there seems little doubt they were intended to be of a disinterested kind, distinguishing the board from a private company. No one was to gain from any profit the industry earned. In fact the boards were not enjoined to make a profit but were rather required to do no more than break even. Further clauses usually made clear that the proper outgoings were to include payments into reserve funds but these, together with any positive surpluses, could only, for most corporations, be applied to the specific public purpose. They could not be taken out of the industry. There were no equity shareholders and all debt was fixed interest. The board members were not to reflect any interest groups and the acts and associated instruments and regulations usually specified the broad background from which they could be drawn (finance, applied science, administration, etc.), perhaps reflecting, if not totally encapsulating, Morrison's famous dictum that they 'must regard themselves as the high custodians of the public interest. In selecting the Board these considerations must be in the mind of the Minister' (1933: 156–7). The content of the public purpose could not stray too far from national policy since the relevant Minister had general powers for acquiring information, was required to set up consumer councils to give him recommendations, could give specific directives to the boards on finance, and 'may, after consultation with the Board, give to the Board directions of a general character as to the exercise and performance by the Board of their functions in relation to matters appearing to the Minister to affect the national interest, and the Board shall give effect to any such directions' (Coal Act section 3 (1)).

The second major theme in the legislation was that the boards were to be independent of government, thereby promoting initiative, enterprise, and a basically commercial ambience. Thus the assets were vested in new bodies which were given a corporate status free from Treasury supervision of personnel and from day-to-day supervision by the Minister or Parliament as in 'a body corporate to be called the British Airports Authority . . . [which] is not to be regarded as the servant or agent of the Crown. The Authority shall have power to do anything which is calculated to facilitate the discharge of its duty under the Act' (section 1 (1), 1 (2), 2 (3) of the Airports Authority Act 1965). Although the Minister decides the tenure and terms of the office of board members, these are for fixed terms deemed to give some immunity from changes in the political party. With the aim of divorcing the corporations' accounts from the national budget, 'the revenues of the Board shall not be less than sufficient for meeting all their outgoings properly chargeable to revenue account . . . on an average of good and bad years' (Coal Act section 4(*c*)). Although capital finance was linked to the Treasury and though for some corporations specific provision was made for deficit grants, the break-even clause did have something of a history as the proper basis for municipal trading. Any threat of wage claims leading to deficits would be converted, it was hoped, to a trade-off between wages and prices. Chester, that close observer of the 1940s nationalizations, described the breakeven clause as the sheet anchor of the thinking of the Ministers who introduced the nationalization legislation (1975: 1046).

The performance of the industries is discussed in the next chapter but the two themes in the legislation did carry several dangers which we can usefully highlight at this stage. First, the public purposes were vague and therefore led to varying interpretations. For consumers it meant 'low' prices; for board members it meant offering a country-wide service not unlike the National Health Service. All interpretations involved potential conflict with the break-even objective. Secondly there was indeed a hope that management would be disinterested. 'Who are better fitted', asked an influential spokesman of this period, 'to judge ... [the public interest] than the people who are running the industry' (Shinwell, Minister of Fuel and Power, 1946 quoted in Chester 1975: 1037). Others have seen in this Tawney's romantic concept of the development of industrial management as a profession like that of doctors. Such people may enhance themselves materially, 'but the meaning of their profession, both for themselves and for the public is not that they make money but that they make health or safety or knowledge or good government or good law. They depend on it for their income but they do not consider that any conduct which increases their income is on that account right' (Tawney 1921: 108–9). All of this proved troublesome in trying to attract top managers from other parts of the economy.

Thirdly the analogy drawn for public corporations of the divorce between ownership and control in private industry was misconceived. Whatever their effectiveness, other sanctions and monitoring devices like take-overs, mergers, the unilateral ability to sell stock, followed the dispersion of private sources of capital. Moreover taking away the direct economic interests of shareholders does not mean there are no interested parties left. In 1943 the Minister of Fuel and Power (G. Lloyd George) felt that 'a conflict of interest between shareholders and consumers will not arise in the case of Public Boards which are operated by persons who are financially disinterested in the profits of the monopoly' (Chester 1975: 868). Wage-earners, ratepayers, consumers all had specific interests and politicians had even loftier ones. Finally we should return to the break-even clause. It may be the case that talk of corporations going bankrupt was, as the parliamentary draftsman of the legislation said, 'poisonous bosh', since the Treasury would always meet a board's payment of principal or interest (Chester 1975: 577–8). But break-even was one of the few statutory provisions that approached measurability and failure carried with it, rightly or wrongly, strong connotations amongst both the general public and professional observers.

CONCLUSIONS

Thus the opportunity created for public intervention had its origin in government concern for industrial performance in the inter-war period, in the limits revealed in that period of arm's length government regulation, and in the reconstruction of the economy needed after the depression and the Second World War. There was a political consensus for the reorganization of the undertakings in the network industries into large business units and for a rescue act for coal and railways. The Labour government in power in addition was committed to economic planning and the redistribution of economic power. The outcome was not simply a new set of regional boards created as legally separate and financially self-contained public corporations but rather, for each industry, a national unified framework with a public purpose which would allow the boards and the central government to redistribute real incomes.

9
The Performance of the Nationalized Industries 1950–1985

INTRODUCTION

Nationalization in the 1940s in Britain was the product of a consensus to increase the size of business units in the network industries, a rescue act for coal and railways, and a commitment by the Labour Party to economic planning and the redistribution of income. The Nationalization Acts set up national units of business organization and created the opportunity for central government to use them as instruments of income redistribution. The last chapter showed that the proponents of nationalization and the drafters of the legislation had financial soundness and efficiently provided services very much in their thoughts. By the late 1970s and early 1980s these were precisely, if not always justifiably, the major grounds for the dissatisfaction with the industries. The absence in the 1980s of defenders for the industries— across the political spectrum—was quite noticeable, allowing Dunkerley and Hare (1991) to conclude that, as a model, nationalization had had its day. In this chapter we look at the industries' performance over the whole of the post-war period. Because of the state monopoly form of ownership, direct comparison of costs and productivity with other ownership forms in the same industry in this period are not possible and several indirect measures of performance have to be used. The main theses of this chapter are, first that the institutional arrangements from the very beginning contained inherent contradictions, secondly that these arrangements allowed governments to use the industries as an instrument of real income redistribution, but that thirdly, and notwithstanding the above, the underlying productivity growth of the industries compared favourably with private industry in the UK and with the fuel and transport sectors in the USA.

INTERPRETING THE INDUSTRIES' OBJECTIVES

The way the industries had been set up as public corporations made them necessarily accountable in a very open way for what they did and how they did it. All tariffs, fares, and other fees and prices had to be published, detailed financial and operating accounts drawn up and presented to Parliament, whilst from the 1950s onwards the industries were subject to scrutiny by Parliamentary Select Committees. The 'insides' of these large corporations were therefore open to public scrutiny in a way that ICI, Unilever, and GEC never were. It made the management of organizations like the National Coal Board and the British Transport Commission, especially in their early years of development, very vulnerable to outside criticisms. Unfortunately the statutory requirements laid on the industries and hence their business objectives rendered management's task particularly difficult.

The analysis in the last chapter of the motives of nationalization and the content of the Nationalization Acts suggests that the industries were expected to serve a public purpose, perform their activities efficiently, and break even taking one year with another. Precisely what did this mean? Let us take each element in turn. A 'public purpose' was, as we have seen, written into the Nationalization Acts. Its essence unfortunately was its vagueness, and this had two major effects. First was the expectation in several quarters that the industries would behave differently from an ordinary commercial organization. The level of prices was particularly important here, as it had been in the nineteenth century, for example in the railways and in the run up to the nationalization of telegraphy. It was not simply the tightrope which the industries had to walk between on the one hand accusations of exploiting monopoly power and on the other hand running deficits and the accusation of managerial incompetence. The prices of the nationalized industries seem to have had a magnified importance for consumers (cf. Jones 1979) in part because of the lump-sum nature of quarterly bills for gas, electricity, and coal and in part because of the few short-run substitutes for fuel and transport. In the late 1940s fuel shortage, prices were not raised to clear the market. The fuel problem continued to the 1950s with clear evidence that coal prices were less than marginal costs but the Ridley Committee (1952) explicitly rejected the proposal to close the gap. In the mid-1970s the electricity and transport industries were especially vulnerable to the OPEC-induced hike of oil prices, but the nationalized industries were prevented from matching the cost increases with price increases (cf. Millward 1976).

A second element of the public purpose was the statutory injunction to provide 'cheap and adequate services'. It is clear from many of the Select Committee reports on the industries and the 1976 report by the National Economic Development Office that many industry managers interpreted this to mean a relatively uniform provision of services throughout the country. Railway tracks and electricity lines were to service rural Wales and the Scottish Highlands as well as more densely populated areas. Charging prices to cover the economic cost of these services would have been inconsistent with this interpretation of the statutory requirement, so that heavily subsidized services to scantily populated areas remained for long a feature of the nationalized industries (see for example the sections on pricing in Thompson and Hunter 1973 and Reid, Allen, and Harris 1973). For a nationalized industry to break even required that the subsidy come from other areas of its activities—the busier and more profitable sectors. Since, as in the case of railways, they often faced competition in these sectors, the necessary raising of prices made them vulnerable to loss of business to road transport. Providing adequate services had a further dimension that relates to the sheer size of the organizations. The strategic role of fuel and transport in any war or related crisis gave some rope to those pressing for increased investment programmes or arguing against service cuts. On coal for example an investigating body in 1966 suggested that for 'the greater part of the period since the outbreak of the Second World War the object of the industry has been to increase or maintain output; output rather than price has dominated the minds of the management' (National Board for Prices and Incomes 1966).

What then of efficiency, the second major objective we identified? This again is a term not defined in the statutes. At least two dimensions are potentially relevant. The first relates to the range of goods and services provided. Many economists have argued that this will be determined by the policy on fares and tariffs and that basically the cost of each service should be identified as far as is practical and the price for each service set equal to that cost. In particular this meant different prices for different services and different prices for similar services if they generated different costs; coal prices would vary geographically, electricity prices by time of day and season, rail services by density of traffic. Prices would always be at such a level as to clear markets since only then would they reflect the opportunity costs. All of this was enshrined in a White Paper on the Nationalized Industries (Treasury 1967) which at the time incorporated much advanced thinking on public sector pricing. Economists who supported such pricing policies recognized the effect on consumer purchasing power and the distribution of real income, but tended to argue that industrial pricing is not a good instrument for effecting policy on income distribution; that is the business of taxation. Clearly however such an approach to efficiency is likely to conflict violently with the way that the 'public purpose' was interpreted; such pricing practices, for example, seemed indistinguishable from those of a private company.

The other dimension to efficiency is sometimes called technical efficiency—to distinguish it from efficiency in resource allocation. Whatever the range of services offered, each should be provided in that way which uses the least volume of resources. As we have already seen in Chapter 6, there is now a body of theoretical literature which for the large part predicts that public firms will be inherently inefficient, in this sense, for two reasons. One is that in contrast to private firms, poor management does not spark off threats of take-over or losses of share values. The other is that because of the vagueness of industry objectives and the scope for ministerial discretion the most cost-effective location of plants, the cheapest source of supplies, will not be chosen. We can try to test these predictions for the post-1945 period.

Finally and crucially, there is the break-even objective. Its presence in the statutes means that the financial record is a relevant measure, if not the only one, of the industry's performance. In fact the industry's finances are important for two very specific reasons. One is that the break-even objective constitutes one of the few statutory requirements which are measurable. Students of managerial performance regard it as vital that business objectives be defined and that clear measures of accountability be available, including in particular a definition of what constitutes failure. A financial loss is the nearest that the statutes get to defining 'failure'. Moreover financial losses raise the spectre that the industries are inefficient, in one or both of the senses discussed above. For the general public and indeed informed observers, losses have often been interpreted, rightly or wrongly, as reflecting incompetent management.

THE FINANCIAL RECORD

The requirements laid on the industries were then contradictory or imprecise. Assessing performance is therefore not straightforward. It seems meaningful to consider the industries as a whole since the issue is the institutional form, the nationalized industry, rather then the ins and outs of fuel and transport policy. We shall consider financial performance since the Nationalization Acts clearly required that the industries' revenue should cover costs and we shall not get too involved with the niceties of how much should be provided for depreciation, etc. The productivity record will also be examined, since this seems a reasonable way of assessing one aspect of efficiency. Finally, the respective roles of government and management will be explored in a case-study of government control of the industries' prices.

For both public and private corporations gross profits for any year are usually measured as revenue net of operating costs and net of some measure of the capital stock used up in that period. Interest charges on debentures and fixed interest stock are much more important for nationalized industries so that profit after interest has a significance for public corporations different from private corporations where profit is devoted more to dividends. A relevant measure of the rate of profit for comparative purposes would therefore be gross profits as a percentage of assets (net of depreciation). The UK National Income Blue Books allow such figures to be calculated for the two sectors with capital consumption used as the measure of depreciation. The post-war financial performance of the nationalized industries, so measured, falls into three phases. In the 1950s in aggregate the industries' annual average rate of profit was zero, which means they did not cover interest charges. There was considerable variation across the different industries. The new technology industries of electricity, airways, telecommunications did best, earning 5–7 per cent. The British Transport Commission made losses even before interest charges, and the main source of this was the railways. In 1961 there was an important White Paper on the Nationalized Industries (Treasury 1961) which advocated a strong element of self-financing for the industries' investment programme. Certainly the 1960s saw a secular improvement towards a rate of profit of 4 per cent for the nationalized sector as a whole. The relative performance of different industries remained roughly the same as in the 1950s; the one major change was that the National Coal Board in the difficult fuel position of the 1950s had shown a reasonable financial return on its assets but in the 1960s its leading role in the energy market was being eroded and it fell towards the lower end of the spectrum of rates of profit. The early 1970s then saw a very strong decline in the profits of the nationalized sector as a whole, such that for most of the 1970s the rate of profit was negative.

The company sector showed a consistently higher rate of profit throughout the post-war period albeit one with a secular decline. The rate of profit averaged some 16 per cent in the 1950s falling to 11 per cent by the end of the 1960s. It then fell in the early 1970s but flattened out at about 8 per cent. Some of the more significant differences between the company and public corporation sector are revealed by looking at the share of profits in income as in Fig. 9.1.

The link between the share of profit in income (that is value added) and the rate of profit discussed earlier is as follows. The rate of profit can obviously be decomposed into profit/value added multiplied by value added/net assets. The latter is the output–capital ratio which has risen slowly but steadily in both sectors. It is profit's share of income that better reflects the main issues in the post-war period. Fig. 9.1 shows the very large gap between the two sectors in the 1950s. In the 1960s specific subsidies were made to the nationalized industries, mainly on the basis of legislation for railway grants. Even net of subsidies however it is clear that the profit share rises in the 1960s, closing some of the gap with the company sector. The 1970s then saw a very sharp deterioration in the nationalized industries' profit share; without subsidies, which were enhanced in this period, the share falls dramatically absolutely as well as relative to the company sector

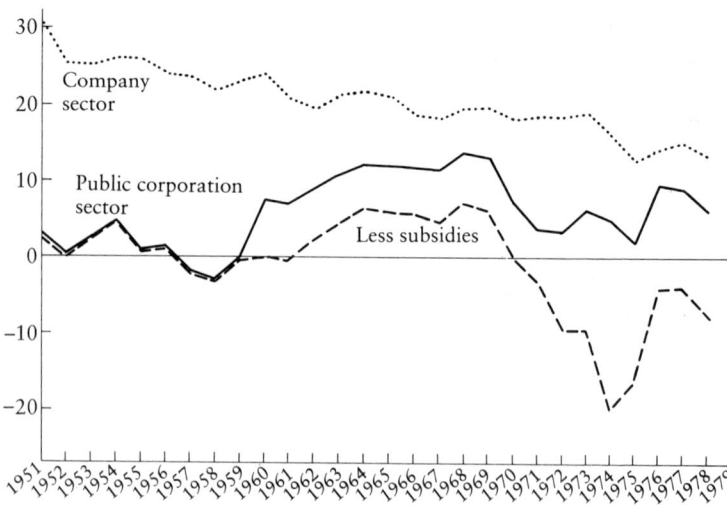

Note: Gross trading surplus as a percentage of domestic value added, both measured net of capital consumption.

Source: Millward (1982).

FIG. 9.1 Share of profits in income of public and private industry in the UK 1951–1979

and the financial losses continued for the rest of the 1970s. In summary then, after a difficult first decade, the nationalized industries in the 1960s went some way to meeting the break-even target but the finances then collapsed in the 1970s. Since this was closely connected with their role in government counter-inflation policy, the latter is considered in more depth later in the chapter.

THE PRODUCTIVITY RECORD

There is now a large body of studies of the performance of public enterprise and private firms in the same industry—electricity, railways, airways, water supply—measured through production and cost functions (see Chapter 6, second section, and Borcheding, Pommerhine, and Schneider 1982; Millward 1982; Picot and Kaulmann 1989). The results support those who argue that more competition improves managerial efficiency. They cast doubt on those who argue that public ownership is less efficient than private. Ownership *per se*, in the Western industrialized nations, does not seem to have had a decisive effect on cost effectiveness, though it does affect the range of services offered and the alignment of prices to private costs. These studies relate however largely to North America.

Assessing the productive efficiency of the UK nationalized industries is difficult in the absence of a significant private sector in the same product groupings. No one, moreover, has yet estimated international production or cost functions for these products. One is left with measures of output per head or total factor productivity in the form of comparisons across countries or over time. The critique of the nationalized industries then takes the form that their productivity growth compares unfavourably with other parts of the British economy, and that their productivity level, *vis-à-vis* other countries, is worse than other parts of the British economy. These points will be disputed. *Of course the measures are far from satisfactory but these are the measures which underlie the critique.*

To this end a sector, 'public enterprise', is defined which embraces in official UK statistics pre-1975 the industries of gas, electricity, water, mining and quarrying, transport, and communication. For 1975 and subsequently, it covers transport, communication, and 'all other energy and water supply', which explicitly excludes oil and gas extraction and processing. For the whole of the post-war period up to 1985, this sector in the UK was populated largely by publicly owned enterprises, most of which were nationalized industries in the official definition. It does include shipping and road transport, which were privately owned but accounted for only some 10 per cent of the capital stock of the public enterprise sector. There are also some omissions, mainly British Steel and British Leyland in the 1960s and 1970s; they are more important as symbols of industrial policy in that period than in terms of the quantitative impact on the productivity measures here considered.

From the mid-1970s onwards, there have been increasing criticisms of the productivity performance of public enterprises. One relates to productivity growth over time. This is not so much a matter of the trend for the sector as a whole. Indeed for the 1960s and much of the 1970s, neither the 1976 National

TABLE 9.1 *Comparative US/UK labour productivity in mining, utilities, transport, and communication: Selected indicators 1967–1975 for the USA (UK = 100)*

	Output	Employment	Productivity
Utilities 1975			
Gas	660	199	332
Electricity	856	242	354
Water	667	339	197
Communications 1972			
Post	775	340	228
Telecommunications	1,118	352	317
Transport 1972			
Rail	1,046	264	395
Local and road passenger	149	103	145
Road haulage	—	—	180
Shipping	155	91	170
Ports	386	155	248
Airlines	842	558	152
Airport passengers	475	} 215	226–310
Airport freight	651		
Mining 1967/8			
Coal	302	34	889
Other mining	1,076	536	202

Notes: The output figures are mainly based on net output at UK prices and weights with US data converted to UK prices at the exchange rate calculated for each product group. In local and road passenger transport, road haulage, shipping, ports, airlines, and airports, output is measured in tons or ton-miles, passenger numbers, or passenger journeys.

Source: Smith *et al.* (1982).

Economic Development Office report nor R. Pryke in his 1981 book could find productivity growing faster in manufacturing than in the public enterprise sector as a whole. Rather the argument was first that the public enterprise high fliers, gas, telecommunications, airways, also experienced large increases in output, which can often drag up productivity, whilst the below-par productivity growth in the also-rans, in Pryke's terminology, cannot wholly be explained by low sales growth. Pryke (1982) has also argued that private firms have performed better in those areas where they do compete with nationalized industries but the activities were, like the sale of gas and electrical appliances, marginal to the main business activities of the industries or, as in airlines, only partial productivity measures, turnover per employee, could be used. The second argument is that the productivity level in British public firms is significantly less than in foreign firms in the same product area (Alford 1988: 48–9; Shackleton 1984: 63; Pryke 1981: 244–50). In fact it is fortunate that for the 1970s there is a National Institute study of US/UK productivity, some of the data in which can be deployed, as in Table 9.1, to reinforce that point. Whereas output per head in US manufacturing was in the 1970s of the order of 2.8 times the level in British manufacturing (with construction at 1.6 and agriculture at 2.2), some of the major nationalized industries (gas, electricity, telecommunications, railways, coal) had a much worse comparative level of labour productivity. Such seems to underline Pryke's conclusions that the performance of the industries during the 1970s was 'third rate', and that 'a substantial waste of resources is occurring within the public enterprise sector due both to technical inefficiency and to misallocation. The nationalized industries must not be judged too harshly because the private sector is also woefully inefficient. Nevertheless, even by British standards, their performance appears to be poor' (1980: 226; 1981: 257). This view has not really been questioned and seems to echo the worries in the 1976 NEDO report about government control.

What needs to be established is whether output changes have truly distorted the productivity growth comparison for UK manufacturing and public enterprise; second, and related, is what the pattern looks like over a long period; a third issue is whether the unfavourable international comparisons are sustained when one looks at periods when fuel and transport were not nationalized. In Table 9.2, trends in productivity are highlighted for three subperiods determined in part by the cycle peaks of 1951, 1964, and 1973 (as used in the Matthews, Feinstein, and Odling-Smee work on long-term British growth, 1982). The year 1985 was adopted as the final benchmark. This was convenient for consistency of different sources for the 1980s and whilst 1988 might have been better as a peak year 1985 does reflect, as Feinstein and Matthews's work (1990) implies, the severity of the 1980s recession. The table shows that up to 1973 manufacturing output was growing at about 3 per cent per annum on a long-term trend.

TABLE 9.2 *Output and productivity in UK manufacturing and public enterprise 1951–1985* (annual average % growth rates)

	1951–64	1964–73	1973–85	1951–85
Manufacturing				
Output	3.2	2.9	(−)0.8	1.7
Labour	0.7	(−)1.1	(−)3.1	(−)1.1
Labour productivity	2.5	4.0	2.3	2.8
Capital	4.0	3.6	1.4	3.0
Capital productivity	(−)0.8	(−)0.7	(−)2.2	(−)1.3
Labour's share[a]	0.66	0.70	0.72	0.70
Total factor productivity	1.9	2.4	1.1	1.6
Public enterprise				
Output	2.7	2.7	0.9	1.9
Labour	(−)0.6	(−)2.3	(−)1.2	(−)1.3
Labour productivity	3.3	5.0	2.1	3.2
Capital	2.3	2.8	0.7	1.8
Capital productivity	0.4	0.1	0.2	0.1
Labour's share[a]	0.71	0.65	0.65	0.67
Total factor productivity	2.4	2.9	1.4	2.2

Notes: Definitions are the same as for Table 9.1 with series for subperiods spliced into each other to allow for changing coverage of each sector. The basic capital stock data are at 1963 replacement cost for 1948–63, at 1975 replacement cost for 1968–75, and at 1980 cost for 1975–85. For output, the weights and factor costs are 1980 for the 1975–85 period, 1975 for 1973–5, 1963 for 1949–56, and 1985 for the year 1948. The employment data 1948–68 refer to the UK and involve some changes in definitions in 1959 and in 1964. The post-1968 data refer to GB and involve a change in definition in 1971.

[a] Arithmetic average of the fraction for each year.

Sources: Central Statistical Office (1960, 1967, 1971, 1979, 1986); Department of Employment, *Employment Gazette* (July 1973, Jan. 1982, Feb. 1987) (Historical Supp. No. 1); Department of Employment (1971: table 132).

This was slightly higher than for public enterprise at 2.7 per cent per annum. However, labour shedding was higher in the latter —its labour force was declining by 1 percentage point per annum *more* than manufacturing. Thus the overall trend in labour productivity was higher in public enterprise. In the 1973–85 period output was falling in manufacturing, but the labour force declined very rapidly and the growth rate of labour productivity was slightly higher than in public enterprise—some 2.3 per cent per annum. Nevertheless, over the whole 1951–85 period labour productivity growth was slightly behind that in public enterprise. Use of man-hours in the labour productivity measure does not alter these conclusions (see Millward 1991*c*: 154 n. 5).

Striking differences appear in the use of capital. In public enterprise the capital stock grew, over the long term, at approximately the same rate as output so that there was close to a zero growth in capital productivity over the whole period. In manufacturing, the capital stock grew consistently faster than output and the two were particularly out of line in the 1973–85 period though the growth of the capital stock may have been overstated because of problems of measuring the scrapping of assets in the recession of the early 1980s. Over the whole post-war period capital productivity in manufacturing appears to have declined on average at over 1 per cent per annum. The net result is that total factor productivity growth per annum is some 0.6 per cent higher in public enterprise over the long term; or to be conservative, making allowance for the problems of measuring the capital stock, we can say that manufacturing does not show a superior productivity record. What has been perhaps overlooked on the public enterprise side is the large amount of labour shedding in the 1950s and 1960s. This was mainly in coal and transport, supplemented by the other fuel industries in the 1960s.

The UK public enterprise sector therefore does not have an inferior productivity growth record to that of private manufacturing. How does it compare internationally over time? Table 9.3 involves a labour productivity comparison of all the industrial sectors in the UK and USA over a long period, based in part on the 1982 study by the National Institute (Smith *et al.* 1982). By drawing on the earlier work of Rostas (1948) for the 1935–9 period and Paige and Bombach (1959) for 1950, we can encompass the period when the British nationalized sector had barely been born. There is an apparent volatility in the data which we should clarify. The big change in the 1940s reflects the massive effect of the Second World War with the British capital stock and hence output per man suffering significantly more than the USA. The figures jump about a bit in the 1970s but this is more a short-term problem and the 1970s detail was included mainly to link with the figures in the 1970s critiques by NEDO and Pryke.

Having made these qualifications three clear points emerge

TABLE 9.3 *Sector output per head 1938–1977: US index* (UK = 100)

	1938	1950	1968	1970	1972	1975	1977
Agriculture	103	222	242	240	207	222	209
Extractive and utilities							
Extractive	415	—	668	692	806	594	342
of which							
Coal mining	380	374	855	892	1,038	697	760
Utilities	180	—	426	397	345	321	307
of which							
Gas	163	—	736	705	492	332	279
Electricity	193	—	406	371	345	354	457
Total	360	769	517	—	—	—	323
Manufacturing	215	292	289	285	293	282	291
Construction	115	150	206	163	165	165	170
Transport and communications							
Transport	270–300	458	240	222	216	204	213
of which							
Railways	297	771	—	395	—	—	—
Airlines	—	388	—	—	152	—	—
Communications	270	264	284	291	302	323	334
Total	280	412	262	251	250	252	264
GRAND TOTAL (all industry)	181	299	278	268	271	266	266

Note: The employment data underlying the calculations are generally total numbers of employees. The output data tend to refer to gross output for 1938 and net output for later years. Aggregates involve calculations using UK prices and weights. The 1938 figure for coal relates to tonnage per man shift and the 1950 figure to tonnage per worker. All the other 1950 data on extractive and utilities exclude (for both countries) output sold within that sector. The data for airlines relate to ton-miles per employee.

Sources: 1968–77 data are taken from Smith *et al.* (1982). The aggregate figure for all industry for all years is also taken from this source, table 3.7. The 1950 data are from Paige and Bombach (1959). The 1938 data are from Rostas (1948), and relate to various years in the period 1935–9.

about the *long-term* trends. First is that, over the whole post-war period, comparative sector productivity in the British and American economies has been stable. In the words of the National Institute study: 'For long periods . . . the British bright spots have been agriculture and construction . . . The laggards have been the extractive industries and public utilities' (Smith *et al.* 1982: 39). The latter, that is, as a group had an inferior relative output per head before nationalization. Second it is clear that, whilst the

comparative labour productivity of manufacturing has not changed (nor that of agriculture and construction significantly), the UK
public enterprise sector has advanced over the post-war period
relative to the US industries in the same product area. US output
per head for the broad group of extractive industries and utilities
declined, taking UK = 100, from 769 in 1950 to 517 in 1968 to
323 in 1977. The figure for transport (which includes all modes)
declined from 458 to 240 to 213 and within that total railways
and airlines have clearly been part of the UK improvement in
relative labour productivity. From the more detailed figures
available annually for 1968–77 we may see that both the gas
industry and the electricity supply industry improved their relative
productivity levels in practically every one of the nine years. The
third point is that some of the improvements are of course simply
structural—the rise in UK oil exploration in the 1970s clearly
affecting the UK figure for extractive industries—whilst in certain
cases (coal, communications) the British performance, in labour
productivity at least, has worsened relative to the USA.

This last point brings us to the question of capital productivity.
Table 9.4 shows total factor productivity growth rates (using
man-hours for labour) for the relevant sectors in the USA and
UK using the data in Griliches (1988) and the British sources
already identified, together with data on mining productivity from
Molyneux and Thompson (1986) and Pryke (1981). Over the
whole period 1950–85 productivity grew on average at 1.8 per
cent per annum in manufacturing in both countries. In mining it
grew at a consistently higher rate in the UK. In gas, electricity, and
water there is not much difference in the first period 1950–65,
but thereafter and averaging over the whole post-war period,
annual productivity growth was higher in the UK. The record in
transport is usually, in every country, inferior to communications.
The separate figures for these two sectors in the USA have not
been aggregated in Table 9.4, but since the transport sector is
clearly bigger than communications by any measure then the
overall productivity growth in the UK is again higher than in
the USA. (See Foreman-Peck 1991*d* for further discussion of
telecommunications and Millward 1991*c*: 155 n. 7 for discussion
of other US productivity measures.) Of course, estimates of productivity change are fragile. Nevertheless, the productivity growth
record of the transport and fuel sectors since coming under public

TABLE 9.4 *Productivity growth in the USA and UK 1950–1985* (average annual % growth in total factor productivity)

	1950–65	1966–73	1973–85	1950–85
Manufacturing				
UK	1.9	2.4	1.3	1.8
USA	1.0	1.8	1.4	1.8
Mining				
UK	1.5	2.2	(−)1.0	0.9
USA	0.5	1.9	(−)4.3	−0.6
Gas, electricity, and water				
UK	3.3	4.3	1.9	3.1
USA	3.7	2.4	1.2	2.6
Transport and communication				
UK	2.4	3.7	1.7	2.5
USA	1.0–2.7	1.6–3.0	0.1–2.3	0.9–2.6

Notes: The US data relate to 1949–66, 1967–73, 1974–85, 1949–85, and 'utilities' is assumed to comprise gas, electricity, and water. The UK data relate to 1951–64, 1964–73, 1973–85, 1951–85.

Sources: Griliches (1988); Matthews, Feinstein, and Odling-Smee (1982); Pryke (1981); Millward (1988); Molyneux and Thompson (1986).

ownership in the UK bears comparison both with the privately owned manufacturing sector in the UK and with the transport and fuel sectors in the USA, where private ownership is much more extensive than in the UK.

GOVERNMENT, INFLATION POLICY, AND NATIONALIZED INDUSTRY PRICING

The differing profitability of public and private industry in the UK cannot therefore be explained by the productivity record. To a large extent the answer lies in the range of products and services supplied in conjunction with the structure and in particular the level of tariffs and fares. This is where governments have intervened in a significant way. Investment planning is another. Here we look at intervention on prices in part because its effects are more quantifiable and in part because it had a significant role in the death-throes of the nationalized sector in the late 1970s.

Inflation really took off in the UK, as well as other Western countries, in the late 1960s rising to some 25 per cent per annum by the mid-1970s. What seem in hindsight much milder inflationary bouts in the earlier part of the post-war period nevertheless prompted the use of administrative instruments to supplement fiscal and monetary policy. There were freezes on money income in 1948, 1956, and 1961/2 supplemented by a 'price plateau' in 1956 and a control on dividends in 1961. Then followed the 'guiding light' of a 2.5 per cent per annum increase in money incomes with public exposure by the National Incomes Commission as the only sanction. However, what is significant for our purpose is that public and private industry were treated on a par both in the details of official policy and in the way that policy was implemented. Official policy on this did not change in the 1960s. The two 1960s White Papers on the Nationalized Industries alluded to earlier were quite firm in proposing that public sector prices closely track costs and with an increasing margin of self-financing for investment. However, during the Wilson government 1964–70 there were increasing signs that the machinery of policy and the manner of its implementation bore more heavily on the nationalized sector. They had to give more advanced warnings of price increases and were subject to more direct official and unofficial pressure from Ministers.

There is now little dispute that during the Heath government, 1970–4, price inflation was controlled more effectively in the public sector and that therefore nationalized industries' prices were held down relative to manufacturing and relative to the movement in their costs. The crude picture from Table 9.5 is that prices in manufacturing were rising in the 1970–3 period at nearly double the rate in nationalized industries. Official policy in the first two years of Conservative government represented no break from the 1964–70 Wilson government in that the industries were officially to be treated on a par to the private sector. None the less, it is clear that the Confederation of British Industry's declaration and initiative on price restraint in 1971 (requesting 200 of its members to limit price changes to 5 per cent p.a.) were more readily enforceable by Ministers who had in any case been exerting informal pressure on the nationalized industries from at least 1965. Moreover, the Stage 2 and 3 Price Codes of 1973 excluded the nationalized industries from the minimum profit provisions which provided a safety net for private firms earning less than an 8 per cent rate of return and more explicitly the nationalized industries were not allowed to reduce deficits by raising prices more than cost increases. By 1973 the Treasury was admitting the existence of price restraint policies in the public sector and this was picked up and reported by the Select Committee on Nationalized Industries (1974). Legislation was then introduced to grant explicit subsidies. Moreover the Labour government in 1974 acknowledged

a need for giving scope for higher price increases by nationalized in-dustries ... [in order to make] progress towards the Government's ob-jective of returning as many of the industries as possible to a position in which their deficits, and the accompanying public expenditure on subsidies, are eliminated. (Secretary of State for Prices and Consumer Protection 1974: 5)

Nevertheless restraint on prices continued, as always in an un-official way (see Millward 1976 and 1991c, for more detail).

How successful was the government in restoring the industries' finances? The annual rate of profit in the public corporation sector as a whole averaged zero in the 1950s, as we have seen. By the end of the 1960s profits net of subsidies had risen to about 8 per cent of value added, as may be seen in Fig. 9.1. This was of course much less than the company sector, but in view of the secular decline in company sector profitability, especially if stock ap-preciation is deducted, the 8 per cent figure is a reasonable bench-mark. By 1972 gross trading profits for the public corporation sector, before subsidy, were only £1,237 million, not even enough to cover estimated capital consumption of £1,552 million. Even with subsidies included, profits accounted for only 3 per cent of value added. Future price increases would have to exceed any future cost increases by a considerable margin.

Now the long-term trends in unit costs facing nationalized industries had two features. First was that labour productivity was growing faster than in manufacturing so that, notwithstanding a much larger rise in wage inflation in the early 1970s, unit labour costs were still growing less than manufacturing. Yet the costs of fuel, raw, materials, and other items bought in by the nationalized industries were growing more rapidly than manufacturing, espe-cially after the oil price rises of 1974, so that overall unit costs in

TABLE 9.5 *Price and cost inflation in the UK 1970–1978* (annual % changes)

	1970	1971	1972	1973	1974	1975	1976	1977	1978
Manufacturing									
Prices	7.1	9.1	5.2	7.4	22.6	22.2	17.3	19.8	9.1
Unit costs	8.1	8.7	4.9	8.9	24.9	21.9	16.7	20.6	7.3
Nationalized industry									
Prices	3.4	8.4	1.6	3.9	28.5	42.3	17.3	9.9	6.2
Unit costs	5.6	9.6	5.2	3.1	35.4	41.2	10.2	9.7	7.7

Source: Monthly *Digests of Statistics* for the wholesale price index for all home sales of manufactured goods. A special price series was constructed for nationalized industries by aggregating, with revenue weights, the following indexes calculated from the annual reports of the corporations: average gas price per therm realized; average electricity revenue per kWh sold to all consumers; average of the postal and telecommunications tariff indices weighted by revenue; proceeds per saleable ton of coal; total revenue per load ton-miles for BEA; for British Rail an average weighted by revenue of average fares per passenger-mile and average receipts per net ton-mile.

Unit costs relate to labour, fuel, and other raw materials. Series on output, employment, and earnings for nationalized industries were developed along the lines of the series for prices. For details write to the author. These data were then used to estimate unit labour costs. Data on raw materials and fuel outlays of public corporations are published in the Blue Books. Hence unit input cost was calculated and added to unit labour costs. Unit labour costs in manufacturing were extracted from data in the *Employment Gazette*. Unit input costs in manufacturing were calculated as a residual from the data on prices, unit labour costs, and profit rates.

the 1970s were rising, on a longer-term trend, at about the same rate as manufacturing. As Table 9.5 shows, however, manufacturing prices tracked costs much more closely than did nationalized industries' prices. Even in the years when the latter prices rose by staggering amounts, 28 per cent in 1974 and 42 per cent in 1975, the increases were actually, overall, slightly less than the rise in unit costs (35 per cent and 41 per cent respectively). The effect on finances is shown in Fig. 9.1. By 1976/7 subsidies and price increases had raised the profit share of income to 12 per cent when subsidies are treated as revenue. It is clear however that price increases were playing a less important role than subsidies. The share net of subsidies rose to only (−)2 per cent, well short of the 8 per cent figure of the late 1960s. By 1979 the nationalized industries' profit, gross or net of subsidies, as a share of value added had slumped. Their annual sales revenue as a group had again fallen below even operating costs and capital consumption.

CONCLUSIONS

The fuel and transport industries were nationalized in the 1940s in part as a means of improving industrial organization and rescuing coal and railways. There was something of a consensus for larger units of business organization in these industries, if only at a regional or subnational level. Within this context the achievements of the nationalized industries have perhaps been ignored. Productivity grew significantly in the postwar period; this was not simply a matter of the high growth new technology industries like telecommunications, electricity, airlines, and gas. Coal and railways saw massive labour shedding in the 1950s and 1960s. The sector as a whole in fact showed a rise in total factor productivity 1951–85 slightly higher than British manufacturing industry and than the fuel and transport sectors in the USA, where private utilities are more common.

At the same time the industries were also set up with the aim of acting as an instrument of economic planning and income redistribution. This area created the most problems. The public purpose objectives of the industries were so vague that scope was provided for policies which conflicted violently with the break-even objective. The offer of specific services at prices below cost, the element of cross-subsidization within each industry, and the frequent overall financial losses received much more public attention than the underlying productivity record. The break-even objective was one of the few measurable objectives in the statutes. The fares and tariffs of public bodies were fair game for comment and criticism. By the mid-1970s the finances of the industries, bolstered by subsidies, were significantly out of hand. By the end of the 1970s little improvement had taken place, leaving the industries vulnerable to proposals for radical change.

10

Privatization of Industry in the 1980s

INTRODUCTION

Policy towards industries based on technological networks veered in a new direction during the 1980s. Monolithic state industries were returned to private ownership, which they had left many decades earlier with far more fragmented structures. The public were to be protected from exploitation by these private monopolies first by new forms of arm's length regulation, and then by attempts to introduce competition. Profit became a clear and overriding objective for enterprises both within and outside the state sector (Ashworth 1991: 56–7; generally on privatization see Bos 1991; Vickers and Yarrow 1988; Swann 1988; Gayle and Goodrich 1990). Nuclear power was exposed as a wildly expensive form of electricity generation which the private sector would not contemplate taking over in view of the potential costs of waste disposal. In industries still owned by the state, where regulation was more internalized, efficiency growth accelerated but cost-cutting was accused of precipitating disasters and accidents such as the King's Cross fire and the Clapham Junction crash.

These nationalized, largely network, industries in 1979 accounted for almost 9 per cent of GDP and over 11 per cent of investment. Primarily because of the privatization programme, a decade later those industries remaining in the public sector supplied only 3.5 per cent of GDP and undertook just over 3 per cent of total investment. They employed about 700,000, whereas forty-two major businesses for which nearly 900,000 people worked had been launched into private ownership by 1990. Some £33 billion had been raised from sales by the end of 1990/1, with an average of £5.5 billion a year planned into the mid-1990s. At the beginning of the decade the proportion of state ownership of industry in Britain was among the highest of any advanced industrial country. By the end, Britain was recognized as the fountainhead of industrial privatization showering the alleged benefits over the rest of the world. The price cap introduced for regulating newly privatized British businesses with monopoly power was emulated in the United States, continental Europe, and Australia.

Why and how this remarkable shift in industrial policy occurred is the subject of present chapter. What effects policy makers thought privatization would have must have been a contributory cause, but they are not necessarily identical with the actual impact. Both motives and outcome are of vital concern for aggregate economic performance, for the network technology sector was fundamental to the economy.

INDUSTRY OWNERSHIP AND PERFORMANCE

Ownership confers a collection of rights and obligations which vary between institutions, as well as between countries. Inter-war electricity generation reform, in which some conventional private property rights were separated from even managerial control, shows how chimerical asset ownership can be. Who owns industrial assets, the state, private individuals, or other businesses, interacts with a number of other possible influences upon how well industry works. Efficient industrial organization is good at acquiring and employing information, and at motivating employees. More generally these factors determine what governments can achieve in their industrial and regulatory policies, what managers can get out of their employees, and what shareholders can expect of their directors (Vickers and Yarrow 1988; Chick 1990).

Political bargaining and lobbying have impinged upon the performance of both private and state-owned network industries. The interests of the taxpayer and 'fair' competition with private industry have often stamped their mark upon state enterprise investment and industrial diversification. The private sector has sought to influence the regulatory processes that determine its profitability as well, but in principle is subject to additional control mechanisms. When claims to industrial assets are traded on stock exchanges, take-overs (after 1945), or direct shareholder action at company meetings, may oust a managerial team whose behaviour is judged unsatisfactory. Alternatively disgruntled shareholders may prefer merely to dispose of their stock, the market price of which then reflects their disdain. If such profit-seeking behaviour is to encourage efficient employment of resources, shareholders must have adequate knowledge of the possibilities open to asset managers. Typically such information is hard to come by from British companies, which have traditionally been subject to, and taken advantage of, rather minimal disclosure rules. State ownership of firms precludes these stock market disciplines but offers instead direct intervention by Ministers at the behest of voters and lobbyists. Which arrangement is preferable may well depend upon what is to be achieved.

Objectives and values determine judgements about how well industry works. Only when an industry raises at least one measure of performance, with no deterioration in the attainment of other targets, can an unambiguous improvement be identified. Otherwise appraisals depend upon trade-offs between goals, about which agreement is generally hard to reach. Assuming, as a first approximation, that government industrial policies are ultimately intended to improve efficiency and perhaps achieve some distributional objectives, the sale of state industries broadly at market prices was not an obvious tactic in 1980. Distributional objectives could be achieved by confiscation, gifts, taxes, or subsidies but not by sale, unless prices were fixed artificially. In the preceding chapters, and from international experience after 1945, there is little evidence that in static efficiency comparisons state or private ownership made much difference either way.

For the post-1945 period British tests of the static cost-efficiency consequences of ownership are sparse, for any given industrial sector has typically been entirely public or entirely private. In some activities marginal to the principal nationalized industries, such as the sale of gas and electrical appliances, and Sealink ferries, private operators were found to have a better record. But the Sealink study, and one of airlines, were hampered by limited data sets, making no allowances for differences in factor prices, in networks or routes, or for scale economies (Pryke 1982). As we saw in Chapter 6 more detailed analysis of railways and airlines in Canada and Australia, where public and private operators coexisted in the years after 1945, suggests no difference in technical efficiency. Much the same can be said for water supplies in the United States. The American Water Works Association collects a large volume of data on water supply undertakings that has encouraged comparative cost analyses. When environmental differences across undertakings were taken into consideration, one study found costs some 24 per cent higher in private firms. Another analysis, including various measures of water quality as well as treating energy and water as explicit inputs, found no difference between public and private costs (Bruggink 1982; Feigenbaum and Teeples 1983; McGuire and Ohsfeldt 1986; and reply by Teeples *et al.* 1986). The costs of producing and supplying electric power appear consistently lower in publicly owned electric utilities in the United States during the 1960s and 1970s than in private firms (Millward and Parker 1983; Atkinson and Halvorson 1986). Chapter 6 showed that in Britain before the Second World War differences in gas and electricity cost functions by ownership type were minimal. And in telecommunications networks, Britain's privately owned system in 1986 was not invariably better or worse than European organizations in which private enterprise played a smaller role (Foreman-Peck and Manning 1988).

Despite the lack of clear empirical evidence linking ownership and cost, the transfer of ownership was represented as a key aspect of the government's drive for efficiency. In 1985 John Moore, then the principal Conservative spokesman on privatization, emphasized that the government would 'continue to return state-controlled industries to the private sector. We will encourage competition where appropriate, but where it does not make business or economic sense, we will not hesitate to extend the benefits of privatization to natural monopolies' (Kay *et al.* 1986: 96). As Moore indicated, the privatized telecommunications industry was subject to minimal competition, with a second licence being given to Mercury. British Gas remained a national monopoly after privatization. The former electricity boards became private regional monopolies and of course so did the water companies. The managers of these firms might have acquired greater freedom to employ assets in the most effective way, but whether they exercised that freedom depended on internal reorganization or the balance between stock market monitoring of profit rates and effective competition, at first sight matters independent of asset ownership. Competition between state and private enterprise has always been controversial in Britain, where the private sector is liable to suspect the competition is subsidized. Provision of greater consumer choice is another aspect of the same supposed advantage of private ownership. It was particularly prominent in arguments for changing the telecommunications regime. But similar considerations apply here as to asset management. What really matter are the incentives to offer customers what they want, and asset ownership alone is not the philosophers' stone.

A more compelling point in favour of private ownership is the rarely stated claim that state industries are more prone to political manipulation of wages, employment, prices, and investment. The central importance of asset ownership is most forcefully argued when contrasted with an unregulated private industry, competing within an immutable institutional framework. That however is a purely theoretical abstraction. In reality private industry has been subject to political pressures and has vigorously attempted to achieve its own ends by lobbying and bargaining with politicians. Airline services in the 1980s were analogous in this respect to railways half a century and more earlier. The exclusion of the Scandinavian airline SAS from bidding for British Caledonian was a political coup for British Airways. BA wanted British Caledonian's routes for themselves and did not relish a sizeable foreign competitor in the domestic British market. SAS's exclusion would only have enhanced the efficiency of airline services in Britain if the market was a natural monopoly, a condition the government did not believe relevant to most other network industries (Graham and Prosser 1991: 207−8).

A test of the efficacy of private ownership is that if private enterprise manages assets more efficiently than the state, the market would be willing to pay for them more than they are worth to the state and everybody gains from privatization. In fact efficiency improvements in state-owned network industries began under the stimulus of impending privatization and were largely attributable to the clarification and narrowing of enterprise objectives. Labour productivity in industries still nationalized at the end of the 1980s grew faster than manufacturing industry through that decade, at an average of 4.4 per cent per annum compared with 4.1 per cent. Between 1979/80 and 1987 British Steel's productivity doubled and the Post Office reduced real unit costs by 11 per cent between 1981/2 and 1986/7 (Treasury 1988).

Experience with the Victorian telegraph industry suggests that the pressures on state enterprise in the long term would make this improved performance hard to sustain. Admittedly the government department (for telecommunications) and the British public corporation were perhaps especially vulnerable to political interference, to which other forms are possibly less prone.

Changes of ownership could be a means of income distribution, the motive for state ownership enshrined in clause 4 of the Labour Party constitution. The government view was that the distribution between the state and private individuals or families was what mattered, not the distribution between individuals. Neither nationalization nor privatization made much difference here. Confiscation of privately owned industrial assets would have produced a more equal interpersonal income distribution but instead, during the nationalizations of the 1945–51 governments, £2.6 billion was paid in compensation. The 'gift' of privatized shares on an equal basis to taxpayers or voters would have created a more egalitarian income distribution as well as giving the population a stake in capitalist enterprise (Brittan 1986). But the need to window dress the Public Sector Borrowing Requirement restricted the redistribution to special offers for buyers of small numbers of shares. This largesse did extend share ownership—13 per cent of the adult population held shares in privatized industries by the end of 1988—but hardly influenced the pattern of wealth and income. That a substantial proportion of the electorate actually paid for their shares had the advantage for the government that it would be more politically costly for the opposition, if elected, to unravel the new arrangements.

How industrial subsidies or prices failing to reflect costs have influenced income distribution has not been investigated in depth. The impact of special prices is hard to predict or control; British Telecom's low user rebate, intended to help low-income households, at first probably conferred the greatest benefit upon relatively wealthy second home owners. A case can be made for addressing income distribution directly through taxation, rather than indirectly, if that is a policy objective. Or if some groups need cheap electricity, gas, telephony, or transport then they, but not everybody else, should receive subsidies. These cases turn on the relative costs of reaching the groups concerned; take-up of targeted benefits is often far less among disadvantaged groups through ignorance, objection to dependence on benefits, or inertia.

The most likely redistribution of income through state industries is in favour of groups with the greatest bargaining power. Customers of state-supported industries find prices below cost agreeable so long as the subsidy is spread among others as well. Workers and management appreciate higher wages partly financed by general taxation. Clearly the policy chosen depends upon the extent to which the government is representative of interests as a whole and how liable it is to be swayed by pressure groups. In turn this is likely to depend upon the size of the unit of government. Large governments present more opportunity for the lobbyist than small, and representative municipal government is less prone to subsidize local industries than national. These may be reasons why ownership–performance comparisons between enterprises in the same country may be less than perfect analogies to ownership–performance relations in general. But the most convincing conclusion is that as far as income distribution and industrial performance are concerned, the British concern with state versus private ownership has been a diversion of energies away from addressing the fundamental determinants.

COMPETITION AND INDUSTRIAL PERFORMANCE

There is more evidence that efficiency gains can be achieved by the introduction of competition, but competition can take many forms, with differing outcomes. Advertising, new product, or service competition will generally benefit customers differently from price competition. Competition may take place by example and emulation (yardstick competition), by the threat of entry to the industry, by franchise bidding, or by offering alternative products. There may be differing degrees of competition in markets for capital, for managers, for technicians, and for consumers all with different effects. Publicly owned electricity utilities in the United States have lower costs, other things being equal, when confronted with a competitor in their area of supply. Deregulation of long-distance coaches in the United Kingdom in the 1980s encouraged cost-cutting in National Express, quite apart from more aggressive marketing by this publicly owned company, as well as from British Rail (Jaffer and Thompson 1986: 62). Even in the absence of competition, emulation of enterprises in other geographical areas may be important. Evidence is still thin but the belief that such yardstick competition is helpful underlies the projected break-up of the Post Office into separately accountable business centres (letters, parcels, counters, Girobank) and perhaps also the water companies (Albon 1988).

Network industries are particularly difficult sectors in which to foster direct product market competition. Often in the past labelled 'natural monopolies', these industries typically have sunk costs that deter entry, while direct competition among established firms can actually raise costs by duplication and underutilization of facilities, at least in the absence of appropriate regulation. In electricity it is unlikely that gas-fuelled generators or any other new entrants will challenge the established dominant duopoly in the foreseeable future (House of Commons Energy Committee 1992). Despite the potential for lowering local telephony costs by joint supply with cable television, local networks were still largely monopolies at the beginning of the 1990s. The 1988 Monopolies and Mergers Commission investigation into price discrimination by British Gas showed how that company was abusing its monopoly position. When introduced into these industries competition can be expensive, as the newly privatized electricity industry demonstrated. The bureaucracy needed to operate the 'pool', the half-hour spot market for electricity contracts, proved costly. All electricity is deemed to flow through this set of agreements, determining which stations are run according to their bid prices, and the costs and prices of electricity traded.

Local bus privatization in contrast to gas, telecommunications, and electricity was accompanied by radical structural change to introduce competition. Competition in buses is not as easy to maintain as the apparent absence of sunk costs in the industry might suggest. The need to operate a regular and reliable service and to be recognized as doing so imposes substantial penalties on new industry entrants and renders them vulnerable to predatory price-cutting (White 1988). Under the 1985 Transport Act, not only was route licensing of local services abolished and entry opened, subject to safety standards, but the nationalized National Bus Company was privatized in about seventy different companies. Moreover any services subsidized by local authorities were obliged to be open to competitive tender. Service in rural areas did not decline much and competition persisted. Medium and larger towns often saw extended and more flexible services, but in large conurbations service tended to be unreliable and to lose custom. Reduced central government financial support contributed. Conflicts between Labour local authorities and Conservative central government also led to the transfer of London Transport to central government in 1984. Tendering for services by London Regional Transport between 1986 and 1989 lowered prices by 15 per cent and increased reliability (Gayle and Goodrich 1990: 8).

Separation of efficiency effects of ownership from those of competition is difficult if changes in both have been introduced at the same time, and in any case a plausible reference counterfactual must be available. Comparing estimates of British Telecom's total factor productivity with those in manufacturing indicates roughly similar progress (Tables 10.1 and 10.2), but that does not show what British Telecom would have achieved under state ownership in the same conditions. Simulation of a model of the nationalized industry over the privatized period suggests some improvement in the privatized industry, but the margins of error in the estimates are large (Foreman-Peck 1991*d*).

Electricity prices in Britain compared unfavourably with many other continental European countries in November 1991 though they were lower than Germany's. More surprising, perhaps, the price structure discriminated less in favour of larger, often footloose, users in Britain than elsewhere. Admittedly only in

TABLE 10.1 *Total factor productivity growth in UK manufacturing 1985–1990 (%)*

1985/6	2.34
1986/7	4.29
1987/8	5.83
1988/9	3.44
1989/90	0.23
Average	3.23

Note: 1990 labour share in total domestic income 0.65 yields a TFP growth of 17.9% 1985–90. With 0.5 labour share weight, the figure is 16.6%.

TABLE 10.2 *Growth of total factor productivity and output 1985–1988 in British telecom (%)*

	TFP			Output
	Optimistic	Base	Pessimistic	
1985	3.6	2.9	2.1	7.8
1986	4.8	4.0	3.2	5.9
1987	3.7	3.4	2.9	8.8
1988	5.4	4.8	4.2	6.2
Average	4.4	3.8	3.1	7.2

Note: Year end 31 Mar.
Source: Subissati (1989).

TABLE 10.3 *Electricity prices paid by large industrial users November 1991 (pence per kWh)*

	25–80 mW-hrs per year	More than 80 mW-hrs per year
Belgium	2.69	2.54
France	2.46	2.24
Italy	3.06	2.74
The Netherlands	2.35	2.29
West Germany	3.67	3.48
United Kingdom	3.05	3.00

Source: House of Commons Energy Committee (1991–2).

March 1990 was the CEGB split into four companies and, together with the regional electricity companies, their sales took place within the following year. The full effects of the radical restructuring may not have been fully felt by the date of Table 10.3.

REGULATION OF NEWLY PRIVATIZED INDUSTRY

Neo-liberal economic doctrine, influential in the government of the 1980s, maintained that competition was a natural state of affairs in the long run, so long as governments did not obstruct it

(Friedman 1962: ch. 8). Even for network technology industries regulation was only an interim measure while full competition emerged, according to Stephen Littlechild (1983*b*, 1986), architect of the two most influential reports on regulation of privatized industries (and subsequently director-general of the electricity regulatory agency OFFER). A price control rule was intended to provide the necessary light and temporary regulation, giving the firm as much freedom as possible to choose its own price structure. The rule was to avoid the allegedly expensive and cumbersome legal regulation and incentives to overinvestment from fixing a maximum allowable rate of return on capital. Price capping had been employed in the nineteenth century but the 'RPI-X' rule was better adapted to the post-gold standard inflationary environment. The regulated enterprise was allowed each year to raise the (revenue-weighted) average of prices of its outputs by no more than the increase in the retail price index minus the X factor. The larger was X, the more the business was obliged to increase its efficiency, or reduce profits, assuming input prices moved approximately in line with retail prices. The first use of this device, on British Telecom, adopted an X of 3 per cent. X was renegotiated every four years or less and raised each time. This rule turned out to be rather similar to rate of return regulation, for the X in telecommunications was fixed by a forecast of BT's profitability and a target rate of return.

Far from withering away, regulation in telecommunications became increasingly detailed and extensive in coverage, despite the licensing of more telecommunications carriers. Enforcement of regulation of all network industries proved more persistent and controversial than policy makers had hoped for. The National Rivers Authority admitted mismanagement at a high level. After persistent conflict with its regulatory agency, in 1992 British Gas chose an investigation by the Monopolies Commission as a means of breaking the deadlock.

In telecommunications and gas the regulatory problem was exacerbated by the failure to break up the enterprises into regional units. In electricity an attempt was made to address the problem but ran into difficulties when the true cost implications of nuclear power were released at a late stage in the planning process. Instead of the originally proposed 70:30 division of capacity between the two privatized generators, with the larger including nuclear reactors, a separate state-owned organization, Nuclear Electric, was created, while fossil fuel capacity was divided as originally planned. The two companies were supposed to bid against each other, and any independent generators, in supplying electricity through the 'pool' to the National Grid Company (NGC). The NGC owned and operated the transmission network and was wholly owned by the regional electricity (distribution) companies.

The 1989 Water Act was obliged to confront not only the regulatory problem of ensuring low and fair prices to customers but also environmental externalities or (appropriately) spillovers. Ten water authorities in England and Wales were sold in 1989. Under the Act their operations were supervised by the National Rivers Authority and by the Office of Water Supply, in some respects analogous to OFTEL, OFGAS, and OFFER. The National Rivers Authority (NRA) assumed responsibility for flood protection, water resource planning (including abstraction licences), pollution control, fisheries, navigation (on some rivers), and recreational uses. The relative costs to the NRA of these functions are reflected in the order in which they are listed (House of Commons Environmental Committee 1991–2). The NRA was organized into regions that matched water catchment areas. All industrial and many commercial customers paid direct user prices. Domestic users were not metered at all; the costs of metering were high. In effect residents acquired the equivalent of a licence to tap into the system, similar to the road fund licence, except that, in the case of water, the fee varied with the rateable value.

Instead of direct regulation by government departments and their own management, the newly privatized network businesses were supervised by an intermediate layer of industry-specific agencies. These agencies were non-ministerial government departments, headed by directors-general appointed by the Secretary of State for Trade and Industry. The DGs were responsible for enforcing the licence conditions under which the regulated companies operated and for providing advice to the Minister. They were obliged to publish information and review complaints. Otherwise duties such as to promote competition in various fields were specific to particular agencies. The licences themselves were granted by the Secretary of State. Although such agencies provided the opportunity to reduce the secrecy of traditional British regulation, the additional information supplied in the public domain was less than under US regulation, such as the reasons for choosing particular values of X in price control formulae.

THE POLITICAL ECONOMY OF PRIVATIZATION

If privatization was primarily intended to regenerate the network industries then there would have been a good deal of wishful thinking by policy makers. In fact the policy , like so much else in British public life, was driven by financial considerations, with some support from ideological change. Apart from a general intellectual and commercial background which predisposed the Conservative Party to reforming the nationalized industries in some way, there are three principal explanations for the turning-point in policy: first, financial stringency and commitment to the Public Sector Borrowing Requirement target that created difficulties for financing state industry investment programmes, second, a changed attitude to unemployment, and third, a desire to constrain union power, which was at its strongest in the public sector. Additional attractions of the policy were that privatization could be represented as a means of regenerating British industry and creating a more stable shareholding democracy.

The timing of the policy shift can be traced to the coincidence of high unemployment and inflation during the mid-1970s, which broke confidence in traditional Keynesian macroeconomic solutions. Tighter budgetary controls and monetary targets were, in effect, enforced by the International Monetary Fund in 1976 through the Letter of Intent that the Chancellor of the Exchequer was obliged to write. These precluded the generous subsidies which the nationalized industries had come to require. Indeed they precipitated the Labour government's sale of some shares in British Petroleum to ease the IMF's constraint on policy. Mrs Thatcher then inherited a budgetary discipline which Mr. Heath mistakenly thought he could avoid by floating the exchange rate in 1972.

Another condition had changed as well. The fragmented industrial structure, the legacy of an early start to sustained economic growth, had been eliminated by the nationalizations of 1945–51. What the market failed to achieve, direct state action had implemented. Then by the late 1970s a new opportunity arose to test the market's capacity for providing the appropriate mix of services, prices, and standards.

The importance of ideological change by the end of the 1970s, itself a reaction to the experience of economic history, is demonstrated by the failure of the first wave of Conservative Party industrial radicalism. The Heath government of 1970–4 at first espoused policies of rolling back the frontiers of state intervention. Rhodes Boyson, MP, later a junior Minister in the Thatcher government, edited in 1971 a volume devoted to the failure of state industries and the need to return them to a competitive framework (Boyson 1971). Rising unemployment and bankruptcies quickly diverted the Heath government from its original policies. Instead it adopted a Keynesian remedy of expansion and a floating exchange rate. Shipbuilding, aerospace, and the motor industry all provided unexpected entrants to the state sector as British manufacturing declined in the 1970s. The trend was accelerated by the next Labour government, which entirely nationalized aerospace, shipbuilding, and iron and steel, and set up the British National Oil Corporation as a means of monitoring and controlling the development of the North Sea oilfields.

Despite this ambitious programme the administrative and organizational principles of nationalized industries remained basically unchanged. NEDO's 1976 report on the sector contrasted the failings of UK nationalized industry organized on the arm's length philosophy with the relative success of France, West Germany, and Sweden, where information was exchanged more frequently and at a number of levels (National Economic Development Office 1976) . The 1978 White Paper replaced the test discount rate for individual projects with a 5 per cent rate of return for investment programmes as a whole. Each industry was also required to publish performance indicators such as productivity and unit cost indices. The Labour government did produce an organizational innovation in the form of the National Enterprise Board, which held shares in a considerable number of companies, including International Computers, with a view to compensating for what some saw as the inadequacies of the capital market for risky projects. This approach to industrial policy was quickly discarded in the Thatcher revolution after 1979.

Although in historical perspective 'revolution' is the appropriate term, within the lives of the first two Thatcher governments privatization of state industries was a policy adopted gradually, as it was demonstrated to satisfy a number of key political objectives. Privatization was not mentioned in the first Thatcher policy statement of 1976, *The Right Approach*. The 1979 election manifesto emphasized the party's opposition to more nationalization, a traditional Conservative theme, and the intention to return aerospace and shipbuilding to the private sector. This was no more radical than the treatment of the steel and road haulage industries during the 1950s but the announced willingness to sell shares in the National Freight Corporation might have been taken as a harbinger of further-reaching policies. By 1983 experience had showed the potential of privatization. Reform of the nationalized industries was central to economic recovery, according to the manifesto of that year. Mrs Thatcher's government asserted that transferring industries to private ownership enhanced their alertness. More would be sold off therefore and they would be exposed to real competition. Only 'substantial parts' of British Steel were to be returned to the private sector, water and railways were not mentioned at all, while gas (ironically) and electricity were considered candidates for the introduction of competition, rather than privatization (Conservative Party 1976, 1979: 15, 1983: 15). As these policy statements imply, during the first Thatcher government only those relatively small companies which operated in competitive markets were sold. After 1983 new regulatory institutions and rules were established and the really big sales of British Telecom and British Gas took place. That privatization policy was only formed slowly is shown by the two Telecommunications Acts of 1981 and 1984. The first partly liberalized the market, the second privatized and introduced competition in basic telephone service. Only in 1986, with the White Paper on Water Privatization, were all the government's objectives for privatization fully stated (Department of the Environment 1986).

From the government's viewpoint a great attraction of privatization was that it allowed the Public Sector Borrowing Requirement target to be fulfilled without imposing the stringency that would otherwise be required. Price stability was a major goal of the Thatcher government and the PSBR was the chief plank in the monetary strategy to achieve this end. Any wavering would

TABLE 10.4 *Gross domestic capital formation 1970–1989 at 1985 market prices*

	1970	1979	1982	1989
Transport	6,300	3,618	1,973	(3,265)
Communication		1,749	1,670	(3,690)
Other energy and water	6,901	3,945	4,235	(4,310)
Total networks	13,201	9,312	7,878	11,265
Manufacturing	10,670	10,136	6,360	10,787

Note: The bracketed figures are estimates.

Source: *UK National Accounts* (CSO, 1990), spliced with 1981 edition.

have sent the wrong signals to the markets. Yet it soon became clear that the target was inappropriate and excessively deflationary. Selling nationalized industry assets actually has the same monetary consequences as government borrowing by selling bonds. The PSBR target conflated current account spending with capital. On the other hand the enormous demands for capital of some of these industries do have implications for national economic efficiency and there are good reasons to offer them a level financial playing field with the rest of British industry.

That finance for investment in the state infrastructure industries was becoming a problem is suggested by the very substantial decline during the 1970s, whereas the decline in manufacturing over that decade was hardly noticeable (Table 10.4). In 1970 total network industries' investment was more than 20 per cent higher than investment in manufacturing. In the year Mrs Thatcher's government was elected it was 8 per cent less. At the trough of the depression with the steep decline of manufacturing, in 1982, both had fallen from 1970 levels by similar proportions. Privatization and greater emphasis on profit in remaining state-owned industries did not encourage a recovery of investment in network industries of comparable dimensions to that of manufacturing. More efficient use of capital and reduced service levels are likely explanations. Inspection of the external financing requirements of nationalized industries during the 1980s offers some pointers. By 1988/9 these industries were generating a surplus of £0.4 million compared with a demand for external funds of £3.6 million in 1981/2, when each pound bought considerably more. After 1988/9 policy changed slightly. Financing requirements rose sharply to £2.3 million in 1990/1 and 1991/2. £1.1 million of this increase was due to greater investment in British Rail and London Transport (the remainder was largely a consequence of losing the profits from electricity on privatization). Thirty-five deaths in the Clapham Junction multiple crash of December 1988 followed the thirty-one fatalities in the King's Cross fire of November 1987 (*The Times* (11, 13 Nov. 1988, 8 Nov. 1989, 5 July 1990); *The Economist* (12. Sept. 1992), 36). The Clapham inquiry blamed unacceptable working practices for the accident, which were associated in some minds with inadequate investment. Higher investment in British Rail in the year after the disaster seemed not wholly fortuitous.

Monetarist doctrines underlying the PSBR target provided the theoretical backing which was at the centre of the policy shift on state ownership. Once it was accepted that there was a natural rate of unemployment which the state could only reduce by improving the working of the market, the government was able to absolve itself from responsibility for job losses from commercializing state enterprises or from refusing to bail out failing large private sector employers ('There is no alternative'). Of course the ideological change did not occur in a vacuum. The experience of macroeconomic 'fine-tuning' in the 1950s and 1960s, culminating in the 'stagflation' of the 1970s, provided the background, as Labour Prime Minister Callaghan's conversion from Keynesianism showed (Desai 1981: 9). Deteriorating British economic performance prepared the ground for the advent of privatization as it did for monetarism.

Dissatisfaction with the great state corporations was a continuing theme of Conservative political doctrine but by comparison with much of the private sector there was little hard evidence of generalized poor performance until the 1970s. Regardless of performance, increasing financial demands of nationalized industry made privatization look more attractive, first when the International Monetary Fund imposed limits on Domestic Credit Expansion in 1976, and subsequently when similar monetary targets were adopted by the Thatcher government. Secretary of State for Trade and Industry Keith Joseph, who was particularly close to Mrs Thatcher, was impressed by telecommunications liberalization in the United States. He was also anxious to break what he saw as the unions' hold on the national 'jugular vein', the telecommunications network. With this second objective Keith Joseph was riding a broader wave of public opinion which had swung in favour of denationalization during the industrial strife of the 1974–5 'winter of discontent' (Newman 1986: 2–4). During the process of trying to reform British telecommunications, the difficulties of finding an institutional arrangement by which the state industry could raise capital without a Treasury guarantee eventually pushed the government into considering the sale of the entire telecommunications organization. After the success of this enormous flotation, there was little reason why other utilities should not go the same way, that is maintaining their nationalized organization.

This organizational conservatism was encouraged by the dependence of the government upon the support or acquiescence of top nationalized industry management which had privileged access to specialized information essential for successful privatization (Chick 1987). Their resistance could at least have proved embarrassing for the government. So long as the policy did not involve a break-up of the industry (and an appeal could be made to natural monopoly arguments which are borne out by Victorian industrial experience), freedom from changing and arbitrary government restrictions on pricing and investment was a pleasing prospect. Successful lobbying by top management in high places first delayed and then determined the structure of the privatized British Airways. Employment legislation, high unemployment, and the perception that times were going to be lean in state industries (reinforced by Monopolies and Mergers Commission investigations from 1980) altered the relative advantage of the private sector. Even so trade union pressure would have caused a reversal of the policy had Labour been elected in 1987 (Labour Party 1986).

Competition was clearly not a major interest of the government in the massive sales of British Telecom and British Gas. If it had been, the corporations would have been broken up before sale. Public concern about their monopoly power delayed electricity privatization until a proposal to divide the Central Electricity Board had been formulated. Indeed the electricity industry is a unique tribute to competition; no other electricity industry in the world has such a disintegrated structure (House of Commons

Energy Committee 1991–2). Some unease about the lack of competition in other areas and the abuse of monopoly power was demonstrated by the creation of industry specific regulatory bodies, beginning with the Office of Telecommunications (OFTEL), but their formal powers have been weak (Veljanovski 1987; Waterson 1988). Even OFTEL, which has greater authority than OFGAS, has had to rely on publicity, moral suasion, and the personality of the director-general rather than formal proceedings to ensure fair competition (Heald 1987). Had the government restructured British Telecom and British Gas into smaller more numerous businesses, monopoly power and profits could have been reduced but then so would the total sales value of the companies. Competition and revenue were at odds. Only profitable enterprises could be sold without government subsidy.

Although they have rightly been subject to substantial criticism, much more consideration and experience underlay the privatizations that terminated state enterprises than went into the organization of the nationalized industries of 1945–51. The performance of privatized industry, on a commercial definition, might be expected to improve both for that reason and because the goals of the new enterprises were simpler, primarily commercial. Whether the industries will be able to avoid the problems that originally gave rise to their acquisition by the state depends largely upon the new regulatory institutions and rules established since 1983. These are genuine innovations and generally mark an advance on the achievements of the Victorians or those of the inter-war period. But that is not to deny that many of the privatized industries were of a size and structure to create fundamental problems for the regulators.

Since Victorian times, technology has changed but in some industries the scope for competition has been improved by reductions in minimum efficient size (MES) (for example, the impact of microwave transmission in telecommunications); in others the MES has increased (such as the need for a national gas distribution network). The railways no longer have a monopoly on long-distance land transport but a national grid, which can be an industry entry barrier, has become necessary for electricity. On average, neither the need for supervision of competition nor the scale of the enterprise which would have to be nationalized if that was judged preferable to regulation, has diminished.

Privatization paid scant regard to the wider social impact of industry, most likely because the notion is a Pandora's Box. For many years the configuration of the telecommunications network was influenced by the desire not to allow any individual exchange to be too large in case it was eliminated by enemy action. With privatization this consideration ceased to be relevant to network design. Defence considerations have never generally loomed large however. More important state industry objectives included the extension of service to as many customers as possible at the same price regardless of cost (the universal service obligation). Local employment has often been an even tighter short-term constraint upon state industry management, if not an objective.

The potential variety of arrangements offers yardsticks for individual industries which the nationalized industry corporate form did not. Even if efficiency did not improve faster than in the best periods of the old regime, reduced government interference with management or with related activities that impinge upon statutory monopolies could be expected to raise the average pace of productivity growth, by an indeterminate amount. Then the question remains as to whether the abandonment of the social and employment objectives of the state corporations more than offset such gains. Even if the relevant magnitudes were known, which they are not, valuations placed upon them will differ and render a final judgement controversial. Either way privatization alone did not and was not really intended to regenerate the network technology industries.

SUMMARY AND CONCLUSION

Although technology has greatly changed since mid-Victorian times, the characteristics that make for difficulties in sustaining competition have become if anything more pervasive in network industries. Would-be competitor users of British Gas's distribution network face similar challenges to those early Victorians who wanted to run their railway engines on other companies' tracks. New telecommunications entrants must surmount difficulties over the terms of interconnection and use of British Telecom's network less extreme but comparable with those experienced by newspapers of the 1860s, dependent for their telegraphic news on the selection provided by the telegraph companies. Technological change is therefore no explanation for the remarkable policy shift on network industry ownership since 1979. The key is rising nationalized industry costs meeting greater financial stringency and ideological change that breaks with the political consensus of the long post-war boom. As faith in the ability of governments to influence the level of employment waned in the stagnation of the 1970s so the scope for industrial reform which cost jobs was enhanced. Monetarist policies favoured reducing the PSBR by selling state assets even though with a more consistent target they would not have done so. Success required more than one period of office, for a Labour government would have reversed the early moves. By swinging Mrs Thatcher back into popular favour, the Falklands War therefore was an essential ingredient for the fulfilment of a long-term privatization programme.

Privatization during the 1980s above all was a response to financial pressure, first from state industries and second from other budgetary demands on the state. But to allay fears of price exploitation and withdrawal of services yet another institutional innovation was born; the industry-specific regulatory office staffed by civil servants and headed by a non-civil servant government appointee. These regulatory offices were charged with intervening to encourage competition, a break with the policy of the past. What remains unclear is whether the regulations that are necessary to ensure competition in the network industries are so pervasive and detailed that effective freedom of action will eventually be removed from the regulated industries. The evolution of telecommunications regulation is consistent with this development. If the trend continues and effects other sectors, eventually there will be little difference between the internalized regulation of the state-owned industry and the regulated private firm. In any case there is little evidence as yet that these institutional innovations have promoted any fundamental changes in the performance of British industry.

I I
Networks in Perspective

INTRODUCTION: NETWORK INDUSTRY CONCEPTS

Privatization is only the latest policy towards network technology industries; their distinctive problems have persisted since the industrial revolution. The sources are their high fixed and sunk costs, common costs, and economies of joint production, which render controversial or questionable the allocation of costs to any particular activity. Their system characteristics place a premium on 'interconnection', integration, and compatibility. Competition in the construction of networks therefore tended to entail duplication and/or fragmentation. Operation of networks encouraged co-ordination, co-operation, and monopoly rather than competition.

Accounting for a proportion of the national capital stock which always substantially exceeded that of manufacturing industry, as well as supplying services essential to modern industries and households, efficient operation of network industries was crucial for the performance of the British economy. Every economic activity may depend upon every other, but some are more closely or more generally related. Most businesses use the infrastructure services of transport, communication, electrical, and water services, but only some use coal. A second pervasive characteristic arises because infrastructure services are generally capital intensive and so in some respects can resemble public goods. Customers can often be supplied at very low marginal (as against average) costs.

A third public aspect of these industries arises from the adverse consequences, beyond those immediately affected, of unsatisfactory infrastructure services. Health and safety considerations arise. Inadequate sewage disposal, as in London of the 1840s, may affect many by outbreaks of cholera other than those who are receiving the inadequate service. This is a negative externality or spillover.

In other cases there are positive externalities arising for example from linking people to transport and communications networks. The value of a railway system to any potential traveller increases with the number of places that can be reached by it. Consequently joining additional communities to the network confers a benefit upon those who already have access.

These industries have long been distinctive because of the tendency for single private suppliers to emerge, able to choose their prices and restrict supply without fear that rivals would steal their business. Hence the traditional policy-laden term 'natural monopoly' used to descibe them. We have preferred 'network technology' industries because the concept captures a key common feature of these industries that accounts for the emergence of monopoly but does not carry any policy implications. By focusing on distribution networks we can explain patterns of industry evolution as well as understanding why some industrial policies were more effective than others.

NETWORK INDUSTRY PERFORMANCE AND INSTITUTIONAL CHANGE

The early nineteenth-century policy of encouraging competition in infrastructure services allowed them to spread rapidly but, as monopoly displaced competition, public concern was voiced about adverse spillovers and exploitation. Limited liability status was restricted until 1856 and therefore, before that date, could be used to limit competition in the interests either of established companies or of the public. Regulation to ensure competition was never enforced even though Parliament in the 1830s intended there to be competition on the railway track. Enforced interconnection and co-operation entailed state-supervised constraints on private property, contrary to the *laissez-faire* doctrine that favoured competition.

After the extension of the franchise in 1867, and with the increasing respectability of general limited liability, restrictions on maximum prices, on rates of return, and on services became common policy instruments, but in a piecemeal fashion. Legislative prohibition of merger contributed to a freezing of the competitive industry structure after competition had ceased. Pressure group politics encouraged tighter regulation, municipalization and nationalization, and a flight from competition.

Competition ceased to be an adequate regulator by the 1870s for gas, water, telegraphs, and railways. In the absence of controls, private monopoly appeared to provide unsatisfactory levels of service at excessive prices. When regulation was imposed, other forms of inefficiency emerged. Municipalization was an effective short-term solution for industries which only needed local networks (gas, water). It was no answer for industries which required national networks (telegraphs, railways). In both cases the long-term effects of state ownership before 1914 were less than ideal; the statutory monopolies which local and national governments acquired may have held back the development of new industries—certainly that was true for telephones. Regulation of privately owned monopoly industry was not obviously more successful. In the four decades before the outbreak of the First World War, the railways maintained an uncoordinated structure, the legacy of competition, without the vitality of the early competitive industry.

Post-war reconstruction and national security pushed policy makers into attempting the reform of infrastructure services between the world wars, introducing the public interest non-governmental corporation as an instrument. In electricity generation the carrot of access to the national grid, backed by statutory force, proved especially effective, almost closing the productivity gap with the United States. With radio broadcasting, whether despite or because of policy, performance was almost as good. But in the older network industries there were few successes to record. The task of integrating service provision was largely left until after the Second World War. Then the hurried nationalizations of 1945–51 established a framework for the public corporation which continued to meet with a great deal of criticism, despite three White Papers. They did however consolidate the generally fragmented industrial structures, a process in other countries achieved by the market, or by banks, or one that was unnecessary. The monolithic nationalized industries with statutory monopolies acquired ideological overtones as instruments of the Labour Party's commitment to state ownership of the 'commanding heights'. Ironically the accumulated avidence of the preceding century indicated that ownership *per se* was a very minor influence upon performance. Integration of distribution networks was achieved but the capital demands of these industries, as well as state attempts to use them as instruments of general economic policy, created increasing tensions. Marginal cost-pricing rules and rate of return targets failed to quench state network industries' thirst for externally generated funds but productivity growth was comparable with that of privately owned manufacturing.

Manufacturing industry has dominated discussions over the last century of the relative decline of the British economy, a matter on which this study can cast some light. The outdated prevalence of the family firm, condemned for poor manufacturing performance, cannot be blamed for low productivity of the networks relative to those of the United States (cf. Chandler 1990), for that distinctive institution never found a foothold in these capital-intensive industries. In view of the central economic position of networks, family firms cannot be a general explanation, although managerial shortcomings may well be. Private versus public ownership differences in enterprise performance within the same country seem to have been relatively small. The big divergences were between nations, in particular between the two sides of the Atlantic. US–UK productivity differentials were present independently of ownership; scale, broadly interpreted, was a promising candidate explanation in the network industries, and, to a lesser extent, natural resources. In any event an emphasis on ownership as such is unlikely to form the basis of an effective industrial policy.

EXPLAINING NETWORK INDUSTRY POLICY AND INSTITUTIONS

The frameworks in which the later network industries operated can be explained by two general intentionalist accounts (those in which outcomes are intended by the actors). First is the optimal adjustment of institutions to economic circumstances—the state was an instrument for correcting market failure. Second is 'capture' by interested parties, either by the industry itself or by groups of customers (such as the Edinburgh and Glasgow Chambers of Commerce). A dynamic component may be added to the explanations by the institutional costs of an early competitive start. The way the industries originated influenced their later evolution: 'path dependence'. Certain organizations, such as the Central Electricity Board and the nationalized industries, later performed the necessary tasks of rationalization. These institutions were unlikely to have been ideal but they brought about improvements.

The doctrine of 'spontaneous order', that in the absence of state intervention, given enough time without human or natural coercion, an evolutionary process will establish institutions that best satisfy social needs (Hayek 1973; Gray 1984), clearly condemns the replacement of mid-Victorian competition because the state played such a central role. No less damning is the theory of 'institutional scelerosis' (Olson 1982). Policy towards the network industries was undoubtedly influenced by special interest groups and therefore must have had adverse effects on the industries and on the economy as a whole. The British political process could obviously be manipulated as the railway interest demonstrated in the 1840s. Which group, customers or directors, pulled the strings seems to have depended in part on the extension of the franchise, from 1867, and in part upon movements of the price level. When the general price level was rising, railway customers were happy enough to pay falling real tariffs and the railways tried to change policy; when prices were falling (with nominal rail tariffs fixed) customers pressed for tariff cuts. The Edinburgh Chamber of Commerce functioned as one of Olson's 'distributional coalitions' in its demand for a telegraph tariff unrelated to distance and so did small rail user lobbyists who managed to exclude volume discounts from the 1893 tariff legislation.

Municipal enterprise, under representative local government, perhaps comes closer to Olson's ideal 'encompassing' organization where decision takers are close to those affected. National regulation or ownership removes decision takers further away from industry customers. In such cases municipal enterprise is more likely to follow efficient market rules. On the other hand local authorities were also the strongest blocking force for new network industries between 1880 and 1940 and in that respect also correspond with Olson's distributional coalitions. For all its achievements with municipal trams, Glasgow Corporation in particular seems to have been a 'Upas tree' (Checkland 1976) where private Edwardian telephony was concerned, at least before being allowed to operate a corporation telephone service; like the reputedly magical tree it prevented or retarded growth within it boundaries.

Olson's scelerosis theory turns on asymmetries between the relatively small distributional coalition and the large affected group who cannot organize, or who do not, because they are not individually sufficiently affected. It is precisely here that state action may be beneficial to correct adverse 'spillover' effects or the exploitation of monopoly power. Safety on the railways, in assuring adequate water for urban fire-fighting, in avoiding domestic gas explosions, were all advanced by state regulation of these industries and did not occur spontaneously. These measures may not have boosted GNP but they did enhance welfare, consistent with the interpretation that state action corrected market failure. On the other hand disasters of the 1980s like the King's Cross fire suggested that public sector owners were no less vulnerable than private enterprise to excessive cost-cutting, under pressure from their political masters.

A large part of social science is devoted to understanding why outcomes are not those that social actors expect, and that type of explanation remains a possibility for policy towards network industries. Schumpeter's (1947) identification of an inexorable 'March into Socialism', the migration of people's economic affairs from the private into the public, or state, sphere, was apparently refuted by policy during the 1980s and the fate of the state-planning regimes of Eastern Europe in 1989. None the less understanding why British network industry experience failed to conform with the trends Schumpeter defined in the 1940s is instructive.

Helped by the experience of production and co-operation during the First World War, the British business class became more organized than ever before during the inter-war years, in two politically influential national bodies (Marrison 1983). Their corporate and individual representatives certainly did not withdraw from politics as Schumpeter predicted as a reason for the onward march of state ownership; City interests, keen on improved communications, were among the lobbyists for privatizing British Telecom in the early 1980s. Although the Second World War created a climate of opinion favourable to socialism and focused the need for industrial reorganization, the resulting state corporations did not acquire the reputations that would have made private companies obsolete, as was necessary if they were to conform with Schumpeter's second predicted trend. The desire for security, the third of Schumpeter's drives for socialism, could largely be met independently of industrial ownership and regulation, and faith in the ability of the state to stabilize the economy began to evaporate by the end of the 1970s. For Casson (1991, 1992), policy towards network industries must be understood as a cultural product, reflecting the values, traditions, and beliefs of society. Industrial policies differ among places and times because of alternative perceptions of issues and missions. Culture determines whether people adopt an interventionist or non-interventionist stance. A key component of culture is the degree of trust in society. The extent to which people can trust each other is reflected in different assumptions of theory that supports various industrial policies. The strategic view of competition policy emphasizes low trust and regulation, rather than state ownership, for 'natural monopoly', but the regulator must still be worthy of trust if this policy is to be effective. Political debate does not necessarily include the optimal industrial policy as a compromise position. In Britain, and the rest of Western Europe since the end of the nineteenth century, political parties divided over capitalism and socialism, reflecting class antagonisms. The post-war Keynesian high-trust consensus temporarily damped the conflict but acquired the seeds of its own destruction from its producer-orientation. Cultural evolution thereafter may have been pulled by traditional ideological debate in the wrong direction for a good industrial performance, away from high trust. In practical terms a better policy towards network industries than privatization and product market competition would emphasize improved management techniques, especially industrial relations, rather than formal regulation.

CONCLUSION

There is little doubt that policy towards the network industries in the one and a half centuries before 1980 cost Britain some GNP growth. State network planning and enforced interconnection, broadly interpreted, could have brought some of the benefits of competition without the wastes, in an ideal world. Although the motives for privatization were not primarily to raise industrial efficiency, it is possible that the sequence of events set in train by the initial decisions could produce novel and effective solutions to some of the persistent shortcomings of British industrial performance. On the other hand widespread and persistent complaints about the quality of service provided by privatized firms in the 1980s could ultimately begin another cycle of transferring industrial assets between state and private hands. If disappointment is the mainspring of human action (Hirschman 1982), alternating 'exit' (voting with the feet or money) and 'voice' (political activism) processes could be sufficient to give Schumpeter's forces another chance.

BIBLIOGRAPHY

BPP = British Parliamentary Papers.

ABEL, D. (1957), 'British Conservatives and State Ownership', *Journal of Politics*, 19: 227–39.

ACWORTH, W. A. (1889), *Railways of England*, London: John Murray.

—— (1891), *The Railways and the Traders*, London: John Murray.

—— (1905), *The Elements of Railway Economics*, Oxford: Clarendon Press.

—— (1923), 'Grouping under the Railways Act 1921', *Economic Journal*, 33: 19–38.

AHARONI, Y. (1981), 'Managerial Discretion', in Y. Aharoni, and R. Vernon (eds.), *State-Owned Enterprise in the Western Economies*, London: Croom Helm.

ALBON, R. (1988), 'Liberalisation of the Post Office', in C. Johnson (ed.), 'Privatisation and Ownership', *Lloyd's Bank Annual Review*, 1: 111–23.

ALCHIAN, A. A. (1959), 'Costs and Outputs', in M. Abramovitz *et al.*, *The Allocation of Economic Resources*, Stanford, Calif.: Stanford University Press.

—— (1965), 'Some Economics of Property Rights', *Il Politico*, repr. in A. A. Alchian, *Economic Forces at Work* (Indianapolis: Liberty Press, 1977).

ALDCROFT, D. H. (1968a), 'The Efficiency and Enterprise of British Railways 1870–1914', *Explorations in Entrepreneurial History*, 5: 158–74.

—— (1968b), *British Railways in Transition*, London: Macmillan.

—— (1974), *Studies in British Transport History 1870–1970*, Newton Abbot: David & Charles.

—— (1975), *British Transport Since 1914*, Newton Abbot: David & Charles.

—— (1986), *The British Economy: The Years of Turmoil 1918–39*, vol. i, Brighton: Harvester.

ALDERMAN, G. (1973), *The Railway Interest*, Leicester: Leicester University Press.

ALFORD, B. W. E. (1988), *British Economic Performance 1945–1975*, London: Macmillan.

ANDERSON, J. (1872), 'On the Statistics of Telegraphy', *Journal of the Statistical Society of London* (Sept.), 284.

ANNS, A. (1911), 'The History of the National Telephone Company', *National Telephone Journal* (Nov.), 156–63; (Dec.), 179–91.

—— (1912), 'A History of the National Telephone Company', *National Telephone Journal* (Jan.), 208–22.

ANON. (1847), *Railways as they Really Are: No. II: The Dover S.E. Company*, London.

—— (1871), *Report on Government Telegraphy in the Netherlands*, London: PO Archives, Post 83/67.

—— (1920–1), 'The Telephone Service', *Post Office Electrical Engineers Journal*, 13: 309–23.

ASHLEY, P. C. (1901), 'Municipal Trading in Great Britain', *Quarterly Journal of Economics*, 15: 458–64.

ASHWORTH, W. (1991), *The State in Business: 1945 to the Mid 1980s*, London: Macmillan.

ASPINALL, B. (1977), 'Glasgow Trains and American Politics, 1894–1914', *Scottish Historical Review*, 56 (Apr.), 197.

ATKINSON, S. E., and HALVORSON, R. (1986), 'The Relative Efficiency of Public and Private of Firms in a Regulated Environment', *Journal of Public Economics*, 29: 281–94.

ATTALI, J., and STOURDZE, Y. (1977), 'The Birth of the Telephone and Economic Crisis: The Slow Death of the Monologue in French Society', in I. de Sola Pool (ed.), *The Social Impact of the Telephone*, Cambridge, Mass.: MIT Press.

AVEBURY, Lord (1900), 'Municipal Trading', *Contemporary Review*, 78 (July), 28–37.

AVERCH, H., and JOHNSON, L. L. (1962), 'Behaviour of the Firm under Regulatory Constraint', *American Economic Review*, 52: 1052–69.

AWTY, B. W. (1975), 'The Introduction of Gas Lighting to Preston', *Transactions of the History Society of Lancashire and Cheshire*, 125: 82–118.

BAGWELL, P. S. (1963), *The Railwaymen: The History of the National Union of Railway Men*, London: Allen & Unwin.

—— (1965), 'The Railway Interest: Its Organization and Influence 1837–1914', *Journal of Transport History*, 7/2: 65–86.

—— (1968), *The Railway Clearing House in the British Economy 1844–1922*, London: Allen & Unwin.

BAIROCH, P. (1976), 'Europe's Gross National Product 1800–1975', *Journal of European Economic History*, 5: 273–340.

BAKER, C. A. (1915), 'Load Factor, Output and Cost', *Electrical Review*, 76: 775–7, 808–10, 841–3.

BAKER, W. J. (1970), *A History of the Marconi Company*, London: Methuen.

BALDWIN, F. G. C. (1938), *History of the Telephone in the United. Kingdom*, London: Chapman & Hall.

Balfour Committee on Industry and Trade (1928–9), *Further Factors in Industrial and Commercial Efficiency*, BPP xxx, London.

BALLIN, H. H. (1946), *The Organisation of Electricity Supply in Great Britain*, London: Electrical Press.

BARNETT, C. (1986), *The Audit of War*, London: Macmillan.

BATSON, L. D. (1929), 'The Extent of the Development of Radio over the World', in I. Steward (ed.), *Radio* (Supp. to *Annals of the American Academy of Political and Social Science*, 142).

BATTEN, J. W. (1884), *The Post Office and the Telephone Companies* (copy in Bodleian Library Oxford).

BAUER, J. M., and LATZER, M. (1988), 'Telecommunications in Austria', in J. Foreman-Peck and J. Muller (eds.), *European Telecommunications Organisation*, Baden-Baden: Nomos.

BAUMOL, W. J. (1977), 'On the Proper Cost Tests for Natural Monopoly in a Multiproduct Industry', *American Economic Review*, 67/3 (Dec.), 809–22.

—— (1982), 'Contestable Markets: An Uprising in the Theory of Industry Structure', *American Economic Review*, 72: 1–15.

——, BAILEY, E. E., and WILLIG, R. D. (1977), 'Weak Invisible Hand Theorems on the Sustainability of Multiproduct Natural Monopoly', *American Economic Review*, 67/3 (June), 350–65.

—— and WILLIG, R. D. (1981), 'Fixed Costs, Sunk Costs, Entry Barriers and the Sustainability of Natural Monopoly', *Quarterly Journal of Economics*, 96 (Aug.), 405–31.

BAXTER, R. D. (1866), 'Railway Extension and its Results', *Journal of the Statistical Society of London*, 29: 549–95.

BEACHAM, A. J. (1945), 'Efficiency and Organisation of the British Coal Industry', *Economic Journal*, 55 (June–Sept.), 206–16.

BEESLEY, M., and LITTLECHILD, S. (1983), 'Privatisation: Principles, Policies and Priorities', *Lloyd's Bank Review*, 149 (July), 1–20.

BENNETT, A. R. (1895), *The Telephone Systems of Western Europe*, London: Longmans Green.

Board of Trade (1845), *Report of the Committee of the Board of Trade on the Various Railway Programmes*, London.

—— (1847, 1850, 1857, 1865, 1866, annual from 1882), *Return Relating to Gas Undertakings in Great Britain*, London.

—— (1901, 1902), *Return Relating to All Authorised Electricity Supply Undertakings in the UK Belonging to Companies in the Year 1899 and Return Relating to All Authorised Electricity Supply Undertakings in the UK Belonging to Local Authorities*, BPP 1901 lxix and 1902 xciii, London.

BONAVIA, M. R. (1981), *Railway Policy between the Wars*, Manchester: Manchester University Press.

BOOTH, B. A. (1951), *The Letters of Anthony Trollope*, Westport, Conn.: Greenwood Press.

BORCHEDING, T. E., POMMERHINE, W. W., and SCHNEIDER, F. (1982), 'Comparing the Efficiency of Private and Public Production: The Evidence from Five Countries', *Zeitschrift für Nationalökonomie*, Supplement 2.

BOS, D. (1991), *Privatisation: A Theoretical Treatment*, Oxford: Clarendon Press.

BOYSON, R. (1971), *Goodbye to Nationalisation*, Enfield: Churchill Press.

BRIGGS, A. (1985), *The BBC: The First Fifty Years*.

—— (1961), *The History of Broadcasting in the United Kingdom*, i: *The Birth of Broadcasting*, London: Oxford University Press.

British Parliamentary Papers (1866), *Railway Traffic Returns*, lxiii, London.

—— (1867–8), *Supplementary Report to the Postmaster General upon Proposals for Transferring to the Post Office the Control and Management of the Electric Telegraph*, xli, London.

—— (1871), *Report by Mr Scudamore on the Reorganisation of the Telegraph Service of the United Kingdom*, xxxvii, London.

—— (1875), *Report of a Committee Appointed by the Treasury to Investigate the Causes of the Increased Costs of the Telegraph since the Acquisition of the Telegraphs by the State*, xx, London.

—— (1910), *56th Report of the Postmaster General*, London: HMSO.

—— (1983), *Energy Act C25*, London: HMSO.

BRITTAN, S. (1986), 'Privatization—A Comment: An Examination the Government Did Not Sit' *Economic Journal*, 96: 33.

BROADBERRY, S. N., and CRAFTS, N. F. R. (1990), 'Explaining Anglo-American Productivity Differences in the Mid-Twentieth Century', *Oxford Bulletin of Economics and Statistics*, 52: 403–22.

BROCK, G. W. (1981), *The Telecommunications Industry: The Dynamics of Market Structure*, Cambridge, Mass.: Harvard University Press.

BROWN, J. C. (1988), 'Coping with Crisis: The Diffusion of Water Works in the Late Nineteenth Century German Towns', *Journal of Economic History*, 48: 307–18.

BROWN, M. J. (1870), *Report on the Working of the French Telegraphic System*, London: PO Archives, Post 83/66.

BROWN, S. J., and SIBLEY, S. A. S. (1986), *Theory of Public Utility Pricing*, Cambridge: Cambridge University Press.

BRUGGINK, T. H. (1982), 'Public versus Regulated Private Enterprise in the Municipal Water Industry: A Comparison of Operating Costs', *Quarterly Review of Economics and Business*, 22/1 (Spring), 111–25.

BULOW, J., GEANAKIPOULOS, J., and KLEMPERER, P. (1985), 'Holding Idle Capacity to Deter Entry', *Economic Journal*, 95: 178–82.

BURN, D. (1958), 'Steel', in D. Burn (ed.), *The Structure of British Industry: A Symposium*, vol. i, Cambridge: Cambridge University Press.

BUSSEL, L. (1988), 'Privatisation: Tramways: A Guide to Policy', *Public Enterprise*, 32 (Mar.).

BUXTON, N. K. (1970), 'Entrepreneurial Efficiency in the British Coal Industry between the Wars', *Economic History Review*, 23: 476–97.

BYATT, I. C. R. (1978), *The British Electrical Industry, 1815–1914*, Oxford: University Press.

Cadman Report (1938), *Report of the Committee of Inquiry into Civil Aviation*, London: Cmd. 5685 (Mar.).

CAIN, P. J. (1972), 'Railway Combination and Government 1900–1914', *Economic History Review*, 25: 623–6.

—— (1980), 'Private Enterprise or Public Utility? Output, Pricing and Investment in English and Welsh Railways, 1870–1914', *Journal of Transport History*, 1: 9–28.

—— (1988), 'Railways 1870–1914: The Maturity of the Private System', in M. J. Freeman, and D. H. Aldcroft (eds.), *Transport in the Victorian Age*, Manchester: Manchester University Press.

CAIRNCROSS, A. (1985), *Years of Recovery: British Economic Policy 1945–51*, London: Methuen.

CARON, F. (1979), *An Economic History of Modern France*, London: Methuen.

—— (1983), 'French Railways', in P. K. O'Brien (ed.), *Railways and European Economic Development 1830–1914*, London: Macmillan.

CASSON, M. C. (1991), *Economics of Business Culture: Game, Theory, Transactions Costs and Economic Performance*, Oxford: Clarendon Press.

—— (1992), 'A Positive Theory of Industrial Policy', European Historical Economics Conference, Oxford, (Dec.).

CAVES, D. W., and CHRISTENSEN, L. R. (1980), 'The Relative Efficiency of Public and Private Firms in a Competitive Environment: The Case of Canadian Railroads', *Journal of Political Economy*, 88: 958–76.

—— and SWANSON, J. A. (1981), 'Productivity Growth, Scale Economies and Capacity Utilization in US Railroads 1955–74', *American Economic Review*, 71: 994.

Census Office (1851, 1861, 1871, 1881, 1891, 1901, 1911, 1921), *Censuses of the Population of England and Wales, Summary Tables*, BPP 1852–3 lxxxv; 1862 li; 1873 lxxii; 1881 xlvi; 1890/1 xliv; 1901 xl; 1911 lxxi; 1921 xl, London.

Central Electricity Board (annual), *Annual Reports*, Archives of Manchester Museum of Science and Engineering.

Central Statistical Office (various years), *United Kingdom National Income and Expenditure*.

CHADWICK, E. (1842), *Report on the Sanitary Conditions of the Labouring Population of Great Britain* (ed. M. W. Flinn, Edinburgh: Edinburgh University Press, 1965).

—— (1859), 'Results of Different Principles of Legislation and Administration in Europe: Of Competition for the Field, as Compared with Competition within the Field, of Service', *Journal of the Royal Statistical Society*, 22 (Sept.), 381–420.

Chancellor of the Exchequer (1947–8), *Financial Relations between the Exchequer and Local Authorities in England and Wales*, London: Cmnd. 7253, BPP xxii.

—— (1978), *The Nationalised Industries*, London: Cmnd. 7131 (Mar.).

CHANDLER, A. D. (1990), *Scale and Scope: The Dynamics of Industrial Capitalism*, Cambridge, Mass.: Belknap Press for Harvard University Press.

CHANDLER, D., and LACEY, A. D. (1949), *The Rise of the Gas Industry in Britain*, London: British Gas Council.

CHANNON, G. (1972), 'A Nineteenth Century Investment Decision: The Midlands Railway's London Extension', *Economic History Review*, 25: 448–70.

—— (1981), 'The Great Western Railway under the British Railways Act of 1921', *Business History Review*, 60: 188–216.

CHANTLER, P. (1938), *The British Gas Industry: An Economic Study*, Manchester: Manchester University Press.

CHATTERTON, D. A. (1972), 'State Control of Public Utilities in the Nineteenth Century: The London Gas Industry', *Business History*, 14/2: 166–78.

CHECKLAND, S. (1976), *The Upas Tree: Glasgow 1875–1975: A Study in Growth and Contraction*, Glasgow: University of Glasgow Press.

CHESTER, Sir N. (1975), *The Nationalisation of British Industry: 1945–51*, London: HMSO.

CHICK, M. (1987), 'Privatization: The Triumph of Past Practice over Current Requirements', *Business History*, 29: 104.

—— (1990) (ed.), *Government, Industries and Markets*, Aldershot: Elgar.

—— (1991), 'Competition, Competitiveness and Nationalisation', in G. Jones, and M. W. Kirby (eds.), *Competitiveness and the State: Government and Industry in 20th Century Britain*, Manchester: Manchester University Press.

CHISHOLM, C. (1937) (ed.), *Marketing Survey of the United Kingdom*, 2nd edn.

CHRISTENSEN, L. R., and GREENE, W. H. (1976), 'Economies of Scale in US Electricity Power Generation', *Journal of Political Economy*, 84: 655–76.

CLAPHAM, J. (1963), *The Economic History of Britain*, Cambridge: Cambridge University Press.

CLEGG, H. A. J. (1952), 'Nationalised Industry' in G. D. N. Worswick, and P. A. Ady (eds.), *The British Economy: 1945–1950*, Oxford: Oxford University Press.

CLEVELAND-STEVENS, E. (1915), *English Railways: Their Development and their Relation to the State*, London: Routledge.

CLINTON, A. (1984), *Post Office Workers: A Trade Union and Social History*, London: Allen & Unwin.

CLUNN, H. (1932), *The Face of London: The Record of a Century's Changes and Development*, London: Simpkin Marshall.

COASE, R. H. (1950), *British Broadcasting: A Study in Monopoly*, London: Longmans.

Commissioners on the State of Large Towns and Populous Districts (1844), *First Report*, London.

—— (1845), *Second Report*.

Commission of the European Communities (1987), *Towards a Dynamic European Community: Green Paper on the Development of the Common Market for Telecommunication Services and Equipment*, Com. (87) 290.

Committee of Enquiry on the Post Office (1932), *Report*, London: Cmd. 4149.

Committee on Industry and Trade (1928), *Further Factors in Industrial and Commercial Efficiency*, (Balfour Report), BPP xxx, London.

Conservative Party (1976), *The Right Approach*, London.

—— (1979), *The Conservative Party Manifesto 1979*, London.

—— (1983), *Our First Eight Years: The Conservative Manifesto 1983*, London.

CRAFTS, N. F. R. (1983), 'Gross National Product in Europe 1870–1910: Some New Estimates', *Explorations in Economic History*, 20: 387–401.

—— (1984), 'Patterns of Development in Nineteenth Century Europe', *Oxford Economic Papers*, 36: 438–58.

CRAIN, W. M., and ZARDKOOHI, A. (1978), 'A Test of the Property-Right Theory of the Firm: Water Utilities in the United States', *Journal of Law and Economics*, 21/2 (Oct.), 395–408.

—— (1980), 'Public Sector Expansion: Stagnant Technology or Attenuated Property Rights', *Southern Economic Journal*, 46/4 (Apr.), 1069–108.

CREW, M. A., and KLEINDORFER, P. R. (1991), 'Rowland Hill's Contribution as an Economist', in M. A. Crew, and P. R. Kleindorfer (eds.), *Competition and Innovation in Postal Services*, Boston, Mass.: Kluwer Academic Publishers.

CROMPTON, G. W. (1985), 'Efficient and Economical Working? The

Performance of the Railway Companies: 1923–1933', *Business History*, 27: 222–37.

CRUTCHLEY, E. T. (1938), *G.P.O.*, Cambridge: Cambridge University Press.

DAKYNS, A. L. (1931), 'The Water Supply of English Towns in 1846', *Manchester School*, 2/1: 18–26.

DANGERFIELD, G. (1936), *The Strange Death of Liberal England*, London: Constable.

DAUNTON, M. J. (1985), *Royal Mail: The Post Office Since 1840*, London: Athlone Press.

DAVIS, E. (1984), 'Express Coaching since 1980: Liberalisation in Practice', *Fiscal Studies*, 5/1: 76–86.

DEMSETZ, H. (1968), 'Why Regulate Utilities?', *Journal of Law and Economics*, 11 (Apr.), 55–65.

—— (1983), 'The Structure of Ownership and the Theory of the Firm', *Journal of Law and Economics*, 26: 375–90.

Departmental Committee (1911), *Railway Agreements and Amalgamations*, London: Cmnd. 5631.

Department of Employment (1971), *British Labour Statistics: Historical Abstract 1886–1968*, London.

—— (various years), *Employment Gazette*.

Department of Industry (1974), *The Regeneration of British Industry*, London: Cmnd. 5710 (Aug.).

—— (1975), *An Approach to Industrial Strategy*, London: Cmnd. 6315 (Nov.).

Department of the Environment (1986), *Privatisation of Water Authorities in England and Wales*, London: Cmnd. 9734.

DESAI, M. (1981), *Testing Monetarism*, London: Pinter.

DICKINSON, H. W. (1954), *The Water Supply of Greater London*, London: Courier Press.

DIEWERT, W. E. (1971), 'An Application of the Shepherd Duality's Theorem: A Generalised Leontief Production Function', *Journal of Political Economy*, 79 (May–June), 481–507.

Director-General of the Belgian Telegraphs (1868), *Memorandum*: *Appendix No. 1 to Report from the Select Committee on the Electric Telegraph Bill*, BPP xi, London.

DODGSON, J. S. (1989), 'Privatising Britain's Railways: Lessons from the Past?', University of Liverpool Discussion Paper in Economics 59.

—— and TOPHAM, N. (1988) (eds.), *Bus Deregulation and Privatisation: An International Perspective*, Avebury: Gower.

DONALD, R. (1903), 'Success of Municipal Ownership in Great Britain', *Street Railway Journal*, 21, 30–4, 72–6.

DOUGLAS, K. A. (1945), *The French Railroads and the State*, New York: Colombia University Press (repr. Octagon Books 1976).

DOUGLAS CAMPBELL, C. (1932), *British Railways in Boom and Depression*, London: P. S. King.

DUNKERLEY, J., and HARE, P. G. (1991), 'Nationalised Industries' in N. F. R. Crafts, and N. Woodward (eds.), *The British Economy since 1945*, Oxford: Clarendon Press.

DYOS, H. J., and ALDCROFT, D. H. (1969), *British Transport: An Economic Survey from the Seventeenth Century to the Twentieth*, Leicester: Leicester University Press.

EDELSTEIN, M. (1982), *Overseas Investment in the Age of High Imperialism: The United Kingdom 1850–1914*, London: Methuen.

EDGERTON, D. E. H. (1984), 'Technical Innovation, Industrial Capacity and Efficiency: Public Ownership and the British Military Aircraft Industry', *Business History*, 26/3: 247–79.

EDMONDS, F. (1987), *Another Bloody Tour*, London: Fontana.

ELBAUM, B., and LAZONICK, W. (1986). *The Decline of the British Economy*, Oxford: Clarendon Press.

ELDON BARRY, E. (1965), *Nationalisation in British Politics: The Historical Background*, London: Cape.

Electricity Commissioners (1938*a*), *The Generation of Electricity in Great Britain*, London: HMSO.

—— (1938*b*), *Electricity Supply: Return of Engineering and Financial Statistics*, London: HMSO.

ELLIS, H. (1959), *British Railway History*, London: Allen & Unwin.

FAHIE, J. J. (1984), *A History of Electric Telegraph to the Year 1837* (1st edn. 1884), New York: Arno Press.

FALKUS, M. E. (1967), 'The British Gas Industry before 1850', *Economic History Review*, 20 (Dec.), 494–508.

—— (1977), 'The Development of Municipal Trading in the Nineteenth Century' *Business History*, 19/2 (July), 134–61.

—— (1982), 'The Early Development of the British Gas Industry, 1790–1815', *Economic History Review*, 35: 217–34.

FAMA, E. (1980), 'Agency Problems and the Theory of the Firm', *Journal of Political Economy*, 88: 288–307.

FARE, T., GROSSKOPH, S., and LOGAN, J. (1985), 'The Relative Performance of Publicity Owned and Privately Owned Utilities', *Journal of Public Economics*, 26: 89–106.

FARRAR, M. F. (1931), *How to Make British Railways Pay: An Economic Survey*, London: Pitmans.

FAULHABER, G. R. (1975), 'Cross-subsidisation: Pricing in Public Enterprises', *American Economic Review*, 65 (Dec.), 966–77.

FEARON, P. (1974), 'The British Airframe Industry and the State 1918–1935', *Economic History Review*, 26: 236–51.

FEIGENBAUM, S., and TEEPLES, R. (1983), 'Public versus Private Water Delivery: A Hedonic Cost Approach', *Review of Economics and Statistics*, 65: 672–8.

FEINSTEIN, C. H. (1965), *Domestic Capital Formation in the United Kingdom 1920–1938*, London: Cambridge University Press.

—— (1972), *National Income, Expenditure and Output of the United Kingdom 1855–1965*, London: Cambridge University Press.

—— and MATTHEWS, R. C. O. (1990), 'The Growth of Output and Productivity in the UK: The 1980s as a Phase of the Post-war Period', *National Institute Economic Review*, (Aug.), 78–90.

—— and POLLARD, S. (1988), (eds.), *Studies in Capital Formation in the UK, 1750–1920*, Oxford: Clarendon Press.

FENELON, K. G. (1933), 'British Railways since the War', *Journal of the Royal Statistical Society*, 96: 381–419.

FIELD, J. W. (1869), *Analysis of Gas Companies*.

FINE, B. (1990), 'Economies of Scale and a Feather-Bedding Cartel? A Reconsideration of the Inter-war British Coal Industry', *Economy History Review*, 43/3 (Aug.), 438–49.

FINER, H. (1941), *Municipal Trading*, London: Allen & Unwin.

FINER, S. E. (1952), *The Life and Times of Sir Edwin Chadwick*, London: Methuen.

FISHLOW, A. (1966), 'Productivity and Technological Change in the Railroad Sector 1840–1910', in D. S. Brady (ed.), *Output, Employment, and Productivity in the United States after 1800*, Studies in Income and Wealth.

FOREMAN-PECK, J. S. (1981), 'The Effect of Market Failure on the British Motor Industry before 1939', *Explorations in Economic History*, 18: 257–89.

—— (1985), 'Competition and Performance in the UK Telecommunications Industry', *Telecommunications Policy*, 9: 215–28.

—— (1987a), 'Death on the Roads: Changing National Responses to Motor Accidents', in T. Barker (ed.), *Economic and Social Effects of the Spread of Motor Vehicles*, London: Macmillan.

—— (1987b), 'Natural Monopoly and Railway Policy in the Nineteenth Century', *Oxford Economic Papers*, 39: 699–718.

—— (1989a), 'Competition, Co-operation, and Nationalization in the Early Telegraph Network', *Business History*, 31: 81–102.

—— (1989b), 'The State and the Development of the Early European Telecommunications Network', *Histoire, economie, sociétés*, 4: 383–402.

—— (1990), 'The 1856 Companies Act and the Birth and Death of Firms', in P. Jobert, and M. Moss (eds.), *The Birth and Death of Companies: An Historical Perspective*, Parthenon.

—— (1991a), 'Railways and Late Victoran Economic Growth', in *New*

Perspectives on the Late Victorian Economy: Essays in Quantitative Economic History 1860–1914, Cambridge: Cambridge University Press.

—— (1991b), 'Industry and Industrial Organisation in the Inter-war Years: A Survey of British Experience', University of Manchester Working Papers in Economic and Social History 5.

—— (1991c), 'International Technology Transfer in Telephony 1876–1914' in D. J. Jeremy (ed.), *International Technology Transfer: Europe, Japan and the USA 1700–1914*, Edward Elgar.

—— (1991d), 'The Efficiency Effects of Privatisation and Liberalisation: The Telecommunications Industry under State and Private Ownship', University of Oxford Applied Economics Discussion Paper Series, No. 124.

—— and HAMMOND, C. J. (1992), 'Closing the Productivity Gap', Hull Economic Research Paper 199, University of Hull.

—— and MANNING, D. (1988), 'How Well is BT Performing? An International Comparison of Total Factor Productivity', *Fiscal Studies*, (Aug.), 54–67.

—— and WATERSON, M. (1984), 'The Comparative Efficiency of Public and Private Enterprise in Britain: Electricity Generation between the World Wars', Univesity of Newcastle upon Tyne Department of Economics Discussion Papers, No. 8.

FRAZER, D. (1970), 'The Politics of Leeds Water', *Proceedings of the Thoresby Society*, 3: 50–70.

—— (1973), *The Evolution of the British Welfare State*, London: Macmillan.

FREEMAN, M. J. (1988), 'Introduction', in M. J. Freeman, and D. H. Aldcroff (eds.), *Transport in the Victorian Age*, Manchester: Manchester University Press.

FREMDLING, R. (1980), 'Freight Rates and State Budgets; The Role of the National Prussian Railways 1880–1913', *Journal of European Economic History*, 9: 21–39.

FRIEDMAN, M. (1962), *Capitalism and Freedom* (1962), Chicago: University of Chicago Press.

FUSS, M. A., and WAVERMAN, L. (1981), 'Regulation and the Multiproduct Firm: The Case of Telecommunications in Canada', in G. Fromm (ed.), *Studies in Public Regulation*, Boston, Mass.: MIT.

GALT, W. (1844), *Railway Reform: Its Expediency and Practicality Considered*, People's Edition.

—— (1865), *Railway Reform: Its Importance and Practicality*, London: Longman.

GARCKE, E. (1907, 1939), *Manual of Electrical Undertakings*.

GAYLE, D. J., and GOODRICH, J. N. (1990) (eds.), *Privatisation and Deregulation in Global Perspective*, London: Pinter.

General Board of Health (1850), *Report on the Supply of Water to the Metropolis*, London.

General Register Office (1952), *Census of England and Wales*, London.

GLAISTER, S., and MULLEY, C. (1983), *Public Control of the British Bus Industry*, Aldershot: Grower.

GLYNN, D. (1988), 'Economic Regulation of the Privatised Water Industry', in C. Johnson (ed.), *Privatisation and Ownership: Lloyd's Bank Annual Economic Review*, 1: 77–92.

GOURVISH, T. R. (1972), *Mark Huish and the London and North-Western Railway: A Study of Management*, Leicester: Leicester University Press.

—— (1980), *Railways and the British Economy 1830–1914*, London: Macmillan.

—— (1986), *British Railways 1948–73: A Business History*, Cambridge: Cambridge University Press.

—— (1988), 'Railways 1830–70: The Formative Years', in M. J. Freeman, and D. H. Aldcroft (eds.), *Transport in the Victorian Age*, Manchester: Manchester University Press.

GRAHAM, C., and PROSSER, A. (1991), *Privatising Public Enterprises: Constitutions, the State and Regulation in Comparative Perspective*, Oxford: Clarendon Press.

GRAY, J. (1984), *Hayek on Liberty*, Oxford: Blackwell.

GREASLEY, D. (1990), 'Fifty Years of Coal Mining Productivity: The Record of the British Coal Industry before 1939', *Journal of Economic History*, 50/4 (Dec.), 877–902.

GRILICHES, Z. (1988), 'Productivity Puzzles and R. & D: Another Non-explanation', *Journal of Economic Perspectives*, 2/4 (Fall), 9–22.

GRINTING, C. H. (1903), *The History of the Great Northern Railway 1845–1902*, London: Methuen.

GUNSTON, W. H. (1933), 'World Telephone Development at the End of 1932', *Telegraph and Telephone Journal* (Dec.), 56.

HAMMOND, C. J. (1992), 'Privatisation and the Efficiency of Decentralised Electricity Generation', *Economic Journal* (May), 538–53.

HANNAH, L. (1976), *The Rise of the Corporate Economy*, London: Methuen.

—— (1977), 'A Pioneer of Public Enterprise: The Central Electricity Generating Board and the National Grid', in B. Supple (ed.), *Essays in British Business History*, Oxford: Clarendon Press.

—— (1979), *Electricity Before Nationalisation*, London: Macmillan.

HANSON, A. H. (1963) (ed.), *Nationalisation: A Book of Readings*, London: Allen and Unwin.

HARCOURT, E. (1987), *Taming the Tyrant: The First 100 Years of Australia's International Telecommunications Services*, Sydney: Allen & Unwin.

HARDING, W. (1848), 'Facts Bearing on the Progress of the Railway System', *Journal of the Statistical Society of London* (Nov.), 322–43.

HART, P. E., and CHAWLA, R. K. (1970), 'An International Comparison of Production Functions: The Coal-Fired Electricity Generating Industry', *Economica*, 37: 164–77.

HASSAN, J. A. (1985), 'The Growth and Impact of the British Water Industry in the 19th Century', *Economic History Review*, 38/4 (Nov.), 531–47.

—— (1991), 'The Goals of the Water Industry', paper presented at the 1991 Economic History Society Conference, Manchester.

HAUSMAN, J. A. (1978), 'Specification Tests in Econometrics', *Econometrica*, 46: 1251–71.

HAWKE, G. R. (1969), 'Pricing Policy of Railways in England and Wales before 1881', in M. C. Reed, *Railways in the Victorian Economy: Studies in Finance and Economic Growth*, Newton Abbot: David & Charles.

—— (1970), *Railways and Economic Growth in England and Wales 1840–1870*, London: Oxford University Press.

HAYEK, F. A. (1973), *Law, Legislation and Liberty: Rules and Order*, vol. i, London: Routledge & Kegan Paul.

HAZLEWOOD, A. (1953), 'The Origin of the State Telephone System in Britain', *Oxford Economic Papers*, 5: 13–25.

HEALD, D. (1980), 'The Economic and Financial Control of United Kingdom Nationalised Industries', *Economic Journal*, 90 (June), 243–65.

—— (1987), 'United Kingdom: The End of Nationalization, and Afterwards?', paper for the Politics of Privatization Conference, Oxford (Nov.).

HEIM, C. E. (1983), 'Industrial Organisation and Regional Development in Inter-war Britain', *Journal of Economic History*, 43/4 (Dec.), 931–52.

—— (1984), 'Limits to Intervention: The Bank of England and Industrial Organisation in the Depressed Areas', *Economic History Review*, 37/4 (Nov.), 533–50.

—— (1986), 'Inter-war Responses to Regional Decline,' in B. Elbaum, and W. Lazonick (eds.), *The Decline of the British Economy*, Oxford: Clarendon Press.

HELM, D., KAY J., and THOMPSON, D. (1988), 'Energy Policy and the Role of the State in the Market for Energy', *Fiscal Studies*, 9/4 (Feb.), 41–61.

HENNOCK, E. P. (1963), 'Finance and Politics in Urban Local Government in England 1835–1900', *Historical Journal*, 6/2: 212–25.

—— (1973), *Fit and Proper Persons: Ideal and Reality in Nineteenth Century Urban Government*, London: Arnold.

Heyworth Report (1945), *Report of the Committee of Inquiry into the Gas Industry 1945*, London; Cmnd. 6699.

HIGHTON, E. (1852), *The Electric Telegraph*, London, John Weale.

HIRSCHMAN, A. (1982), *Shifting Involvements: Private Interest and Public Action*, Oxford: Blackwell.

HOLCOMBE, A. N. (1911), *Public Ownership of Telephones in Continental Europe*, Cambridge, Mass.: Harvard University Press.

Home Office (1884–5), *Return of the Municipal Boroughs*, HC Paper C260, BPP lxvii, London.

—— (1902), *Return of Municipal Charters of Incorporation*, BPP lxxxviii, London.

HOTELLING, H. (1929), 'Stability in Competition', *Economic Journal*, 39: 41–57.

House of Commons Energy Committee (1992), *Consequences of Electricity Privatisation*, Second Report 1991–2, vol. i, London: HMSO.

House of Commons Environmental Committee (1991–2), *Government Proposals for an Environmental Agency*, London: HMSO.

HOWE, F. C. (1906), 'Municipal Ownership in Great Britain', *Bulletin of the Bureau of Labour*, 62 (Jan.), 1–123.

HUNT, E. H. (1973), *Regional Wage Variations in Britain 1850–1914*, London: Oxford University Press.

HUTH, A. (1942), *Radio Today: The Present State of Broadcasting*, Geneva.

IRVING, R. J. (1976), *The North Eastern Railway Company 1870–1914: An Economic History*, Leicester: Leicester University Press.

—— (1978), 'The Profitability and Performance of British Railways 1870–1914', *Economic History Review*, 31: 46–66.

JACKMAN, W. T. (1916), *The Development of Transportation in Modern England* (1st edn.), Cambridge: Cambridge University Press.

JAFFER, S. M., and THOMPSON D. J. (1986), 'Deregulating Express Coaches: A Reassessment', *Fiscal Studies*, 7/4 (Nov.), 45–68.

JEANS, J. S. (1887), *Railway Problems: An Inquiry into Economic Conditions of Railway Working in Different Countries*, London: Longman.

JEVONS, W. S. (1867), 'On the Analogy between the Post Office, Telegraphs and Other Systems of Conveyance of the United Kingdom as Regards Government Control', *Manchester Statistical Society*, 91–104.

—— (1874), 'The Railways and the State', in *Essays and Addresses of the Owens College Manchester*, London: Macmillan.

JOHNES and CLEGG (1847), 'Observations or General Report on the Existing System of Lighting Towns with Gas, by Messrs, Johnes and Clegg, Surveying Officers', BPP xxii, London.

JOHNSTON, J. (1960), *Statistical Cost Analysis*, New York: McGraw-Hill.

JOHNSTON, K. H. (1949), *British Railways and Economic Recovery: A Sociological Study of the Transport Problem*, London: Clerke & Cockeran.

Joint Select Committee of the House of Lords and the House of Commons (1872), *Report on Railway Amalgamation* BPP xxxviii, London.

—— (1900, 1903), *Report on Municipal Trading*, BPP, 1900 vii and 1903 vii, London.

JONES, K. (1978), 'Policy Towards the Nationalized Industries', in F. T. Blackaby (ed.), *British Economic Policy 1960–1974*, London: Heinemann.

JONES, L. J. (1983), 'Public Pursuit of Private Profit: Liberal Businessmen and Municipal Politics in Birmingham, 1845–1900', *Business History*, 25/3: 240–59.

JONES, Lewis W. (1980), 'The Municipalities and the Electricity Supplies Industry in Birmingham', *West Midlands Studies*, 13: 19–26.

JONES, T. T. (1979), 'The Retail Price Index of Nationalised Industries 1962–1978', UMIST Department of Management Sciences Occasional Paper 7905 (Oct.)

KATZ, M., and SHAPIRO, C. (1985), 'Network Externalities, Competition and Compatibility', *American Economic Review*, 75: 424–40.

KAY, J. A., MAYER, C., and THOMPSON, D. J. (1986), *Privatisation and Regulation: The United Kingdom Experience*, Oxford: Clarendon Press.

—— and SILBERSTON, Z. A. (1984), 'The New Industrial Policy: Privatisation and Competition', *Midland Bank Review* (Spring), 8–16.

KEITH-LUCAS, B. (1952), *The English Local Government Franchise: A Short History*, Oxford: Blackwell.

KELF-COHEN, R. (1958), *Nationalization in Britain: The End of a Dogma*, London: Macmillan.

KELLETT, J. R. (1978), 'Municipal Socialism, Enterprise and Trading in the Victorian City', *Urban History Year-Book*, 36–45.

KENDRICK, J. W. (1987), 'Service Sector Productivity' *Business Economics*, 22/2 (Apr.), 18–24.

KENNEDY, W. P. (1987), *Industrial Structure, Capital Markets and the Origins of British Economic Decline*, Cambridge: Cambridge University Press.

KIEVE, J. L. (1973), *Electric Telegraph: A Social and Economic History*, Newton Abbot: David & Charles.

KINGSBURY, J. (1915), *The Telephone and the Telephone Exchange*, London: Longmans.

Kingston upon Hull (1964), *Souvenir Diamond Jubilee 1904–1964*, Hull: Corporation of Kingston upon Hull.

Kingston upon Hull Telephones (1954), *Golden Jubilee*, Hull: Corporation of Kingston upon Hull.

KIRBY, M. W. (1973a), 'The Control of Competition in the Coal Mining Industry in the Thirties', *Economic History Review*, 26: 273–84.

—— (1973b), 'Governmental Intervention in Industrial Organisation: Coal Mining in the 1930s', *Business History*, 15: 160–73.

—— (1974), 'The Lancashire Cotton Industry in the Inter-war Years: A Study in Organisational Change', *Business History*, 16: 145–59.

—— (1977), *The British Coal Mining Industry 1870–1946*, London: Macmillan.

—— (1979), 'The Politics of State Coercion in Inter-war Britain: The Mines Department of the Board of Trade', *Historical Journal*, 22/2: 373–96.

KLEIN, M. (1990), 'Competition and Regulation: The Railroad Model', *Business History Review*, 64: 311–25.

KNOOP, D. (1912), *Principles and Methods of Municipal Trading*, London: Macmillan.

KNOX, V. (1901), 'The Economic Effects of the Tramways Act of 1870', *Economic Journal*, 11: 492–510.

Labour Party (1986), *Social Ownership: Statement to the Labour Party Conference 1986*, London.

LARDNER, D. (1866), *The Electric Telegraph Popularised* (3rd edn.), London: Walton.

LAWFORD, G. L., and NICHOLSON, L. R. (1950), *The Telcon Story 1850–1950*, London: The Telegraph Construction and Maintenance Co. Ltd.

LAZONICK, W. (1986), 'The Cotton Industry', in B. Elbaum, and W. Lazonick (eds.), *The Decline of the British Economy*, Oxford: Clarendon Press.

LEWIN, H. G. (1925), *Early British Railways 1801–1844*, London: Locomotive Publishing Co.

—— (1936), *The Railway Mania and its Aftermath 1845–52*, London: Railway Gazette.

LIKIERMAN, A. (1979), 'The Financial and Economic Framework for Nationalised Industries', *Lloyd's Bank Review* (Oct.), 16–32.

LITTLECHILD, S. C. (1979), 'Controlling the Nationalised Industries: Quis custodiet ipsos custodes', University of Birmingham, Faculty of Commerce and Social Science Series B Discussion Paper 5 (Aug.).

—— (1983a), 'The Effects of Ownership on Telephone Penetration', *Telecommunications Policy*, 7/3: 246–7.

—— (1983b), *The Regulation of British Telecommunications Profitability*, Department of Industry, London: HMSO.

LITTLECHILD, S. C. (1986), *Economic Regulation of Privatized Water Authorities*, London: HMSO.

LIVESEY, G. (1948), 'The Inception and Development of Gas Lighting', *Journal of Gas Lighting and Water Supply* (2 Oct.), 646–9.

Local Government Board (1893–4), *Return Relating to the Areas and Population of the Counties of England and Wales*, BPP lxxvii, London.

—— (1899a), *Annual Local Taxation Return: England and Wales 1897–1898*, BPP lxxxii, London.

—— (1899b, 1902), *Return Relating to Municipal Corporations (Reproductive Undertakings)*, HC Paper 88, BPP 1899 lxxxiii and 1902 lxvii, London.

—— (1909, 1910), *Annual Local Taxation Return: England and Wales 1907–1908*, BPP 1909 lxxv and 1910 lxxvii, London.

—— (1913), *Return*, HC Paper 119, BPP lv, London.

—— (1915), 'Return of Particulars Regarding Every Water Undertaking in Every District in England and Wales', BPP lxxix, London.

LOMAX, K. S. (1952), 'Cost Curves for Electricity Generation', *Economica*, 19: 193–7.

LOWE, R. (1978), 'The Erosion of State Intervention in Britain 1917–24', *Economic History Review*, 31: 270–86.

LUBENOW, W. C. (1971), *The Politics of Government Growth: Early Victorian Attitudes Towards State Interventions 1833–1848*, London: Archon Books.

LYTH, P. (1990), 'A Multiplicity of Instruments: The 1946 Decision to Create a Separate British European Airline and its Effects on Airline Productivity', *Journal of Transport History*, 11/2: 1–17.

MCCALMONT, F. H. (1971), *Maccalmont's Parliamentary Poll Book: British General Election Results*, Brighton: Harvester.

McGowan Report (1936), *Report of the Committee on Electricity Distribution*, London: Ministry of Transport (May).

MCGUIRE, R. A., and OHSFELDT, R. (1986), 'Private versus Public Water Delivery: A Critical Analysis of Hedonic Cost Function', *Public Finance Quarterly*, 14/3 (July), 339–50.

MCKAY, J. P. (1976), *Tramways and Trolleys: The Risk of Urban Mass Transporting Europe*, Princeton, NJ: Princeton University Press.

MADDISON, A. (1982), *Phases of Capitalist Development*, Oxford: Oxford University Press.

MALTBIE, M. R. (1900), 'Gas Lighting in Great Britain', *Municipal Affairs*, 4: 538–73.

MANKIW, N. G., and WHINSTON, M. D. (1986), 'Free Entry and Social Inefficiency', *Rand Journal of Economics*, 17: 48–58.

MARLAND, E. A. (1964), *Early Electrical Communication*, London: Abelard-Schumann.

MARRISON, A. J. (1983), 'Businessmen, Industries and Tariff Reform in Great Britain 1903–30', *Business History*, 25: 8–78.

MARTIN, R. BIDDULPH (1873), 'Notes on the Purchase of the Railways by the State', *Journal of the Statistical Society (of London)*, 36: 177–202.

MATTHEWS, D. (1985), 'Rogues, Speculators and Competing Monopolies: The Early London Gas Companies, 1812–1860', *London Journal*, 2: 39–50.

—— (1986), 'Laissez-faire and the London Gas Industry in the 19th Century: Another Look', *Economic History Review*, 39/2: 244–63.

MATTHEWS, R. C. O., FEINSTEIN, C. H., and ODLING-SMEE, J. C. (1982), *British Economic Growth 1856–1973*, Oxford: Clarendon Press.

MEDLYN, W. J. (1929–30), 'Telephone Finance and Statistics of the American Bell Co and the British Post Office', *Post Office Electrical Engineers Journal*, 22: 143–8.

MEYER H. R. (1907), *Public Ownership and the Telephone in Great Britain*, New York: Macmillan.

MILL, J. S. (1965), *Principles of Political Economy*, London: Routledge & Kegan Paul.

MILLWARD, R. (1976), 'Price Restraint, Anti-inflation Policy and Public and Private Industry in the United Kingdom 1947–1973', *Economic Journal*, 86 (June), 226–42.

—— (1982), 'The Comparative Performance of Public and Private Ownership', in Lord Roll of Ipsden (eds.), *The Mixed Economy*, London: Macmillan.

—— (1986), 'Some Implications of the New Theory of Natural Monopoly', Salford Papers in Economics 86–1.

—— (1988), 'The United Kingdom Services Sector, Productivity Change and the Recession in Long Term Perspective', *Service Industries Journal* (July), 263–76.

—— (1989), 'Privatisation in Historical Perspective: The United Kingdom Water Industry', in D. Cobham, R. Harrington, and G. Zis, (eds.), *Money Trade and Payments: Essays in Honour of D. J. Coppock*, Manchester: Manchester University Press.

—— (1990), 'Productivity in the UK Services Sector: Historical Trends 1856–1985 and Comparisons with the USA 1950–85', *Oxford Bulletin of Economics and Statistics*, 52/4: 423–35.

—— (1991a), 'The Emergence of Gas and Water Monopolies in Nineteenth-Century Britain: Contested Markets and Public Control', in J. Foreman-Peck (ed.), *New Perspectives on the Late Victorian Economy*, Cambridge: Cambridge University Press.

—— (1991b), 'The Market Behaviour of Local Utilities in Pre-World War I Britain: The Case of Gas', *Economic History Review*, 44/1: 102–27.

—— (1991c), 'The Nationalised Industries', in M. Artis and D. Cobham (eds.), *Labour's Economic Policies 1974–79*, Manchester: Manchester University Press.

—— and PARKER, D. (1983), 'Public and Private Enterprise: Comparative

Behaviour and Relative Efficiency', in R. Millward *et al.*, *Public Sector Economics*, London: Longman.

—— and WARD, R. (1987), 'The Costs of Public and Private Gas Enterprises in Late Nineteenth-Century Britain', *Oxford Economic Papers*, 39: 719–37.

—— (1993), 'From Private to Public Ownership of Gas Undertakings in England and Wales, 1851–1947: Chronology, Incidence and Causes', *Business History* 35/3: 1–21.

Ministry of Civil Aviation (1945), *British Air Transport*, London: Cmd. 6605 (Mar.).

Ministry of Fuel and Power (1948), *Engineering and Financial Statistics of all Authorised Undertakings 1946/7*, Electricity Supply Act (41–213–0–47), London.

Ministry of Health (1929, 1936), *Annual Local Taxation Returns: England and Wales*, London (for 1926/7 and 1933/4).

MITCHELL, B. R. (1980), *Abstract of European Historical Statistics* (2nd edn.), London: Macmillan.

MOLYNEUX, R., and THOMPSON, D. J. (1986), 'The Efficiency of the Nationalised Industries Since 1978', Institute of Fiscal Studies Working Paper 100.

—— —— (1987), 'Nationalised Industry Performance: Still Third Rate?', *Fiscal Studies* (Feb.), 48–82.

Monopolies and Mergers Commission (1988), *Gas*, Cmd. 500, London.

MORRISON, H. (1933), *Socialisation and Transport*, London: Constable.

MULHALL, M. G. (1892), *Dictionary of Statistics*, London: Routledge.

NABB, H. (1986), 'A History of the Gas Industry in South West England before 1949', Ph.D. thesis, University of Bath.

National Board for Prices and Incomes (1966), *Coal Prices*, Report No. 12, London Cmnd. 2919, (Feb.).

National Civic Federation (1907), *Municipal and Private Ownership of Public Utilities*, vols. i, ii, and iii, New York: City of New York.

National Economic Development Office (1976), *A Study of United Kingdom Nationalised Industries: Their Role in the Economy and Control in the Future*, London (Nov.).

NERLOVE, M. (1963), 'Returns to Scale in Electricity Supply', in C. F. Christ, *et al.*, *Measurement in Economics: Studies in Mathematical Economics and Econometrics in Memory of Yehuda Grunfeld*, Standford, Calif: Stanford University Press.

NEWMAN, K. (1986), *The Selling of British Telecom*, London: Holt, Rinehart & Winston.

O'BRIEN, P. (1977), *The New Economic History of Railways*, London: Croom Helm.

—— (1983) (ed.), *Railways and the Economic Development of Western Europe 1830–1914*, London: Macmillan.

OCHOJNA, A. D. (1978), 'The Influence of Local and National Policies on the Development of Urban Passenger Transport in Britain 1850–1900', *Journal of Transport History* 4/3 (Feb.) 125–46.

Office of Telecommunications (1987), *Quality of Telecommunications Services*, London: HMSO.

OLSON, M. (1982), *The Rise and Decline of Nations*, New Haven, Conn.: Yale University Press.

O'MEARA, W. A. J. (1910–11), 'Some Notes on a Trip to the North American Continent', *Post Office Electrical*, Engineers Journal 3: 97–118.

—— (1913), *Report on the Telegraph and Telephone Services of the German Empire*, London: PO Archives Post, 83/78.

—— (1915) *Report on the Telegraph and Telephone Services of Sweden*, London: PO Archives Post, 83/88.

Ostergaard, G. N. (1954), 'Labour and the Development of the Public Corporation', *Manchester School*, 22: 192–226.

PAIGE, D., and BOMBACH, G. (1959), *A Comparison of National Output and Productivity of the United Kingdom and United States of America*, Paris: OEEC.

PAISH, G. (1902), *The British Railway Position*, London: The Statist.

PALMER, A. M. F. (1943), *The Future of Electricity Supply*, Fabian Society Research Series No. 69.

PANZAR, J. C., and WILLIG, R. D. (1977), 'Free Entry and the Sustainability of Natural Monopoly', *Bell Journal of Economics*, 8 (Spring), 1–22.

PARRIS, H. (1965), *Government and the Railways in Nineteenth Century Britain*, London: Routledge & Kegan Paul.

PARSONS, R. H. (1939), *Early Days in the Power Station Industry*, Cambridge: Cambridge University Press for Babcock & Wilcox.

PARSONS, W. (1988), *The Political Economy of British Regional Policy*, London: Routledge.

PELTZMAN, S. (1976), 'Towards a More General Theory of Regulation', *Journal of Law and Economics*, 19: 211–40.

PERRY, C. R. (1977), 'The British Experience 1876–1912: The Impact of the Telephone During the Years of Delay', in I. de Sola Pool (ed.), *The Social Impact of the Telephone*, Cambridge, Mass.: MIT Press.

PESCATRICE, D. R., and TRAPANI, J. M., III (1980), 'The Performance and Objectives of Public Utilities Operating in the United States', *Journal of Public Economics*, 13: 259–76.

PHILLIPS, EDWIN (1877), *The Railway Autocracy*.

PICOT, A., and KAULMANN, T. (1989), 'Comparative Performance of Government Owned and Privately-Owned Industrial Corporations: Empirical Results from Six Countries', *Journal of Institutional and Theoretical Economics*, 145: 298–316.

PITT, D. C. (1980), *The Telecommunications Function in the British Post Office: A Case Study of Bureaucratic Adaption*, Saxon House.

Political and Economic Planning (1936), *Electricity Supply Industry*, London.

POLLARD, A. (1978), *Anthony Trollope*, London: Routledge & Kegan Paul.

POLLARD, S. (1989), *Britain's Prime and Britain's Decline: The British Economy 1870–1914*, London: Edward Arnold.

—— (1992), *The Development of the British Economy 1914–90*, London: Edward Arnold.

POLLINS, H. (1952), 'A Note on Railway Constructional Costs 1825–1850', *Economica*, NS 19: 395–407.

—— (1969), 'Aspects of Railway Accounting before 1868', in M. C. Reed, (ed.), *Railways in the Victorian Economy*, Newton Abbot: David & Charles.

—— (1971), *Britain's Railways: An Industrial History*, Newton Abbot: David & Charles.

PORTER, R. P. (1902), 'The Failure of Municipal Ownership in England', *Street Railway Journal* (Aug. and Sept.), 109–14, 216–20.

Postmaster-General (1880), *Report*, London: HMSO.

Post Office (1861), *Prospectus and Directors' Report of the United Kingdom Telegraph Company*, London: PO Archives, Post 81/105.

—— (1887), *The Post Office of Fifty Years Ago*, London: Cassell.

—— (1893), *Report of W. H. Preece's Visit to the USA: 1893*, London: PO Archives, Post, 87/6.

—— (1911), *The Post Office: An Historical Summary*, London.

—— (1929), *The Cost of Construction and Maintenance of Telephone Plant in the American Bell and the British Telephone Services*, London: PO Archives.

PREECE, W. H. (1875), *Report on Continental Systems of Telegraphy*, London: PO Archives, Post 83/68.

—— and FISCHER, H. C. (1877), *Report on the American Telegraph System*, London: PO Archives, Post 83/69.

—— —— (1896), *Report on the German and Scandinavian Telephone Systems*, London: PO Archives Post, 3/21.

PRICE WILLIAMS, R. (1881), 'The Question of the Reduction of the Postal Telegraph Tariff', *Journal of the Statistical Society of London* (Mar.), 14–15.

PRYKE, R. (1980), 'Public Enterprise in Practice: The British Experience of Nationalisation during the Past Decade', in W. J. Baunol (ed.), *Public and Private Enterprise in a Mixed Economy*, London: Macmillan.

—— (1981), *The Nationalised Industries: Policies and Performance Since 1968*, Oxford: Martin Robertson.

—— (1982), 'The Comparative Performance of Public and Private Enterprise', *Fiscal Studies*, 3/2: 68–81.

PURVES, T. F. (1911–12), Telephones in England and the USA', *Post Office Electrical Engineers Journal*, 4: 97–110.

RAWSON, R. W. (1839), 'On Railways in Belgium', *Journal of the Statistical Society of London*, 2: 47–62.

READER, W. J. (1977), 'Imperial Chemical Industries and the State 1925–45', in B. Supple (ed.), *Essays in British Business History*, Oxford: Clarendon Press.

REES, R. (1979), 'The Pricing Policy of the Nationalised Industries', *3 Banks Review* 122 (June), 3–31.

Registrar-General (1852–3 and 1866), *Return of Towns and Boroughs*, BPP 1852/3 lxxvii and 1866 lx, London.

REID, G. L., ALLEN, K., and HARRIS, D. T. (1973), *The Nationalised Fuel Industries*, London: Heinemann.

Reid Report (1945), *Report of the Technical Advisory Committee on Coal Mining*, London: Cmnd. 6610.

RENNISON, R. W. (1978), *Water to Tyneside: A History of the Newcastle and Gateshead Water Company*, Newcastle: Newcastle and Gateshead Water Co.

ROBERTSON, J. H. (1947), *The Story of the Telephone*, London: Pitman.

ROBINS, F. W. (1948), *The Story of Water Supply*, Oxford: Oxford University Press.

ROBINSON, H. (1948), *The British Post Office: A History*, Princeton, NJ: Princeton University Press.

ROBSON, W. A. (1935), 'The Public Utility Services', in H. J. Laski, W. J. Jennings, and W. A. Robson (eds.), *A Century of Municipal Progress: The Last Hundred Years*, London: London: Allen & Unwin.

—— (1963), *Nationalised Industry and Public Ownership*, London: Allen & Unwin.

ROSTAS, L. (1948), *Comparative Productivity in British and American Industry*, National Institute of Economic and Social Research, Cambridge: Cambridge University Press.

ROUTH, G. (1954), 'Civil Service Pay, 1875–1950', *Economica* (Aug.), 201–23.

ROUTLEDGE, R. (1891), *Discoveries and Inventions of the Nineteenth Century* (8th edn.), London: Routledge.

ROWLEY, C. K., and MULLEY, C. (1983), 'Transport Deregulation in the United Kingdom: A Theoretical and Empirical Analysis', *International Journal of Transport Economics*, 10: 443–80.

—— and YARROW, G. K. (1981), 'Property Rights, Regulation and Public Enterprise: The Case of the British Steel Industry 1957–1975', *International Review of Law and Economics*, 1: 63–96.

ROWLINSON, P. J. (1984), 'The Regulation of the Gas Industry in the

Early Nineteenth Century, 1800–60', D. Phil. thesis, Linacre College, Oxford.

Royal Commission on Railways (1867), *Report*, BPP xxxviii, London.

Royal Commission on Transport (1931), *Final Report: The Coordination and Development of Transport*, London: HMSO.

Royal Commission on Water Supply (1869), *Report of the Commissioners*, London.

Royal Economic Society (1912), *The State in Relation to Railways*, London: P. S. King.

Royal Sanitary Commission (1871), *Report*, London.

Samuel Commission (1925), *Report of the Royal Commission on the Coal Industry*, London: Cmnd. 2600.

Sankey Commission (1919), *Coal Industry Commission Act: Interim Report*, London: Cmnd. 84.

SAVAGE, C. I. (1966), *An Economic History of Transport*, London: Huntingdon.

SCHUMPETER, J. (1943), *Capitalism, Socialism and Democracy*, London: Allen & Unwin.

SCHWARTZ, P. (1966), 'John Stuart Mill and Laissez Faire: London Water', *Economica*, 33 (Feb.), 71–83.

Secretary of State for Energy (1988), *Privatising Electricity: The Government's Proposals for the Privatisation of the Electricity Supply Industry in England and Wales*, London: Cmnd. 322 (Feb.).

Secretary of State for Prices and Consumer Protection (1974), *Review of the Price Code: A Consultative Document*, London: Cmnd 5779, (Nov.).

Secretary of State for the Environment, Secretary of State for Wales, Ministry of Agriculture, Fisheries and Food (1986), *Privatisation of the Water Authorities in England and Wales*, London (Feb.).

Select Committee on Amalgamation of Railways and Canals (1852), *Report*, BPP xxxviii, London.

Select Committee on London Water Supply (1880), *Report*, London (Aug.).

Select Committee on Nationalized Industries (1974), *Capital Investment Procedures*, 1st Report, Session 1973/4, HC 65, London.

Select Committee on the Health of Towns (1840), *Report*, London (June).

Select Committee on the Post Office (Telegraph Department) (1876), *Report Together with Proceedings of the Committee*, BPP xiii, London.

Select Committee on the Supply of Water to the Metropolis (1821), *Report*, London (May).

—— (1828), *Report*, London (July).

SHACKLETON, J. R. (1984), 'Privatisation: The Case Examined', *National Westminster Bank Review* (May), 59–73.

SHARKEY W. W. (1981), 'Existence of Sustainable Prices for Natural Monopoly Outputs', *Bell Journal of Economics*, 12 (Spring), 144–54.
—— (1982), *The Theory of Natural Monopoly*, Cambridge: Cambridge University Press.
SHAW, A. (1890), 'Glasgow: A Municipal Study', *Century*, 39: 721–36.
SHEAIL, J. (1983), 'Planning, Water Supplies and Ministerial Power in Inter-war Britain', *Public Administration*, 61: 386–95.
SHERRINGTON, C. E. R. (1934), *A Hundred Years of Inland Transport 1830–1933* (repr. London: Cass, 1969).
SHORT, E. (1946), *Railways and The State: The Problems of Nationalisation*, London: Hollis & Carter.
SMART, W. (1901), 'Municipal Industries and the Rate-Payer', *Economic Journal*, 11/2: 169–79.
—— (1905), 'Glasgow and its Municipal Industries', *Quarterly Journal of Economics*, 9/2, (Jan.), 188–94.
SMELLIE, K. B. (1968), *A History of Local Government*, London: Allen and Unwin.
SMITH, A. (1848), *The Bubble of the Age or the Fallacies of Railway Investment*.
SMITH, A. D., HITCHENS, D. M. W. N., and DAVIES, S. W. (1982), *International Industrial Productivity: A Comparison of Britain, America and Germany*, National Institute of Economic and Social Research, Cambridge: Cambridge University Press.
SOMMERFIELD, V. (1923), *The Railway Grouping Scheme: A Handbook for Stockholders and Investors*, London: Financial News.
STERN, W. M. (1954), 'Water Supply in Britain: Development of a Public Service', *Royal Sanitary Institute Journal*, 74: 998–1004.
STIGLER, G. J. (1968), *The Organization of Industry*, Homewood, Ill.: R. D. Irwin.
STURMEY, S. G. (1958), *The Economic Development of Radio*, London: Duckworth.
SUBISSATI, E. E. (1989), 'Some Evidence Regarding British Telecom's Performance Under Price Cap Regulation', paper presented at Conference on Telecommunications Costing in a Dynamic Environment, San Diego.
Submarine Telegraph Company (1861), *Report of Committee of Consultation*, London: PO Archives, Post 81/105.
SUPPLE, B. (1986), 'Ideology or Pragmatism? The Nationalisation of Coal 1916–1946' in N. McKendrick, and R. B. Outhwaite (eds.), *Business Life and Public Policy: Essays in Honour of D. C. Coleman*, Cambridge: Cambridge University Press.
—— (1987), *The History of the British Coal Industry*, iv: *1913–1946: The Political Economy of Decline*, Oxford: Clarendon Press.

SUTCLIFFE, A. (1982), 'The Growth of Public Intervention in the British Urban Environment during the Nineteenth Century: A Structural, Approach' in J. H. Johnson , and C. G. Purley (eds.), *The Structure of Nineteenth Century Cities*, London: Croom Helm.

SWANN, D. (1988), *The Retreat of the State: Deregulation and Privatisation in the UK and the US*, Brighton: Harvester Wheatsheaf.

TAWNEY, R. W. (1921), *The Acquisitive Society*, London: Bell.

TEEPLES, R., FEIGENBAUM, S., and GLYER, D. (1986), 'Public Versus Private Water Delivery: Cost Comparisons', *Public Finance Quarterly*, 14/3 (July), 351–66.

TELSER, L. G. (1987), *A Theory of Efficient Co-operation and Competition*, Cambridge: Cambridge University Press.

THOMPSON, A. W. J., and HUNTER, L. C. (1973), *The Nationalised Transport Industries*, London: Heinemann.

THOMPSON, R. L. (1947), *Wiring a Continent*, Princeton, NJ: Princeton University Press.

TOLLIDAY, S. (1986), 'Steel and Rationalisation Policies 1918–1950', in B. Elbaum, and W. Lazonick (ed.), *The Decline of the British Economy*, Oxford: Clarendon Press.

TREASURY (1961), *The Financial and Economic Obligations of the Nationalised Industries*, London: Cmnd. 1337.

—— (1967), *Nationalised Industries: A Review of Economic and Financial Objectives*, London: Cmnd. 3437 (Nov.).

—— (1988), *The Government's Expenditure Plans 1988–9 to 1990–1*, London: Cmnd. 288.

URQUHART, M. C., and BUCKLEY, K. A. H. (1965), *Historical Statistics of Canada*, Cambridge: Cambridge University Press.

VELJANOVSKI, C. (1987), *Selling the State*, London: Institute of Economic Affairs.

VICKERS, J., and Yarrow, G. (1988), *Privatisation: An Economic Approach*, Cambridge, Mass.: MIT Press.

WALLER, P. J. (1983), *Town, City and Nation: England 1850–1914*, Oxford: Oxford University Press.

WATERSON, M. (1988), *Regulation of the Firm and Natural Monopoly*, Oxford: Blackwell.

WEAVER, A. (1867), *Letter Book*, London: PO Archives, Post 81/27.

WEBB, A. D. (1911), *A New Dictionary of Statistics*, London: Routledge.

WEBB, H. Lawes (1895), *Report on Europe*, AT & T. Archives.

—— (1908), 'Letter to the Editor', *Financial Times* (5 Feb.).

WHITE, P. R. (1988), 'British Experience with Deregulation of Local Bus Services', in Dodgson and Topham (1988).

WIENER, M. J. (1981), *English Culture and the Decline of the Industrial Spirit 1850–1980*, Cambridge: Cambridge University Press.

WILLIAMS, F. S. (1852), *Our Iron Roads: Their History, Construction and Social Influence*, London: Ingram, Cooke & Co.

WILLIAMS, T. I. (1981), *A History of the British Gas Industry*, Oxford: Oxford University Press.

WILLIAMSON, O. E. (1964), *The Economics of Discretionary Behaviour: Managerial Objectives in the Theory of the Firm*, Englewood Cliffs, NJ: Prentice Hall.

—— (1968), 'Economies as an Antitrust Defense', *American Economic Review*, 58: 18–36.

WILSON, J. F. (1990), 'Competition in the Early Gas Industry: The Case of Chester Gas Light Company 1817–1856', *Transactions of the Antiquarian Society of Lancashire and Cheshire*, 86: 87–110.

—— (1991*a*), *Management and Finance in Victorian Public Utilities: A History of the North West Gas Industry*, London; Chapman.

—— (1991), 'Ownership, Management and Strategy in Early North West Gas Companies 1815–1830', *Business History*, 33/2 (Apri.), 203–21.

Wilson Fox Committee (1918), *Report from the Select Committee on Transport*, London (Nov.).

WISHAW, S. (1969), *Railways of Great Britain and Ireland*, Newton Abbot, David & Charles (repr. of 1842 edn.).

WOHL, P. and ALBITRECCIA, A. (1935), *Road and Rail in Forty Countries*, Oxford: Oxford University Press.

WOOD, G. (1976), 'Telephone History at Newcastle upon Tyne and Sunderland'. Newcomen Society Paper.

WOOD, W. V., and Sherrington, C. E. R. (1929), *The Railway Industry of Great Britain 1927*, London and Cambridge Economic Service, Special Memorandum 27 (Jan.).

WRIGHT, M. (1987), 'Government Investments and the Regulation of Natural Monopolies in the United Kingdom: The Case of British Gas', *Eñrgy Policy*, 15/3 (June), 193–216.

INDEX